P9-BYN-776

REA: SERIOUS PREP FOR THE MAT

6th Edition

MAT® MILLER ANALOGIES TEST®

TestWare® Edition

Updated by Suzanne Scafuri

Tracy Budd
Instructor of English
Rutgers, The State University of NJ
New Brunswick, NJ

Heather Craven
Library Sciences Consultant
Morristown, NJ

Marc Davis
English Consultant
Somerset, NJ

Mitchel Fedak, M.S.
Instructor of Chemistry,
Physics, and Mathematics
Community College of Allegheny County
Pittsburgh, PA

John P. Frade
Social Sciences Consultant
Hillsborough, NJ

Bernice Goldberg, Ph.D.
Educational Consultant
Falmouth, ME

Gary Land, Ph.D.
Instructor and Chair
Department of History
Andrews University
Berrien Springs, MI

Carol Rush, Ph.D.
Instructor of Science
La Roche College
Pittsburgh, PA

Research & Education Association

Visit our website: www.rea.com

i283318

NOV 2 0 2010

Planet Friendly Publishing
✔ Made in the United States
✔ Printed on Recycled Paper
Text: 10%   Cover: 10%
Learn more: www.greenedition.org

GREEN EDITION

At REA we're committed to producing books in an Earth-friendly manner and to helping our customers make greener choices.

Manufacturing books in the United States ensures compliance with strict environmental laws and eliminates the need for international freight shipping, a major contributor to global air pollution.

And printing on recycled paper helps minimize our consumption of trees, water and fossil fuels. This book was printed on paper made with **10% post-consumer waste**. According to Environmental Defense's Paper Calculator, by using this innovative paper instead of conventional papers, we achieved the following environmental benefits:

Trees Saved: 11 • Air Emissions Eliminated: 2,524 pounds
Water Saved: 2,232 gallons • Solid Waste Eliminated: 745 pounds

For more information on our environmental practices, please visit us online at **www.rea.com/green**

Research & Education Association
61 Ethel Road West
Piscataway, New Jersey 08854
E-mail: info@rea.com

Miller Analogies Test (MAT)
With TestWare® on CD-ROM

Copyright © 2011 by Research & Education Association, Inc.
Prior editions copyright © 2006, 2005, 2003, 2000, 1998, 1996 by
Research & Education Association, Inc. All rights reserved. No part
of this book may be reproduced in any form without permission of
the publisher.

Printed in the United States of America

Library of Congress Control Number 2010933950

ISBN-13: 978-0-7386-0875-4
ISBN-10: 0-7386-0875-0

Windows® is a registered trademark of Microsoft Corporation.

REA® and TestWare® are registered trademarks of
Research & Education Association, Inc.

H10-0101

CONTENTS

ABOUT RESEARCH & EDUCATION ASSOCIATION

Founded in 1959, Research & Education Association (REA) is dedicated to publishing the finest and most effective educational materials—including software, study guides, and test preps—for students in elementary school, middle school, high school, college, graduate school, and beyond.

Today, REA's wide-ranging catalog is a leading resource for teachers, students, and professionals.

We invite you to visit us at *www.rea.com* to find out how "REA is making the world smarter."

ACKNOWLEDGMENTS

In addition to our authors, we would like to thank Larry B. Kling, Vice President, Editorial, for his overall guidance, which brought this publication to completion; Pam Weston, Publisher, for setting the quality standards for production integrity and managing the publication to completion; John Cording, Vice President, Technology, for coordinating the design and development of REA's TestWare®; Mike Reynolds and Diane Goldschmidt, Senior Editors, for project management; Alice Leonard, Senior Editor, for preflight editorial review; Heena Patel, Technology Project Manager, for design contributions and software testing efforts; and Christine Saul, Senior Graphic Designer, for designing our cover.

We also gratefully acknowledge Suzanne Scafuri for her editorial review and Kathy Caratozzolo of Caragraphics for typesetting this edition.

INDEPENDENT STUDY SCHEDULE

The following study schedule allows for thorough preparation for the MAT. Although it is designed for eight weeks, it can be condensed into a four-week course by condensing two weeks into one. If you are not enrolled in a structured course, be sure to set aside enough time—at least two or three hours each day—to study. But no matter which study schedule works best for you, the more time you spend studying, the more prepared and relaxed you will feel on the day of the exam.

WEEK	ACTIVITY
1	Take Practice Test 1 on CD-ROM as a diagnostic exam. Your score will be an indication of your strengths and weaknesses. Carefully review all explanations, because although a piece of information may be wrong in one analogy, it may be useful in another.
2	Study REA's Main Analogy Review to familiarize yourself with the analogy format. Take Practice Test 2 on CD-ROM, and pay close attention to the types of analogies that are difficult for you.
3 and 4	Study REA's Quick Study Lists. Use any other supplementary materials that may help you absorb as much information as possible. This includes reference books, encyclopedias, trivia questions, etc. Take Practice Tests 3 and 4 on CD-ROM.
5	Create tests for yourself using index cards. These cards will be particularly helpful in learning vocabulary words and word parts. Take written Practice Test 5.
6	Continue testing yourself using your index cards. You may want to have a friend or colleague quiz you on key facts and items. Take written Practice Test 6. Track your progress over all your practice tests and determine which types of analogies are still difficult for you.
7	Study any areas you consider to be your weaknesses by using your study materials, references, and notes. Take written Practice Test 7. Remember to study the explanations for all the questions, because they may provide valuable information.
8	Take the final practice test. Review all explanations and continue to study using your index cards and REA's Quick Study Lists. If you care to, and time allows, retake the practice tests. This will help strengthen the areas in which your performance may still be lagging and build your overall confidence.

one

Section 1

Introduction

Chapter 1

Scoring High on the MAT

▌ ABOUT THIS BOOK AND TESTWARE®

This book and the accompanying software provide a complete and accurate representation of the Miller Analogies Test (MAT). Our comprehensive review details specific strategies for attacking analogy questions, and glossary-style subject reviews provide the information you will need to achieve a high score on this unique and challenging exam. REA's tests contain every type of question you can expect to see on the actual exam, and following each practice test are detailed explanations of every analogy to help you better understand the test material.

In addition to the printed tests in this book, Practice Tests 1 through 4 are also included on CD-ROM as part of our special interactive MAT TestWare®. **We strongly recommend that you begin your preparation with the TestWare® practice exams.** The software provides the added benefits of instantaneous, accurate scoring, and enforced time conditions.

▌ ABOUT THE TEST

Who takes the test and what is it used for?

The Miller Analogies Test is a graduate admissions and scholarship exam required by over 2,300 schools in both the United States and Canada. In addition, some corporations use the test to place their executives.

Who administers the test?

Pearson Education's PsychCorp unit administers the Miller Analogies Test.

When should the MAT be taken?

The MAT is usually taken shortly after a candidate graduates from college. You may be applying to a number of graduate schools that require the MAT, or a prospective employer may ask that you take the test. You should determine whether or not the exam will be required of you so that you have enough time to prepare. You may also wish to allow yourself time to take the MAT again, in case you are not pleased with your initial score. Give yourself enough time to carefully study our review material, and familiarize yourself with the format of the exam. This will spare you the anxiety of having to learn about the MAT during the actual exam.

When and where is the test given?

The MAT is administered through a network of Controlled Testing Centers licensed by Pearson Education, Inc. These testing centers comply with Pearson's rigorous standards for test administration; however, they are free to set their own fees and schedules. To apply for the test, you must apply directly to the testing center.

For more information regarding Controlled Testing Centers, their fees, and schedules, you may contact:

> Pearson Education, Inc.
> Miller Analogies Test
> Attn: Customer Service
> 19500 Bulverde Road
> San Antonio, Texas 78259-3701
> Phone: (800) 627-7271
> Website: *www.milleranalogies.com*

Is there a registration fee?

Yes, you must pay a fee to take the MAT. As stated above, fees are set by individual testing centers. A complete list of Controlled Testing Centers is available in the Miller Analogies Test registration bulletin, which is available from Harcourt Assessment.

Accommodations for Students with Disabilities

Students needing extra time, large-print or audio editions, or other special accommodations for taking the MAT will be given a non-standard administration of the test and must notify their chosen Controlled Testing Center several weeks before their test date. Submission of an Accommodations Request Form is required. See the Miller Analogies website for more information.

HOW TO USE THIS BOOK

What should I study first?

Your first step to a high score on the MAT is a comprehensive understanding of the analogy format and the challenges it presents. For this reason, a careful reading of our main analogies review is essential. When you have completed this section, take the first practice test. This will help you get a clear idea of those areas that are most challenging to you. From there, you will be able to devise the plan of study that will be most beneficial to you.

When should I start studying?

It is never too early to begin studying for the MAT. Do not procrastinate! Last-minute studying and cramming are not effective ways to learn. The more time you allow yourself to study for the MAT, the better your chances of achieving a high score. Give yourself enough time to become familiar with the format of the test and the material it covers. This will allow you to arrive at the testing center with confidence.

FORMAT OF THE MILLER ANALOGIES TEST

The format of the MAT is very straightforward. You are given 60 minutes to complete 120 analogies. Twenty of the analogies are for experimental purposes and will not be scored. The practice tests in this book contain 100 questions to be completed in 50 minutes, maintaining the correct time available per question.

The test is given in a single session; there are no breaks and no divisions between different types of analogies. You'll be presented with three of the four elements of an analogy; you must complete the analogy by choosing the best answer from the four multiple-choice options provided.

The MAT is available in either the traditional paper-and-pencil version or a computer-based version. In either format, the content is the same. The only difference is that with the computer-based test you receive a *preliminary* score report as soon as you finish.

ABOUT THE REVIEW SECTIONS

There are two main sections to our MAT review material. The first section covers the nature of an analogy itself and specific strategies for answering problems posed in the analogy format. This section is very important because unless you have a very clear understanding of the analogy format, you may mistakenly choose answers that seem correct, but are actually only meant to confuse you. Verisimilitude, in fact, will be your greatest challenge when taking the MAT.

The second section of the MAT review material contains numerous glossary-type quick study lists, designed to provide as much information as possible to prepare you for the wide variety of subject matter that you are likely to encounter on the Miller Analogies Test. The MAT is unlike most other standardized tests in that it not only tests your ability to critically analyze the relationships between given items, but also how you apply knowledge of the world around you. Thus, nothing will be more helpful to you in preparing for the MAT than a well-rounded education.

SCORING AND SCORE REPORTS

Approximately 10 to 15 working days after you take the MAT, you will receive your personal score report. This report will list your name, address, and social security number as you entered them on your answer document, your raw score, your percentile scores, and your score recipient codes. When you take our practice tests, you will only be able to determine your raw score, because your percentile scores are based on your performance compared to other MAT candidates. One percentile score will be based on the current normative data of the general population of MAT candidates. The other percentile score is based on current normative data of MAT candidates with whom you share an intended major.

There is one important difference between your personal score report and the official score report submitted to those institutions that you specify when you take the MAT. The official score report will list your MAT scores for any administration taken in the last five years. Scores for tests taken longer than five years ago will not be reported.

If, while you are taking the MAT, you decide that you are truly unhappy with your performance, you may exercise the no-score option. How to exercise this option will be explained to you at the Controlled Testing Center. If you choose not to have your exam scored, no score reports will be sent to your specified recipients, and there will be no reportable record of you ever having taken the MAT. However, before you exercise this option, consider the ramifications carefully. No refunds are available to candidates who choose the no score option, and once this decision is made, it is irrevocable. You will be sent a personal score report, however it will not show any score. Any future requests to have your test scored and your scores reported will be denied.

STUDYING FOR THE MAT

It is very important that you choose the time and place for studying that works best for you. Some candidates set aside a few hours in the morning to study, while others retain more information by studying just before going to sleep. Some students require absolute silence while studying, and some others are undisturbed by what many candidates would consider intolerable distractions. Only you can determine when and where your study time will be most effective, but you must be consistent and use your time wisely. Work out a routine and stick to it.

You may study our review material under any circumstances you like; however, when you are taking our practice tests, you should try to duplicate the actual testing conditions as closely as possible. Turn off the stereo or television, and sit at a clean table free from distractions. Be sure to time yourself accurately so you can establish a set pace.

As you complete each practice test, score your test and thoroughly review each explanation. You may even want to review the explanations for the analogies you answer *correctly* because, whenever possible, each analogy imparts up to eight pieces of information. An answer choice that is incorrect for one analogy may turn out to be correct for another, so no bit of knowledge should be wasted.

TEST-TAKING TIPS

While the subject matter of the MAT may be unlike any other standardized test that you have encountered in the past, there are several ways to acclimate yourself to this type of exam that will help alleviate any test-taking anxiety that you may feel. Following are some of the most effective tried-and-true methods to help you master the MAT.

Become comfortable with the format of the MAT. When you take our practice tests, simulate actual testing conditions as closely as possible. Stay calm and focused. You'll have half a minute for each analogy, so pace yourself accordingly. You will probably notice that pacing becomes much easier after only a few practice tests. This will boost your confidence and greatly increase your chances of doing well on the actual exam.

Read all of the possible answers. This is more important on the MAT than virtually any other standardized test, because relationships between MAT analogy items can be very subtle. If you ignore even minor nuances in word meanings, you are more likely to choose an answer that is only partially correct. Be sure to choose the best answer, rather than one that looks correct on its face.

Use the process of elimination. If you are having difficulty with a particular analogy, go through all the possible answer choices and eliminate as many as possible. Even if you can only eliminate one answer choice, you have increased your chance of picking a correct answer by 25 percent.

Work on the easiest analogies first. Remember, time spent on one analogy is time not spent on another. Go through the entire test answering questions in those subject areas that come easiest to you, then return to the more difficult ones. If you spend too much time working on difficult analogies, time may run out before you've had the opportunity to answer easier ones.

Guess. Your score on the MAT will be based on the number of questions answered correctly. Therefore, you should never leave a question blank. Even if you have absolutely no idea what the correct answer to a given analogy might be, guessing still gives you a 25 percent chance of getting it right. If you leave a question blank, that chance is reduced to zero.

Be sure that the oval you are marking on your answer sheet corresponds to the number of the analogy in the test booklet. The graders of the MAT, whether your answer sheets are hand scored or machine scored, have no sympathy for clerical errors. One incorrectly placed answer could disrupt your entire answer sheet, and even if you are fortunate enough to discover the problem early, you will waste valuable time correcting your answer sheet. Be extremely careful when filling in your answer choices.

If you're taking the computerized MAT, be sure to mouse-click your intended choice. And when making your choice, check the screen to ensure your command has been accepted. This is a good habit to keep yourself from having the computer lull you into inattentiveness.

▍THE DAY OF THE TEST

Before the Test

On the day of the test, you should wake up early after a good night's rest and have a full breakfast. Dress comfortably, and in layers that can be added or removed as conditions in the testing center require. You should make sure that you will not be distracted by hunger, or by being too hot or too cold. Plan to arrive at the testing center early. No one will be permitted into the testing center after the test has begun, and arriving early will allow you to become acclimated to the surroundings of the testing center. This will minimize the chance of distraction during the test.

To facilitate your early arrival, you may want to prepare everything you will need the night before the test. Be sure that you have

- your admission ticket

- two forms of identification (at least one with a recent photograph)

- several sharpened No. 2 pencils with erasers, as none will be provided at the testing center.

If you wish, you may wear a watch to the testing center; just be sure to disable any alarms or signals that may be present. These might distract you and the other candidates. No dictionaries, calculators, notebooks, briefcases, or packages may be taken into the testing center. Drinking, smoking, and eating are also prohibited.

During the Test

Once you have entered the testing center, follow all directions of the test supervisor carefully. If you do not, you risk being dismissed from the testing center, forfeiting your testing fees, and having your scores canceled.

When all of the testing materials have been distributed, the test supervisor will give you instructions for filling out the answer sheet. You must fill out this sheet carefully, because any errors may affect your score reports.

Once the test is under way, be sure to fill in your answer choices carefully, completely, and neatly. If you change your answer, be sure to completely erase your previous choice. Any stray marks or incompletely erased answer choices may be misinterpreted by the scoring machine, thus depriving you of valuable points.

After the Test

Once you have finished the test, turn in your testing materials and proceed to the exit in an orderly fashion. Your score report will arrive in approximately 10 to 15 working days.

Chapter 2

Main Analogy Review

▌ INTRODUCTION

The Miller Analogies Test is unlike any test you have taken previously, and probably unlike any test you will ever encounter again. The MAT is a high-level, analytic ability test. It is used by graduate schools and employers to identify candidates who are logical thinkers, whose knowledge goes beyond memorizing and repeating information. The Miller Analogies Test contains analogy questions that test reasoning ability in a multitude of subject areas.

The following lists some of the relationships that you will be asked to discern:

RELATIONSHIP TYPES:

- **SEMANTIC**
  Meaning, definition, synonym, antonym, contrast, degree, intensity, word parts, expressions

- **CLASSIFICATION**
  Hierarchy, classification, category, membership, whole/part

- **ASSOCIATION**
  Object/characteristic, order, sequence, transformation, agent/object, creator, creation, function, purpose

- **LOGICAL/MATHEMATICAL**
  Mathematical equivalence, multiples, negation, letter or sound patterns

The content areas from which the analogies will be taken include:

CONTENT AREAS:

- **SOCIAL SCIENCES**
  Sociology, Psychology, History, Anthropology, Philosophy, Economics, Geography

- **NATURAL SCIENCES**

  Chemistry, Botany, Biology, Physics, Geology, Health Sciences

- **FINE ARTS AND HUMANITIES**

  Art, Art History, Music, Literature

- **MATHEMATICS**

  Ability to perform mathematical operations such as multiplication, division, square roots, etc., in order to analyze numerical relationships, knowledge of Roman numerals

- **VOCABULARY**

  Words that would be considered difficult

- **GENERAL INFORMATION**

  This is a catchall category which contains information not included in the previous categories, but which may be considered common information

At this point you may be awestruck at the diversity and number of subject areas covered in the Miller Analogies Test. After all, you probably didn't study some of these courses in your career as a student so far. What's more, you might not have any interest in them at all.

Don't let the types or quantity of subjects deter you. You are not expected to have in-depth knowledge in all these subjects. Rather, the Miller Analogies Test expects you to have a superficial acquaintance with these topics.

In fact, the Miller Analogies Test contains what you could consider trivial information about these subjects. If you can answer Jeopardy quiz show questions, or play a decent game of Trivial Pursuit, you have about as much knowledge as you need in the subject areas. Remember, that this is an ANALOGY test. You need to show that you can discern the RELATIONSHIP between the words in the questions.

Within any of the various topics, there are certain ideas that would be known to you even if you didn't study the course. For example,

- You don't have to be a history major to know that Ceylon is the former name of the nation now known as Sri Lanka.

- You don't have to be a chemistry major to know that a pH of 7 is neutral.

- You don't have to be an English major to know that Mark Twain was the pseudonym for Samuel Clemens.

- You don't have to be a music major to know that "fortissimo" means "very loudly."

- You don't have to be a math major to know that 3 squared is 9 or that the Roman numeral I is one and X is ten.

- You don't have to be an English major to know that Candide is a character in a novel by Voltaire.

These are examples of the types of information that are demanded by the Miller Analogies Test. As you can tell by these few examples, although there are many subjects tested, there is little esoteric or profound knowledge required within the subject area.

The major difficulty that you will encounter on the test is the same as any test that contains analogies—in each question, you must determine the relationship between the given words and then decide which word in the answer choices best maintains that relationship.

TEST FORMAT: FIND THE RELATIONSHIP BETWEEN THE WORDS

An analogy is a relationship between two things that may not be alike in some respects, but are similar in at least one way. It is this similarity that is the key to the analogy. It is therefore important that you know the definitions of the words to be compared, because what you will be doing on the Miller Analogies Test is finding how the definitions of these words relate to each other.

Actually, an analogy can be considered the verbal equivalent of a proportion in mathematics. In math, you recall that a colon between a pair of numbers indicates that the numbers are a ratio; as, for example, 4:1 means, "the odds are 4 to 1." The relationship 4 to 1 is the same as the relationship 8 to 2. If we translate the ratio 4:1 into words, we can say that: for every four times that something happens in one case, it happens one time in the other case.

In a verbal comparison, a colon also separates two words that can be compared. We would read a verbal comparison as: Word A has a relationship to Word B—A : B. A double colon between two such comparisons means that the relationship Word A to Word B is the same as the relationship Word C to Word D—A : B :: C : D.

It is essential that you identify the relationship between Word A and Word B in order to complete the pattern that exists between C and D.

DESOLATE : JOYOUS—The relationship between these words can be stated as DESOLATE is the opposite of JOYOUS. Similarly, the relationship between

DESPAIR : HOPE can be stated as DESPAIR is the opposite of HOPE. Therefore, we could write these analogies as: DESOLATE : JOYOUS :: DESPAIR : HOPE.

In the Miller Analogies Test, one word in the verbal equation has been replaced by four choices. Only one choice accurately completes the relationship. The analogy may appear in the test as any one of the following combinations:

$$(a, b, c, d) : B :: C : D$$

$$A : (a, b, c, d) :: C : D$$

$$A : B :: (a, b, c, d) : D$$

$$A : B :: C : (a, b, c, d)$$

Example

CASSETTE : AUDITORY :: BOOK : (a. tactile, b. visual, c. olfactory, d. savory)

Answer: (b) visual. A CASSETTE provides an AUDITORY experience, and a BOOK provides a VISUAL experience.

Any one of the terms in the analogy may be replaced in the question.

Example

HOUSE : SHELTER :: (a. animal, b. friendship, c. food, d. job): SUSTENANCE

Answer: (c) food. A HOUSE provides a person with SHELTER, and FOOD provides a person with SUSTENANCE.

Example

KEYBOARD : (a. typewriter, b. screen, c. puzzle, d. element) :: DASHBOARD : CAR

Answer: (a) typewriter. A KEYBOARD is part of a TYPEWRITER, and a DASHBOARD is part of a CAR.

Example

(a. campus, b. building, c. tribe, d. army) : REGIMENTS :: SCHOOL : GRADES

Answer: (d) army. An ARMY unit is organized by REGIMENTS, and a SCHOOL unit is organized by GRADES.

No matter how you rearrange the words, a relationship exists between their definitions. An ARMY and a SCHOOL are both institutions, and REGIMENTS and GRADES are both methods of organization within them. The key to completing analogies is to recognize the pattern within them.

PARITY OF PARTS OF SPEECH

The Miller Analogies Test is essentially a test of your ability to recognize the relationship between the meanings of words. Parts of speech are always consistent within individual analogies. If the choices in the question are ADJECTIVE : NOUN, then the answer must be ADJECTIVE : NOUN. Some words can be used as both verbs and nouns. Don't get confused. The specific parts of speech that are given will remain constant.

Example

(a. drill, b. string, c. board, d. nail) : HAMMER :: FLUTE : PIANO

Answer: (a) drill. If you look at the total question, FLUTE and PIANO are both nouns. The relationship between them can be stated as the following: Both a FLUTE and a PIANO are instruments. The word we would be seeking is a noun also, and would be related to HAMMER in the same way. Both a DRILL and a HAMMER are tools (instruments). DRILL is also a verb, but by looking over the total analogy, we know that we are looking for a noun.

Although INAUGURATE: PRESIDENT :: CORONATION : KING seems to be correct on the surface, this is not a valid analogy. "Inaugurate" is a verb and "coronation" is a noun. The two words are not the same part of speech. Don't be fooled by words that seem to go together.

TYPES OF ANALOGIES: IDENTIFYING CONNECTIONS

The most important element of the MAT is identifying the connections between words and fill in the missing blank with the best choice. Though this action sounds rather simple, there are actually several different types of connections that you should be familiar with before going into the test.

SEMANTIC

1. Word : Synonym/Definition

This type of analogy is the relationship between a word and its synonym. You could say that any given word can be replaced by the other.

Example

HABITATION : (a. nest, b. earth, c. dome, d. abode) :: VOID : BLANK

Answer: (d). First, we establish the relationship between the given words. VOID (emptiness) is a synonym for BLANK: therefore, we are looking for a word which is a synonym for HABITATION. The correct answer is (d) abode. A HABITATION is an ABODE. The words are synonyms of each other.

2. Word : Antonym/Contrast

This analogy type is the relationship between a word and its opposite.

Example

FRAGMENT : ASSEMBLE :: IMPOVERISH : (a. enrich, b. money, c. egocentric, d. humble)

Answer: (a) enrich. The first thing to do is establish the relationship between the given words. What is the relationship between FRAGMENT and ASSEMBLE? We know that FRAGMENT can be either a noun meaning "a part broken off," or a verb meaning "to break into fragments." In order to determine which part of speech we will be working with, it's necessary to check the part of speech of its verbal equivalent, which is IMPOVERISH. IMPOVERISH is a verb, and therefore FRAGMENT must also be a verb. We can then say, that FRAGMENT (break into fragments) is the opposite of ASSEMBLE (put together.) The correct answer is (a) enrich. IMPOVERISH (make poor) is the opposite of ENRICH (make rich).

A similar analogy is word extension : antonym. In this case the words have opposite meanings, but different parts of speech.

Example

> PASSIVE : ACTIVITY :: OBJECTIVE: (a. prejudice, b. humor, c. envy, d. elegance)

Answer: (a) PREJUDICE. Looking at the given words, we determine that if you are PASSIVE, then you don't show any ACTIVITY. The correct answer would maintain that relationship. If you are OBJECTIVE, then you don't show any PREJUDICE. PASSIVE and OBJECTIVE are adjectives describing a condition, and ACTIVITY and PREJUDICE are nouns.

3. Condition/Intensity : Greater or Lesser Degree

This analogy compares one situation and its greater or lesser degree of intensity.

Example

> HAPPY : EXHILARATED :: (a. punish, b. hit, c. respond, d. relate) : CASTIGATE

Answer: (a) PUNISH. If we create a sentence using the given words, we could say that HAPPY is a less extreme feeling than EXHILARATED, and (a) PUNISH is a less severe action than CASTIGATE which means "to punish severely." The pattern can also be reversed.

Example

> FORTIFY : BUILD :: SANITIZE : (a. germs, b. building, c. clean, d. length)

Answer: (c) CLEAN. If you FORTIFY something, you build it with strength so FORTIFY is a greater degree than BUILD. If you SANITIZE something, you clean it with more emphasis than normal.

4.   Word Part/Meaning

This analogy is when a term describes or explains the purpose of the other word.

Example

BI : TWO :: ANNUAL : (a. one b. two c. three d. four)

Answer: (a.) 1. BI means TWO, while ANNUAL only means ONCE a year.

CLASSIFICATION

5.   Part : Whole (or Whole : Part)

This analogy type represents the relationship between a segment and the whole entity.

Example

SONG : (a. tune, b. repertory, c. instrument, d. conductor) :: CHAPTER : BOOK

Answer: (b) REPERTORY. If we establish the relationship between the given words, we would say that a SONG is part of a whole REPERTORY, and a CHAPTER is part of a whole BOOK.

The pattern can also be reversed. For example, BANK : VAULT or ZOO : CAGE. If we assume that a BANK is a whole building or organization, then a VAULT is a smaller part of it. Also, in the organization we call a ZOO, a CAGE is a part of this whole.

Example

SPECTRUM : RED :: ELEMENTS : (a. hydrogen, b. zinc, c. copper, d. oxygen)

Answer: (a) HYDROGEN. The relationship between the given words can be stated that the SPECTRUM contains RED as the first color of the group of colors in the passage of light through a prism. Therefore, the correct answer is (a) HYDROGEN. Of all the ELEMENTS in the chemical chart, we would find that HYDROGEN is the first element listed in the group. This is a difficult analogy. Not only are we looking for a word that is part of the whole, but we are also seeking its relative position within the group.

6.   Person or Thing : Characteristic (or Characteristic : Person or Thing)

This analogy type requires that you establish a relationship between a given person or thing and the characteristic that it represents.

Example

PREVARICATOR: (a. builds, b. travels, c. lies, d. sings) :: THIEF : STEALS

Answer: (c) LIES. If we work from the given words, the sentence would be a THIEF is a person who STEALS. We are then looking for a word that describes a PREVARICATOR. A PREVARICATOR is a person who deviates from the truth when speaking, therefore, a PREVARICATOR is a person who LIES.

This category is similar to the one in which a thing or person is compared with the action or job that they perform.

Example

ACTOR : PORTRAYS :: JURY : (a. evaluates, b. convenes, c. rules, d. influences)

Answer: (a) EVALUATES. An ACTOR is a person whose job it is to PORTRAY a character, and a JURY is made up of people whose job it is to EVALUATE evidence. The pattern can also be reversed. For example: REVOLTS : REBEL or DECORATES : GARNISH.

Example

GEOPHYSICS : (a. solids, b. stars, c. motion, d. earth) :: GEOLOGY : MATTER

Answer: (d) EARTH. Using the given analogy, we would create a sentence that states GEOLOGY is the study of MATTER. We then need to find which word represents the object of the study of GEOPHYSICS. The correct answer is (d) earth. GEOPHYSICS is the study of the EARTH.

7. Group : Member (or Member : Group)

This analogy represents the relationship between a group and a member or representative of that group. It is similar to part : whole in that one word represents a piece of the other.

Example

(a. pride, b. flock, c. coven, d. pack) : LION :: SENATE : SENATOR

Answer: (a) PRIDE. A PRIDE is the group to which a LION belongs, and the SENATE is the group to which a SENATOR belongs. The pattern can also be reversed as member : group, for example CAT : FELINE, or SALMON : FISH, or GRAPE : FRUIT.

Example

DATA : CENSUS :: (a. symposium, b. congregation, c. resort, d. retreat) : OPINIONS

Answer: (a) SYMPOSIUM. Using the given words, we would create a sentence that states that DATA is a piece of information that comes from a CENSUS. We are then looking for a word that represents many opinions. The correct answer is (a) symposium. A SYMPOSIUM is a collection of opinions about a topic.

ASSOCIATION

8. Cause : Effect (or Effect : Cause)

This type of analogy involves a word and the outcome it causes. However, the analogy could reverse the relationship by starting with the outcome and following with the word itself.

Example

BACTERIA : DISEASE :: (a. planet, b. sun, c. noon, d. day) : HEAT

Answer: (b) SUN. The relationship between the given words can be stated as BACTERIA causes DISEASE. We then have to determine which of the words best fits that same relationship to HEAT. The correct answer is (b) sun. BACTERIA is a cause of DISEASE and SUN is a cause of HEAT.

The reverse pattern is Effect : Cause. Examples are:

FOOD : AGRICULTURE :: LAUGHTER : JOKE

Here, FOOD is the result of AGRICULTURE which causes it to be produced. LAUGHTER is the result that follows (or should follow), a JOKE.

9. User : Tool (or Tool : User)

This analogy type represents a name of a person who uses a specific tool.

Example

(a. doctor, b. singer, c. captain, d. dentist) : DRILL :: CARPENTER : HAMMER

Answer: (d) dentist. Using the given words, we could say that a CARPENTER is a person who uses a HAMMER. Therefore, we would be looking for an answer that represents the type of person who would use a DRILL. A DENTIST uses a DRILL.

The pattern can also be reversed.

Example

BOBBIN : (a. musician, b. equestrian, c. weaver, d. radiologist) :: LATHE : MACHINIST

Answer: (c) weaver. Using the given words, we would create a sentence that states a LATHE is used by a MACHINIST. We are then looking for the name of the person who would use a BOBBIN. A BOBBIN is a cylinder or spindle for dispensing thread. Therefore, A BOBBIN is used by a WEAVER.

A variation of this pattern might be instrument : application or tool : application, and its reversal. For example,

WORD PROCESSOR : WRITING :: TROWEL : GARDENING

A WORD PROCESSOR is used in WRITING and a TROWEL is used in GARDENING.

10. Trait : Example (or Example : Trait)

This type of analogy states the relationship between a distinguishing quality and an example of that quality.

Example

> INGENIOUS : (a. convoluted, b. intelligent, c. dishonest, d. courageous) :: BRAZEN : EXTROVERTED

Answer: (b) intelligent. Using the given words, we would say that a BRAZEN (marked by boldness) person is EXTROVERTED (a person interested in things outside the self). If a person is INGENIOUS (has skill or cleverness), then that person has to be INTELLIGENT.

> The pattern can also be reversed.

Example

> TUNELESS : DISCORDANT :: FRAGRANT : (a. ambrosial, b. pungent, c. rancid, d. lackluster)

Answer: (a) ambrosial. Using the given words, we would say that TUNELESS is an example of something that is DISCORDANT (a harsh combination of musical sounds). We are then seeking a word of which FRAGRANT is an example. The correct answer is (a) ambrosial (capable of being a food for a god). An example of something that is FRAGRANT would be an example of a food that is AMBROSIAL.

11. Trait : Location : Setting

Example

> EURO: ITALY :: PESO: (a. SPAIN b. YEN c. MEXICO d. CANADA)

Answer: (c) MEXCIO. EURO is the currency of Italy and PESO is the currency of MEXICO.

12. Trait : Grammar Transformation

Example

ME : MINE :: THEY : (a. HIS b. HERS c. OUR d. THEIRS)

Answer: (d) THEIRS. The possession form of THEY is THEIRS, which corresponds to ME: MINE.

13. Trait : Object : Material (or Material : Object)

This analogy type represents an object and the material of which it is made.

Example

SKIRT : (a. book, b. gabardine, c. picture, d. window) :: SHIRT : COTTON

Answer: (b) gabardine. GABARDINE is a material that SKIRTS can be made of, and COTTON is a material that SHIRTS can be made of.

The pattern can also be reversed.

Example

SILK : PARACHUTE :: METAL : (a. coins, b. money, c. currency, d. debt)

Answer: (a) coins. Using the given words, we would say that SILK is the material that a PARACHUTE is made out of. METAL is the material that (a) COINS are made out of. Remember that although (b) money and (c) currency are plausible choices, they are not the correct answers. Not all money is made of metal, nor is all currency.

14. Symbol : Institution (or Institution : Symbol)

This analogy type represents the relationship between a specific symbol and the institution it represents.

Example

> (a. pamphlet, b. vote, c. flag, d. bouquet) : GOVERNMENT :: CROWN : MONARCHY

Answer: (c) flag. Using the given words, a CROWN is the symbol of a MONARCHY (a nation or state governed by a monarch). A FLAG is the symbol of institutional GOVERNMENT. The pattern can also be reversed.

Institution : Symbol

Example

> HAWAII : HIBISCUS :: NEW YORK : (a. pansy, b. rose, c. carnation, d. lily)

Answer: (b) rose. Using the given words, we would state that HAWAII is a state whose flower symbol is represented by the HIBISCUS flower. We are then looking for the flower that represents the state of NEW YORK. The correct answer is (b) rose. The ROSE is the state flower of NEW YORK.

LOGICAL/MATHEMATICAL

Some of the questions will have mathematical equations, fractions, negation, pattern identification, and multiples.

Fraction or Multiple

25:5	25 is 5 squared
FORTNIGHT: WEEK	A fortnight is twice as long as a week.
25%: ¼	25% and ¼ have the same numerical values, but they are written in different ways.

Relation that is non-semantic, but has some other obvious similarity such as rhyme, wordplay, or letter reversal.

THOUGH: KNOW   THOUGH and KNOW sound alike, but they are not spelled alike.

STAR: RATS   STAR is RATS spelled backwards.

SEPARATE: RAT   The word RAT is inside the word SEPARATE.

TOPICS

The Miller Analogies Test challenges you to reason the relationships between words in the following subject areas: Social Sciences, Natural Sciences, Fine Arts and Humanities, Mathematics, History, Vocabulary, and General Information.

SOCIAL SCIENCES

This category includes subjects within the area considered social sciences. These types of subjects could include: sociology, psychology, anthropology, philosophy, economics, and geography. Although these are wide ranging categories, you don't have to be a social science major to be able to answer the questions. For the most part the questions will be on general topics that pertain to the subject area. Look at the following examples.

Sociology

Example

(a. society, b. role, c. action, d. government) : INDIVIDUAL :: POPULATION : UNIT

Answer: (a) society. A SOCIETY is comprised of INDIVIDUALS, and a POPULATION contains UNITS. This is an example of whole : part.

Psychology

Example

PIAGET: COGNITIVE :: (a. Kohlberg, b. Skinner, c. Freud, d. Dewey) : MORAL

Answer: (a) Kohlberg. PIAGET studied the COGNITIVE development in children, and KOHLBERG studied the moral development of children. This is an example of person : characteristic.

Anthropology

Example

> EVOLUTION : DARWIN :: (a. culture, b. fossils, c. language, d. conflict) : MEAD

Using the given analogy words, we would say that the study of EVOLUTION was pursued by DARWIN. Therefore, we need to choose which aspect of anthropology was studied by MEAD. The correct answer is (a) culture. The CULTURE of primitive societies was studied by Margaret Mead. This is an example of person : characteristic.

Philosophy

Example

> (a. realism, b. naturalism, c. pluralism, d. hedonism) : SCIENTIFIC EXPLANATION :: EMPIRICISM : SENSE PERCEPTIONS

Answer: (b) naturalism. Using the given words, we would create a sentence that states EMPIRICISM (a philosophical term that means that all knowledge is derived from experience by way of sense perception) is based on sense perceptions. We are then looking for the philosophical term on which SCIENTIFIC EXPLANATION is based. The answer is NATURALISM. This is a philosophical term that says that because all objects in nature are regular and not haphazard, they are all subject to a scientific explanation. This is an example of a trait : example type of analogy.

Economics

Example

> Washington : 1 :: (a. 5, b. 10, c. 20, d. 50) : Lincoln

Answer: (a) 5. Using the given analogy we would create the following sentence: The portrait of Washington is on the $1 bill. Therefore, we are looking for the denomination of the bill on which Lincoln is depicted. The correct answer is that Lincoln is on the $5 bill. This is an example of part to whole. The portrait of Lincoln is part of the $5 bill.

Geography

Example

ALASKA : RHODE ISLAND :: MAINE : (a. Alabama, b. Pennsylvania, c. Florida, d. Virginia)

Answer: (c) Florida. If we look at the given words in the analogy, we could say that ALASKA is the largest state in land area while RHODE ISLAND is the smallest state in land area. Therefore, we are looking for opposites. We are looking for a state that has an opposite relationship to MAINE. Since MAINE is the northernmost state on the eastern seaboard, what is the southernmost state? The correct answer is FLORIDA. This analogy type is closest to word : antonym.

NATURAL SCIENCES

This category includes subjects from the following areas: chemistry, botany, biology, physics, geology, and health sciences. The types of analogy questions that you will be asked are based on information from these topics. As before, it is not necessary for you to be an expert in these areas. Look at the following examples. The information necessary for you to know is of a general type, and doesn't require much in-depth knowledge of all the subjects.

Chemistry

Example

ATOM : ELEMENT :: MOLECULE : (a. compound, b. mass, c. mixture, d. energy)

Answer: (a) compound. When we look at the given words, we can say that an ATOM is the smallest part of an ELEMENT that retains the element's properties. Therefore, we are looking for a word that can complete the following sentence: A MOLECULE is the smallest part of a ? that contains the properties of it. A COMPOUND is the correct answer. A molecule is the smallest part of a compound that retains that compound's properties. This is an example of a part : whole analogy.

Botany

Example

> GENUS : (a. division, b. class, c. order, d. kingdom) :: MISTLETOE :
> PLANT

Answer: (d) kingdom. Using the given words, we would say that MISTLETOE is a part of the whole category of PLANTS. In botany, plants are placed in categories from the most to the least specific. GENUS is the most specific name (the part) and KINGDOM is the least specific (the whole category). If we rearrange the analogy, we could say that the GENUS is MISTLETOE, and the KINGDOM is PLANT.

Biology

Example

> (a. cellulose, b. water, c. chlorophyll, d. carbon dioxide) : PLANT CELL ::
> PROTEIN : ANIMAL CELL

Answer: (a) cellulose. The given analogy could be stated as PROTEIN is the material that makes up the membrane of an ANIMAL CELL. We are then looking for a word which makes up the membrane of a PLANT CELL. The cell membrane of a typical PLANT CELL is made up of CELLULOSE. This analogy type is mostly related to trait : characteristic. Because the membrane has cellulose it must be a plant cell.

Physics

Example

> ROBOTS : MACHINES :: CONSTELLATIONS : (a. planets, b. gravity,
> c. moons, d. stars)

Answer: (d) stars. Using the given words, we could create a sentence which states that ROBOTS are MACHINES made up of many machines arranged in a specific way. Therefore, we would need a word that retains this relationship. CONSTELLATIONS are made up of many STARS arranged in a specific way. This analogy is closest to whole : part.

Geology

Example

LAPIDARY : (a. concrete, b. glass, c. stone, d. plant) :: SCULPTOR : CLAY

Answer: (c) stone. A LAPIDARY is a person who turns a common, rough STONE into a gem. If we use the given words, we would create a sentence that states that a SCULPTOR turns CLAY into a work of art. This is an example of a person : job type of analogy.

Health Sciences

Example

ANEMIA : IRON :: SCURVY : (a. beta carotene, b. calcium, c. vitamin A, d. vitamin C)

Answer: (d) vitamin C. Using the given words, the relationship can be stated as ANEMIA is a disease caused by a lack of IRON in your diet. We are then looking for a word that would fit into the sentence SCURVY is a disease caused by a lack of ? in your diet. SCURVY is caused by a lack of vitamin C. This analogy type is most similar to extension : antonym. If you have SCURVY then you don't have any vitamin C in your diet.

FINE ARTS AND HUMANITIES

This category can be broken down into four general areas: art, art history, music, and literature. As with the previous subject areas, it is not necessary to be an expert in the individual subject areas. It is important for you to have a general conceptual understanding of the topics.

Art

Example

> (a. easel, b. canvas, c. palette, d. brush) : COLORS :: BOWL :
> INGREDIENTS

Answer: (c) palette (a board used by an artist to mix colors). If we use the original words, we could say that a BOWL is what a cook uses to mix INGREDIENTS. Therefore we are looking for an object that is used to mix COLORS. PALETTE is the only correct choice. This is an example of a thing : action analogy.

Art History

Example

> GILBERT STUART : PORTRAITS :: CLAUDE MONET : (a. abstract
> shapes, b. impressionistic art, c. fantasy, d. realism)

Answer: (b) impressionistic art. Using the given analogy we can state the relationship between the words as GILBERT STUART painted mostly PORTRAITS. Therefore we would have to find the type of art that CLAUDE MONET was most famous for. That would be Impressionism. This would be a type of person : characteristic analogy.

Music

Example

> APPALACHIAN SPRING : UNITED STATES :: SWAN LAKE :
> (a. Austria, b. England, c. Italy, d. Russia)

Answer: (d). Using the given words, we could state the relationship in a sentence that says: APPALACHIAN SPRING is music composed in the UNITED STATES by Aaron Copeland. Therefore, in what country was SWAN LAKE composed? The correct answer is SWAN LAKE was composed in RUSSIA by Peter Tchaikovksy. This is an example of a thing : characteristic analogy.

Literature

Example

> *MACBETH* : *HAMLET* :: *TAMING OF THE SHREW* : (a. *The Little Foxes,*
> b. *Cyrano de Bergerac,* c. *King Lear,* d. *The Iliad*)

Answer: (c) *King Lear.* The relationship between *MACBETH* and *HAMLET* is that they are both plays written by Shakespeare. *TAMING OF THE SHREW* is also a play written by Shakespeare; therefore, we are looking for an answer which would also be a Shakespearean play. In a way, this could be considered a synonym analogy. *MACBETH, HAMLET, TAMING OF THE SHREW,* and *KING LEAR* are all plays written by the same author.

MATHEMATICS

This category contains mathematically-oriented analogy questions that could include knowledge of mathematical operations, such as your ability to do multiplication, division, and square roots. You have to determine the relationships between numbers. You might also be tested on your knowledge of Roman numerals. Included in this category could be a type of question testing your general knowledge of math related information. This topic would be found in the following analogies.

Example

> (a. troy, b. gram, c. ton, d. yard) : LENGTH :: QUART : CAPACITY

Answer: (d) yard. Using the given words, we would state that a QUART is a measure of CAPACITY. Therefore, which word would indicate a measure of LENGTH? The YARD is a measure of LENGTH. This could be considered a thing : characteristic analogy. A YARD characterizes LENGTH and a QUART characterizes CAPACITY.

Example

> MILLION : 6 :: TRILLION : (a. 9, b. 10, c. 11, d. 12)

Answer: (d) 12. A MILLION is represented by 6 zeros, and a TRILLION is represented by 12 zeros. This could be considered a characteristic : thing analogy. A MILLION is represented, or characterized by 6 zeros.

Other types of analogy questions may require that you perform mathematical operations in order to determine the relationship between the given numbers.

Example

3 : 81 :: (a. 4, b. 5, c. 6, d. 7) : 625

Answer: (b) 5. The relationship of 3 and 81 is that the number 3 is multiplied by itself four times. Therefore, you have to determine which number multiplied by itself four times equals 625.

Another type of mathematical analogy may be:

Example

(a. 0.35, b. 1.45, c. 0.75, d. 1.00) : 0.25 :: 1.56 : 0.52

Answer: (c) 0.75. If you look at the given numbers, you will determine that by dividing 1.56 by 3, you will get 0.52. Therefore, you need to figure out which number divided by 3 will give you 0.25.

Another type of mathematically oriented question you may encounter on the Miller Analogies Test is based on your knowledge of Roman numerals:

Example

L : C :: (a. X , b. M, c. D, d. V) : XX

Answer: (a) X. If you know that V = 5, X = 10, XX = 20, L = 50, C = 100, D = 500, and M = 1,000, then you can determine that the relationship between L and C could be stated as follows: L is one-half of C. Therefore you will need a number that is one-half of XX. Since 10 (X) is one-half of 20 (XX), that is the correct answer.

HISTORY

The Miller Analogies Test requires you to have some general knowledge of American History and Government, as well as some knowledge of World History. You don't have to be a history major in order to answer the types of questions found on the test. The types of questions are so general that you've probably studied the topics throughout your school career.

American History

Example

> (a. Casey Jones, b. Paul Revere, c. Franklin Roosevelt, d. Martin Luther King, Jr.) : PATRICK HENRY :: HARRY TRUMAN : DOUGLAS MacARTHUR

Answer: (b) Paul Revere. If you look at the given relationship, you may determine that the most obvious one is that DOUGLAS MacARTHUR was a general who served under President HARRY TRUMAN. Therefore, they were contemporaries. You then need to find which of the choices was a contemporary of PATRICK HENRY.

PAUL REVERE and PATRICK HENRY were contemporaries, just as HARRY TRUMAN and DOUGLAS MacARTHUR were. This could be considered a type of synonymous analogy. Both parts of the analogy are similar in that the people were contemporaries.

American Government

Example

> INTERNAL REVENUE : TREASURY :: (a. prisons, b. consumer affairs, c. public affairs, d. mint) : JUSTICE

Answer: (a) prisons. The INTERNAL REVENUE service is part of the TREASURY department and the PRISONS are part of the JUSTICE department in American government. This could be considered a whole : part analogy.

World History

Example

> FRENCH REVOLUTION : NAPOLEON BONAPARTE :: RUSSIAN REVOLUTION : (a. Lenin, b. Stalin, c. Khruschev, d. Nicholas)

Answer: (a) Lenin. After the French Revolution, NAPOLEON BONAPARTE came to power as a dictator over France, and after the RUSSIAN REVOLUTION the person who came to rule Russia was LENIN. This could be considered a person : characteristic analogy. NAPOLEON BONAPARTE is associated with the FRENCH REVOLUTION as LENIN is associated with the RUSSIAN REVOLUTION.

VOCABULARY

As with most of the analogies you are familiar with, those on the Miller Analogies Test require your knowledge of relationships between vocabulary words. These words may be considered difficult for two reasons. One, because they are not the common types of words that you would normally use in everyday language, and two, because they may be related in a way that is not obvious.

Example

> PUERILE : SUBTLETY :: INJUDICIOUS : (a. sagacity, b. repentance, c. candor, d. uncertainty)

Answer: (a) sagacity. The relationship between PUERILE (childish, silly) and SUBTLETY (shrewd, keen), may be stated as follows: Someone who acts in a PUERILE manner will show no SUBTLETY. Someone who behaves in an INJUDICIOUS (not exercising sound judgment) manner will have no SAGACITY (wisdom, prudence). This could be considered a trait : example type of analogy.

Example

> ALIENATION : ENMITY :: (a. examination, b. rejoicing, c. depression, d. repentance) : BLITHE

Answer: (b) rejoicing. The analogy between the given words can be stated as follows: During a time of ALIENATION (estrangement) you might feel ENMITY (hatred) towards something. In order to complete the analogy, we need to find a word that tells you when you would feel BLITHE (happy, lighthearted) toward something. During a time of REJOICING you would feel BLITHE towards something. This could be considered a thing : characteristic type of analogy.

GENERAL INFORMATION

This is a catchall category. It applies to any information not covered in the aforementioned categories. General information is knowledge that you have picked up from various and diverse places, such as magazines, textbooks, recreational readings, etc. It is the kind of general knowledge that you would assume any educated person would know.

Example

JACK NICKLAUS : (a. tennis racket, b. golf club, c. boxing gloves, d. basketball) :: GEORGE GERSHWIN : PIANO

Answer: (b) golf club. The given analogy contains the relationship between GEORGE GERSHWIN and PIANO. GEORGE GERSHWIN is a famous pianist, and therefore his talent lies in playing the PIANO. You then have to determine in what field JACK NICKLAUS is famous. Unless you have been totally hidden away in a dark cave for years, you have to know that JACK NICKLAUS is a famous golfer. So the correct answer has to be GOLF CLUB. This is a user : tool type of analogy.

Example

CITIZEN : VISA :: SOLDIER (a. gun, b. uniform, c. pass, d. detention)

Answer: (c) pass. Using the given analogy, we can say that a CITIZEN requires a VISA to gain entry to or leave a country. In order to maintain the relationship we need to determine what a SOLDIER needs in order to go into or out of his/her base. A SOLDIER requires a PASS to facilitate movement. This would be considered a thing : characteristic type of analogy.

As you can tell by the examples, these types of questions do not fall into any particular subject category, and yet they require you to have an understanding of the given words in order to determine the relationship and complete the analogy.

Example

ROBIN HOOD : ENGLAND :: (a. George Washington, b. Eugene O'Neill, c. Johnny Appleseed, d. Paul Revere) : AMERICA

Answer: (c) Johnny Appleseed. The relationship that you should have determined from the given words is that ROBIN HOOD was or was not a myth in ENGLAND. You then have to find the person who has the same status in America. JOHNNY APPLESEED may or may not have been a myth.

TEST-TAKING STRATEGIES

Consider Alternative Meanings

Sometimes words can have more than one meaning. When looking over the test question, you may be confused at first by the word choices.

Example

(a. pride, b. flock, c. coven, d. pack) : LION :: SENATE : SENATOR

Answer: PRIDE may be a verb (meaning to indulge in pride) or it may be a noun (meaning conceit or a group of lions). If you look over the total analogy, you will realize that the verb form cannot be correct because all the words in the analogy are nouns. Therefore, you have to decide if any of the noun definitions fit into the analogy. It then becomes obvious that PRIDE is the correct answer because one of the definitions of PRIDE refers to a group of LIONS. The relationship that the analogy is testing is that of group : member.

The same reasoning can also apply to the word : synonym analogy PIECE : (a. bowl, b. text, c. handle, d. fragment) :: GLINT : GLEAM. PIECE is a versatile word. It can be used as either a noun (meaning fragment, a written work, a coin, or a gun) or a verb (meaning to repair by adding pieces). If you establish that the relationship between GLINT : GLEAM is that GLINT is a synonym of GLEAM, then you need the word that would be a synonym to PIECE. All the words in the analogy are nouns; therefore, we have to consider the noun meaning of PIECE. Using process of elimination on all PIECE definitions, you will discover that the correct meaning of PIECE in the analogy is that of FRAGMENT.

Some of the words used in the Miller Analogies Test may be unfamiliar to you. If this happens, then it is necessary for you to make the best educated guess you can. Learning the meaning of prefixes, roots, and suffixes may make this task a lot easier. Study the following lists of the most commonly used prefixes, roots, and suffixes. Be sure to use index cards for the items you don't know or find unusual. Look over the examples given, and then try to think of your own. Testing yourself in this way will allow you to see if you really do know the meaning of each item. Even if you aren't sure, be sure to answer every question!

Verify the Part of Speech

When looking at the words in the analogies, one quick and easy method for choosing the correct answer is to look at the parts of speech.

Example

WATER : SWIMMING :: FIELD : (a. grass. b. football c. game d. playing)

Answer: (d) playing is correct. The analogy ratio is WATER, which is a noun, to SWIMMING, which is usually a verb. The other part of the analogy is FIELD, which is a noun. Therefore, it would be best to choose a verb to take the place of the unknown. PLAYING is the only verb given; therefore, it is the correct choice.

HOW TO ANSWER MILLER ANALOGY QUESTIONS

The questions on the Miller Analogies Test are not as straightforward as those you've encountered on other tests that include analogy questions. Other analogy tests rely on your knowledge of the definitions of vocabulary words. The Miller Analogies Test relies not only on your knowledge of words, but also of names in various subjects or fields. In addition, you will be required to perform mathematical computations.

Although the diversity of topics you are tested on may seem to make it impossible for you to study for the MAT, that isn't the case. Most of the information you are required to know is so general and trivial that you are probably already knowledgeable in the subject. The questions are designed to test your familiarity with words or numbers and their relationships—that's all. You will not be expected to know detailed amounts of information. Just be able to establish the relationship between the given analogy words or numbers and maintain that relationship to determine the answer to each question.

Individual questions on the Miller Analogies Test are written in the following way: A : B :: C : D. Any one of these variables may be omitted. On either side of the equation there will be a complete set of words. You have to determine the relationship between the two words on the completed side. It is then necessary for you to choose which would be the best word out of the four choices, which when inserted into the equation, would make both sides have similar relationships.

If an analogy question seems difficult or unclear, you have the option of rearranging the words. Because an analogy is comparable to a mathematical equation, it is feasible for you to rearrange the items so that they might make more sense. For example, a given analogy is A : B :: C : D, and it can be reordered without losing validity, so that B : A :: D : C.

Given Analogy:	ITINERARY : TRIP :: AGENDA : MEETING
Reordered:	TRIP : ITINERARY :: MEETING : AGENDA

This can be interpreted as follows:

Given:	An ITINERARY is used to plan a TRIP, and an AGENDA is used to plan a MEETING.
Reordered:	An ITINERARY is a plan used on a TRIP and an AGENDA is a plan used at a MEETING.

The best way to approach analogy questions is to create a sentence that states a clear and direct relationship between the two given capitalized words on either side of the equation. Substitute the choices into a sentence you create between the choices and the given capitalized word on the other side of the equation. Make sure you look at all the choices before you choose an answer. Eliminate any choice which does not make sense in your answer. Sometimes, there may be two or more possible choices that seem to fit the analogy. In this case, you must go back to your original relationship sentence and revise it.

SHELL : WALNUT :: (a. section, b. juice, c. rind, d. fruit) : ORANGE

The first question you have to ask yourself is, "What is the relationship between the two given capitalized words SHELL and WALNUT?" The most obvious sentence is: SHELL is part of the WALNUT. You then substitute the words in the answer choices and see if they relate to ORANGE in the same way.

(a) SECTION is part of the ORANGE.

(b) JUICE is part of the ORANGE.

(c) RIND is part of the ORANGE.

(d) FRUIT is part of the ORANGE.

So far, choices (a), (b), and (c) are correct. It is therefore necessary to revise our initial sentence to make it more precise.

The SHELL is the outer covering of a WALNUT.

   (a)   SECTION is the outer covering of an ORANGE.

   (b)   JUICE is the outer covering of an ORANGE.

   (c)   RIND is the outer covering of an ORANGE.

   (d)   FRUIT is the outer covering of an ORANGE.

Answer: (c) RIND.

   Lastly, **be careful to fill in your answers carefully**. Only fill the bubble for the question you are currently answering—always double-check that you are on track.

Guessing Strategies

   Unlike some other standardized tests, there is no penalty for guessing. There-fore, it is to your advantage to guess intelligently on every question. You will not be penalized for getting an answer wrong. After you have established a relationship be-tween the two given words, you should then eliminate the obviously incorrect choices, and guess from the remaining ones. If you immediately choose an answer, you have a one in four chance of getting it correct. If you eliminate one choice, you then have a one in three chance, and if you can eliminate two choices, you have a one in two, or 50%, chance of getting it correct. If you leave a question blank, then you will auto-matically get it wrong.

   If you know the meaning of both capitalized words on one side, form a sentence with a clear relationship and then insert the choices to form a relationship with the given word on the other side of the question.

   (a. ape, b. fish, c. zoo, d. swim) : MINNOW :: GEM : AGATE

   A sentence that states the relationship between two given words on the same side is: group : member—A GEM is the group of which AGATE is a member. You then have to find the word which relates to MINNOW in the same way.

   (a)   APE is a group of which MINNOW is a member.

   (b)   FISH is a group of which MINNOW is a member.

   (c)   ZOO is a group of which MINNOW is a member.

   (d)   SWIM is a group of which MINNOW is a member.

Answer: (b) FISH.

Reduce the Number of Choices

Always look for options to eliminate. Occasionally you can save a lot of time if you just happen to note the perfect match from the start. In that case, you should quickly review the other options, just to be sure you are correct.

If you don't know all the words in the question, use the sentence you have already formed, and substitute the answer whose meanings you do know, and eliminate those which don't fit. It's possible that you may be able to use your knowledge of prefixes, roots, and suffixes to help you arrive at the correct answer.

> BIOLOGY : (a. plants, b. life, c. planets, d. death) :: PSYCHOLOGY : MIND

"OGY" is a suffix meaning "the study of," and therefore if you know that "BIO" is a root word meaning "life," then BIOLOGY is the study of life. "PSYCH" is a root word meaning "mind," and so PSYCHOLOGY means the study of the mind. The relationship between the two given words on the same side of the analogy can be expressed as: PSYCHOLOGY is the study of the MIND. You now have to choose which of the following choices is correct.

(a) BIOLOGY is the study of PLANTS.

(b) BIOLOGY is the study of LIFE.

(c) BIOLOGY is the study of PLANETS.

(d) BIOLOGY is the study of DEATH.

Answer: (b) LIFE.

Leave the Difficult Questions for Last

If you do not know the meanings of some of the words, and knowledge of prefixes, roots, and suffixes isn't appropriate, then try to recall in what context you might have heard the words used. Keep in mind that you are looking for a match with the same relationship as the capitalized given word pair, you are not looking for a word that matches in meaning.

> (a. stratosphere, b. environment, c. gravity, d. technology) : JET STREAM :: CRUST : GEOLOGIC FAULT

If you can't recall the meaning of STRATOSPHERE, try and recall some sentence you might have heard in the past that could provide a context for you. "His head is never here on Earth. It's always in the stratosphere." or "That kite flew so high it reached the stratosphere." These sentences give you an idea that "stratosphere" is a word meaning very high up. As before, we follow the first step in approaching an analogy question by creating a relationship between the two given words on one side of the verbal equation:

Within the Earth's CRUST is found GEOLOGIC FAULT.

    (a)   Within the Earth's STRATOSPHERE is found JET STREAM.

    (b)   Within the Earth's ENVIRONMENT is found JET STREAM.

    (c)   Within the Earth's GRAVITY is found JET STREAM.

    (d)   Within the Earth's TECHNOLOGY is found JET STREAM.

Answer: (a) STRATOSPHERE. If you are looking for a word that means "high up," then ENVIRONMENT, GRAVITY, and TECHNOLOGY can be eliminated. STRATOSPHERE is the choice that is left, and happens to be the most precise relationship for the analogy.

Sometimes prefix, root, suffix or context knowledge can't be used. In this case, try to work backwards from the answer choices.

> STORMY : TEMPESTUOUS :: SCARED : (a. compassionate, b. soothing, c. frightened, d. elegant)

If you don't know the meaning of TEMPESTUOUS, try working the analogy this way:

    (a)   Is there a relationship between SCARED and COMPASSIONATE?

    (b)   Is there a relationship between SCARED and SOOTHING?

    (c)   Is there a relationship between SCARED and FRIGHTENED?

    (d)   Is there a relationship between SCARED and ELEGANT?

There are two possible choices: (b) SCARED and SOOTHING and (c) SCARED and FRIGHTENED. If you are SCARED, then something SOOTHING would calm you down. In (c), if you are SCARED, then you are FRIGHTENED. There are logical relationships within these two answer choices.

Look back at the word STORMY. You know that there are many definitions, among them, to rain or snow with violence, or to have rage. Since the choices for SCARED are adjectives, the best definition of STORMY would be an adjective also.

Let's reorder the analogy.

> STORMY : SCARED :: TEMPESTUOUS : (b. soothing, c. frightened)

If it is STORMY, then you might be SCARED. Therefore:

If it is TEMPESTUOUS, then you might be SOOTHING

If it is TEMPESTUOUS, then you might be FRIGHTENED

Reordered this way, your best guess would be FRIGHTENED. FRIGHTENED is an adjective describing a feeling. By the way, TEMPESTUOUS means "full of storm." So the original analogy STORMY : TEMPESTUOUS describes a word : synonym relationship. SCARED and FRIGHTENED are also synonyms.

Remember

- Always establish a relationship between the given words and use that relationship to complete the analogy.

- Make an educated guess even if you are not sure of the answer. This means using your knowledge of prefixes, roots, suffixes, and context. Sometimes you have to work backwards from the answer.

- Sometimes an uncommon meaning of a word fits the analogy better than a common one. Always be flexible enough to revise your original relationship sentence.

- Look for parts of speech. The part of speech of a word in an analogy is always the same as the part of speech of the corresponding answer choices.

- Look for the relationships between the given numbers. Be flexible enough to work all sorts of mathematical computations on them. Be prepared to work with squares and cubes.

TIME MANAGEMENT

The Miller Analogies Test is a timed test. You will have 60 minutes to answer 120 questions. This means you have 30 seconds to answer each analogy question. All of the analogy questions have the same value. Therefore, you do not want to spend your time deliberating over questions that you don't know at first glance. Get all your sure points. Do not spend a lot of time deliberating over analogy questions with tricky answers or those where you have little confidence.

The best way to approach this test is to quickly go through each question, answering the easiest ones first. By following this strategy, you will be skipping over some questions that you don't know immediately. Make sure that you circle those questions in your question booklet. Skip the corresponding questions on your answer sheet. You do not want to lose points for putting answers in the wrong spaces. After you have answered all the questions that you can, go back to the ones you have skipped, and try working them out by using the strategies mentioned previously. Do not leave any answers blank. Make your best educated guess.

two

Section 2

Quick Study Lists

INTRODUCTION

Because of the wide scope of material covered by the Miller Analogies Test, the most reliable way to review for the exam is to absorb as much information as possible before taking the test. Although you could study for years and not cover everything that *may* be encountered on the exam, you can study the subject reviews in this section to become familiar with the most frequently tested information. When deconstructing an analogy, the more terms you are familiar with, the better your chance of discerning the relationship between the remaining elements. You need not memorize all the information included in this section. You can, however, familiarize yourself with as much of the information as possible, so that you can confidently take the exam.

This section includes reviews for the following subjects:

- Vocabulary (General and Specific)
- Literature
- Art and Architecture
- Music
- History
- Philosophy
- Mythology
- Geography
- Religion
- Science
- Mathematics

VOCABULARY

1. WORD PARTS

Prefix

ab –, a –, abs: **away, from**	absent—away, not present abstain—keep from doing, refrain
ad: **to, toward**	adjacent—next to address—to direct towards
ante: **before**	antecedent—going before in time anterior—occurring before
anti: **against**	antidote—remedy to act against an evil antibiotic—substance that fights against bacteria
be: **over, thoroughly**	bemoan—to mourn over belabor—to exert much labor upon
bi: **two**	bisect—to divide biennial—happening every two years
cata –, cat –, cath: **down**	catacombs—underground passageways catalogue—descriptive list
circum: **around**	circumscribe—to draw a circle around circumspect—watchful on all sides
com: **with**	combine—join together communication—to have dealing with
contra: **against**	contrary—opposed contrast—to stand in opposition
de: **down, from**	decline—to slope downward decontrol—to release from government control

di: **two**   dichotomy—cutting in two
                                            diarchy—system of government with two authorities

dis –, *di*: **apart, away**   discern—to distinguish as separate
                                            dismiss—send away

epi –, *ep* –, *eph*:   epidemic—happening among many people
upon, among   epicycle—circle whose center moves on the
                                            circumference of a greater circle

ex –, *e*: **from, out**   exceed—go beyond the limit
                                            emit—to send forth

extra: **outside, beyond**   extraordinary—beyond or outside the common method
                                            extrasensory—beyond the senses

hyper: **beyond, over**   hyperactive—above the normal activity level
                                            hypercritic– one who is critical beyond measure

hypo: **beneath, lower**   hypodermic—pertaining to or injected beneath the skin
                                            hypocrisy—to be under a pretense of goodness

in –, *il* –, *im* –, *ir*: **not**   inactive—not active
                                            irreversible—not reversible

in –, *il* –, *im* –, *ir*:   instill—to add or introduce slowly
in, on, into   impose—to lay on

inter: **among, between**   intercom—a system allowing for communication
                                                between people
                                            interlude—an intervening period of time

intra: **within**   intravenous—within a vein
                                            intramural—within a single college or its student body

meta: **beyond, over,**   metamorphosis—change in form or nature
along with   metatarsus—part of foot beyond the flat of the foot

mis: **badly, wrongly**   misconstrue—to interpret wrongly
                                            misappropriate—to use wrongly

mono: **one**
monogamy—marriage to one person at a time
monotone—a single, unvaried tone

multi: **many**
multiple—of many parts
multitude—a great number

non: **no, not**
nonsense—lack of sense
nonentity—not existing

ob: **against**
obscene—offensive to modesty
obstruct—to hinder the passage of

para –, par: **beside**
parallel—continuously at equal distance apart
parenthesis—sentence inserted within a passage

per: **through**
persevere—to maintain an effort
permeate—to pass through

poly: **many**
polygon—a plane figure with many sides or angles
polytheism—belief in existence of many gods

post: **after**
posterior—coming after
postpone—to put off until a future time

pre: **before**
premature—ready before the proper time
premonition—a previous warning

pro: **in favor of, forward**
prolific—bringing forth an abundance of offspring
project—throw or cast forward

re: **back, against**
reimburse—pay back
retract—to draw back

semi: **half**
semicircle—half a circle
semiannual—half-yearly

sub: **under**
subdue—to bring under one's power
submarine—travel under the surface of the sea

super: **above**
supersonic—above the speed of sound
superior—higher in place or position

tele –, tel: **across**	telecast—transmit across a distance telepathy—communication between mind and mind at a distance
trans: **across**	transpose—to change the position of two things transmit—to send from one person to another
ultra: **beyond**	ultraviolet—beyond the limit of visibility ultramarine—beyond the sea
un: **not**	undeclared—not declared unbelievable—not believable
uni: **one**	unity—state of oneness unison—sounding together
with: **away, against**	withhold—to hold back withdraw—to take away

Root

act, ag: **do, act, drive**	activate—to make active agile—having quick motion
alt: **high**	altitude—height alto—highest singing voice
alter, altr: **other, change**	alternative—choice among two things altruism—living for the good of others
am, ami: **love, friend**	amiable—good-natured amity—friendship
anim: **mind, spirit**	animated—spirited animosity—violent hatred
annu, enni: **year**	annual—every year centennial—every hundred years

aqua: water	aquarium—tank for water animals and plants aquamarine—semiprecious stone of sea-green color
arch: first, ruler	archenemy—chief enemy archetype—original pattern from which things are copied
aud, audit: hear	audible—capable of being heard audience—assembly of hearers
auto: self	automatic—self-acting autobiography—story about a person who also wrote it
bell: war	belligerent—a party taking part in a war bellicose—war-like
ben, bene: good	benign—kindly disposition beneficial—advantageous
bio: life	biotic—relating to life biology—the science of life
brev: short	abbreviate—make shorter brevity—shortness
cad, cas: fall	cadence—fall in voice casualty—loss caused by death, injury, or illness
capit, cap: head	captain—the head or chief decapitate—to cut off the head
cede, ceed, cess: to go, to yield	recede—to move or fall back proceed—to move onward
cent: hundred	century—hundred years centipede—insect with a hundred legs
chron: time	chronology—science dealing with historical dates chronicle—register of events in order of time
cide, cis: to kill, to cut	homicide—the killing of one human being by another incision—a cut

clam, claim: to shout | acclaim—receive with applause
proclamation—a public announcement

cogn: to know | recognize—to know again
cognition—awareness

corp: body | incorporate—combine into one body
corpse—dead body

cred: to trust,
to believe | incredible—unbelievable
credulous—too prone to believe

cur, curr, curs: to run | current—flowing body of air or water
excursion—short trip

dem: people | democracy—government by the people
epidemic—affecting all people

dic, dict: to say | dictate—to read aloud for another to transcribe
verdict—decision of a jury

doc, doct: to teach | docile—easily instructed
indoctrinate—to instruct

domin: to rule | dominate—to rule
dominion—territory of rule

duc, duct: to lead | conduct—act of guiding
induce—to overcome by persuasion

eu: well, good | eulogy—speech or writing in praise
euphony—pleasantness or smoothness of sound

fac, fact, fect, fic: to
do, to make | factory—location of production
fiction—something invented or imagined

fer: to bear, to carry | transfer—to move from one place to another
refer—to direct to

fin: end, limit | infinity—unlimited
finite—limited in quantity

***flect, flex*: to bend**	flexible—easily bent reflect—to throw back
***fort*: luck**	fortunate—lucky fortuitous—happening by chance
***fort*: strong**	fortify—strengthen fortress—stronghold
***frag, fract*: break**	fragile—easily broken fracture—break
***fug*: flee**	fugitive—fleeing refugee—one who flees to a place of safety
***gen*: class, race**	engender—to breed generic—of a general nature in regard to all members
***grad, gress*: to go, to step**	regress—to go back graduate—to divide into regular steps
***graph*: writing**	telegram—message sent by telegraph autograph—person's own handwriting or signature
***ject*: to throw**	projectile—capable of being thrown reject—to throw away
***leg*: law**	legitimate—lawful legal—defined by law
***leg, lig, lect*: to choose, gather, read**	illegible—incapable of being read election—the act of choosing lecture—a prepared speech read to several people
***liber*: free**	liberal—favoring freedom of ideas liberty—freedom from restraint
***log*: study, speech**	archaeology—study of human antiquities prologue—address spoken before a performance

luc, lum: **light**	translucent—slightly transparent
	illuminate—to light up
magn: **large, great**	magnify—to make larger
	magnificent—great
mal, male: **bad, wrong**	malfunction—to operate incorrectly
	malevolent—evil
mar: **sea**	marine—pertaining to the sea
	submarine—below the surface of the sea
mater, matr: **mother**	maternal—motherly
	matriarch—female head of family or group
mit, miss: **to send**	transmit—to send from one person or place to another
	mission—the act of sending
morph: **shape**	metamorphosis—a changing in shape
	anthropomorphic—having a human shape
mut: **change**	mutable—subject to change
	mutate—to change
nat: **born**	innate—inborn
	native—a person born in a place
neg: **deny**	negative—expressing denial
	renege—to deny
nom: **name**	nominate—to put forward a name
	anonymous—no name given
nov: **new**	novel—new
	renovate—to make as good as new
omni: **all**	omnipotent—all powerful
	omnipresent—all present
oper: **to work**	operate—to work on something
	cooperate—to work with others

pass, path: to feel	pathetic—affecting the tender emotions passionate—moved by strong emotion
pater, part: father	paternal—fatherly patriarch—male head of family or group
ped, pod: foot	pedestrian—one who travels on foot podiatrist—foot doctor
pel, puls: to drive, to push	impel—to drive forward compulsion—irresistible force
phil: love	philharmonic—fond of or devoted to music philanthropist—one who loves and seeks to do good for others
port: carry	export—to carry out of the country portable—able to be carried
psych: mind	psychology—study of the mind psychiatrist—specialist in mental disorders
quer, ques, quir, quis: to ask	inquiry—to ask about question—that which is asked
rid, ris: to laugh	ridiculous—laughable derision—to mock
rupt: to break	interrupt—to break in upon erupt—to break through
sci: to know	science—systematic knowledge of physical or natural phenomena conscious—having inward knowledge
scrib, script: to write	transcribe—to write over again script—text of words
sent, sens: to feel, to think	sentimental—expressive or appealing to tender feelings sensitive—easily affected by changes

***sequ, secut*: to follow**	sequence—connected series consecutive—following one another in unbroken order
***solv, solu, solut*: to loosen**	dissolve—to break up absolute—without restraint
***spect*: to look at**	spectator—one who watches inspect—to look at closely
***spir*: to breathe**	inspire—to breathe in respiration—process of breathing
***string, strict*: to bind**	stringent—binding strongly restrict—to restrain within bounds
***stru, struct*: to build**	misconstrue—to interpret wrongly construct—to build
***tang, ting, tack, tig*: to touch**	tangent—touching, but not intersecting contact—touching
***ten, tent, tain*: to hold**	tenure—holding of office contain—to hold
***term*: to end**	terminate—to end terminal—having an end
***terr*: earth**	terrain—tract of land terrestrial—existing on Earth
***therm*: heat**	thermal—pertaining to heat thermometer—instrument for measuring temperature
***tort, tors*: to twist**	contortionist—one who twists violently torsion—act of turning or twisting
***tract*: to pull, to draw**	attract—draw toward distract—to draw away
***vac*: empty**	vacant—empty evacuate—to empty out

ven, vent: **to come**	prevent—to stop from coming intervene—to come between
ver: **true**	verify—to prove to be true veracious—truthful
verb: **word**	verbose—use of excess words verbatim—word for word
vid, vis: **to see**	video—picture phase of television vision—act of seeing external objects
vinc, vict, vang: **to conquer**	invincible—unconquerable victory—defeat of enemy
viv, vit: **life**	vital—necessary to life vivacious—lively
voc: **to call**	provocative—serving to excite or stimulate to action vocal—uttered by voice
vol: **to wish, to will**	involuntary—outside the control of will volition—the act of willing or choosing

Suffix

–able, –ble: **capable of**	believable—capable of being believed legible—capable of being read
–acious, –icious, *–ous*: **full of**	vivacious—full of life wondrous—full of wonder
–ant, –ent: **full of**	eloquent—full of eloquence expectant—full of expectation
–ary: **connected with**	honorary—for the sake of honor disciplinary—enforcing instruction

–ate: **to make**	facilitate—to make easier
	consecrate—to make or declare sacred
–fy: **to make**	magnify—to make larger
	testify—to make witness
–ile: **pertaining to, capable of**	docile—capable of being managed easily
	civil—pertaining to a city or state
–ism: **belief, ideal**	conservationism—ideal of keeping safe
	sensationalism—matter, language designed to excite
–ist: **doer**	artist—one who creates art
	pianist—one who plays the piano
–ose: **full of**	verbose—full of words
	grandiose—striking, imposing
–osis: **condition**	neurosis—nervous condition
	psychosis—psychological condition
– tude: **state**	magnitude—state of greatness
	multitude—state of quantity

2. COMMONLY TESTED VOCABULARY WORDS

WORD	DEFINITION	SYNONYMS
abaft	*adv.*—on or toward the rear of a ship	astern, posterior, hind
abdicate	*v.*—to reject, denounce, or abandon	disown, reject, renounce, give up, refuse, relinquish, repudiate, abandon, turn one's back on, wash one's hands of, forgo, waive
abjure	*v.*—to renounce upon oath	renounce, relinquish, reject, forgo, disavow, abandon, deny, repudiate, give up, wash one's hands of; eschew, abstain from, refrain from

WORD	DEFINITION	SYNONYMS
abnegation	*n.*—a denial	renunciation, rejection, refusal, abandonment, abdication, surrender, relinquishment, repudiation, denial
abscond	*v.*—to go away hastily or secretly often with the intention to hide; to avoid capture by the authorities	run away, escape, bolt, flee, take flight, take off, decamp; take to one's heels, run for it, make a run for it, disappear, vanish, slip away, split, steal away, sneak away; clear out
abstemious	*adj.*—1. sparing in diet; 2. sparingly used	self-denying, temperate, abstinent, moderate, self-disciplined, restrained, self-restrained, sober, austere, ascetic, puritanical, spartan, hair-shirt
abysmal	*adj.*—bottomless; extraordinarily bad	dreadful, awful, terrible, frightful, atrocious, disgraceful, deplorable, shameful, hopeless, lamentable; rotten, appalling, crummy, pathetic, pitiful, woeful, useless, lousy, dire
acerbity	*n.*—harshness or bitterness	acidity, asperity, astringency, mordancy, sourness, tartness
acrimony	*n.*—sharpness	bitterness, anger, rancor, resentment, ill feeling, ill will, bad blood, animosity, hostility, enmity, antagonism, waspishness, spleen, malice, spite, spitefulness, peevishness, venom
addle	*adj.*—confused	muddled, muzzy, fuddled, befuddled, dazed, disoriented, disorientated, fuzzy
adjure	*v.*—to entreat earnestly and solemnly	asseverate, authenticate, implore, importune, petition

WORD	DEFINITION	SYNONYMS
adulation	*n.*—praise in excess	worship, idolization, adoration, admiration, veneration, awe, devotion, glorification, praise, flattery, blandishments
adulterate	*v.*—to corrupt, debase, or make impure	degrade, debase, spoil, taint, contaminate; doctor, tamper with, dilute, water down, weaken; bastardize, corrupt
agrarian	*adj.*—relating to land and the equal divisions of land	agricultural, rural, rustic, pastoral, countryside, farming
alchemy	*n.*—any imaginary power of transmitting one thing into another	chemistry; magic, sorcery, witchcraft
allegory	*n.*—symbolic narration or description	parable, analogy, metaphor, symbol, emblem
anachronism	*n.*—representation of something existing at other than its proper time	chronological error, metachronism, misdate, misplacement, postdate, prolepsis, solecism
annihilate	*v.*—to reduce to nothing	destroy, wipe out, obliterate, wipe off the face of the earth; eliminate, liquidate, defeat
apocalyptic	*adj.*—pertaining to revelation or prophecy	doomsday, doom-laden, ominous, portentous; catastrophic, momentous
arrogate	*v.*—to claim or demand unduly	assume, take, claim, appropriate, seize, expropriate, wrest, usurp, commandeer

WORD	DEFINITION	SYNONYMS
artifice	*n.*—skill; ingenuity; craft; deception; trickery	deceit, deception, duplicity, guile, cunning, artfulness, wiliness, slyness, chicanery; fraud, fraudulence
askance	*adv.*—1. sideways; 2. with suspicion	skeptically, cynically, mistrustfully, distrustfully, doubtfully, dubiously; disapprovingly, contemptuously, scornfully, disdainfully
assay	*n.*—the determination of any quantity of a metal in an ore or alloy	evaluation, assessment, appraisal, analysis, examination, test/tests, testing, inspection, scrutiny
attenuate	*v.*—1. to make thin or slender; 2. to lessen or weaken	1. slender, narrow, slim, skinny, spindly, bony; rare 2. reduced, lessened, decreased, diminished, impaired
avarice	*n.*—inordinate desire of gaining and possessing wealth	greed, greediness, acquisitiveness, cupidity, covetousness, rapacity, materialism
batten	*v.*—to fix in place	fasten, secure, clamp (down), lash, make fast, nail (down), seal
beholden	*adj.*—obliged; indebted	obligated, under an obligation, grateful, owing a debt of gratitude
bellicose	*adj.*—warlike; disposed to quarrel or fight	belligerent, aggressive, hostile, warlike, warmongering, hawkish, antagonistic, pugnacious, truculent, confrontational, contentious, militant, combative

WORD	DEFINITION	SYNONYMS
besmirch	*v.*—to soil or discolor	sully, tarnish, blacken, drag through the mud/mire, stain, taint, smear, disgrace, dishonor, bring discredit to, damage, debase, ruin, slander, malign, defame
bestial	*adj.*—having the qualities of a beast	savage, brutish, brutal, barbarous, barbaric, cruel, vicious, violent, inhuman, subhuman; depraved, degenerate, perverted, debauched, immoral, warped
betroth	*v.*—to promise or pledge in marriage	engagement, pledge
blighted	*adj.*—destroyed; frustrated	ruin, wreck, spoil, mar, frustrate, disrupt, undo, end, scotch, shatter, devastate, demolish, foul up, stymie
bode	*v.*—to foreshadow something	augur, portend, herald, be a sign of, warn of, be an omen of, presage, indicate, signify, promise, threaten, spell, denote, foretell, prophesy, predict
boorish	*adj.*—rude; ill–mannered	coarse, uncouth, rude, ill-bred, uncivilized, unrefined, rough, thuggish, loutish, oafish, lubberly, vulgar, unsavory, gross, brutish, Neanderthal
brindled	*adj.*—streaked or spotted with a darker color	brownish, brown; dappled, streaked, mottled, speckled, flecked, marbled
broach	*v.*—1. to pierce; 2. to introduce into conversation	1. puncture, tap; open, uncork 2. bring up, raise, introduce, talk about, mention, touch on, air

WORD	DEFINITION	SYNONYMS
bucolic	*adj.*—pastoral	rustic, rural, pastoral, country, countryside
burlesque	*v.*—to imitate comically	parody, caricature, satire, lampoon, skit, farce, takeoff, spoof
cadaver	*n.*—a dead body	corpse, remains, carcass
caliber	*n.*—1. the diameter of a bullet or shell; 2. Quality	1. bore, gauge 2. merit, distinction, stature, excellence, preeminence; ability, expertise, talent, capability, capacity, proficiency
callow	*adj.*—immature	inexperienced, juvenile, adolescent, naive, green, raw, untried, unworldly, unsophisticated
calumny	*n.*—slander	defamation (of character), character assassination, libel, vilification, obloquy, verbal abuse
canard	*n.*—a false statement or rumor	dishonesty, dissimulation, erroneousness, fabrication, fakery, fallaciousness, prevarication, untruism, untruth, untruthfulness
candid	*adj.*—open; frank; honest	outspoken, forthright, blunt, truthful, sincere, direct, plain-spoken, straightforward, ingenuous, bluff
carnage	*n.*—slaughter	massacre, mass murder, butchery, bloodbath, bloodletting, gore
carte blanche	*n.*—unlimited power to decide	free rein, a free hand, a blank check

WORD	DEFINITION	SYNONYMS
castigate	*v.*—to chastise	reprimand, rebuke, admonish, chastise, chide, censure, upbraid, reprove, reproach, scold, berate, take to task, lambaste
cataclysm	*n.*—1. an overflowing of water; 2. an extraordinary change	2. disaster, catastrophe, calamity, tragedy, devastation, holocaust, ruin, ruination, upheaval, convulsion, apocalypse, act of God
catharsis	*n.*—purgation	emotional release, relief, release, venting, purging, purification, cleansing
cavil	*v.*—to find fault without good reason	quibble, carp
celibate	*adj.*—unmarried, single; chaste	unwed, spouseless, virginal, virgin, maidenly, maiden, intact, abstinent, self-denying
cessation	*n.*—a ceasing; a stop	end, ending, termination, stopping, halting, finish, finishing, stoppage, conclusion, winding up, discontinuation, abandonment, suspension, breaking off, cutting short
chafe	*v.*—1. to rage; to fret; 2. to rub so much that skin or feelings are raw and irritated	1. be angry, be annoyed, be irritated, fume, be exasperated, be frustrated 2. abrade, graze, rub against, gall, scrape, scratch
chaffing	*n.*—1. banter; 2. teasing	repartee, ragging, joking, jesting, raillery, badinage, wisecracks, witticism(s)

WORD	DEFINITION	SYNONYMS
chaste	*adj.*—virtuous; free from obscenity	virginal, virgin, intact, maidenly, unmarried, unwed; celibate, abstinent, self-restrained, self-denying, innocent, pure, sinless, undefiled, unsullied, immaculate, nonsexual
choleric	*adj.*—easily irritated; angry	bad-tempered, irascible, irritable, grumpy, grouchy, crotchety, testy, cranky, crusty, cantankerous, curmudgeonly, ill-tempered, peevish, cross, fractious, crabby, waspish, prickly, peppery, touchy, short-tempered, snappish, short-fused, ornery
circumvent	*v.*—to go around	avoid, get around, get past, evade, bypass, sidestep, dodge
clandestine	*adj.*—secret; private; hidden	covert, furtive, surreptitious, stealthy, closet, backstairs, backroom; hush-hush
cogent	*adj.*—urgent; compelling; convincing	forcible, inducing, puissant, weighty, well-grounded
cohort	*n.*—a group; a band	unit, force, corps, division, brigade, battalion, regiment, squadron, company, troop, contingent, legion, phalanx
collusion	*n.*—secret agreement for a fraudulent or illegal purpose	conspiracy, connivance, complicity, intrigue, plotting, secret understanding, collaboration, scheming
comport	*v.*—to agree; to accord	behave, conduct oneself

WORD	DEFINITION	SYNONYMS
conclave	*n.*—any private meeting or closed assembly	meeting, gathering, assembly, conference, council, summit
connivance	*n.*—passive cooperation	collusion, complicity, collaboration, involvement, assistance, tacit consent, conspiracy, intrigue
consort	*n.*—1. a companion; *v.*—2. to be in harmony or agreement	1. partner, life partner, companion, mate; spouse, husband, wife, helpmate 2. associate, keep company, mix, go around, spend time, socialize, fraternize, have dealings
contravene	*v.*—to go against; to oppose	conflict with, be in conflict with, be at odds with, be at variance with, run counter to
contusion	*n.*—a bruise; an injury where the skin is not broken	discoloration, injury
copious	*adj.*—abundant; in great quantities	plentiful, ample, profuse, full, extensive, generous, bumper, lavish, fulsome, liberal, overflowing, in abundance, many, numerous
covenant	*n.*—a binding and solemn agreement	contract, undertaking, commitment, guarantee, warrant, pledge, promise, bond, indenture, pact, deal, settlement, arrangement, understanding
coy	*adj.*—1. modest; bashful; 2. pretending shyness to attract	simpering, coquettish, flirtatious, kittenish; demure, shy, modest, reticent, diffident, self-effacing, shrinking, timid

WORD	DEFINITION	SYNONYMS
crass	*adj.*—gross; thick; coarse	stupid, insensitive, mindless, thoughtless, ignorant, witless, oafish, boorish, asinine, graceless, tasteless, tactless, clumsy, heavy-handed, blundering
cursory	*adj.*—hasty; slight	perfunctory, desultory, casual, superficial, token; sketchy, half-done, incomplete, quick, hurried, rapid, brief, passing, fleeting
dally	*v.*—to delay; to put off	dawdle, loiter, linger, waste time; lag, trail, straggle, fall behind; amble, meander, drift
dauntless	*adj.*—fearless; not discouraged	determined, resolute, indomitable, intrepid, spirited, mettlesome; undaunted, undismayed, unflinching, unshrinking, bold, audacious, valiant, brave, courageous, daring
debonair	*adj.*—1. having an affable manner; courteous; 2. suave; urbane	sophisticated, cultured, self-possessed, self-assured, confident, charming, gracious, courteous, gallant, chivalrous, gentlemanly, refined, polished, well-bred, genteel, dignified, courtly; well-groomed, elegant, stylish, smart, dashing
decadence	*n.*—a decline in force or quality; moral decay	dissipation, degeneracy, debauchery, corruption, depravity, vice, sin, moral decay, immorality, immoderateness, intemperance, licentiousness, self-indulgence, hedonism

WORD	DEFINITION	SYNONYMS
deciduous	*adj.*—falling off at a particular season or stage of growth	fugacious, fugitive, impermanent
decry	*v.*—to denounce or condemn openly	criticize, censure, attack, rail against, run down, pillory, lambaste, vilify, revile, disparage, deprecate
defunct	*adj.*—no longer living or existing	disused, unused, inoperative, nonfunctioning, unusable, obsolete, discontinued, extinct
deliquesce	*v.*—to melt away	liquefy, melt away, thaw
delusion	*n.*—act or process of deception	misapprehension, misconception, misunderstanding, mistake, error, misinterpretation, misconstruction, fallacy, illusion, fantasy
deposition	*n.*—1. a removal from a position of power; 2. a testimony	statement, affidavit, attestation, affirmation, assertion; allegation, declaration; testimony, evidence
depredation	*n.*—a plundering or laying waste	looting, pillaging, robbery; devastation, destruction, damage, rape; ravages, raids
descant	*v.*—to comment at length on a theme	comment, criticize, discussion
despoil	*v.*—to strip; to rob	plunder, pillage, rob, ravage, raid, ransack, rape, loot, sack; devastate, lay waste, ruin.
despotism	*n.*—1. tyranny; 2. absolute power or influence	authoritarianism, autocracy, dictatorship

WORD	DEFINITION	SYNONYMS
desultory	*adj.*—without order or natural connection	casual, cursory, superficial, token, perfunctory, half-hearted, random, aimless, erratic, unmethodical, unsystematic, chaotic, inconsistent, irregular, intermittent, sporadic
dexterous	*adj.*—having or showing skill of hands, body, or mind	deft, adept, adroit, agile, nimble, neat, handy, able, capable, skillful, skilled, proficient, expert, practiced, polished, efficient, effortless, professional, masterly
diffidence	*n.*—1. lack of self-confidence; 2. distrust	shyness, bashfulness, modesty, self-effacement, meekness, unassertiveness, timidity, humility, hesitancy, reticence, insecurity, self-doubt, uncertainty, self-consciousness
dilapidated	*n.*—falling to pieces or into disrepair	run-down, tumbledown, ramshackle, broken-down, shabby, battered, beat-up, rickety, shaky, unsound, crumbling, in ruins, ruined, decayed, decaying, decrepit, neglected
dilettante	*n.*—an admirer of the fine arts; a dabbler	amateur, nonprofessional, layman, layperson
dint	*n.*—a blow; a stroke	indentation, nick, cavity, con-cavity, crater, crenel
disarray	*n.*—1. disorder; confusion; 2. incomplete or disorderly attire	chaos, untidiness, disorganization, dishevelment, mess, muddle, clutter, jumble, tangle, shambles

WORD	DEFINITION	SYNONYMS
divulge	*v.*—to make known	disclose, reveal, tell, communicate, pass on, publish, broadcast, proclaim; expose, uncover, make public
dormant	*adj.*—as if asleep	sleeping, resting; inactive, passive, inert, latent, quiescent
doting	*adj.*—excessively fond	adoring, loving, besotted, infatuated; affectionate, fond, devoted, caring, uxorious
doughty	*adj.*—brave; valiant	fearless, dauntless, determined, resolute, indomitable, intrepid, plucky, spirited, bold, stouthearted, courageous
dregs	*n.*—waste or worthless matter	residue, scum, refuse, riffraff, outcasts, underclass, untouchables
ecclesiastic	*adj.*—pertaining or relating to a church	priestly, ministerial, clerical, ecclesiastic, canonical, sacerdotal, church, churchly, religious, spiritual, holy, divine
edify	*v.*—1. to build or establish; 2. to instruct and improve the mind	educate, instruct, teach, school, tutor, train, guide; enlighten, inform, cultivate, develop, better
efface	*v.*—to erase; to remove from the mind	eradicate, expunge, blot out, rub out, wipe out, eliminate, delete, cancel, obliterate
effrontery	*n.*—impudence	impertinence, insolence, cockiness, audacity, temerity, presumption, nerve, gall, shamelessness, impoliteness, disrespect, bad manners

WORD	DEFINITION	SYNONYMS
effusive	*adj.*—pouring out or forth; overflowing	gushing, gushy, unrestrained, extravagant, fulsome, demonstrative, lavish, enthusiastic
egregious	*adj.*—remarkably bad, outrageous	shocking, appalling, terrible, awful, horrendous, frightful, atrocious, abominable, abhorrent, monstrous, heinous, dire, unspeakable, shameful, unforgivable, intolerable, dreadful
egress	*v.*—to depart; to go out	departure, exit, withdrawal, retreat, exodus
elegy	*n.*—a poem of lament and praise for the dead	requiem, threnody, dirge
elucidate	*v.*—to make clear or manifest; to explain	explain, illuminate, clarify, clear up, sort out, unravel, spell out, interpret, explicate
emanate	*v.*—to send forth; to emit	issue, spread, radiate
embellish	*v.*—to improve the appearance of	decorate, adorn, ornament, beautify, enhance, grace, trim, garnish, gild, bedeck, festoon, emblazon
enamored	*adj.*—filled with love and desire	infatuated with, besotted with, smitten with, captivated by, enchanted by, fascinated by, bewitched by, beguiled by; keen on, taken with
encroach	*v.*—to trespass or intrude	impinge on, obtrude on, impose oneself on, invade, infiltrate, interrupt, infringe on, violate, interfere with, disturb

WORD	DEFINITION	SYNONYMS
encumber	*v.*—to hold back; to hinder	hamper, obstruct, impede, cramp, inhibit, restrict, limit, constrain, restrain, bog down, retard, slow (down), inconvenience, disadvantage, handicap
enrapture	*v.*—to fill with pleasure	delight, enchant, captivate, charm, enthrall, entrance, bewitch, beguile, transport, thrill, excite, exhilarate, intoxicate
epilogue	*n.*—closing section of a play or novel providing further comment	afterword, coda, codicil, appendix, supplement, addendum, postlude, rider, conclusion
epiphany	*n.*—an appearance of a supernatural being	revelation, adumbration, divination, divulgement
epitaph	*n.*—an inscription on a monument, in honor or memory of a dead person	commemoration, elegy
epitome	*n.*—a part that is typical of the whole	personification, embodiment, incarnation, paragon, essence, quintessence, archetype, paradigm
equivocate	*v.*—to be purposely ambiguous	prevaricate, be evasive, be noncommittal, be vague
eschew	*v.*—to escape from; to avoid	abstain from, refrain from, give up, forgo, shun, renounce, steer clear of, have nothing to do with, fight shy of, relinquish, reject, disavow, abandon, spurn
estranged	*adj.*—kept at a distance; alienated	antagonize, turn away, drive away

WORD	DEFINITION	SYNONYMS
ethereal	*adj.*—1. very light; airy; 2. heavenly; not earthly	delicate, exquisite, dainty, elegant, graceful, fragile, fine, subtle
euphemism	*n.*—the use of a word or phrase in place of one that is distasteful	polite term, indirect term, circumlocution, substitute, alternative, understatement, genteelism
euphoria	*n.*—a feeling of well-being	elation, happiness, joy, delight, glee, excitement, exhilaration, jubilation, exultation, ecstasy, bliss, rapture
exhume	*v.*—to unearth; to reveal	disinter, dig up
expunge	*v.*—to blot out; to delete	erase, remove, wipe out, efface, cross out, strike out, destroy, obliterate, scratch, eradicate, eliminate
exude	*v.*—to flow slowly or ooze in drops	ooze, seep, issue, escape, discharge, flow, leak, radiate, display
faction	*n.*—a number of people in an organization having a common end view	clique, coterie, caucus, cabal, bloc, camp, group, grouping, sector, section, wing, arm, branch, set
fallible	*adj.*—liable to be mistaken or erroneous	error-prone, errant, liable to err, open to error; imperfect, flawed, weak
fathom	*v.*—to reach or penetrate with the mind	understand, comprehend, work out, grasp, divine, interpret, decipher, decode
fatuous	*adj.*—silly; inane; unreal	foolish, stupid, inane, idiotic, vacuous, asinine, pointless, senseless, ridiculous, ludicrous, absurd

WORD	DEFINITION	SYNONYMS
fealty	*n.*—fidelity; loyalty	allegiance, divined, constancy, obligation
feign	*v.*—to invent or imagine	simulate, fake, sham, affect, give the appearance of, make a pretense of
ferment	*v.*—to excite or agitate	fever, furor, frenzy, tumult, storm, rumpus; turmoil, upheaval, unrest, disquiet, uproar, agitation, turbulence, disruption, confusion, disorder, chaos, mayhem
fervid	*adj.*—1. very hot; burning; 2. intensely fervent or zealous	fervent, ardent, passionate, impassioned, intense, vehement, wholehearted, heartfelt, sincere, earnest
fetish	*n.*—an object to which one gives excessive devotion or blind adoration	fixation, obsession, compulsion, mania, weakness, fancy, fascination, fad
fidelity	*n.*—faithfulness; honesty	loyalty, constancy, trueheartedness, trustworthiness, dependability, reliability
fissure	*n.*—a dividing or breaking into parts	opening, crevice, crack, cleft, breach, crevasse, chasm, fracture, fault, rift, rupture, split
flaccid	*adj.*—1. hanging in loose folds or wrinkles; 2. lacking force; weak	1. soft, loose, flabby, slack, lax; drooping, sagging 2. lackluster, lifeless, listless, uninspiring, unanimated, tame, dull, vapid

WORD	DEFINITION	SYNONYMS
flamboyant	*adj.*—ornate; too showy	colorful, brightly colored, bright, vibrant, vivid, dazzling, eye-catching, bold, ostentatious, gaudy, garish, lurid, loud
foible	*n.*—a slight frailty in character	weakness, failing, shortcoming, flaw, imperfection, blemish, fault, defect, limitation, quirk, kink, idiosyncrasy, eccentricity, peculiarity
foist	*v.*—1. to put in slyly or stealthily; 2. to pass off as genuine or valuable	impose on, force on, thrust on, offload on, unload on, dump on, palm off on
foray	*v.*—to raid for spoils, plunder	attack, assault, incursion, swoop, strike, onslaught, sortie, sally, push, thrust
forensic	*adj.*—pertaining to legal or public argument	debatable, dialectic, dialectical, disputative, juridical, juristic, polemical
fortitude	*n.*—firm courage; strength	bravery, endurance, resilience, mettle, strength of character, strong-mindedness, backbone, spirit, grit, steadfastness
fractious	*adj.*—rebellious; apt to quarrel	grumpy, bad-tempered, irascible, irritable, crotchety, grouchy, cantankerous, short-tempered, tetchy, testy, curmudgeonly, ill-tempered, ill-humored, peevish, cross, waspish, prickly, touchy
fraught	*adj.*—loaded; charged with	full of, filled with, rife with; attended by, accompanied by

WORD	DEFINITION	SYNONYMS
fulminate	*v.*—1. to explode with sudden violence; 2. to issue thunderous verbal attack or denunciation	protest, rail against, rant about, vociferate against, declaim, denounce, decry, condemn, criticize, censure, disparage, attack, execrate
galvanize	*v.*—to stimulate as if by electric shock; startle; excite	jolt, impel, stir, spur, prod, urge, motivate, stimulate, electrify, rouse, arouse, awaken, invigorate, fire, animate, vitalize, energize, exhilarate, thrill, catalyze, inspire
gamut	*n.*—1. a complete range; 2. any complete musical scale	spectrum, span, scope, sweep, compass, area, breadth, reach, extent, catalog, scale, variety
garish	*adj.*—gaudy; showy	lurid, loud, harsh, glaring, violent, showy, glittering, brassy, brash, tasteless, tawdry, vulgar, unattractive, bilious
gauche	*adj.*—awkward; lacking grace	gawky, inelegant, graceless, ungraceful, ungainly, maladroit, klutzy, inept, uncultured, uncultivated, unrefined, raw, inexperienced, unworldly
gauntlet	*n.*—a long glove with a flaring cuff covering the lower part of the arm	gage
germane	*adj.*—closely related; pertinent	relevant, applicable, apposite, material, apropos, appropriate, apt, fitting, suitable, connected, related, akin

WORD	DEFINITION	SYNONYMS
glib	*adj.*—smooth and slippery; speaking or spoken in a smooth manner	fast-talking, smooth-talking, disingenuous, insincere, facile, shallow, superficial, flippant, silver-tongued, urbane
gnarled	*adj.*—full of knots	knobbly, gnarly, lumpy, bumpy, nodular, twisted, bent, crooked, distorted, contorted
gourmand	*n.*—a greedy or ravenous eater; glutton	overeater, big eater, gobbler, gorger
gregarious	*adj.*—fond of the company of others	sociable, company-loving, convivial, companionable, outgoing, friendly, affable, amiable, genial, warm, comradely
grisly	*adj.*—frightful; horrible	gruesome, ghastly, fearful, hideous, macabre, horrendous, grim, awful, dire, dreadful, terrible, shocking, appalling, abominable, loathsome, abhorrent, odious, unspeakable, disgusting, repulsive, repugnant, revolting, repellent, sickening
guffaw	*n.*—a loud, coarse burst of laughter	roar, bellow, cackle
guise	*n.*—1. customary behavior; 2. manner of dress; 3. false appearance	2. likeness, outward appearance, appearance, semblance, form, shape, image; disguise. 3. pretense, disguise, front, facade, cover, blind, screen, smokescreen
halcyon	*adj.*—calm; quiet; peaceful	happy, golden, idyllic, carefree, blissful, joyful, joyous, contented, flourishing, thriving, prosperous, successful, serene, tranquil

WORD	DEFINITION	SYNONYMS
hapless	*adj.*—unlucky; unfortunate	unlucky, luckless, out of luck, ill-starred, ill-fated, jinxed, cursed, doomed, unhappy, forlorn, wretched, miserable, woebegone
harangue	*v.*—to speak in an impassioned and forcible manner	tirade, diatribe, lecture, polemic, rant, fulmination, broadside, attack, onslaught, criticism, condemnation, censure, admonition, sermon, declamation, speech
heretic	*n.*—one who holds opinion contrary to that which is generally accepted	dissenter, nonconformist, apostate, freethinker, iconoclast, agnostic, atheist, nonbeliever, unbeliever, idolater, idolatress, pagan, heathen
hiatus	*n.*—an opening or gap; slight pause	pause, break, lacuna, interval, intermission, interlude, interruption, suspension, lull, respite, time out, time off, recess
hoary	*adj.*—very aged; ancient; gray or white with age	grizzled, elderly, aged, old, ancient, venerable
homily	*n.*—discourse or sermon read to an audience	lecture, discourse, address, lesson, talk, speech, oration
hybrid	*n.*—anything of mixed origin	cross, mixture, blend, amalgamation, combination, composite, compound, fusion
idiosyncrasy	*n.*—any personal peculiarity, mannerism, etc.	oddity, eccentricity, mannerism, trait, singularity, quirk, tic, whim, vagary, caprice
igneous	*adj.*—having the nature of fire	burning, blazing, flaming, on fire, ablaze

WORD	DEFINITION	SYNONYMS
ignominious	*adj.*—1. contemptible; 2. degrading	humiliating, undignified, embarrassing, mortifying, ignoble, inglorious, disgraceful, shameful, dishonorable, discreditable
immaculate	*adj.*—1. perfectly clean; perfectly correct; 2. Pure	1. spotless, ultraclean, pristine, unsoiled, unstained, unsullied, shining, shiny, gleaming, neat, tidy 2. perfect, pristine, mint, as good as new; flawless, faultless, unblemished, unspoiled, undamaged, excellent, impeccable
imminent	*adj.*—appearing as if about to happen	impending, coming, forthcoming, expected, anticipated, brewing, looming, threatening, menacing
impasse	*n.*—a situation that has no solution or escape	deadlock, dead end, stalemate, standoff, standstill, halt, stoppage, stop
impenitent	*adj.*—without regret, shame, or remorse	unrepenting, uncontrite, remorseless, unashamed, unapologetic, unabashed
impiety	*n.*—1. irreverence toward God; 2. lack of respect	1. godlessness, ungodliness, unholiness, irreligion, irreverence, sinfulness, sin, vice, transgression, wrongdoing, immorality, unrighteousness, blasphemy, sacrilege 2. irreverence, disrespect, impertinence, insolence, mockery, derision

WORD	DEFINITION	SYNONYMS
impolitic	*adj.*—unwise; imprudent	injudicious, incautious, irresponsible, ill-advised, misguided, rash, reckless, foolhardy, foolish, shortsighted
imprecate	*v.*—to pray for evil; to invoke a curse	anathematize, damn, hex, jinx
imputation	*n.*—attribution	quality, characteristic, trait, feature, element, aspect, property, sign, mark, distinction
incarcerate	*v.*—to imprison or confine	put in prison, send to prison, jail, intern, confine, detain, hold, immure
incommodious	*adj.*—uncomfortable; troublesome	small, cramped, tiny
incorporeal	*adj.*—not consisting of matter	intangible, impalpable, nonphysical, bodiless, disembodied, discarnate, immaterial, spiritual, ethereal, unsubstantial, insubstantial, transcendental
incorrigible	*adj.*—not capable of correction or improvement	chronic, irredeemable, hopeless, beyond hope, impenitent, unrepentant, unapologetic, unashamed, bad, naughty, terrible
incubate	*v.*—to sit on and hatch (eggs)	produce, procreate, nurture
inculcate	*v.*—to impress upon the mind by frequent repetition or urging	implant in, fix in, impress in, imprint in, drum into, drive into, drill into
indemnify	*v.*—to protect against or keep free from loss	reimburse, compensate, guarantee

WORD	DEFINITION	SYNONYMS
indigenous	*adj.*—innate; inherent; inborn	native, original, aboriginal, autochthonous; local, domestic, homegrown
indomitable	*adj.*—not easily discouraged or defeated	invincible, unconquerable, unbeatable, unassailable, invulnerable, unshakable, indefatigable, unyielding, stalwart, stout-hearted, lionhearted, strong-willed, strong-minded, steadfast, staunch, resolute, firm, determined, intransigent, inflexible, adamant; unflinching, courageous, brave, valiant, heroic, intrepid, fearless, impenetrable, impregnable
indubitable	*adj.*—unquestionable; sure	undoubtable, indisputable, unarguable, undebatable, incontestable, undeniable, irrefutable, incontrovertible, unmistakable, unequivocal, certain, sure, positive, definite, absolute, conclusive, watertight, ironclad
inimical	*adj.*—unfriendly; adverse	harmful, injurious, detrimental, deleterious, prejudicial, damaging, hurtful, destructive, ruinous, pernicious, antagonistic, contrary, antipathetic, unfavorable, opposed, hostile, unkind, unsympathetic, unfriendly
iniquitous	*adj.*—unjust; wicked	sinfulness, immorality, impropriety, vice, evil, sin, villainy, criminality, odiousness, atrocity, egregiousness, outrage, monstrosity, obscenity, reprehensibility

WORD	DEFINITION	SYNONYMS
inordinate	*adj.*—not regulated; excessive	undue, unreasonable, unjustifiable, unwarrantable, disproportionate, unwarranted, unnecessary, needless
intrepid	*adj.*—fearless; brave	unafraid, undaunted, unflinching, unshrinking, bold, daring, gallant, audacious, adventurous, heroic, dynamic, spirited, indomitable
inured	*adj.*—accustomed	harden, toughen, season, temper, condition, habituate, familiarize, acclimatize, adjust, adapt, desensitize
irascible	*adj.*—easily provoked or inflamed to anger	irritable, quick-tempered, short-tempered, hot-tempered, testy, touchy, tetchy, edgy, crabby, petulant, waspish, dyspeptic, snappish, cross, surly, crusty, grouchy, grumpy, cranky, cantankerous, curmudgeonly, ill-natured, peevish
irreparable	*adj.*—cannot be repaired or regained	irreversible, irrevocable, irrecoverable, beyond repair, unrectifiable; hopeless
jettison	*n.*—a throwing overboard of goods to lighten a vehicle in an emergency	dump, drop, ditch, discharge, throw out, unload
jocund	*adj.*—merry; gay; cheerful	happy, jolly, merry, bright, glad, sunny, joyful, joyous, lighthearted, sparkling, bubbly, exuberant, buoyant, ebullient, elated, gleeful

WORD	DEFINITION	SYNONYMS
lacerate	*v.*—1. to tear or mangle; 2. to wound or hurt	gash, slash, tear, rip, rend, shred, score, scratch, scrape, graze, wound, injure, hurt.
lambent	*adj.*—giving off a soft radiance	flickering, fluttering, incandescent, twinkling, dancing, radiant, brilliant
lassitude	*n.*—a state or feeling of being tired or weak	lethargy, listlessness, weariness, languor, sluggishness, tiredness, fatigue, torpor, lifelessness, apathy
lewd	*adj.*—lustful; wicked	lecherous, licentious, lascivious, dirty, prurient, salacious, lubricious, libidinous; debauched, depraved, degenerate, decadent, dissipated, dissolute, perverted, wanton
libertine	*n.*—one who indulges his desires without restraint	philanderer, playboy, rake, lecher, seducer, womanizer, adulterer, debauchee, profligate, wanton
licentious	*adj.*—disregarding accepted rules and standards	dissolute, dissipated, debauched, degenerate, immoral, naughty, wanton, decadent, depraved, sinful, corrupt, lustful, lecherous, lascivious, libidinous, prurient, lubricious, lewd, promiscuous, lickerish
lithe	*adj.*—easily bent; pliable; marked by effortless grace	agile, graceful, supple, limber, lithesome, loose-limbed, nimble, deft, flexible, lissome, slender, slim, willowy
loquacious	*adj.*—talkative	voluble, communicative, expansive, garrulous, unreserved, chatty, gossipy, gossiping

WORD	DEFINITION	SYNONYMS
lugubrious	*adj.*—mournful; very sad	gloomy, sad, unhappy, doleful, glum, melancholy, woeful, miserable, woebegone, forlorn, somber, solemn, serious, sorrowful, morose, dour, cheerless, joyless, dismal
lurid	*adj.*—ghastly pale; gloomy	bright, brilliant, vivid, glaring, shocking, fluorescent, flaming, dazzling, intense, gaudy, loud, showy, bold, garish, tacky
magnate	*n.*—a very influential person in any field of activity	tycoon, mogul, captain of industry, baron, lord, king, magnifico; industrialist, proprietor; informal big shot, big cheese
malefactor	*n.*—one who commits a crime	wrongdoer, miscreant, offender, criminal, culprit, villain, lawbreaker, felon, evildoer, delinquent, hooligan, hoodlum; sinner, transgressor
malign	*v.*—to defame; speak evil of	harmful, evil, bad, baleful, hostile, inimical, destructive, malignant, injurious
marauder	*n.*—a rover in search of booty or plunder	raider, plunderer, pillager, looter, robber, pirate, freebooter, bandit, highwayman, rustler
maudlin	*adj.*—foolishly and tearfully sentimental	emotional, overemotional, tearful, lachrymose
mendacious	*adj.*—addicted to deception	lying, untruthful, dishonest, deceitful, false, dissembling, insincere, disingenuous, hypocritical, fraudulent

WORD	DEFINITION	SYNONYMS
mercurial	*adj.*—quick, volatile; changeable	capricious, temperamental, excitable, fickle, changeable, unpredictable, variable, protean, mutable, erratic, quicksilver, inconstant, inconsistent, unstable, unsteady, fluctuating, ever-changing, moody, flighty
meretricious	*adj.*—alluring by false, showy charms; fleshy	worthless, valueless, cheap, tawdry, trashy, Brummagem, tasteless, kitsch, kitschy
mettle	*n.*—high quality of character	spirit, fortitude, strength of character, moral fiber, steel, determination, resolve, resolution, backbone, grit, true grit, courage, courageousness, bravery, valor, fearlessness, daring
mien	*n.*—manner; external appearance	look, expression, countenance, aura, demeanor, attitude, air, manner, bearing
misanthropy	*n.*—hatred of mankind	cynic, recluse, hermit
mite	*n.*—1. very small sum of money; 2. very small creature	1. morsel, portion, pinch, smidgen 2. acarid, atom, molecule, mote, nit
modulate	*v.*—1. to regulate or adjust; 2. to vary the pitch of the voice	1. adjust, set, modify, moderate 2. adjust, change the tone of, temper, soften
mollify	*v.*—to soften; to make less intense	appease, placate, pacify, conciliate, soothe, calm

WORD	DEFINITION	SYNONYMS
moot	*adj.*—subject to or open for discussion or debate	debatable, arguable, questionable, at issue, disputable, controversial, contentious, disputed, unresolved, unsettled
mordant	*adj.*—biting, cutting, or caustic	trenchant, biting, acerbic, sardonic, sarcastic, scathing, acid, sharp, keen; critical, bitter, virulent, vitriolic
mutinous	*adj.*—inclined to revolt	rebellious, insubordinate, subversive, seditious, insurgent, insurrectionary, rebel, riotous
nefarious	*adj.*—very wicked; abominable	evil, sinful, iniquitous, egregious, heinous, atrocious, vile, foul, odious, depraved, monstrous, fiendish, diabolical, unspeakable, despicable, villainous, criminal, corrupt, illegal, unlawful
nemesis	*n.*—just punishment; retribution; one that inflicts relentless vengeance	retribution, vengeance, punishment, just deserts, fate, destiny
nexus	*n.*—a connection	center, core, link
nostrum	*n.*—a quack medicine	potion, elixir, panacea, cure-all, wonder drug, quack remedy
noxious	*adj.*—harmful to health or morals	poisonous, deadly, dangerous, pernicious, damaging, destructive, unpleasant, nasty, disgusting, awful, dreadful, horrible, vile, revolting, foul, nauseating, appalling, offensive, malodorous, fetid, putrid

WORD	DEFINITION	SYNONYMS
nugatory	*adj.*—trifling; futile; insignificant	useless, vain, unavailing, null, invalid
obeisance	*n.*—a gesture of respect or reverence	bow, curtsy, bob, genuflection
obfuscate	*v.*—to darken; to confuse	obscure, confuse, make unclear, blur, muddle, complicate, muddy, cloud, befog
objurgate	*v.*—to chide vehemently	upbraid, berate, reprimand, reprove, rebuke, admonish, censure, lambaste, lecture
obloquy	*n.*—verbal abuse of a person or thing	insult, be rude to, swear at, curse, taunt, revile, bawl out, vilify, slander
obtrude	*v.*—to thrust forward; to eject	bail out, escape, get out
odious	*adj.*—hateful; disgusting	revolting, repulsive, repellent, repugnant, offensive, objectionable, vile, foul, abhorrent, appalling, reprehensible, deplorable, insufferable, intolerable, despicable, contemptible, unspeakable, atrocious, dreadful, frightful, obnoxious, unsavory, unpalatable, unpleasant, disagreeable, nasty
oligarchy	*n.*—form of government in which the supreme power is placed in the hands of a small exclusive group	absolutism, authoritarianism, autocracy, despotism, fascism, high-handedness, imperiousness, totalitarianism, totality, unreasonableness

WORD	DEFINITION	SYNONYMS
opalescent	*adj.*—iridescent	prismatic, kaleidoscopic, multicolored, many-hued, lustrous, shimmering, glittering, sparkling, variegated, scintillating, shot, milky, pearly
opprobrious	*adj.*—reproachful or contemptuous	abusive, vituperative, derogatory, disparaging, pejorative, deprecatory, insulting, offensive, defamatory, vitriolic, libelous, venomous, scornful, contemptuous, derisive
palatial	*adj.*—large and ornate, like a palace	luxurious, deluxe, magnificent, sumptuous, splendid, grand, opulent, lavish, stately, regal, fancy, upscale
palindrome	*n.*—a word, verse or sentence that is the same when read backward or forward	Example: racecar
paltry	*adj.*—worthless; trifling	small, meager, trifling, insignificant, negligible, inadequate, insufficient, derisory, pitiful, pathetic, miserable, beggarly
pandemonium	*n.*—a place of wild disorder, noise, or confusion	bedlam, chaos, mayhem, uproar, turmoil, tumult, commotion, confusion, anarchy, furor, hubbub, rumpus
parapet	*n.*—a wall or railing to protect people from falling	balustrade, barricade, rampart, bulwark, bank, embankment, fortification, defense
pariah	*n.*—an outcast; someone despised by others	outcast, persona non grata, black sheep, leper, undesirable

WORD	DEFINITION	SYNONYMS
parity	*n.*—state of being the same in power, value, or rank	equality, equivalence, uniformity, consistency, correspondence, congruity, levelness, unity, coequality
parley	*v.*—to speak with another; to discourse	conference, summit, discussion, powwow
parry	*v.*—to ward off; to avoid	fend off, deflect, hold off, block, counter, repel, repulse
parsimonious	*adj.*—miserly; stingy	cheap, miserly, mean, close-fisted, close, penny-pinching, ungenerous
paucity	*n.*—scarcity; small number	scarcity, sparseness, dearth, shortage, poverty, insufficiency, deficiency, lack, want
peculate	*v.*—to embezzle	misappropriate, steal, thieve, pilfer, purloin, appropriate, pocket, abstract
pecuniary	*adj.*—relating to money	financial, monetary, money, fiscal, economic
pellucid	*adj.*—transparent	translucent, clear, crystal clear, crystalline, glassy, limpid, unclouded
penury	*n.*—lack of money or property	extreme poverty, destitution, pennilessness, impecuniousness, impoverishment, indigence, pauperism, privation, beggary
perdition	*n.*—complete and irreparable loss	damnation, eternal punishment, doom

WORD	DEFINITION	SYNONYMS
peremptory	*adj.*—1. barring future action; 2. that cannot be denied, changed, etc.	irreversible, binding, absolute, final, conclusive, decisive, definitive, categorical, irrefutable, incontrovertible
perfidious	*adj.*—violating good faith or vows	treacherous, duplicitous, deceitful, disloyal, faithless, unfaithful, traitorous, treasonous, false, untrustworthy
perquisite	*n.*—a fee, profit, etc., in addition to the stated income of one's employment	perk, fringe benefit, additional benefit, benefit, advantage, bonus
peruse	*v.*—to read carefully and thoroughly	study, scrutinize, inspect, examine, wade through, look through; browse through, leaf through, scan
pied	*adj.*—spotted	multicolored, variegated, black and white, brown and white, piebald, skewbald, dappled, brindle, spotted, mottled, speckled, flecked
pinioned	*adj.*—1. having wings; 2. having wings or arms bound or confined	hold down, pin down, restrain, hold fast, immobilize, tie, bind, truss (up), shackle, fetter, hobble, manacle, handcuff
platonic	*adj.*—1. idealistic or impractical; 2. not amorous or sensual	nonsexual, nonphysical, chaste, intellectual, friendly
plenary	*adj.*—full; entire; complete	unconditional, unlimited, unrestricted, unqualified, absolute, sweeping, comprehensive, plenipotentiary

WORD	DEFINITION	SYNONYMS
plethora	*n.*—the state of being too full; excess	overabundance, superabundance, surplus, glut, superfluity, surfeit, profusion
portend	*v.*—to foreshadow	presage, augur, foreshadow, foretell, prophesy, indicate, herald, signal, bode, promise, threaten, signify, spell, denote
potable	*adj.*—drinkable	palatable, fit to drink, pure, clean, safe, unpolluted, untainted, uncontaminated
prate	*v.*—to talk much and foolishly	babble, gab, gabble, jabber, tattle
precept	*n.*—a rule or direction of moral conduct	principle, rule, tenet, canon, doctrine, command, order, decree, dictate, dictum, injunction, commandment
precocious	*adj.*—developed or matured earlier than usual	advanced for one's age, forward, mature, gifted, talented, clever, intelligent, quick
prefatory	*adj.*—introductory	preliminary, opening, initial, preparatory, initiatory, precursory
preponderate	*v.*—to outweigh	dominate, dictate, command, domineer, control
prerogative	*n.*—a prior or exclusive right or privilege	predominate, prevail, dominate, reign
prevaricate	*v.*—to evade the truth	hedge, fence, shilly-shally, dodge (the issue), sidestep (the issue), equivocate, waffle

WORD	DEFINITION	SYNONYMS
prognosis	*n.*—a forecast, especially in medicine	prediction, prognostication, prophecy, divination, augury
prolific	*adj.*—fruitful	plentiful, abundant, bountiful, profuse, copious, luxuriant, rich, lush, fecund
propagate	*v.*—to reproduce or multiply	breed, grow, cultivate
propitiate	*v.*—to win the good will of	appease, placate, mollify, pacify, make peace with, conciliate, soothe, calm
protocol	*n.*—an original draft or record of a document	agreement, treaty, entente, concordat, convention, deal, pact, contract, compact
provident	*adj.*—prudent; economical	farsighted, judicious, shrewd, circumspect, forearmed, wise, sagacious, sensible, thrifty, economical
proviso	*n.*—conditional stipulation to an agreement	provision, clause, rider, qualification, restriction, caveat
pseudonym	*n.*—a borrowed or fictitious name	pen name, nom de plume, assumed name, false name, alias, professional name, sobriquet, stage name, nom de guerre
puerile	*adj.*—childish; immature	infantile, juvenile, babyish, inane, fatuous, jejune, asinine, foolish, petty
purloin	*v.*—to steal	thieve, rob, take, snatch, pilfer, loot, appropriate

WORD	DEFINITION	SYNONYMS
purview	*n.*—the range of control, activity, or understanding	amplitude, confines, diapason, extensity, parameters, radius, scope
quaff	*v.*—to drink or swallow in large quantities	gulp (down), guzzle, slurp, down, empty, imbibe, partake of, consume, swig, swill, slug, knock back, toss off, chug
quagmire	*n.*—a difficult position, as if on shaky ground	muddle, mix-up, mess, predicament, mare's nest, can of worms, quandary, tangle, imbroglio, trouble, confusion, difficulty
qualm	*n.*—sudden feeling of uneasiness or doubt	misgivings, doubts, reservations, second thoughts, worries, concerns, anxiety, hesitation, hesitance, hesitancy, demur, reluctance, disinclination, apprehension, trepidation, unease, scruples, remorse
quintessence	*n.*—1. the ultimate substance; 2. the pure essence of anything	perfect example, exemplar, prototype, stereotype, picture, epitome, embodiment, ideal, apotheosis
quixotic	*adj.*—extravagantly chivalrous	idealistic, romantic, visionary, extravagant, starry-eyed, unrealistic, unworldly
quizzical	*adj.*—1. odd; comical; 2. suggesting puzzlement; questioning	inquiring, questioning, curious, puzzled, perplexed, baffled, mystified, amused, mocking, teasing
ramification	*n.*—the arrangement of branches; consequence	result, aftermath, outcome, effect, upshot; development, implication

WORD	DEFINITION	SYNONYMS
rampant	*adj.*—violent and uncontrollable action	unrestrained, unchecked, unbridled, widespread, rife
rancor	*n.*—a continuing and bitter hate or ill will	spite, resentment, malice, malevolence, animosity, antipathy, enmity, hostility, acrimony, venom, vitriol
raze	*v.*—to scrape or shave off	destroy, demolish, tear down, pull down, knock down, level, flatten, bulldoze
recalcitrant	*adj.*—refusing to obey authority	uncooperative, intractable, obstreperous, truculent, insubordinate, defiant, rebellious, willful, wayward, headstrong, self-willed, contrary, perverse, difficult
recidivism	*n.*—habitual or chronic relapse	backslide, backsliding, regression, relapse, retrogradation, retrogression
recumbent	*adj.*—leaning or reclining	lying, flat, horizontal, stretched out, sprawled, prone, prostrate, supine, lying down
recusant	*adj.*—disobedient of authority	agitator, dissenter, misbeliever, nonconformist, protester, separatist
redolent	*adj.*—sweet-smelling; fragrant	evocative, suggestive, reminiscent
reminiscence	*n.*—a remembering	nostalgic
remonstrate	*v.*—to exhibit strong reasons against an act	protest, complain, expostulate
rendition	*n.*—a performance or interpretation	rendering, presentation, execution

WORD	DEFINITION	SYNONYMS
repertoire	*n.*—stock of plays which can be readily performed by a company	collection, stock, range, repertory, reserve, store, repository, supply
reprehend	*v.*—to reprimand; to find fault with	rebuke, admonish, chastise, chide, upbraid, reprove, reproach, berate, take to task, lambaste, lecture, criticize, censure
reprieve	*v.*—to give temporary relief	save, rescue, pardon, spare, amnesty
resonant	*adj.*—resounding; re-echoing	deep, low, sonorous, full, full-bodied, vibrant, rich, clear, ringing, loud, booming
resplendent	*adj.*—dazzling; splendid	magnificent, brilliant, glittering, gorgeous, impressive, imposing, spectacular, striking, stunning, majestic
resurgent	*adj.*—rising or tending to rise again	renewal, revival, recovery, comeback, reawakening, resurrection, reappearance, reemergence, regeneration
revile	*v.*—to be abusive in speech	criticize, censure, condemn, attack, castigate, lambaste, denounce, slander, libel, malign, vilify, abuse, excoriate, calumniate
risible	*adj.*—able or inclined to laugh	ridiculous, absurd, comical, comic, amusing, funny, hilarious, humorous, droll, farcical, silly, ludicrous, hysterical
roseate	*adj.*—bright, cheerful, or optimistic	sanguine, bright, buoyant, favorable, auspicious, propitious

WORD	DEFINITION	SYNONYMS
rote	*n.*—a fixed, mechanical way of doing something	automatically, unthinkingly, mindlessly
rotund	*adj.*—rounded out or plump	stout, portly, paunchy, ample, heavyset, corpulent, obese
rudimentary	*adj.*—elementary	basic, primary, fundamental, essential
ruminate	*v.*—to muse on	contemplate, consider, meditate
sapid	*adj.*—having a pleasant taste	savory, palatable, tasty
sardonic	*adj.*—bitterly ironical	mocking, satirical, sarcastic, ironical, ironic; cynical, scornful, contemptuous, derisive, derisory, sneering, jeering; scathing, caustic, trenchant, cutting, sharp, acerbic
savant	*n.*—a learned person	intellectual, scholar, sage, philosopher, guru, master
schism	*n.*—a division in an organized group	split, rift, breach, rupture, break, separation, severance, chasm, gulf, discord, disagreement, dissension
scourge	*v.*—to whip severely	horsewhip, lash, strap, birch, switch, bullwhip, rawhide
scurrilous	*adj.*—using low and indecent language	defamatory, slanderous, libelous, scandalous, insulting, offensive, gross, abusive, vituperative, malicious
sedentary	*adj.*—1. characterized by sitting; 2. remaining in one locality	inactive, lethargic, lazy, idle

WORD	DEFINITION	SYNONYMS
serendipity	*n.*—an apparent aptitude for making fortunate discoveries accidentally	fortuity, providence
sloth	*n.*—disinclination to action or labor	laziness, idleness, indolence, slothfulness, inactivity, inertia, sluggishness, shiftlessness, apathy, acedia, listlessness, lassitude, lethargy, languor, torpidity
slovenly	*adv.*—careless in habits, behavior, etc.; untidy	scruffy, untidy, messy, unkempt, ill-groomed, slatternly, disheveled, bedraggled, tousled, rumpled, frowzy
sordid	*adj.*—filthy; foul	tawdry, cheap, debased, degenerate, dishonorable, disreputable, discreditable, contemptible, ignominious, shameful, abhorrent
specious	*adj.*—appearing just and fair without really being so	misleading, deceptive, false, fallacious, unsound, spurious, casuistic, sophistic
splenetic	*adj.*—bad-tempered; irritable	peevish, petulant, pettish, irritable, irascible, choleric, dyspeptic, testy, tetchy, querulous, resentful, rancorous, bilious, spiteful, malicious, hostile, acrimonious, malevolent, malignant, malign
staid	*adj.*—sober; sedate	respectable, quiet, serious, steady, conventional, traditional, unadventurous, decorous, formal, stuffy, stiff, priggish
staunch	*v.*—to stop or check the flow of blood	restrain, restrict, control, contain, lessen, reduce, diminish, retard

WORD	DEFINITION	SYNONYMS
stigmatize	*v.*—to characterize or brand as disgraceful	denounce, disparage, vilify, pillory, defame
stoic	*adj.*—a person who is seemingly indifferent to joy, grief, pleasure, or pain	uncomplaining, forbearing, accepting, tolerant, resigned, phlegmatic, philosophical
stolid	*adj.*—unexcitable; dull	phlegmatic, unemotional, placid, unexcitable, dependable, unimaginative
striated	*adj.*—marked with fine parallel lines	streak, dapple, variegate
strident	*adj.*—creaking; harsh; grating	harsh, raucous, rough, grating, rasping, jarring, loud, shrill, screeching, piercing
stymie	*n.*—to hinder or obstruct;	impede, inhibit, retard, balk, thwart, foil, curb, delay
succor	*n.*—aid; assistance	assistance; comfort, ease, relief, support
sumptuous	*adj.*—involving great expense	lavish, luxurious, opulent, magnificent, resplendent, gorgeous
sundry	*adj.*—1. various; miscellaneous; 2. separate; distinct	various, varied, miscellaneous, assorted, mixed, diverse, diversified; several, numerous, many, manifold, multifarious, multitudinous
supplant	*v.*—to take the place of	replace, supersede, displace, take over from, substitute for, override
suppliant	*adj.*—asking earnestly and submissively	petitioner, supplicant, pleader, beggar, applicant

WORD	DEFINITION	SYNONYMS
surfeit	*v.*—to feed or supply in excess	surplus, abundance, oversupply, superabundance, superfluity, glut, avalanche, deluge, overdose
swathe	*v.*—to wrap around something; envelop	wrap, envelop, bind, swaddle, bandage, cover, shroud, drape, wind, enfold, sheathe
tawdry	*adj.*—gaudy or cheap	flashy, showy, garish, tasteless, vulgar, trashy, junky, shoddy, shabby, gimcrack, chintzy
teem	*v.*—1. to be stocked to overflowing; 2. to pour out; to empty	1. swarming with, be aswarm with; be packed with, be crawling with, be overrun by, bristle with, seethe with, be thick with 2. pelt down, beat down
tenet	*n.*—any principle, doctrine, etc., which a person, school, or institution believes or maintains	principle, belief, doctrine, precept, creed, credo, article of faith, axiom, dogma, canon, theory, thesis, premise, conviction, idea, view, opinion, position
termagant	*n.*—a boisterous, scolding woman; a shrew	disobedient, undisciplined, intemperate, refractory, riotous, ungovernable, unmanageable
terrestrial	*adj.*—pertaining to the earth	earthly, worldly, mundane, earthbound
thrall	*n.*—a slave	bondage, servitude, enslavement, helotry
throe	*n.*—a violent pang or spasm of pain	agony, pangs, spasms, torment, suffering, torture

WORD	DEFINITION	SYNONYMS
timorous	*adj.*—fearful	nervous, scared, frightened, cowardly, pusillanimous, spineless
tortuous	*adj.*—pertaining to or involving excruciating pain	racking, struggling, tearing, tormenting, excruciating, harrowing
traduce	*v.* –to slander	defame, misrepresent, malign, vilify, denigrate, disparage, slur, impugn, smear, besmirch
transmute	*v.*—to transform	alter, adapt, transform, convert, metamorphose, morph, translate
travail	*v.*—to harass; to torment; struggle with difficulty	tribulation, trouble, hardship, privation, stress, drudgery, toil, slog, effort, exertion, endeavor, sweat, struggle
trenchant	*adj.*—1. keen; penetrating; 2. clear-cut; distinct	incisive, penetrating, sharp, keen, insightful, acute, focused, shrewd, razor-sharp, piercing, vigorous, forceful, strong, potent, telling, emphatic, forthright, mordant, cutting, biting, acerbic, pungent
tribunal	*n.*—the seat of judge	bench, magistrate, committee, forum, judiciary
troth	*n.*—belief; faith; fidelity	arbitration committee, jury, forum
turbid	*adj.*—1. thick; dense; 2. confused; perplexed	murky, opaque, cloudy, unclear
tutelage	*n.*—the condition of being under a guardian or a tutor	guardianship, coaching, custody, ministration, protection, safekeeping, superintendence, supervision

WORD	DEFINITION	SYNONYMS
umbra	*n.*—shade; shadow	adumbration, blackness, coolness, gloominess, obscuration, penumbra
uncouth	*adj.*—uncultured; crude	uncivilized, uncultivated, unrefined, unpolished, unsophisticated, rough, coarse, loutish, boorish, oafish, churlish, uncivil, rude, impolite, discourteous, disrespectful, unmannerly, bad-mannered, ill-bred, indecorous, crass, indelicate, vulgar, raunchy
unfeigned	*adj.*—genuine; real; sincere	true, honest, unaffected, unforced, heartfelt, wholehearted, bona fide
untrowable	*adj.*—incredible	magnificent, wonderful, marvelous, spectacular, remarkable, phenomenal, prodigious, breathtaking, extraordinary, unbelievable, amazing, stunning, astounding, astonishing, awe-inspiring, staggering, formidable, impressive, supreme, great, awesome, superhuman
uxoricide	*n.*—the murder of a wife by her husband	murder, killing, slaughter, butchery, massacre; assassination, execution, extermination
vagary	*n.*—1. an odd action or idea; 2. a wandering	change, fluctuation, variation, quirk, peculiarity, oddity, eccentricity, unpredictability, caprice, foible, whim, whimsy, fancy
vantage	*n.*—advantage; gain; profit	Convenience, dominance, ascendancy, prevalence, precedence, superiority, supremacy

WORD	DEFINITION	SYNONYMS
vaunt	*v.*—to brag or boast	parade, flaunt, acclaim, trumpet, praise, extol, celebrate
venal	*adj.*—that can be readily bribed or corrupted	corruptible, bribable, open to bribery, dishonest, dishonorable, untrustworthy, unscrupulous, unprincipled, mercenary, greedy
veneer	*n.*—1. a thin surface layer; 2. any attractive but superficial appearance	1. lamination, overlay, facing, covering, finish, exterior, cladding, laminate 2. facade, front, false front, show, impression, semblance, guise, disguise, mask, masquerade, pretense, camouflage, cover
verbiage	*n.*—wordiness	verbosity, wordiness, prolixity, long-windedness, loquacity, rigmarole, circumlocution, superfluity, periphrasis
verity	*n.*—truthfulness	accuracy, veracity, verisimilitude
vertigo	*n.*—a sensation of dizziness	giddiness, lightheadedness, loss of balance
vestige	*n.*—a trace of something that no longer exists	bit, touch, hint, suggestion, suspicion, shadow, scrap, tinge, speck, shred, jot, iota, whit, scintilla, glimmer
vicarious	*adj.*—taking the place of another person or thing	indirect, secondhand, secondary, derivative, derived, surrogate, substitute; empathetic, empathic

WORD	DEFINITION	SYNONYMS
vicissitude	*n.*—changes or variation occurring irregularly in the course of something	alteration, shift, reversal, twist, turn, downturn, variation, inconstancy, instability, uncertainty, chanciness, unpredictability, fickleness, variability, changeability, fluctuation, vacillation
vigilance	*n.*—watchfulness	observant, attentive, alert, eagle-eyed, hawk-eyed, on the lookout, wide awake, wakeful, circumspect, heedful, mindful
visage	*n.*—appearance	face, countenance, look, (facial) features, (facial) expression
vitriolic	*adj.*—extremely biting or caustic	acrimonious, rancorous, bitter, caustic, mordant, acerbic, trenchant, virulent, spiteful, savage, venomous, poisonous, malicious, splenetic, nasty, mean, cruel, unkind, harsh, hostile, vindictive, vicious, scathing, barbed, wounding, sharp, cutting, withering, sarcastic
vociferous	*adj.*—making a loud outcry	outspoken, forthright, plain-spoken, expressive, blunt, frank, candid, open, vehement, strident, vigorous, emphatic, insistent, forceful, zealous, clamorous, loudmouthed
volition	*n.*—the act of willing	voluntarily, willingly, readily, freely, intentionally, consciously, deliberately, on purpose, purposely, gladly

WORD	DEFINITION	SYNONYMS
voracious	*adj.*—greedy in eating	insatiable, unquenchable, unappeasable, prodigious, uncontrollable, compulsive, gluttonous, greedy, rapacious, enthusiastic, eager, keen, avid, desirous, hungry, ravenous
vouchsafe	*v.*—1. to be gracious enough to grant; 2. to guarantee as safe	permit, bestow, concede, acquiesce, endow, tender
wan	*adj.*—pale; pallid	ashen, white, gray, anemic, colorless, bloodless, waxen, chalky, pasty, peaked, sickly, washed out, drained, drawn, ghostly
wily	*adj.*—cunning; sly	shrewd, clever, sharp, sharp-witted, astute, canny, smart; crafty, artful, scheming, calculating, devious
wizened	*adj.*—withered; shrunken	wrinkled, lined, creased, shriveled, withered, weather-beaten, shrunken, gnarled, aged
wreak	*v.*—to give vent or free play	inflict, bestow, mete out, administer, deliver, impose, exact, create, cause, result in, effect, engender, bring about, perpetrate, unleash, let loose,
wrest	*v.*—1. to turn or twist or grab from; 2. usurp; 3. to distort or change the true meaning of	wrench, snatch, seize, pry, pluck, tug, pull, jerk, dislodge, removed

3. FOREIGN WORD PHRASES

ad hoc	*Latin*	literally, "to this"—for a specific purpose
ad infinitum	*Latin*	literally, "to infinity"—for a long time
ad nauseum	*Latin*	to the point of nausea
alfresco	*Italian*	out of doors, in the open
alma mater	*Latin*	literally "fostering mother"—the school one attended
ars gratia artis	*Latin*	literally, "art for art's sake"
au naturel	*French*	naked, unadorned
avant-garde	*French*	on the cutting edge
bête noire	*French*	literally "black beast"—a minor personal annoyance
bon vivant	*French*	someone who gets great enjoyment from life
carpe diem	*Latin*	literally, "seize the day"
carte blanche	*French*	literally, "white card"—complete freedom
cause célèbre	*French*	an infamous event or scandal
comme il faut	*French*	appropriate
corpus delecti	*Latin*	literally, "body of the crime"—evidence
coup de grace	*French*	the death blow
de facto	*Latin*	literally, "in fact"
deus ex machina	*Latin*	literally, "god from the machine"—a solution created out of desperation because no plausible one exists
enfant terrible	*French*	an unmanageable child
ex cathedra	*Latin*	literally, "from the chair"—with unquestionable authority
fait accompli	*French*	literally, "accomplished fact"
faux pas	*French*	literally, "false step"—a breach in etiquette or social protocol

flagrante delicto	*Latin*	literally, "with the crime blazing"—caught red-handed
in vino veritas	*Latin*	literally, "in wine, truth"
ipso facto	*Latin*	literally, "by the fact itself"
joie de vivre	*French*	literally, "joy of living"—high spirits, enthusiasm
lingua franca	*Italian*	literally, "the Frankish tongue"—a common language between people who do not speak the other's native language
mea culpa	*Latin*	literally, "my fault"
noblesse oblige	*French*	the obligation of those of noble heritage
prima facie	*Latin*	literally, "on the face of it"—at first glance
quod erat demonstratum	*Latin*	literally, "as has been demonstrated"—often abbreviated Q.E.D.
raison d'être	*French*	literally, "reason for being"
savoir-faire	*French*	literally, "to know what to do"
status quo	*Latin*	the current circumstances
tabula rasa	*Latin*	literally, "erased tablet"—not yet affected by environment
tempus fugit	*Latin*	literally, "time flies"
tête-à-tête	*French*	literally, "head to head"—a private conversation
veni, vidi, vici	*Latin*	literally, "I came, I saw, I conquered"
verboten	*German*	forbidden
Zeitgeist	*German*	the mood of the moment

LITERATURE

1. IMPORTANT LITERARY FIGURES AND THEIR MAJOR WORKS

Aeschylus (525 B.C.E.–456 B.C.E.)—Responsible for the origin and development of Greek drama; introduced 2nd speaking character and concept of conflict (*Oresteia, Agamemnon, Chophori, and Eumenides*)

Aristophanes (450 B.C.E.–385 B.C.E.)—Considered the father of Greek comedy (*Lysistrata, The Clouds, The Birds*)

Aristotle (384 B.C.E.–322 B.C.E.)—Introduced and popularized the concept of literary criticism (*The Poetics*)

Euripides (485 B.C.E.–405 B.C.E.)—Chiefly responsible for introducing the technique of deus ex machina (*The Trojan Women, Helen, The Bacchae*)

Homer (c. 9th Cen. B.C.E.)—Products of a non-literate culture. 1st works of Western literature (*Odyssey, Iliad*)

Ovid (43 B.C.E.–18 C.E.)—(Publius Ovidius Naso) Brought erotic verse to popularity (*Metamorphoses, Love's Remedy*)

Plato (428 B.C.E.–399 B.C.E.)—Father of Western philosophy (*Republic, Apology, Symposium*)

Sappho (c. 612 B.C.E.—?)—Verse fragments (Early Greek poetry)

Sophocles (496 B.C.E.–406 B.C.E.)—Added 3rd speaking character and moved Greek drama further from religious commentary to more basic human interaction (*Oedipus Tyrannus, Antigone, Electra*)

Virgil (70 B.C.E.–19 B.C.E.)—(Publius Vegilius Maro) Popularized the pastoral poem and the concept of civic virtue (*The Aeneid*)

The Middle Ages and the Renaissance

Alighieri, Dante (1265–1321)—Considered to have single-handedly founded modern European literature; perfected "terza rima" (rhyme in threes) (Divine Comedy, *The Inferno, Purgatorio, Paridiso*)

Bacon, Francis (1561–1626)—Founder of the inductive method of modern science and philosophical writings about science (Essays, *The New Atlantis*)

Boccaccio, Giovanni (1313–1375)—Introduced the use of the vernacular in classically focused literature (*The Decameron*)

Chaucer, Geoffrey (1340–1400)—Chiefly responsible for bringing literature to the middle class (*The Canterbury Tales, Troilus and Criseyde*)

de Cervantes Saavedra, Miguel (1547–1616)—Wrote the 1st modern novel (*Don Quixote*)

Jonson, Ben (1573–1637)—English playwright (*Every Man in His Humour*)

Machiavelli, Nicolò (1469–1527)—*The Prince* outlined a governmental structure based on the self-interest of the ruler; such rule is still called "Machiavellian." (*The Prince, La Madrigola*)

Marlowe, Christopher (1564–1593)—Author of 1st real historical drama and 1st English tragedy (*The Tragedy of Doctor Faustus, Edward the Second*)

Milton, John (1608–1674)—Puritan poet noted for allegorical religious epics (*Paradise Lost, Paradise Regained*)

Petrarch, Francesco (1304–1374)—His works provided the basis for love poetry and popularized the theme of humanism. (*The Canzoniere*)

Rabelais, François (1494–1553)—Introduced satiric narrative (*Gargantua, Pantagruel*)

Shakespeare, William (1564–1616)—Considered the greatest English poet and dramatist (*Hamlet, King Lear, Macbeth, Romeo and Juliet, Twelfth Night, Richard III, Julius Caesar, Much Ado About Nothing,* Sonnets)

Spenser, Edmund (1552–1599)—Popularized the use of allegory (*The Faerie Queen, Amoretti*)

The Neoclassical Period

Dryden, John (1631–1700)—Influential in establishing the heroic couplet (*Alexander's Feast, Heroic Stanzas*)

Molière (Jean-Baptiste Poquelin) (1622–1673)—Perfected literary conversation and introduced everyday speech to theatre (*Don Juan, Tartuffe, The Misanthrope*)

Racine, Jean (1639–1699)—Renowned for lyric poetry based on Greek and Roman literature (*Andromaque, Bernice and Phaedre*)

The Enlightenment

Addison, Joseph (1672–1719)—Outstanding poet, critic, and playwright whose numerous essays marked political free thinking of his time (*The Tattler, The Spectator, Cato*)

Blake, William (1757–1827)—Visual artist and poet who defied neoclassical convention with subjects of truth and beauty (*Songs of Innocence, Songs of Experience*)

Franklin, Benjamin (1706–1790)—Scientist, educator, abolitionist, philosopher, economist, political theorist, and statesman who defined the colonial New World in his writings; principle figure of the American Enlightenment (*Poor Richard's Almanac, Observations on the Increase of Mankind,* numerous essays and state papers)

Pope, Alexander (1688–1744)—Classicist and wit who formulated rules for poetry and satirized British social circles (*The Dunciad, The Rape of the Lock*)

Rousseau, Jean-Jacques (1712–1778)—Libertine whose focused prose inspired the French Revolution (*Social Contract, The New Heloise*)

Swift, Jonathan (1667–1745)—Noted for his direct style, clear, sharp prose and critical wit (*Gulliver's Travels, Tale of a Tub*)

Voltaire (François-Marie Arouet) (1694–1778)—Progressive philosopher and freethinker best known for synthesizing French and English critical theory (*Candide, Zadig*)

Romantic, Victorian, and Realists

Austen, Jane (1775–1817)—Principally known for novels of manners and middle class English society (*Sense and Sensibility, Pride and Prejudice*)

Baudelaire, Charles (1821–1867)—French Symbolist poet (*Flowers of Evil (Les Fleurs du Mal)*)

Brontë, Charlotte (1816–1855)—Victorian novelist, sister to Emily Brontë (*Jane Eyre*)

Brontë, Emily (1816–1848)—Victorian novelist (*Wuthering Heights*)

Browning, Elizabeth Barrett (1806–1861)—English poet, married to Robert Browning (*Sonnets from the Portuguese, Aurora Leigh*)

Browning, Robert (1812–1889)—English poet, married to Elizabeth Browning (*Bells and Pomegranates*)

Byron, George Gordon (Lord) (1788–1824)—Major figure in Romantic movement, and inspiration for the Byronic hero (*Don Juan,* classic poetry)

Coleridge, Samuel Taylor (1772–1834)—Foremost literary critic of the Romantic period (*Rime of the Ancient Mariner*)

Conrad, Joseph (1857–1924)—Ukrainian born of Polish parents, major English post-colonialist novelist (*Heart of Darkness, Lord Jim*)

Dickens, Charles (1812–1870)—English novelist (*Great Expectations, Oliver Twist*)

Dickinson, Emily (1830–1886)—American poet (*Because I Could Not Stop for Death*)

Dostoyevsky, Fyodor (1821–1881)—Russian novelist (*Crime and Punishment, Notes From the Underground*)

Eliot, George (1819–1880)—English author (*Mill on the Floss*)

Flaubert, Gustave (1821–1880)—French novelist (*Madame Bovary*)

Hawthorne, Nathaniel (1804–1864)—American transcendentalist (*The Scarlet Letter, House of the Seven Gables*)

Ibsen, Henrik (1828–1906)—Norwegian playwright and forerunner of the Expressionist movement (*A Doll's House*)

Kafka, Franz (1883–1924)—Major existentialist novelist (*The Metamorphosis, The Castle*)

Keats, John (1795–1821)—Most versatile of the Romantics (*Hyperion, On a Grecian Urn*)

Lawrence, D.H. (1885–1930)—English novelist (*Lady Chatterly's Lover, The Rainbow*)

Melville, Herman (1819–1891)—American transcendentalist (*Moby-Dick, Billy Budd*)

Poe, Edgar Allan (1809–1849)—American transcendentalist who dealt with macabre issues of insanity and horror (*Fall of the House of Usher, The Tell-Tale Heart, The Raven*)

Rossetti, Christina (1830–1894)—English poet (*Goblin Market*)

Shelley, Mary (1797–1851)—Romantic novelist whose liberal social and political views underscore her work, sister to Percy Shelly (*Frankenstein, The Last Man*)

Shelley, Percy Bysshe (1792–1822)—Romantic poet who mastered metaphor and metrical form, brother to Mary Shelley (*Adonais*)

Stowe, Harriet Beecher (1811–1896)—American novelist, wrote the most important novel of the abolitionist movement (*Uncle Tom's Cabin*)

Thoreau, Henry David (1818–1848)—American transcendentalist and social theorist (*Walden*)

Tolstoy, Leo Nikolayevich (1828–1910)—Major Russian novelist (*War and Peace, Anna Karenina*)

Twain, Mark (Samuel Clemens) (1835–1910)—American novelist, essayist, and satirist (*Huckleberry Finn, Tom Sawyer*)

Whitman, Walt (1819–1892)—American poet (*Leaves of Grass*)

Wilde, Oscar (1854–1900)—English novelist, dramatist, and social critic (*The Importance of Being Earnest, Picture of Dorian Gray*)

Wordsworth, William (1770–1850)—Romantic poet who broke with neoclassical theory in much of his nature poetry (*The Prelude, Lyrical Ballads*)

Modernism and Post-Modernism

Baldwin, James (1924–1987)—American poet and novelist (*The Fire Next Time*)

Beckett, Samuel (1906–1989)—Irish-born French playwright and novelist; themes include existentialism and absurdity (*Waiting for Godot, Happy Days*)

Bishop, Elizabeth (1911–1979)—American poet (*Collected Works*)

cummings, e.e. (1894–1962)—Known for non-traditional forms of poetry (*Tulips and Chimneys*)

Eliot, T.S. (1888–1965)—Christian poet and theorist (*The Waste Land*)

Faulkner, William (1897–1962)—Major author of the American South (*The Sound and the Fury, Absalom! Absalom!*)

Frost, Robert (1874–1963)—Major American poet (*Birches, The Road Not Taken*)

Ginsberg, Allen (1926–1997)—American Beat poet (*Howl*)

Gordimer, Nadine (1923–)—South African novelist (*A Sport of Nature*)

Hemingway, Ernest (1899–1961)— Known for lean prose and ardently masculine themes and characters (*The Old Man and the Sea, A Farewell to Arms*)

Hughes, Langston (1902–1967)—Harlem Renaissance poet (*Collected Works*)

Hurston, Zora Neale (1901–1960)—American novelist and folklorist (*Their Eyes Were Watching God, Tell My Horse*)

Joyce, James (1882–1941)—Premier Modernist novelist of Ireland, pioneered stream of conscious and non-linear narratives (*Portrait of an Artist as a Young Man, Ulysses*)

Kerouac, Jack (1922–1969)—American Beat poet and novelist (*On the Road, Dharma Bums*)

Lee, Harper (1926–)—American writer. *To Kill a Mockingbird* is only novel.

Lewis, Sinclair (1885–1951)—American novelist and social critic (*Babbitt, Elmer Gantry*)

Miller, Arthur (1915–2005)—American Playwright (*Death of a Salesman, The Crucible*)

Miller, Henry (1891–1980)—Controversial American novelist (*The Tropic of Cancer, The Tropic of Capricorn*)

Morrison, Toni (1931–)—American novelist (*The Bluest Eye, Song of Solomon, Beloved*)

Nabokov, Vladimir (1899–1977)—Russian novelist (*Lolita, Invitation to a Beheading*)

Naipaul, V.S. (1932–)—Post-Colonialist novelist, born in Trinidad of Indian parents, raised in England (*Enigma of Arrival, House for Mr. Biswas*)

O'Neill, Eugene (1888–1953)—Major American dramatist (*Anna Christie, The Hairy Ape*)

Plath, Sylvia (1932–1963)—American poet and novelist (*Ariel, The Bell Jar*)

Pound, Ezra (1885–1972)—American poet (*The Cantos*)

Pynchon, Thomas (1937–)—Reclusive American novelist (*Vineland, Gravity's Rainbow, The Crying of Lot 49*)

Rich, Adrienne (1929–)—American poet (*Aunt Jennifer's Tigers*)

Rushdie, Salman (1947–)—Known for death sentence (*fatwa*) placed upon him by Ayatollah Khomeni because Khomeni believed Rushdie's subject matter to be blasphemous. (*The Satanic Verses, Shame*)

Salinger, J.D. (1919–2010)—Reclusive American writer (*Catcher in the Rye, Franny and Zooey*)

Shaw, George Bernard (1856–1950)—Irish born British author and playwright (*Arms and the Man, Saint Joan*)

Sinclair, Upton (1878–1968)—American novelist and social critic, characterized as a "muckraker" (*The Jungle*)

Solzhenitsyn, Aleksander Isayevitch (1918–2008)—Major Russian novelist and social critic (*The Gulag Archipelago*)

Stein, Gertrude (1874–1946)—American modernist author (*3 Lives*)

Steinbeck, John (1902–1968)—American novelist whose major theme was the life of the American worker (*Grapes of Wrath, Cannery Row*)

Walker, Alice (1944–)—American novelist (*The Color Purple, Possessing the Secrets of Joy*)

Williams, Tennessee (1911–1983)—American playwright (*A Streetcar Named Desire, The Glass Menagerie*)

Woolf, Virginia (1882–1941)—Modernist novelist and early feminist (*A Room of One's Own, To the Lighthouse*)

Yeats, William Butler (1865–1939)—Irish poet and dramatist (*The Wind Among the Reeds, The Winding Stair*)

2. LITERARY VOCABULARY

Allegory	Poetry or prose in which abstract ideas are represented by individual characters, events, or objects.
Alliteration	Rapid repetition of consonants in a given line of poetry or prose.
Allusion	Reference to one literary work in another.
Anachronism	A chronological error in which a relationship between events or objects is historically impossible.
Anapest	A metrical foot where two unstressed syllables are followed by a stressed syllable.
Antagonist	The character in a literary work that goes against the actions of the hero.
Antihero	The protagonist of a literary work who has none of the characteristics associated with the hero.
Apostrophe	Direct address to someone or something not present.
Assonance	Rapid repetition of vowels in a given line of poetry or prose.
Ballad	A poem, often intended to be sung, that tells a story.
Bathos	Deliberate anticlimax used to make a definitive point.
Bildungsroman	A coming-of-age story, usually autobiographical.
blank verse	Unrhymed poetry usually written in iambic pentameter.

Caesura	A deliberate pause in a line of poetry.
Canto	Analogous to a chapter in a novel, a division in a poem.
Climax	The peak of action in a literary work.
Conceits	Elaborate comparisons between unlike objects.
Consonance	Repetition of consonant sounds with unlike vowels—similar to alliteration.
Couplet	A pair of rhyming lines of poetry in the same meter.
Dactyl	A metrical foot composed of one stressed syllable followed by two unstressed syllables.
Denouement	The action following the climax in a literary work.
Diction	Word choice or syntax.
Doggerel	Crudely written poetry, in which words are often mangled to fit a rhyme scheme.
Elegy	A poem lamenting the passage of something.
Enjambment	In poetry, the continuation of a phrase or sentence onto the following line.
Epistolary	Refers to a novel or story told in the form of letters.
Fable	A story used to illustrate a moral lesson.
Foot	A group of syllables that make up a metered unit of a verse.
Haiku	A Japanese poetical form, having three lines and 17 syllables, five in the first line, seven in the second, and five in the third.
Hubris	In tragic drama, excessive pride leading to the fall of a hero.
Hyperbole	Exaggeration for effect.

Iamb	A foot containing two syllables, a short then a long (in quantitative meter).
Irony	A deliberate discrepancy between literal meaning and intended meaning.
Malapropism	Often used for humorous effect; it is the substitution of a word for one that sounds similar but has a radically different meaning.
Metaphor	A form of comparison in which something is said to be something else, often an unlikely pairing.
Meter	The combination of stressed and unstressed syllables that creates the rhythm of a poem.
Metonymy	A phrase or statement that takes on a larger meaning.
Motif	The recurrence of a word or theme in a novel or poem.
Onomatopoeia	A word whose sound suggests its meaning; for example, "crash."
Oxymoron	Two contradictory words used together to create deeper meaning; for example, sweet sorrow.
Paradox	A seemingly contradictory phrase, which proves to be true upon comparison.
Pathos	An appeal that evokes pity or sympathy.
Scansion	The annotation of the meter of a poem.
Simile	Means of comparison using either "like" or "as."
Sonnet	A verse form consisting of fourteen lines arranged in an octet (eight lines) and a sextet (six lines), usually ending in a couplet; in common English form, arranged in three quatrains followed by a couplet.
Spondee	A metrical foot comprised of two stressed syllables.
Synecdoche	The use of part of a thing to represent the whole; for example, "wheels" for a car.

Tone   Attitude of the speaker, setting the mood for a given passage.

Trochee   A metrical foot composed of a stressed syllable followed by an unstressed syllable.

Villanelle   A verse form consisting of five tercets and a quatrain, the first and third lines of the tercet recur alternately as the last lines of the other tercets and together as the last lines of the quatrain.

ART AND ARCHITECTURE

1. ARTISTS AND ARCHITECTS

Bacon, Henry (1866–1924)—American architect: Lincoln Memorial

Botticelli, Sandro (1445–1510)—Botticelli, Italian painter, known for concentration on line, depth of feeling, delicacy of style: *Birth of Venus* (Venus on a Half-Shell), tempera on canvas

Brancusi, Constantin (1876–1957)—Romanian pioneer of abstract sculpture: *Bird in Space,* in marble

Brunelleschi, Filippo (1377–1446)—founder of Renaissance style in architecture: *Pazzi Chapel* in Santa Croce, Florence

Cassatt, Mary (1845–1926)—American Impressionist painter: soft surface, snapshot vision in paintings, subjects almost exclusively female: *The Bath,* oil on canvas

Cézanne, Paul (1839–1906)—French Post-Impressionist painter, used color to construct form, painted abstractly, "Father of Modern Art": *Still Life with Apples and Oranges, Woman with the Coffeepot,* oil on canvas

Dali, Salvador (1904–1989)—sexual symbolism, master of draftsmanship and color: *The Persistence of Memory* (the melting clock picture), oil on canvas

(David) Jacques Louis David (1748–1825)—known as David, Rococo painter, revival of classicism: *Oath of the Horatii, Death of Marat,* oil on canvas

da Vinci, Leonardo (1452–1519)—High Renaissance Italian painter, sculptor, architectural engineer, inventor: *Last Supper,* mural, oil and tempera on plaster, *Mona Lisa,* oil on panel

Degas, Edgar (1834–1917)—French Impressionist painter, did not share the Impressionist interest in landscape, fascinated by the dance, known for his paintings of dance: *The Rehearsal,* oil on canvas

(Donatello) Donato di Niccolo Bardi (1386?–1466)—commonly known as Donatello, leading sculptor in Italy, one of the founders of the new Renaissance style: bronze sculpture *David* (first nude David), *Mary Magdalen* in gilded wood

Dürer, Albrecht (1471–1528)—founder of German High Renaissance, known for his graphic art—woodcuts, copper engravings: *Four Horsemen of the Apocalypse,* woodcut, *Adam and Eve,* engraving, *Saint Jerome,* engraving

Eiffel, Gustave (1832–1923)—French engineer: Eiffel Tower

Gauguin, Paul (1848–1903)—no formal art training, departed from Western artistic tradition, return to archaic, primitive styles: *The Day of the God, Vision After the Sermon,* oil on canvas

(Goya) Fransisco José de Goya y Lucientes (1746–1828)—known as Goya, Romantic Spanish painter: *The Third of May, 1808, at Madrid: The Shootings on Principe Pio Mountain,* oil on canvas

Javachef, Christo (1935–)—Bulgarian Earth artist, packages inert objects and nature in plastic and fabric: *Surrounded Islands, Biscayne Bay, Greater Miami, Florida,* woven synthetic fabric, 6 million square feet

Jefferson, Thomas (1743–1826)—American architect: *Monticello* in the style of a neoclassic temple

Klimt, Gustav (1862–1918)—greatest of Art Nouveau painters: *The Kiss*

Latrobe, Benjamin (1764–1820)—English American architect and engineer: Waterworks of Philadelphia, assisted in the design and construction of the Capitol Building in Washington, D.C.

Le Vau, Louis (1612–1670)—creator of the basic body of Versailles in France, later expanded and altered by others

Lichtenstein, Roy (1923–1997)—American Pop artist, "comic strip art": *Wham,* two panels, magna on canvas

Manet, Edouard (1832–1883)—French Impressionist painter, forefather of Impressionism: *Luncheon on the Grass, A Bar at the Folies-Bergere,* oil on canvas

Matisse, Henri (1869–1954)—French Expressionist, experimented with simplified figures, masses stated with bold areas of pigment, brilliant color: *The Green Stripe (Madame Matisse),* oil and tempera on canvas

Mazzola, Francesco (1503–40)—commonly known as Parmigianino, Mannerist Italian painter, known for the distortion in his renderings: *Madonna with the Long Neck,* panel painting

Merisi, Michelangelo (1573–1610)—known as Caravaggio, Baroque Italian painter, known for his naturalism, hard pictorial style, but mostly for his intense light and dark contrasts: *Conversion of St. Paul,* oil on canvas

(Michelangelo) Michelangelo Buonarroti (1475–1564)—commonly known as Michelangelo, High Renaissance Italian painter, sculptor: marble sculpture *David,* ceiling fresco for the Sistine Chapel

Mills, Robert (1781–1855)—American architect: *Washington Monument, U.S. Treasury*

Mondrian, Piet (1872–1944)—Dutch painter, master of the De Stijl movement, reduced all formal elements to flat surfaces bounded by straight lines intersected at right angles, colors in black, white, gray, and primary colors: *Composition,* oil on canvas

Monet, Claude (1840–1926)—French impressionist painter painted outdoors, began with reality and painted into it the objective perception of color: *Nympheas (Water Lilies), Rouen Cathedral in Full Sunlight,* oil on canvas

Moore, Henry (1898–1986)—English sculptor, adaptation of empty spaces and Cubist Structure: *Interior-Exterior Reclining Figure,* in bronze

Munch, Edvard (1863–1944)—Norwegian painter, forerunner of Expressionism, themes involving sex and death, psychological subjects: *The Scream,* oil on canvas

O'Keeffe, Georgia (1887–1986)—American Modern painter, free flow of rhythmic shapes, known for her studies of flowers: *Blue and Green Music,* oil on canvas

Picasso, Pablo Ruiz y (1881–1973)—father of Cubism: *Les Demoiselles d'Avignon, Seated Woman,* oil on canvas

Pollock, Jackson (1912–1956)—American Abstract Expressionist painter, free motion of arm, drip painting, used gobs of color, "action painting": *Blue Poles,* oil, Duco, and aluminum paint on canvas

Rauschenberg, Robert (1925–)—American Pop artist, used objects in his works: *Trapeze,* oil on canvas with silkscreen

(Rembrandt) Rembrandt van Rijn (1606–69)—Baroque Dutch painter, known for his spirituality in art, radiant light against and through warm, glowing, vibrant shadow: *Supper at Emmaus, Return of the Prodigal Son,* both oil on canvas

Renoir, Pierre Auguste (1842–1919)—French Impressionist painter, known for the warmth, physical delight, enjoyment of the moment of light and air in his paintings: *Le Moulin de la Galette,* oil on canvas

Renwick, James Jr. (1818–1895)—American architect and engineer: St. Patrick's Cathedral in New York, Smithsonian Institution in Washington

Rodin, Auguste (1840–1917)—Impressionist sculptor: exclusively concerned with the human figure, particularly in moments of great physical and emotional stress: *The Age of Bronze, The Kiss* (in marble)

Rubens, Peter Paul (1577–1640)—Baroque Flemish painter; in many of his paintings, the figures form a spiral up into the picture: center panel of a triptych *Raising of the Cross*

Sanzio, Raffaello (1483–1520)—commonly known as Raphael, High Renaissance Italian painter, his ideals of figural and compositional harmony came to be recognized as the High Renaissance principles: fresco *School of Athens,* panel painting *Madonna of the Meadows*

Segal, George (1924–2000)—American Pop artist, began as painter, abandoned color almost entirely in his sculptural treatment of the human figure: *The Bus Riders,* plaster, metal, and vinyl

Seurat, Georges Pierre (1859–1891)—French Post-Impressionist painter, began with divisionism, in which each touch of the brush represents a separate color so the shades mix only in the eye, not on the palette, later developed into pointilism: *Sunday Afternoon on the Island of La Grande Jatte,* oil on canvas

Thetokopoulos, Domenikos (1541–1614)—commonly known as El Greco, born in Crete, recreated in contemporary Renaissance style the Byzantine pictorial tradition: *Resurrection, The Burial of Count Orgaz, Toledo,* all oil on canvas

Tiffany, Louis Comfort (1848–1933)—American artisan, known for his stained glass creations

van Eyck, Jan (1385–1441)—Early Renaissance Flemish painter known for the naturalism, minute detail, and representation of atmospheric space in his works: *Ghent Altarpiece,* 20 panels, oil

van Gogh, Vincent (1853–1890)—Dutch Post-Impressionist painter, used thick pigment, blazing color, strong strokes: *Starry Night, The Night Cafe,* oil on canvas

Vecellio, Tiziano (1490–1576)—commonly known as Titian, High Renaissance painter in Venice, established color as the major determinant in his paintings: *Venus of Urbino, Man with the Glove, Sacred and Profane Love,* all oil on canvas

(Velázquez) Diego Rodriguez de Silva y Velázquez (1599–1660)—known as Velázquez, Spanish Baroque painter, known for his optical method of painting, nature as revealed to human vision through light: *Las Merinas,* oil on canvas

Warhol, Andy (1930–1987)—American Pop artist, specialized in the boring, impersonal, mechanized sameness: *Marilyn Monroe,* oil, acrylic, and silkscreen enamel on canvas

Wright, Frank Lloyd (1867–1959)—American architect: *Solomon R. Guggenheim Museum*

2. MOVEMENTS

Abstract Expressionism (began about mid-1900s)—Opposed to strict formalism that characterizes much of abstract art: Arshile Gorky (1904–48)—American artist, one of the founders.

Cubism (early 1900s)—Imposed formal structure of largely monochromatic planes upon an object; its chief exponents were Pablo Picasso and Georges Braque, who saw it as a stark expression of the impact of modernity.

Early Renaissance art (about 1400–1480))—In Italy: artists began to approximate reality in form, space, color.

Earth Art (began about 1960s)—Creating art in nature: Robert Smithson (1938–1973)—Spiral Jetty in Utah.

Expressionism (about 1900s)—Daring treatment of unexpected and shocking themes, sharp contrast of colors and shapes, bold brushwork, arbitrary color, harshly unreal drawing.

Futurism (about 1900s)—Motion brought to Cubism: Umberto Boccioni (1882–1916)—Orpheus

Gothic style (about 1590 to 1750)—Began in northern France before the middle of the 12th century and in the rest of western Europe slightly later, most distinctive are the Gothic cathedrals: Notre-Dame in Paris.

High Renaissance (about 1500–1580)—Central Italy: spatial depth and harmony, natural proportions, graceful poses.

Impressionism (about 1860–1875)—Considered photography false to the psychological perception of reality in color and motion, fascination with transformations wrought by light on natural objects, surfaces, atmospheric spaces.

Mannerism—Nervous, spaceless, crowded with twisting, turbulent figures, unnaturally lengthened.

Minimal Art (began about 1960s)—Simple objects, shorn of all suggestion of meaning or of human receptiveness (e.g., bookshelves), Donald Judd, art based on pure proportion: Untitled, seven identical quadrangular cubic masses of galvanized iron.

Neo-classicism (1775–1825)—Held Baroque in abhorrence, return to discipline in form drawing and composition.

Paleolithic art (Old Stone Age) (30,000–10,000 B.C.E.)—Cave art, large-scale paintings in caves.

Performance Art—Intended to shock, combines theatricism with art, first performance artist: Allan Kaprow: 18 Happenings in 6 Parts.

Photo-Realism (began about 1980s)—Picture was painted, unaltered, with an airbrush from a photographic slide projected on the canvas, as long as the subject was as banal as possible: Richard Estes (1936–)—Hotel Empire, oil on canvas.

Pop Art (began about 1960s)—Characterized by wit, anti-aestheticism, positive nihilism.

Op Art (Optical Art) (began about 1960)—Denies representation altogether, strong optical illusions of depth, mass, motion: Richard Anuszkiewicz, American artist: Trinity.

Post-Impressionism (about 1880–1890)—Retained the bright palette of Impressionism, but acquired new shape and function, unique to the personal style of each painter

Process Art (began about 1960)—Any material was art, as long as it was shapeless and impermanent

Realism (about 1825–1870)—Lowering of tonality of color, as well as action and emotion, insistence on priority of vision over abstraction, emotion

Rococo—Softness, vagueness, voluptuousness

Romanticism (about 1780–1825)—Interest in the sublime, picturesque

Surrealism (began about 1930)—Exploring illogic on Freudian principles to uncover and utilize for creative purposes the "actual" processes of thought

3. ART AND ARCHITECTURE VOCABULARY

Aqueduct   artificial channel for conducting water, in Roman times, usually built over ground and supported on arches

Atrium   open entrance or central hall of an ancient Roman house

Basilica   barn-like building form, central long space flanked by side aisles

Bungalow   Indian (Bengali) word for single-storied house with veranda

Cameo   a carving in relief upon a gem, stone, or shell

Cenotaph   abstract monument to a person buried elsewhere: *Washington Monument*

Chiaroscuro   painting term, the opposition of light and dark

Cinquefoil   Gothic tracery pattern, reminiscent of a five-leaf clover

Cromlech   circle of standing unhewn stones: *Stonehenge*

Crosshatching   crossing sets of parallel lines to produce the effect of shading

Engraving   print made by incising a design onto a copper plate, inking the plate, wiping off the excess ink, and pressing the plate onto a moistened piece of paper

Façade   front or principal face of a building

Foreshortening   in drawing, painting, the object seems to recede in space and conveys the illusion of three dimensions

Fresco   painting on wet plaster with watercolors, so plaster absorbs colors and the painting becomes part of the wall

fresco secco   painting on dry plaster, less durable as the paint tends to flake off over time

gargoyle   roof spout in the shape of a grotesque human or animal figure, e.g., Gothic gargoyles on the Notre Dame Cathedral

genre painting	scenes from everyday life for their own sake, usually with no religious or symbolic significance
hatching	in drawing or engraving, use of parallel lines to produce the effect of shading
hieroglyphs	characters in the picture-writing system of ancient Egyptians
hypostyle	in the style of ancient Egyptian temple architecture, a hall of many columns, e.g., *Parthenon* in Athens
illumination	decorating manuscripts, scrolls, with illustrations or designs in gold, silver, or bright colors
lithograph	print made by drawing with a crayon on a porous stone or metal plate, applying greasy printing ink which adheres only to the lines of the drawing, and pressing the plate on a moistened piece of paper
megalithic architecture	monuments made partially or wholly of giant stones
mosaic	surface decoration in which bits of colored stone or glass are laid in cement in a design or decorative pattern
obelisk	a tapering four-sided shaft of stone, usually monolithic, with a pyramidal apex, used as a freestanding monument, as in ancient Egypt, or as an architectural decoration
perspective	representation of three-dimensional objects on a flat surface so as to produce the same impression of distance and relative size as that received by the human
relief	sculpture that is not freestanding but projects from the background of which it is a part, can be high relief and low relief depending on the amount of projection; incised relief is when the background is not cut out, as in some Egyptian architecture
stippling	method of representing light and shade by the use of dots in painting, drawing, and engraving,

tempera   Widely used in Italian panel painting before the sixteenth century, ground colors mixed with yolk of egg, instead of oil

triptych   Altarpiece or devotional picture consisting of three panels joined together, frequently hinged, so that the center panel is covered when the side panels are closed

woodcut   Print made by cutting a design in relief on a block of wood and printing only the raised surfaces

ziggurat   Tiered, truncated pyramid of mud brick

4. ART AND ARCHITECTURE SCHOOLS

Bauhaus   Architectural design school opened in Germany in 1919, tried to blend art and architecture with industrial techniques

Chicago School   Around the middle of the nineteenth century, architects who became known as the Chicago School; their architecture more functional than artistic, characteristic new architectural forms were the factory, warehouse, office building, department store, apartment house

École des Beaux-Arts In Paris, national French architectural school, architecture of 19th century France

MUSIC

1. MUSIC VOCABULARY

Absolute music

Instrumental music with no text, or story. Abstract music which stands for itself.

Baroque (1600–1750)

Elaborate, intense and full of spirit. Opera was explored.

Classical (1750–1820)

Centered in Vienna. Stressed balance, form, and restraint in music.

Fugue

Polyphonic. Two or more voices, with independent melodies, sounded together. Employed by Bach.

Gregorian chant

Plainchant music. Monophonic, single melodic lines with no accompaniment. Vocal music of the church.

Jazz (1800s–)

Truly "American" music. Originated from the black American musical traditions of folk music, ragtime and the blues. Contains a strong beat, relies on improvisation. Rhythmic with a swing feel.

Medieval Period (500–1420)

Both secular (nonreligious) and sacred music were composed, although mostly sacred survived as monks transcribed the music used for worship in Christian mass.

Madrigal

Musical form which utilizes composed poetry and new music for each verse.

Mass

Polyphonic service.

Motet

Vocal polyphony for use in church.

Nationalism

A patriotic influence, spirit, and flavor within the musical composition.

Orchestral symphony	A large work for orchestra, usually in four movements, of which the first is in sonata form.
Passions	Choral. Oratorios based on the Crucifixion of Christ.
Polyphony	Two or more lines of melody; distinct thoughts performed together.
Program music	Descriptive music which represents ideas, thoughts, and feelings.
Recitative	Words and speech set to music. Pitches reflect the inflections of the voice.
Renaissance (1420–1600)	A "rebirth" and revival of humanistic thoughts.
Romantic (1820–1900)	Employed emotional feelings in music.
Song cycles	Works of music related by content or musical thoughts. Used by Schumann.
Tone poem	Music which is dramatic and incorporates elements of a poetic nature

2. IMPORTANT MUSICIANS

Armstrong, Louis (1900–1971)—American. Known as the "Father of Jazz." Used the Trumpet, scat singing, and call and response. Nickname: "Satchmo"

Bach, Johann Sebastian (1685–1750)—German. Church musician, composer, and teacher. Works: *Mass in B minor; Little Fugue in G minor*

Bartók, Béla (1881–1945)—Hungarian. Neo-classical, nationalistic. Researched and revived Hungarian folk music. He made music for the people. Works: *Mikrokosmos; Music for Strings, Percussion and Celesta*

Berg, Alban (1885–1935)—Austrian. Expressionist. Works: *Wozzeck*

Berlioz, Hector (1803–1869)—French. Compositions incorporated imagery and musical effects. Program music. Works: Symphony *Fantastique*

Bernstein, Leonard (1918–1990)—American. Conductor, composer, educator, and innovator. Composed for orchestras, Broadway shows, and small ensembles. Works: *Candide; West Side Story; Age of Anxiety*

Brahms, Johannes (1833–1897)—German. Stubborn use of classical intentions with Romantic nuances. Works: *Academic Festival Overture*

Britten, Benjamin (1913–l976)—England. Composed patriotic music and operas. Works: *Peter Grimes; Billy Budd*

Brubeck, Dave (1920–)—American. "Cool Jazz" innovator. Used a classical style, with swing and unusual meter combinations.

Chopin, Frédéric (1810–1849)—Polish. Composed miniatures for piano. Considered the "poet of the piano."

Coltrane, John (1926–1967)—American. Saxophonist who played hard bop. A composer, arranger, and performer known for a forceful, full, and dark sound. Experimented with modal music and researched African and Asian music to incorporate into his playing. Works: "Giant Steps"

Copland, Aaron (1900–1990)—American. Neo-classical and nationalistic. Used jazz, rhythmic variety and folk songs. Works: *Rodeo; Billy the Kid; Appalachian Spring*

Corelli, Arcangelo (1653–1713)—Italian. Instrumental music. Concerto grosso-string orchestra and a group of solo instruments.

Count Basie (1904–1984)—American. Created the "stride" style of piano playing which involved "comping" with a bouncy, flexible, and syncopated style.

Davis, Miles (1926–1992)—American. Trumpet player. Flexible performer of cool jazz, modal jazz, and rock-fusion.

Debussy, Claude (1862–1918)—French. Works involved musical impressionism which suggested an idea or feeling. Works: *Prelude to the Afternoon of a Faun*

Diaghilev, Sergei (1872–1929)—Russian. Created the Russian ballet, commissioned contemporary composers and choreographed ideas which were the beginnings of modern dance.

Ellington, Edward Kennedy "Duke" (1899–1974)—American. Jazz pianist, big band leader and arranger. Innovated the jazz piano and defined African-American styles on the instruments.

Gabrielli, Giovanni (1557–1612)—Italian. Organist, teacher, and composer. Art song: poem set to music. Works: *Sonata Pian'e Forte*

Gershwin, George (1898–1937)—American. Nationalist who composed symphonic and jazz music as well as musicals. The "American Sound." Works: *Rhapsody in Blue; Porgy and Bess*

Gillespie, Dizzy (1917–1993)—American. Trumpet player, big band leader composer and performer. Utilized melodic and high register playing. Works: *A Night in Tunisia; Groovin' High*

Goodman, Benny (1909–1986)—American. Clarinetist and big band leader. "King of Swing"

Handel, George Frideric (1685–1759)—German. Oratorio, religious opera, voice, and orchestra. Works: *Messiah*

Haydn, Franz Joseph (1732–1809)—Austrian. Employed by the Esterhazy family. Composer and performer. Utilized symphonic form. Works: *Symphony No. 94*

Hindemith, Paul (1895–1963)—German. Neo-classical composer. Influenced music education and composition. Works: *Mathis der Maler; Gebrauchmusik*

Ives, Charles (1874–1954)—American. An experimentalist who explored the possibilities of sound. His works combined melodies, hymns, and patriotic tunes. Works: *Decoration Day; The Circus Band*

Jaques-Dalcroze, Émile (1865–1950)—French. Music educator. Used eurhythmics which entailed a physical response to music, ear training, and improvisation to teach music.

Joplin, Scott (1868–1917)—American. Considered the "King of Ragtime." Works: *Maple Leaf Rag*

Kodaly, Zoltan (1882–1967)—Hungarian. Believed that music is for all people so he centered his teaching on using nationalistic themes and folksongs. He combined efforts with Béla Bartók. Developed symbols and hand signals for music. Works: *Hary Janos Suites*

Liszt, Franz (1811–1886)—Hungarian. Nationalistic style, symphonic poems, and tone poems. Works: Hungarian Rhapsodies; *Les Preludes*

Lully, Jean-Baptiste (1632–1687)—Italian. Worked in France. Comedy ballets, lyrical tragedies, and overtures.

Mahler, Gustav (1860–1911)—Austrian. Composer and conductor. Composed powerful and emotional symphonies which were influenced by folklore. Works: *The Song of the Earth; Symphony No. 2 Resurrection*

Mendelssohn, Felix (1809–1847)—German. Conductor and composer. Followed the classical ideas but his music conveyed the bold spirit of the Romantics.

Monteverdi, Claudio (1567–1643)—Italian. Choirmaster at St. Mark's. Polyphonic church music, madrigals, and opera. Works: *Orfeo*

Moussorgsky, Modest (1839–1881)—Russian. Nationalist who incorporated folk songs in compositions. Works: *A Night on Bald Mountain; Pictures at an Exhibition*

Mozart, Wolfgang Amadeus (1756–1791)—Austrian. Worked in Vienna. Child prodigy with a natural gift. Composed with a lyrical touch. His work was rhythmic and inventive, and utilized melodic variety. Works: *Don Giovanni, The Marriage of Figaro*

Orff, Carl (1895–1982)—German. Concentrated on the rhythmic nature of music and developed percussion instruments to teach music to children Works: *Carmina Burana*

Palestrina, Giovanni (1525–1594)—Italian. Composed motets and masses.

Parker, Charlie (1920–1955)—American. Jazz saxophonist. Innovated the "Be-bop" style of jazz which used melody and improvisations based on chord progressions. Nickname: "The Bird"

Porter, Cole (1891–1964)—American. Composed popular music, musical comedies and theater. Works: *Anything Goes*

Prokofiev, Sergei (1891–1953)—Russian. Conservative whose compositions were influenced by the Soviet power structure. Works: *Peter and the Wolf*

Purcell, Henry (1659–1695)—English. Composed opera and church music. Known as a melodist. Works: *Dido and Aeneas*

Ravel, Maurice (1857–1937)—French. Nationalist known for his orchestrational skills. Works: *Bolero; Daphnis and Cloe*

Reed, Alfred (1921–   )—American. Composer and arranger with a worldwide influence on band music and education.

Rimsky-Korsakov, Nicolai (1844–1908)—Russian. Orchestrator, also known for opera. Works: *Sheherazade; Russian Easter Overture*

Rossini, Gioachino (1792–1868)—Italian. Known for opera.

Schönberg, Arnold (1874–1951)—Austrian. Used Expressionism which is emotional and often sounds disturbing. He was progressive and incorporated sprechstimme (speech voice). Works: *Pierrot Lunaire*

Schubert, Franz (1797–1828)—Austrian. Melodic solo voice usually with piano. Works: *Der Doppelganger; Morning Greeting*

Schumann, Robert (1810–1856)—German. Intellectual, critic, and composer of art songs and piano music. Works: *Carnaval*

Schutz, Heinrich (1585–1672)—German. Organist who composed opera and madrigals. Works: *Orpheus und Euridice*

Shostakovich, Dmitri (1906–1974)—Russian. His compositions were politically influenced.

Sibelius, Jean (1865–1957)—Finnish. Nationalist who composed folk music, tone poems, and incidental music. Works: "Finlandia," Finnish national anthem

Smith, Bessie (1894–1937)—American. Known as the "Empress of the Blues." Powerful vocal skills and expressive nature. Influenced by folksongs.

Sousa, John Philip (1854–1932)—American. Composer and band leader who popularized the march, patriotic songs, and band music. Works: *Stars and Stripes Forever*

Strauss, Richard (1864–1949)—German. His compositions often followed the classical form with Romantic emotions. Realistic symphonic poems and opera. Works: *Salome*; Also *Sprach Zarathustra*

Stravinsky, Igor (1882–1971)—Russian. Used Primitivism which is uncivilized and exotic, with uninhibited rhythms and much dissonance. Works: *El Sacre du Printemps; Petrushka; The Firebird*

Suzuki, Shinichi (1898–1998)—Japan. Educator. Mother-tongue method of education. Learning by rote.

Tchaikovsky, Peter Ilyich (1840–1893)—Russian. Romantic who combined Russian folk songs with a German style. Works: *Romeo and Juliet; The Nutcracker*

Verdi, Giuseppe (1813–1901)—Italian. Known for opera. Nationalist. Used human emotion and drama. Works: *Aida; Otello*

van Beethoven, Ludwig (1770–1827)—German. Innovative in his use of emotion and expressive human feelings; a bridge to the Romantic Period. Works: *Moonlight Sonata; Eroica; Fifth Symphony*

Vivaldi, Antonio (1678–1741)—Italian. Ordained priest. Known for his concerto grosso. Works: *Four Seasons*

Wagner, Richard (1813–1883)—German. Poet, and musician. Musical drama. Innovated German opera. Works: *Lohengrin; Tristan and Isolde*

HISTORY

1. EXPLORERS AND DISCOVERERS

Armstrong, Neil (1930–)—American astronaut. First man to walk on the moon.

Cabot, Sebastian (1474–1557)—Italian explorer. Led one of the first expeditions to find a North-West passage across North America.

Cartier, Jacques (1491–1557)—French explorer. He claimed Canada for France.

Columbus, Christopher (1451–1506)—Italian explorer. His explorations across the Atlantic made Europe aware of the Americas. He was responsible for the Spanish, and eventually the European, colonization of the Western Hemisphere.

Cortez, Hernán (1485–1547)—Spanish explorer. He claimed Mexico for Spain after conquering the Aztecs.

da Gama, Vasco (1460–1524)—Portuguese explorer. Discovered oceanic route from Portugal to India.

Dias, Bartolomeu (1457–1500)—Portuguese explorer. First to sail around the Cape of Good Hope.

Drake, Sir Francis (1540–1596)—English explorer. First Englishman to circumnavigate the Earth.

Ericson, Lief (c. 970-c. 1020)—Viking explorer. First person to land in North America, some 500 years before Columbus.

Hillary, Sir Edmund Percival (1919–2008)—New Zealand explorer. First person to reach the summit of Mount Everest.

Lewis, Meriwether (1774–1809) and **William Clark** (1770–1838)—Opened the new West in the United States to traders, trappers, and settlers. Accompanied by Native American female, Sacagawea.

Magellan, Ferdinand (1480–1521)—Portuguese explorer. First person to sail around the Earth.

Pizzaro, Francisco (1478–1541)—Spanish explorer/warrior. Accidentally discovered Incan empire, stealing gold, silver, and precious riches.

Polo, Marco (1254–1324)—Italian voyager. He spent over 24 years traveling around Asia with his father and uncle, even meeting Kubla Khan in Beijing.

Ponce de Leon, Juan (1460–1521)—Spanish explorer. First explorer to set foot in Florida. Believed in a "fountain of youth."

Prince Henry the Navigator (1394–1460)—Portuguese prince and patron of explorers. Financed several sailing expeditions to Africa.

Vespucci, Amerigo (1454–1512)—America was named after him. Discovered the Americas were not a part of Asia, but a separate land structure.

2. HISTORICAL FIGURES

Anthony, Susan B. (1820–1906)—American suffragette. Helped women earn the right to vote.

bin Laden, Osama (1947-)—Saudi revolutionary. Founded militant Islamist group al-Qaeda, who are best known for taking responsibility for the September 11, 2001, terrorist attacks in the United States.

Bonaparte, Napoleon (1769–1821)— French ruler. First named consul for life, he declared himself emperor in 1804. Established civil reforms and introduced the Civic Code. Though a brilliant general, he was defeated by overwhelming forces. He died in exile on a small island, St. Helena.

Castro, Fidel (1926-)—Cuban dictator and revolutionary. Strong believer in communism.

Calvin, John (1509–1564)—French theologian. Father of the theological system known as Calvinism; believed in predestination.

Charles III (1716–1788)—Spanish king. Enacted reforms and eliminated laws that restrict internal trade. Strongly Catholic, but expelled the Jesuits from Spain. Entered the American Revolution on the American side.

d'Arc, Joan (c. 1412–1431)—French saint. Rallied the French for several victories, was captured by the French allies of England, and was sold to the English. She was tried for heresy and burned at the stake in 1431.

Douglass, Frederick (1817–1895)—Author and abolitionist. An escaped slave, eloquent speaker, who brought the story of slavery to thousands. Close relationship with Lincoln helped to persuade the president to work to free the slaves.

Erasmus, Desiderius (1466–1536)— Dutch Renaissance humanist. Most notable Christian humanist; wrote "In Praise of Folly." Leader of the Humanist movement. Believed in human capacity for self-improvement through education. A priest, highly critical of the abuses of the church.

Frederick the Great (1740–1786)—King of Prussia. Pondered questions of religion, morality, and power. First 23 years of reign spent at war, the second 23 spent building an honest government, establishing trials by impartial judges and abolishing torture of prisoners.

Gandhi, Mohatma (1869–1948)—An Indian spiritual leader, he was the leader of non-violent opposition to an oppressive British government in India. A great humanitarian and a catalyst for change in areas of civil disobedience.

Guevara, Che (1928–1967)—South American revolutionary and major figure in the Cuban Revolution who fought against the Batista regime.

Henry IV (Henry of Navarre) (1553–1610)—A French Calvinist who became king in 1589. His conversion to Catholicism helped unite his country. Henry issued the Edict of Nantes in 1589 which extended religious tolerance to Huguenots.

Henry VIII (1491–1547)—King of England. Separated the Church of England from the Roman Catholic Church, and effectively eradicated the papacy from the Church of England, making himself the Supreme Head of the Church.

Hussein, Saddam (1937–2006)—Iraqi President from 1979–2003. Member of the revolutionary Ba'ath party. U.S. forces deposed Hussein after invading Iraq for supposedly housing weapons of mass destruction. He was tried, convicted and executed in 2006.

King, Martin Luther (1929–1968)—African American activist and prominent leader in the Civil Rights Movement. A human rights icon, most noted for his "I Have a Dream" speech. Received Nobel Peace Prize for his work in ending racial discrimination through non-violent civil disobedience. Assassinated in 1968.

Leopold I (1658–1705)—Austrian emperor. Patron of arts, devout Catholic, drove Turkish army from Austria (1683).

Lenin, Vladimir (1870–1924)—Articulate, beloved leader in Communist Soviet Union. He led the Bolshevik Revolution.

Louis XIV (1643–1715)—King of France. Longest documented reign of a European monarch. Believed in the divine right of kings. Sought to eliminate feudalism.

Luther, Martin (1483–1546)—An Augustinian friar and teacher who initiated the Reformation in his native Germany. Luther questioned basic teachings of the church and held that salvation was possible only through faith.

Marx, Karl (1818–1883)—Author and philosopher who created the principles and ideology of communism.

More, Thomas (1478–1535)—Lawyer and Lord Chancellor to Henry VIII of England. He invented the term "utopia," and wrote a novel about this theory called *Utopia*. He was executed by Henry VIII for refusing to recognize him as Supreme Head of the Church in England.

Kempis, Thomas à (1380–1471)—German mystic sought direct knowledge of God through inner feelings, possibly wrote *The Imitation of Christ*.

Peter the Great (1682–1725)—Tsar of Russia. Seven feet tall with great strength and boundless energy. Great drive to modernize Russia. Visited Europe in disguise to learn techniques and cultures. Sent many technicians and craftsmen back to Russia. Treaty of Nystad with Sweden granted Russia the areas of Livonia and Estonia. Built city of St. Petersburg.

Philip V (1700–1746)—Spanish king. Modernized Spanish army. Industry, agriculture, and ship-building revived, his son, Ferdinand VI, rules 1746–1759.

Rockefeller, J.D. (1839–1937)—Leader in American corporate industrialism; revolutionized the petroleum industry

Stalin, Joseph (1879–1953)—Supreme leader of the Soviet Union. Strident Communist leader who ruled with an iron hand in the Soviet Union. Turned the Soviet Union into a world power. Millions died because of his policies.

Wycliffe, John (1324–1384)—An English friar, he believed the church should follow only the Scriptures. Translated the Bible into English. Called the "Morning Star" of the Reformation.

Zedong, Mao (Mao Tse-tung) (1893–1976)—Leader of the Chinese Cultural Revolution who instituted Communism in what he named the People's Republic of China.

3. WARS AND BATTLES

American War for Independence (1775–1783)—France and Spain join Americans to regain territories lost to Britain.

American Civil War (1861–1865)—War between the Southern states and the Northern states, mostly based around issues with the expansion of slavery, states rights, and economic and social differences.

Battle of Waterloo (1815)—An area in present day Belgium, the defeat at Waterloo ended Napoleon's reign as emperor.

Battle of Wounded Knee (1889–1890)—Also known as the Wounded Knee Massacre. A group of nearly 300 unarmed Lakota Indian men, women, and children were killed by U.S. military who feared an uprising. Took place in South Dakota.

English Civil War (1642–1649)—Conflict between King Charles I of England and a large body of his subjects. Underlying issue was whether the King could govern without the consent of Parliament.

French Civil War (1562–1589)—The bloodiest event was the St. Bartholomew's Day Massacre of 1572 in which 20,000 Huguenots were killed.

French Revolutionary War (1789–1795)—The uprising of the common people in France which also led to a series of conflicts fought between the French government and other European nations over expanding French control.

Hundred Years' War (1337–1453)—A series of separate wars between England and France. "Modern" techniques in warfare were developed and a growing sense of nationalism sprouted in each country.

Iraq War (Operation Iraqi Freedom) (2003–)—War between Iraq and the United States and a coalition of allies, the most prominent being Great Britain. After terrorist attacks on the United States in 2001, government officials believed Iraq housed weapons of mass destruction. When Iraq refused to give up information, the U.S. invaded Iraq.

Korean War (1950–1953)—War between the Republic of Korea (South Korea) and the Democratic People's Republic of Korea (North Korea). The United Nations called for cessation of hostilities and withdrawal of North Korean army. United Nations troops, composed mostly of U.S. personnel, went to the aide of South Korea. China later entered the "police action" to defend North Korea.

Mexican-American War (1846–1848)—Conflict between Mexico and the United States. At its end, the U.S. acquired one-half million miles of territory and Mexico was left devastated.

Persian Gulf War (1990–1991)—War between Iraq and a coalition of 32 nations led by United States' General Schwarzkopf. Conflict ignited by Iraq's invasion of Kuwait.

Second Dutch War (1665–1667)—Between England and Holland. Treaty of Breda generally favored the Dutch (Holland).

The Seven Years' War (1756–1763)—First global conflict. Included all of Europe as well as the colonies of Britain, France, and Spain.

The Thirty Years' War (1618–1648)—Rooted in the ongoing Protestant and Catholic struggle across Europe. In addition, Protestants fought one another for control. Since Germany was the main battleground it suffered major destruction and was weakened politically.

Vietnam War (1955–1975)—War fought between the communist North Vietnam and Western-supported South Vietnam. Because America felt threatened by Communism and communist forces, the United States sided with South Vietnam. All countries suffered devastating casualties.

War of 1812 (1812–1815)—War between the United States and the British Empire over continued British navy's arrogance on the seas. It confirmed American independence.

War of Devolution (1667–1668)—Louis XIV of France claims Spanish Netherlands after death of Phillip IV. Triple alliance formed (England, Holland, Sweden)

War of the Roses (1455–1485)—War episodes, in England, in which many nobles were exterminated. Conflict was principally between the houses of York and Lancaster over political power.

World War I (1914–1918)—War that started in Europe and engulfed the world before its end. Caused by imperialistic foreign policies of the great nations of Europe. The end of war created a new Russia, and the four major imperial powers—Germany, France, Austro-Hungarian and Ottoman Empires—were defeated, suffering economic and physical destruction. Growing nationalism in these countries is said to have caused the beginning of World War II.

World War II (1939–1945)—The most widespread war in history, with traumatic civilian causalities. France declared war on Germany when Nazis invaded Poland. Germany moved across Central and Eastern Europe, finally going to war with Russia. China and Japan had been at war with each other, and Japan launched an attack on the United States. This act of war spurred others to declare war against Japan. The United States dropped atomic bombs on Nagasaki and Hiroshima, Japan; Japan surrendered a few days later. The war ended with complete victory over Japan and Germany by the Allied countries.

4. UNITED STATES PRESIDENTS

Bush, George H. W. (1924–)—41st President. A president during a time of political change, he worked toward stabilizing the United States military in the Middle East during the Persian Gulf War.

Bush, George W. (1946–)—43rd President. President during the September 11, 2001 terror attacks, and, after declaring a war on terrorism, issued an invasion in Afghanistan and later in Iraq. Laws included No Child Left Behind and Medicare benefits.

Carter, James E. (1924–)—39th President. Created the Department of Education and the Department of Energy, also established a national energy policy. He highlighted human rights and remains a strong advocate for peace.

Clinton, Bill (1946–)—42nd President. Called the "New Democrat," he created the North American Free Trade Agreement (NAFTA) with the support of his three predecessors. He was impeached for implications in a White House scandal, but was later acquitted.

Grant, Ulysses S. (1822–1885)—Military commander for the North during the Civil War. Later elected 18th President of the United States. Wrote magnanimous terms of surrender for the South to end the Civil War.

Jefferson, Thomas (1743–1826)—3rd President and the main author of the Declaration of Independence.

Kennedy, John F. (1917–1963)—35th President. Effectively led America through the Cuban Missile Crisis. He created the Peace Corps and was an advocate of the Civil Rights Movement.

Lincoln, Abraham (1809–1865)—16th President. Led the U.S. through the Civil War, helping to abolish slavery. Assassinated just as the war ended.

Nixon, Richard (1913–1994)—37th President. Only president to resign from office. He was facing impeachment because of the Watergate scandal. He believed that desegregation would improve education, and he approved the space shuttle program.

Obama, Barack (1961–)—44th President. First African American President. He signed an economic stimulus package to help citizens cope with an economic recession, as well as the American Recovery and Investment Act.

Roosevelt, Franklin D. (1882–1945)—32nd President. Only president elected for more than two terms. He ably led the United States through World War II. FDR created the New Deal Coalition, which, among other things, effectively united labor unions and started Social Security.

Roosevelt, Theodore (1858–1919)—26th president. A previous explorer and historian, he became leader of the Progressive Movement and the Republican Party. He negotiated the end of the Russo-Japanese War, for which he won a Nobel Peace Prize.

Washington, George (1732–1799)—First U.S. President. Known as "the Father of our Country." Had been the leader of the American army in the successful culmination of the American Revolutionary war against England. Only president elected unanimously.

5. HISTORICAL TERMS

Abolitionism	The movement in western Europe and the Americas to abolish slavery
Absolutism	Political theory that absolute power should be vested in one ruler
Allies (Allied Nations)	In World War II, the countries who opposed the Axis powers, including the British Empire, the Soviet Union, the U.S., and China (also France before its defeat in 1940)
Axis	In World War II, the countries, Germany, Italy, and Japan, who opposed the Allied Nations, namely the United States, England, China, the Soviet Union, and France.

Apartheid racial segregation that involved political, legal, and economic rights. Formerly practiced in the Republic of South Africa.

Baroque Age (1600–1750) a period in history that emphasized grandeur, spaciousness, unity, and emotional impact

Bill of Rights The first 10 amendments of the United States Constitution

Bourgeoisie According to Karl Marx, the middle class.

Caste One of the hereditary social classes in Hinduism that restricts members according to a social structure; it can also refer to any class or group of people who inherit elite rights or are perceived as socially distinct.

Calvinism Religious doctrines of John Calvin. Noted for its stern and militant stance and its rejection of most of the medieval church's practices and traditions. Emphasized salvation of the elect by God's grace alone.

Cold War (1947–1991) A state of political hostility between the United States and Russia and its surrounding states. It was a state of competitive political conflict, propaganda, arms race for nuclear weapons, and space exploration. It ended after the collapse of the Soviet Union in 1991.

Communism Economic system where all the people control the means and distribution of production.

Conciliar Movement In the 14th, 15th, and 16th centuries, a movement that attempted to overcome the problems caused by the existence of two popes – and later three popes—at the same time. Proposed that the church be ruled by bishops, cardinals, abbots, and laity

Constitutionalism Rules limited government; consent of the governed provided the basis for the legitimacy of the regime

Cultural Revolution In 1966–1976 in China, the Chinese military, led by Mao Zedong, upheld a system of beliefs that the bourgeoisie (bringers of Westernized culture) were a negative influence on Chinese culture.

Czar (tsar) A male monarch or emperor, especially one of the emperors who ruled Russia until the revolution of 1917.

Dred Scott Slave Dred Scott sued for freedom on grounds that his owner took him into a free state. U.S. Supreme Court ruled that residence in a free state did not make a slave free and that Congress could not exclude slavery from any territory.

Empiricists Relied on inductive reasoning, with emphasis on sensory experience

Feminism Movement to give equal rights for females, originally linked to abolitionists.

Geneva Conference Conference that developed humanitarian laws about the treatment of enemy combatants, prisoners, and civilian persons in a time of war.

Great Schism Two popes claimed authority over the Catholic Church; one resided in Rome, the other in France during a 40-year period of the Late Middle Ages

Great Depression A time of economic depression before World War II. The stock market crash, coupled with high unemployment and agricultural devastation in the Midwest, brought the United States economy to a standstill.

Homestead Act of 1862 Gave 160 acres of unoccupied public land to anyone farming it for five years; land could be acquired after six months of residency and at a price of $1.25 per acre. Led to settlement of much of the West.

Imperialism The political or economic domination of one country over another.

Laissez-faire capitalism	The government does not advocate regulation of the economic market.
Magna Carta	A charter of English political and civil liberties granted by King John in 1215; document that formed the origin of English law.
Manifest Destiny	A policy of imperialism rationalized as inevitable (as if granted by God).
Missouri Compromise (1820)	A measure passed by Congress to end the first of a series of crises over slavery. Missouri's application for statehood raised the issue of slavery's extension into the territories. Henry Clay's compromise admitted Missouri as a slave state, balanced with free Maine, but drew a line to the Pacific Coast, limiting the extension of slavery above the 36° 30′ latitude.
Muckraker	A writer who primarily reports about provocative social and political issues concerning major leaders.
NATO (North Atlantic Treaty Organization)	Formed in 1949 for the perceived threat of Soviet attack. Main purpose is to safeguard countries against aggression.
Pluralism	The holding of more than one office.
Prohibition	Manufacture and sale of alcohol prohibited in 18th amendment to the Constitution passed by Congress; lasted from 1920 until 1933 when it was repealed by the 21st amendment.
Proletariat	According to Marx, the hard-working, laboring class
Rationalists	Those who stressed deductive reasoning or mathematical logic.
Renaissance (1300–1600)	Secular movement that stressed the individual, the growth of the arts, and human abilities. Began in Italy.

Red Scare	Russia's fall to Communism-prompted scare, which led to many being arrested and deported as undesirable foreigners or communists.
The Reformation (1517–1560)	Abuses in the church led some to question the church's authority in determining the individual's role vis-à-vis God. Begun by Martin Luther; gave rise to Protestant churches
Republic	Government where the people elect representatives.
The Restoration (1660–1688)	In England. New Parliament restores a limited monarchy. Charles II (1660–85) agreed to abide by decisions of Parliament. Royalists allowed to recover their lands in court. Feudalism abolished.
Sherman Anti-Trust Act (1890)	Prohibited combinations or conspiracies in restraint of trade; the U.S. Supreme Court eventually applied it to unions and farmer cooperatives as well as corporations.
Simony	The purchase of church positions
Suffrage	The right to vote

6. INVENTORS/INTELLECTUAL ACHIEVERS

Bacon, Francis (1561–1626)—English philosopher; formalized empiricism with the Baconian method, a system of procedures similar to the scientific method.

Brahe, Tycho (1546–1601)—Danish astronomer who devised the most precise instruments available before the invention of the telescope. Made important observations of the heavens that swept away age-old myths of the unchanging sky.

Copernicus, Nicolaus (1473–1543)—Polish astronomer who formulated the heliocentric (Sun-centered) theory of the universe; discovers planets revolve around Sun; Earth not the center of the universe.

Descartes, René (1596–1650)—French mathematician who formulated analytic geometry and believed scientific laws could be found by deductive reasoning; develops deductive analysis; leader in math and physics

da Vinci, Leonardo (1452–1519)—A renowned Italian painter, da Vinci also worked with solar power, outlined a theory of plate tectonics, and the idea of a helicopter. He extensively studied anatomy, the movement of water, and engineering.

Edison, Thomas (1847–1941)—American inventor. Invented kinetoscope making motion pictures possible, and is credited with inventing the light bulb, phonograph, and communicative devices.

Galilei, Galileo (1564–1642)—Italian physicist, mathematician, and philosopher; known as the "father of science," he utilized the telescope, investigated gravity, and the basic law of falling bodies

Gutenberg, Johannes (1398–1468)—German goldsmith and printer. Inventor of moveable type, which made modern book printing possible.

Kepler, Johannes (1571–1630)—German mathematician and astronomer; discovered that the Earth and planets travel around the Sun in elliptical orbits.

Newton, Isaac (1643–1727)—English physicist, mathematician, and astronomer; discovered the principle of universal gravitation and the laws of motion

Whitney, Eli (1765–1825)—American inventor. Developed the cotton gin, a machine used to separate cotton, helping to make the cotton industry profitable.

PHILOSOPHY

1. **PHILOSOPHICAL FIGURES**

Anselm of Canterbury (c. 1033–1109)—11th century philosopher; best known for his ontological argument for the existence of God.

Aquinas, Thomas (c. 1225–1274)—13th century philosopher; best known for his "Five Ways," which are five proofs of the existence of God

Aristotle (384–322 B.C.E.)—3rd century B.C.E.; extremely influential Greek philosopher; criticized Plato's theory of Forms; was the first to systematize logic

Augustine of Hippo (354–430)—4th and 5th century bishop and philosopher; Neo-platonist; had a profound influence on medieval religious thought

Austin, J.L. (1911–1960)—British philosopher of language; developed speech act theory

Bentham, Jeremy (1748–1832)—British philosopher of law; utilitarian

Bergson, Henri-Louis (1859–1941)—French philosopher; dualist; rejected mechanistic and deterministic approach to understanding reality

Berkeley, George (1685–1753)—Irish philosopher; idealist; empiricist

Bradley, F.H. (1846–1924)—English philosopher; idealist; wrote *Appearance and Reality*

Brentano, Franz (1838–1917)—German philosopher and psychologist; remembered for his "doctrine of intentionality"

Carnap, Rudolf (1891–1970)—German philosopher; logical positivist

Chomsky, Noam (1928–)—American linguist and philosopher; argues that there is an innate universal grammar

Clarke, Samuel (1675–1729)—English philosopher and theologian

Davidson, Donald (1917–2003)—American philosopher of language and philosopher of mind; proposed theory of anomalous monism about the mind-body relationship

Democritus (c. 460–370 B.C.E.)—4th and 3rd century B.C.E. Greek philosopher; formulated an atomic theory

Descartes, René (1596–1650)—Extremely influential French rationalist philosopher and mathematician; held a view of the relation between mind and body, which has come to be known as Cartesian dualism; famous for the statement "coqito ergo sum," or "I think therefore I am."

Dewey, John (1859–1952)—American pragmatist philosopher and educational theorist

Engels, Friedrich (1820–1895)—Marx's collaborator; dialectical materialist

Frege, Friedrich (1848–1925)—German mathematician and philosopher; one of the founders of modern logic; generally considered to be the father of analytic philosophy

Goodman, Nelson (1906–1998)—American philosopher; nominalist; wrote (most notably) *Fact Fiction and Forecast* and *Languages of Art*

Hegel, Georg (1770–1831)—German idealist philosopher; famous for his theory of dialectic, a process of argument which proceeds from a thesis and its antithesis to a synthesis of the two

Heidegger, Martin (1889–1976)—German philosopher; commonly regarded as an existentialist although he claimed not to be one

Hempel, Carl (1905–1997)—German empiricist philosopher of science; his theories of confirmation and explanation have been extremely influential

Heraclitus (c. 535–475)—4th century B.C.E. pre-Socratic philosopher; said to have believed that everything is always in a state of flux

Hobbes, Thomas (1588–1679)—British materialist philosopher and political scientist; wrote *Leviathan*

Hume, **David** (1711–1776)—Scottish philosopher, historian and empiricist; drew attention to the problem of induction

Husserl, Edmund (1859–1938)—German philosopher; phenomenologist

James, William (1842–1910)—American philosopher and psychologist; empiricist; pragmatist

Kant, Immanuel (1724–1804)—German idealist philosopher; most famous for putting forward the categorical imperative ("Act only on that maxim which you can at the same time will to become a universal law") as a test of moral principles

Kierkegaard, Søren (1813–1855)—Danish philosopher; existentialist

Kripke, Saul (1940–)—American philosopher and logician; his most influential work is "Naming and Necessity," which launched the causal theory of reference

Leibnitz, Gottfried (1646–1716)—German rationalist philosopher; argued (in his Theodicy) that this is the best of all possible worlds

Leucippus—5th century B.C.E. Greek philosopher; thought to have originated atomic philosophy

Locke, John (1632–1704)—English philosopher and physician; influential Enlightenment thinker; wrote *Essay Concerning Human Understanding*, an attempt to give an empiricist's account of the origins, nature, and limits of human reason

Marx, Karl (1818–1883)—German social theorist; wrote *Das Kapital*

Merleau-Ponty, Maurice (1908–1961)—French philosopher; worked on ethics and on problems of consciousness

Mill, James (1773–1836)—Scottish philosopher and economist; father of the better-known philosopher J.S. Mill

Mill, J.S. (1806–1873)—English empiricist philosopher; best known for his System of Logic and for his ethical writings, which include *Utilitarianism* and *On Liberty*

Moore, George (1873–1958)—British philosopher; best-known for his *Principia Ethica*

Nagel, Ernest (1901– 1985)—American philosopher of science; author of *The Structure of Science*

Neurath, Konstantin (1882–1945)—Austrian logical positivist philosopher; member of the Vienna Circle

Nietzsche, Friedrich (1844–1900)—German philosopher; best known for introducing the concept of the Ubermensch (Overman)

Ockham, William of (c. 1288–1348)—14th century English philosopher and cleric; famous for Ockham's Razor, which is the dictum, "Do not multiply entities beyond necessity."

Pascal, Blaise (1623–1662)—French philosopher, mathematician, and theologian; most famous for an argument called "Pascal's Wager" which provides prudential reasons for believing in God

Peirce, Charles (1839–1914)—American philosopher; founder of pragmatism

Plato B.C.E. (427–347 B.C.E.)—Greek philosopher; wrote dialogs, many of which have Socrates as their main character, which provided the starting point for many later developments in ethics, epistemology and metaphysics; his best-known theory is the theory of Forms (or Ideas), according to which the objects of knowledge are universals (such as The Good and The Just), and things in this world (such as a just person) are mere reflections of the Forms and can only be the objects of opinion.

Plotinus (c. 204–270)—3rd century Neoplatonist philosopher

Popper, Karl (1902– 1994)—Philosopher of science; wrote *The Logic of Scientific Discovery*; best known for his claim that falsifiability is the hallmark of science

Pre-Socratics—General term for all of the Greek philosophers before Socrates

Pythagoras—6th century B.C.E. pre-Socratic philosopher and mathematician; as well as making many scientific and mathematical discoveries, he believed in the transmigration of souls

Quine, Willard (1908–2000)—American empiricist philosopher of language and logician

Rawls, John (1921–2002)—American political philosopher and ethicist; best known for *A Theory of Justice*

Reid, Thomas (1710–1796)—Scottish philosopher; defended the commonsense view that through our senses we can have knowledge of a mind-independent reality

Rousseau, John Jacques (1712–1778)—Political philosopher and philosopher of education

Russell, Bertrand (1872–1970)—British philosopher; with Whitehead, the author of the extremely influential *Principia Mathematica*; argued (in such seminal papers as "On Denoting" and "The Principles of Logical Atomism") that the structure of the world can be revealed by the proper analysis of language

Ryle, Gilbert (1900–1976)—British philosopher of language and philosopher of mind; proponent of logical behaviorism

Santayana, George (1863–1952)—American Platonist philosopher, novelist, and poet

Sartre, Jean-Paul (1905–1980)—French philosopher; Marxist; existentialist

Schlick, Mortiz (1882–1936)—Logical positivist philosopher; a founding member of the Vienna Circle

Schopenhauer, Arthur (1788–1860)—German philosopher; Kantian; best known for *The World As Will and Idea*

Smith, Adam (1723–1790)—Scottish philosopher and political economist; wrote *The Wealth of Nations*

Spinoza, Benedict de (1632–1677)—Rationalist philosopher; best known for his *Tractatus Theologico-Politicus*

Socrates—4th century BCE Greek philosopher; did not write any philosophical treatises; his ideas have survived only through the writings of his followers, most notably Plato, and it is unclear to what extent the views attributed to the character of Socrates in Plato's dialogs were the views of the actual historical Socrates.

Strawson, Sir Peter (1919–2006)—British philosopher of language and metaphysician; best known for arguing (in "On Referring") that some meaningful sentences have no true value

Tarski, Alfred (1901–1983)—American logician and mathematician; famous for his definition of the concept of truth for formal logical languages, which has been used extensively by philosophers of language as a basis for theories of natural language

Thales of Miletus (c. 624–526)—6th and 5th century B.C.E. pre-Socratic philosopher; sometimes called "the father of Western philosophy"; held that the first principle of nature (the substance that everything in the universe is made out of) is water

Thomism—The theological and philosophical system of St. Thomas Aquinas and his followers

Vienna Circle—The group of logical positivists which centered around the University of Vienna in the 1920s and 1930s; included Schlick, Carnap and Neurath

Wittgenstein, Ludwig (1889–1951)—Viennese-born philosopher who has had an enormous influence on later philosophy of language; his first and most famous work was *Tractatus Logico-Philosophicus*, in which he defended a picture theory of meaning, and which contains such often-quoted aphorisms as "The world is everything that is the case."

Zeno of Elea—4th century B.C.E. pre-Socratic philosopher; famous for a set of paradoxes which are intended to show that plurality and motion do not really exist

2.   PHILOSOPHICAL VOCABULARY

Aristotelianism	medieval study and development of Aristotle's philosophy
atomism	the belief that matter consists of atoms
dialectical materialism	a metaphysical doctrine originally propounded by Engels and held by many Marxists, according to which matter (rather than mind) is primary, and is governed by dialectical laws
empiricism	the view that all knowledge is derived from experience; Locke, Berkeley, and Hume are notable empiricists
existentialism	the view that the subject of philosophy is *being*, which cannot be made the subject of objective inquiry but can only be investigated by reflection on one's own existence. Kierkegaard was probably the first existentialist; Sartre is another notable existentialist.
idealism	the view that the so-called "external world" is actually a creation of the mind. Berkeley and Hegel are notable idealists
logical positivism	a radical empiricist position; the doctrine that the meaning of a proposition consists in the method of its verification; also known as "logical empiricism"
Marxism	the body of doctrines originally propounded by Marx and Engels; includes dialectical materialism
neoplatonism	the dominant philosophy in Europe from 250–1250 CE; begun by Plotinus; a combination of Plato's ideas with those of other philosophers including Aristotle and Pythagoras
phenomenology	a method of inquiry which begins from the scrupulous inspection of one's own conscious thought processes; developed by Husserl

pragmatism   originally (as used by Peirce) a theory of meaning; later (as used by James) a theory of truth according to which "ideas become true just so far as they help us to get into satisfactory relations with other parts of our experience"

rationalism   the view that knowledge of the external world can be derived from reason alone, without recourse to experience; notable rationalists include Descartes, Leibnitz, and Spinoza

MYTHOLOGY

1. GREEK AND ROMAN GODS AND GODDESSES

Aphrodite Goddess of love. Goddess of pure and ideal love as well as of marriage and of lust and venal love. Essence of feminine beauty. Daughter of Zeus. Roman counterpart—Venus.

Apollo A sun-god, god of the light. Cultivated and protected crops. God of divination and prophecy. Associated with music. Represented as an archer. Son of Zeus and Leto. Roman counterpart—Apollo.

Ares God of war, of blind, brutal courage, and of bloody rage and carnage. Son of Zeus and Hera. Roman counterpart—Mars.

Artemis Agricultural deity. Goddess of the chase and of forests. Associated with moonlight. Represented as an archer. Apollo's twin sister, also daughter of Zeus and Leto. Roman counterpart—Diana.

Athena Warrior goddess, goddess of arts of peace, and goddess of prudent intelligence. Zeus's daughter, she was born, fully armed, out of his skull. Roman counterpart—Minerva.

Charybdis and Scylla Dwelt in same Sicilian sea as the Sirens. Charybdis, daughter of Poseidon and the earth, was a whirlpool who swallowed ships. Scylla, once a beautiful woman, was changed into a monster, with six ugly heads.

Cronus Son of titans. Married his sister, Rhea. They gave birth to three daughters—Hestia, Demeter, and Hera, and three sons— Poseidon, Hades and Zeus. Roman counterpart—Saturn.

Demeter Goddess of the earth and the underworld, represents motherhood and fertile, cultivated soil. Earth mother. Daughter of Cronus and Rhea. Roman counterpart—Ceres.

Dionysus
God of wine and pleasure. Son of Zeus. Roman counterpart—Bacchus.

Eros
Youngest of the gods, a winged child, gracious and rebellious. Armed with bow and arrows which would cause people to fall in love if hit by them. Son of Aphrodite. Roman equivalent—Cupid.

Hades
God of the underworld. Invisible, god of buried treasure and agricultural wealth. Son of Cronus and Rhea, brother of Zeus. Roman equivalent—Pluto.

Helen
Woman whose beauty launched a thousand ships and began the Trojan War. Wife to Menelaus, but carried off by love struck Paris.

Hera
Zeus's wife. Woman deified, presided over all stages of feminine existence, primarily marriage and maternity. Represents idealized wife. Roman counterpart—Juno.

Heracles
Not a god, but a hero. Personification of physical strength. Founder of Olympic Games. Had to perform twelve superhuman labors. Son of Zeus and a mortal woman. Roman counterpart—Hercules.

Hermes
God of travelers. Conducted the souls of the dead to the underworld. God of commerce and profit. Tireless runner, messenger of Zeus. Son of Zeus and Maia. Roman counterpart—Mercury.

The Muses
Apollo's habitual companions. Goddesses of memory and poetic inspiration. Clio—history. Euterpe—flute. Thalia—comedy. Melpomene—tragedy. Terpsichore—lyric poetry and dance. Erato—love poetry. Polyhymnia—mimic art. Urania—astronomy. Calliope—epic poetry and eloquence.

Oedipus
Son of King of Thebes. Unwittingly killed his father and married his mother, which caused him to blind himself. Answered the riddle of the Sphinx.

Orion	Beautiful giant, son of Mother Earth. Passionate hunter, accompanied by his dog, Sirius. Banished to live in the sky, and now an easily recognized constellation.
Orpheus	One of the few Greek heroes not known for warlike exploits. Son of Apollo, sang and played the lyre so beautifully that trees and savage beasts would follow him. Performed miracles on the voyage of the Argonauts to find the Golden Fleece.
Pan	Son of Hermes. Not a satyr, though he also was half-goat. Shepherd god of woods and pastures, protector of shepherds and flocks.
Pandora	The first woman. Created by all the divinities. Unleashed terrible afflictions which spread over the earth.
Persephone	Daughter of Demeter, wife of Hades. Spent part of the world in the underworld and part on earth, and therefore associated with seasons of the year and myths of regeneration. Roman counterpart—Proserpina.
Perseus	Son of a mortal woman and Zeus, who impregnated her disguised as a shower of gold. Also a hero, not a god, who had many adventures. Killed the snake headed monster Medusa. Also killed a sea monster to save a beautiful princess named Andromeda.
Poseidon	God of the sea. Personification of water—god of vegetation and fecundity. Son of Cronus. Roman equivalent—Neptune.
Prometheus	Created humans from earth and water. Though a titan, he was allowed to live on Olympus.
Satyrs	Part of the retinue of Dionysus. Represented the elementary spirits of forests and mountains. Half-man and half-goat, they were sensual and lascivious.
Sirens	Sea monsters with bird's bodies and women's heads. Sang sweetly and irresistibly to lure travelers and then killed them.

Theseus	Not a god, but a hero. Like Heracles destroyed many monsters, including the Minotaur on Crete. Son of a mortal woman, a mortal man, and the god, Poseidon.
Titans	The first divine race. Ultimately honored as ancestors of humans. Credited with the invention of the arts and of magic.
Tritons	Strange sea creatures, half-men, half-fish, with scales, sharp teeth, claws, fins and forked tails. Hedonistic and lascivious.
Zeus	Supreme god. Unites in himself all attributes of divinity—omnipotent, omniscient, omnipresent. Ruled according to fate and his own will. Lived on Mount Olympus. Roman counterpart—Jupiter.

2. NORSE GODS

Balder	Son of Odin and Frigg. So beautiful he shed radiance all around himself. Wisest and favorite of gods.
Freja	Female equivalent of Frey—his sister. Lived in Folkvang, a rich dwelling in the sky where she received the deceased warriors and assigned them seats in her banqueting hall. First and supreme commander of the Valkyries.
Frey	Njord's son. Also peaceful, benevolent and mighty. Also a Vanir, though he lived among the Aesir. Had all the same qualities as his father. Had a powerful horse and sword and a golden boar.
Frigg	An Aesir. Odin's wife. Most revered of goddesses. Our word "Friday" is derived from her name. Possessed of great wisdom and foresight. Sometimes known as "Frija."
Gerda	Frey's wife, also the daughter of a giant.
Heimdall	God of light. Presided over ambiguous beginnings of things. Guardian of all the gods.

Idun	The goddess who owned the magic apples which gave all of the gods and goddess eternal youth and immortality.
Jord	The earth goddess. Thor's mother.
Kvasir	Made from the mingled saliva of the two races of gods—Aesir and Vanir. Surpassed all men in wisdom. He was killed and his blood was mixed with honey in a cauldron to make a liquid which would cause the drinker to become a sage and poet.
Loki	A superior demon. Always making mischief. Served the gods but also undermined their power whenever possible. Handsome and attentive to goddesses. Thor's blood brother.
Magni and Modi	Thor's sons. Magni was strength and Modi was anger. They would inherit Thor's hammer and replace him in a newly-made world.
Mimir	A water demon. Odin's uncle and wisest counselor. Lived by the roots of the ash tree Yggdrasil known as "world tree." Lived in a fountain in which all wisdom and knowledge were hidden.
Njord	A Vanir rather than an Aesir. Peaceful, benevolent and mighty. The greatest of the Vanir. Provided fields and pastures with sun and rain. God of harvests, game, riches, commerce, and navigation. Guarantor of oaths.
Odin	Of the Aesir race. Principal god of Teutonic peoples. Our word "Wednesday" is derived from his name, which suggests frenzy and fury. Decided human's fates. Handsome and eloquent, magician god of the other world, god of spiritual life. Warlike, but did not fight in battles himself, intervened magically. Lived in great glittering hall of gold called Valhalla. Sometimes know as "Woden."
Sigmund	A hero, not a god. Mortal descendant of Odin. Pulled a magical sword out of a tree trunk in which Odin had placed it, and had many adventures with it. Died willingly at Odin's insistence.

Sigurd   Sigmund's son, inheritor of his sword. Also a hero not a god, also had many adventures. Sometimes known as "Siegfried."

Skadi   Njord's wife. Daughter of a giant.

Thor   An Aesir. God of thunder and war. Our word "Thursday" is derived from his name. Much feared. It was believed that thunder was caused by his chariot wheels and that thunderbolts were his fiery weapons. Rude, simple, noble. Often represented with a hammer. Sometimes known as "Donan."

Tiw   Sky god and god governing battles. His spear was a sign of judicial power. Our word "Tuesday" is derived from his name. Sometimes known as "Tyr."

Valkyries   Supernatural women who lived in Valhalla. Guardians and servants to the gods. Had both domestic and martial duties— they mingled with combatants in wars. Rode on fiery chargers.

GEOGRAPHY

1. GEOGRAPHICAL MAP VOCABULARY

Antarctic Circle	66.5 degrees north
Arctic Circle	66.5 degrees south
Cartography	Construction of maps
Conic projection	Projection of a globe onto a cone (parallels are spaced evenly along the central meridian)
Contour interval	Vertical distance separating two adjacent contour lines.
Contour line	Line along which all points are of equal elevation above or below a datum (single) plane, usually indicating mean sea level.
Cylindrical projection	Projection of the earth onto a cylinder (e.g., navigation uses).
Equidistant	Can be centered anywhere, facilitating the correct measurement of distances from that point to all others.
Gnomonic projections	All great circles appear as straight lines.
Lines of Latitude (parallels)	Run east-west. Measure the distance (in degrees, minutes, seconds) north and south of the equator (0 degrees latitude), the lowest latitude possible. The highest latitude possible is 90 degrees north (North Pole) and south (South Pole).
Lines of Longitude (meridians)	Run north-south. Measure the distance (in degrees, minutes, seconds) east and west of the Prime Meridian (0 degrees longitude). The highest longitude possible is 180 degrees (east and west), called the International Date Line.
Planar (azimuthal)	Projection of a globe grid onto a plane (used in atlases).

Scale	Ratio between the measurement of something on a map and the corresponding measurement on the earth (e.g., 1 inch to 1 mile).
Topographical features	Portray the surface terrain of small areas, usually in detail (e.g., routes, boundaries, streams).
Tropic of Cancer	23.5 degrees north.
Tropic of Capricorn	23.5 degrees south

2. PHYSICAL GEOGRAPHY—LAND FORMATION VOCABULARY

Chemical weathering	Breaking down rock mass into smaller particles by the interaction between surface or underground water and chemicals present in rock mass.
Continents	Great divisions of the land on the globe: Asia, Africa, North America, South America, Antarctica, Europe, and Australia/ Oceania.
Erosion	Wearing away of the earth's surface by moving ice (glaciers), water, or wind.
Extrusive vulcanism	Molten material hardens on the earth's surface (e.g., basalt).
Faulting	Break in the earth's crust, break can occur as a rock mass is pulled apart (tensional or normal fault) by irresistible forces in the crust.
Folding	More intense bending of the earth's crust—produces accordion effect—series of upfolds (anticlines) and downfolds (synclines), referred to as ridge and valley topography.
Glaciation	Movement of continental and alpine ice and snow that rubs and shapes topography.

Geomorphology   The study of landform origins, characteristics, and evolutions and their processes.

Gravity transfer   The force of gravity is the attraction of the earth's mass for bodies at or near its surface.

Igneous rocks   Formed by cooling and hardening of earth material.

Intrusive vulcanism   Molten material hardens before it reaches the earth's surface (e.g., granite), not exposed on the earth's surface.

Lava   Above ground molten material.

Loess   Fine fertile soil that is transported by wind (in glaciated regions).

Magma   Underground molten material.

Metamorphic rocks   Igneous and sedimentary rocks transformed due to heat, pressure, or chemical reaction (e.g., marble, slate).

Pacific Ring of Fire   Series of volcanoes surrounding the Pacific Ocean, includes 80% of the world's active volcanoes.

Pangaea   Represents a supercontinent of 200 million years ago—later separated into two large sections: Gondwana and Laurasia, which further separated into today's continents.

Physical weathering   Breaking down rock mass into smaller particles by force or pressure.

Plate tectonic processes   Portions of the earth's mantle and crust on separate slowly moving "plates." Responsible for mountain-building, volcanoes, and earthquakes.

Sedimentary rocks   Composed of particles of gravel, sand, silt (fine particles of soil), and clay that were eroded from other rocks (e.g., shale, coal, sandstone).

Vulcanism   The outpouring of molten material from cracks in the earth.

Warping	Gentle bending of the earth's crust.
Weathering	Breaking down rock mass into smaller particles.

3. PHYSICAL GEOGRAPHY—WATER VOCABULARY

Delta	Triangular soil deposit at the mouth of a river.
Distributaries	Channels carrying water off of the main stream of the river.
Mouth	Where a river empties into another body of water.
River basin	Area drained by a river system.
Source	Place of origin for a river.
Tributaries	Small bodies of water that feed into the main stream of a river.

4. PHYSICAL GEOGRAPHY—WEATHER VOCABULARY

Air pressure	The weight of the air as measured at a point on the earth's surface (barometric pressure).
Air temperature	Controlled by the intensity and duration of radiation from the sun (solar energy). Generally, air temperature decreases with increasing elevation.
Atmospheric moisture	Precipitation is water (can be rain, sleet, snow, hail) deposited on the earth's surface.
Convection	Results from the flow of air that replaces warm, rising air and the rapid movement of replacement air.

Convectional precipitation	Caused by rising, heated, moisture-laden air (rain or hail can occur).
Cyclonic (frontal) precipitation	Occurs in mid-altitudes as cool and warm air masses meet.
Ocean currents	Wind direction and the differences in density (of water) cause water to move in paths from one part of the ocean to another.
Orographic precipitation	Occurs as warm air is forced to rise because of some obstruction (hill or mountain).
Pressure gradients	Occur with differences in air pressure between areas that induce air to flow from areas of high to areas of low pressures.
Storms	Occur whenever two air masses come into contact (cyclone, hurricane, tornado).
Wind belts	Prevailing surface wind movements responding to pressure gradients (e.g., jet stream, monsoon).

5. PHYSICAL GEOGRAPHY—CLIMATE VOCABULARY

Desert	High daily temperature range. Less than 10 inches of annual precipitation. Sandy soils that lack humus (organic matter.
Dry-summer subtropical (Mediterranean)	Mild rainy winters; hot, dry summers. Warm climate with long growing season. Lack of humus in soils. Vegetation (chaparral or maquis) with large roots and small leaves, to survive the summer drought.

Humid continental   Found in the middle of large landmasses in the mid-latitudes. Often broken into long summer and short summer types. Plenty of moisture, cold winters, and hot summers are normal.

Humid subtropical   Soil may become leached and slightly acidic. Located on the southeast corner of large landmasses in middle latitudes. Mild winters; hot, humid summers

Ice cap   Constant cold; less than 10 inches of precipitation annually.

Steppe   Soils are chernozems; thick, black earth rich in humus. Annual precipitation 10–20 inches; natural vegetation is short grasses (used for livestock grazing)

Sub-arctic   Temperatures above 50°F for at least 1–3 months. Heavy snowfalls can occur.

Tropical rain forest   Generally centered on the equator, rainy and warm, and no distinct dry season.

Tropical Savanna   Warm and wet, but not as much as rain forest. No distinct dry season. Soils heavily leached.

Tundra   Land of the permafrost. Monthly temperature averages below 50°F.

6. POPULATION GEOGRAPHY VOCABULARY

Crude birth rate (CBR)   Annual number of live births per population of 1,000 (without regard to sex or age).

Crude death rate (CDR) or mortality rate   Annual number of deaths per population of 1,000.

Crude population density	The number of people per unit area of land, usually within the boundaries of a political entity.
Demographic Transition Model	Traces the changing levels of human fertility and mortality over time. Gives a relationship between population growth and economic development in stages.
Rate of natural increase	The crude death rate is subtracted from the crude birth rate (excluding the effects of immigrations or emigration).
Total fertility rate (TFR)	More accurate, since it gives the average number of children that would be born to each woman if during her child-bearing years she bore children at the current year's rate for women her age.

7. GEOGRAPHICAL CULTURE VOCABULARY

Assimilation	Process of merging into a composite culture and becoming culturally homogenized (i.e., one culture).
Culture hearth	Cultural innovation—ideas that diffuse from this origin to other places around the world (e.g., Mesopotamia was an early cultural hearth in southwest Asia.)
Cultural landscape	Part of the landscape modified by humans.
Culture traits	The smallest distinctive items of a culture.
Dialect	Regional or socioeconomic variation of a more widely spoken language.
Environmental determinism	Belief that the physical environment by itself shapes humans, their actions, and their thoughts.
Ethnocentrism	Believing one's own people and culture as setting the proper standard for others.

Language family	A group of languages thought to have a common origin in a single, earlier tongue.
Possibilism	The viewpoint that people are the dynamic forces of cultural development (more widely accepted).

8. POLITICAL AND URBAN GEOGRAPHY VOCABULARY

Antecedent (cultural classification)	Placed before the cultural landscape developed
Anthropogeographic boundaries	Show a change in the cultural landscape or dominant cultural or ethnic group.
Centrifugal forces	Destabilize and weaken a state
Centripetal forces	Bind together the people of a state.
City	Urban area acquiring a second important function.
Country (nation)	Group of people with a common culture occupying the same territory, bound together by shared beliefs and customs.
Geometric boundaries	Straight-lined or curved and follow some precise measurement.
Metropolis	A center of specified activities, including local, national, and worldwide.
Metropolitan Area	Several urbanized areas, built up discretely, but economically coherent.
Nation-state	A state whose territory is identical to that occupied by a particular nation.
Nationalism	Sense of unity binding the people of a state together.

Natural (physical) boundaries	Follows topographical features such as rivers, valleys, or mountains.
Relict (cultural classification)	Political boundary that has ceased to function but still has an imprint on the cultural landscape (e.g., former East/West German border).
State	An independent political unit occupying a permanent territory with full sovereign control over its internal and foreign affairs.
State characteristics	The size, shape, and location of a state.
Subsequent (cultural classification)	Set after the cultural landscape developed.
Superimposed (cultural classification)	Set in place as a result of wars or colonialism.
Town	Single urban function dominates.

9. GEOGRAPHICAL ECONOMIC VOCABULARY

Commercial economy	Producers market goods and services, laws of supply and demand set price and quantity, and marketing is essential for production decisions and distributions.
Economic activities	Involve the occupational structure, or the proportion of workers found in each economic activity.
Planned economy	Communist-controlled society controls the development of goods and services and also supply and price.
Primary activity	Agriculture, mining, and other extractive activities.
Quaternary activity	Services related to information and research.
Secondary activity	Manufacturing and processing of primary products.

Subsistence economy	Goods and services are produced for the use of the producers. Little exchange of goods and marketing is limited.
Tertiary activity	Called "service activity," retailing and other services.

10. GEOGRAPHICAL ENVIRONMENTAL VOCABULARY

Acid rain	From the burning of fossil fuels, generally with a pH <5.
Aquifer	Layer of water-bearing, porous rocks lying between impermeable layers (e.g., Ogallala aquifer (Midwest)—largest underground water supply in the U.S.)
Biocides	Herbicides and pesticides
Ecosystem	Population of organisms existing together in an area with the resources (air, water, soil, chemicals) upon which it depends.
Fertilizers	Excess nutrients in water (eutrophication).
Food chain	Transfer of energy and material from one organism to another.
Greenhouse Effect	Gases released concentrate in the atmosphere, thus providing an insulation barrier for heat, causing warming of the earth.
Hydrologic cycle	Involves the cycling of water in different forms and composition through evaporation and transpiration (emission of water vapor from plants).
Hydrosphere	Surface and subsurface waters (e.g., oceans, lakes, groundwaters, glaciers) not immediately available for use.

Nonrenewable resource   Are generated in nature slowly and in small quantities (crude oil, natural gas, coal, synthetic fuels).

Ozone   Formed from automobile and industrial gas emissions.

Renewable resource   Materials that can be regenerated in nature faster than society can recover them (biomass [living matter], wood, waste, hydroelectric power, solar power).

Resource   A naturally occurring, recoverable material that a society perceives to be useful to its economic and material well-being (natural resource).

Resource reserves   Nuclear energy (fission process).

Troposphere   The layer of air closest to the earth, extending upward about 7–8 miles.

RELIGION

1. MAJOR WORLD RELIGIONS AND THEIR GODS

Christendom—Although Christians worship one God, they identify him three separate ways

> **Holy Trinity**—comprised of God the Father, Jesus the Son, and the Holy Ghost

Hinduism (although there are actually millions, these are the major Gods)

> **Bhrama**—the creator of life

> **Brahman (or Brahm)**—supreme all-powerful entity of the universe

> **Kali**—a goddess of destruction, the bloodthirsty goddess of death

> **Mitra**—the god of light

> **Shiva (or Siva)**—a god of fertility and life, destruction, and death

> **Vishnu**—the god who preserves life

Islam (a monotheistic religion)

> **Allah**—creator of the universe and all mankind, worshipped by Muslims

Judaism (a monotheistic religion)

> **Yahweh (Jehovah)**—the creator of universe and every living thing; worshipped by the Hebrews.

Shintoism

> **Amatersau Omikami**—the sun goddess, principle god of Shinto

> **Amenominakanushi-no-kami**—god of the universe, based on Christian God

> **Takami-musubi**—the high-producing subordinate of universe god

> **Emperor Hirohito**—World War II Emperor of Japan; said to be a descendant of sun goddess

> **Kami-musubi**—divine producing god; subordinate of universe god

Taoism (there are numerous gods, goddesses, fairies, and immortals)

> **Pa Hsien/The Eight Immortals**—immortal ancestors of China
>
> **Tsao Shen/The god of hearth**—god of fire
>
> **Ch'eng Huang/city gods**—gods who protected ancient Chinese cities
>
> **Men Shen/Guardians of the door**—spirits who protect the way to the spirit world

2. WORLD RELIGIONS AND THEIR MAJOR FIGURES

Buddhism	**Siddharatha Gautama**	Buddha—or enlightened One, founder and teacher of Buddhism
Christianity	**Jesus Christ**	Founder of Christianity, son of the Hebrew God; Although Christ was born a Jew, he directed the Israelites towards another way of worship.
Confucianism	**Confucius**	Founder of Confucianism, taught moral codes and ethics. Confucius taught that everyone must learn what role they play in society, and live accordingly.
Islam	**Muhammad**	Founder of Islam; a prophet sent by Allah to teach followers the pure way of worship
Jainism (off-shoot of Hinduism)	**Nataputta Vardhamana**	Also known as Vardhamana Mahavira his title meant Great Hero. Founder of Jainism, he taught self-denial, self-discipline, and nonviolence.
Judaism	**Abraham**	(Abram) the forefather of the Israelites; he worshipped Yahweh (Jehovah) over 4,000 years ago. He believed in adherence to Divine commandment.
	Moses	Leader of the nation of Israel; provided the Jews with a copy of "the law" from God
Sikhism (off-shoot of Hinduism)	**Guru Nanak**	Founder of Sikhism; taught that all mankind are brothers and sisters and should treat one another accordingly.

Taoism	**Lao-tzu**	"Old Master" founder of Taoism; taught that mankind should leave behind the world and become one with nature.

3. MAJOR WORLD RELIGIONS, THEIR HOLY CITIES, AND OTHER LOCATIONS

Christendom	**Rome**	Holy city where the Vatican is located, acknowledged mostly by Catholics
Hinduism	**Ganges River**	Hindus believe that this river has the power to cleanse, purify, and release its believers
Islam	**Mecca**	Holy city for Muslims. All male Muslims must journey to Mecca at least once in their lifetime.
Judaism	**Jerusalem**	Up until 70 C.E., Solomon's temple in Jerusalem was the center of worship for the Israelites. The city is still acknowledged as a holy one; there is also a holy wall located in the city.
Sikhism	**Amristar**	The Sikh holy city located in India.

4. MAJOR WORLD RELIGIONS AND THEIR FESTIVALS OR HOLY DAYS

Christendom	**Christmas**	The celebration of the birth of the Messiah, mankind's redeemer
	Easter	Celebration of the Messiah's death and subsequent resurrection
Judaism	**Yom Kippur**	Day of Atonement; day of fasting and spiritual self-examination

	Sukkot	Festival of Booths, or Huts; autumnal celebration of the harvest, the end of an agricultural year
	Pesach	Passover Festival; commemorates Israel's deliverance from Egyptian captivity
Shinto	**Sho-gatu**	The New Year festival days (January 1–3)
	Setsubun	The tossing of beans in and outside of homes, done to keep the evil spirits out and good ones in (February 3)

5.   MAJOR WORLD RELIGIONS AND THEIR HOLY WRITINGS

Christianity	**The Bible**	The most widely published and read book in history; comprised of 66 small books translated from Hebrew, Aramaic, and Greek.
Islam	**Koran**	Holy book of Muslims; said to have superseded the Bible
Judaism	**Tanakh**	Comes from the three divisions of the Jewish Bible, consisting of the *Torah* (five books of Moses), Nevi'im (the Prophets), and Kethuvin (the Writings)
	Talmud	given as a supplement to the original law of Moses
Hinduism	**Vedas**	the earliest of sacred writings of Hinduism
Confucianism	**The Four Books**	The Great Learning, The Doctrine of the Mean, The Analects, The Book of Mencius. All collections of sayings and teaching of Confucius.
	The Five Classics	Writings that deal with poetry, rituals, and ancient Chinese history: The Book of Poetry, The Book of History, The Book of Changes, The Book of Rites, Annuals of Spring and Autumn

6. MAJOR WORLD RELIGIONS AND THEIR PLACES OF WORSHIP

Judaism	**Temple**	Place of meeting for Jews
Christianity	**Church**	Meeting place of worship for most Christian religions
Islam	**Mosque**	Place of worship for Muslims

SCIENCE

1. EXPERTS AND COLLECTORS

Anatomist   expert in dissection and body parts

Arabist   expert in Arabic language and culture

Arachnologist   spider expert

Arlologist   expert on primitive people

Astrophysicist   an expert in astronomy in a branch dealing with the physical
                       and chemical makeup of celestial matter

Bacteriologist   expert in bacteria in medicine, industry, and agriculture

Botanist   a specialist in plant life

Discophile   expert on music that is recorded

Ecumenist   expert in, or one who practices, principles and practices of
                       religious groups, mostly Christian

Entomologist   expert in insects

Epidemiologist   expert in disease incidence, distribution, and control

Gastroenterologist expert in stomach diseases

Genealogist   expert in tracing the descent of people

Ichthyologist   fish expert

Metallurgist   expert in the science of metals

Numismatist   an expert in the study or collection of coins, tokens, and paper
                       money and related objects (such as medals)

Oncologist	expert in tumors
Ophthalmologist	expert in the structure, function, and disease of the eye
Ornithologist	bird expert
Orthodontist	expert in irregularities of teeth
Parasitologist	expert in parasites
Pathologist	expert in the changes caused by disease in tissues and body fluids
Periodontist	expert in diseases of the gums and other structures surrounding the teeth
Podiatrist	foot doctor
Teratologist	expert in the biological study of monsters
Thanatologist	expert in death
Urologist	expert in urinary or urogenital tract
Virologist	expert in viruses
Vulcanologist	expert in volcanic phenomena

2. CLASSIFICATION OF LIVING THINGS

Moneran Kingdom

Bacteria, blue-green algae, and primitive pathogens

Characteristics	prokaryotic organisms, single-celled; autotrophic though a few are heterotrophic
Structures	flagella capsules

Functions	food gathering, respiration, reproduction
Systems	none
Growth	cell membrane and availability of food set growth limit
Reproduction Method	binary fission

Protista Kingdom

Animal-like organism, distinguished by method of locomotion

Characteristics	eukaryotes, mainly microscopic, single-celled or multi-cellular; some autotrophic and many heterotrophic
Structures	cilia, flagella, cell organelles membrane bound, photo-synthetic
Functions	organelles function as organ systems
Systems	none
Growth	cell membrane and availability of food set growth limit
Reproduction Method	asexual or sexual

Fungi Kingdom

Characteristics	eukaryotes, mainly multicellular, parasitic, symbiotic, mycorrhizae
Structures	root-like, caps, filaments, reproductive
Functions	digestive-like, respiration, reproductive

Systems	beginning to develop
Growth	based on food source and availability
Reproduction Method	asexual, sexual

Plantae Kingdom

Characteristics	eukaryotes, multicellular, nonmotile, autotrophic
Structures	cellulose cell walls
Functions	based on cell and tissue chemistry
Systems	developed and functioning
Growth	based on hormone action
Reproduction Method	asexual, sexual by spores, seeds, flowers, and cones

Animalia Kingdom

Characteristics	eukaryotes, multicellular, heterotrophic, most are motile at some point in lifetime
Structures	all present and unique to organism
Functions	based on nutrition, cell and tissue chemistry, and individual demands
Systems	developed and functioning
Growth	based on hormone action and nutrition
Reproduction Method	asexual, sexual

3. ANIMAL GROUPS

ANIMAL	YOUNG	MALE	FEMALE	GROUP
Badger	Kit/Cub	Boar	Sow	Cete
Bear	Cub	Boar	Sow	Sleuth
Bee	Larva	Drone	Queen	Swarm
Boar	Piglet/Shoat/Farrow	Boar	Sow	Sounder
Cats	Kitten	Tomcat	Queen	Clowder
Chicken	Chick, Pullet (hen) Cockrell (rooster)	Rooster	Hen	Brood
Cow **Elk** **Elephant** **Porpoise** **Whale** **Rhinoceros**	Calf	Bull	Cow	Herd

Crash (Rhinoceros) |
Deer	Fawn	Buck/Stag	Doe	Herd
Duck	Duckling	Drake	Duck	Team (flight) Paddling (in water)
Eagle	Fledgling/Eaglet			Convocation
Ferrets	Kit	Hob	Jill	Business
Fish	Fry/Fingerling			Shoal
Frog	Tadpole/Polliwog/Froglet			Army

ANIMAL	YOUNG	MALE	FEMALE	GROUP
Fox	Kit/Cub/Pup	Reynard/ Dog/Tod	Vixen	Skulk
Goat	Kid	Buck/ Billy	Doe/ Nanny	Herd/Tribe
Goose	Gosling	Gander	Goose	Skein
Gull **Heron** **Jay** **Lark** **Nightingale**	Chick	Cock	Hen	Colony Siege (heron) Band (jay) Exaltation (Lark) Watch (Nightingale)
Hare	Leveret	Buck	Doe	Trace
Hawk	Eyas	Tiercel	Hen	Flight
Horse	Foal/Coat (male) Filly (female)	Stallion/ Stud	Mare/ Dam	Herd
Kangaroo	Joey	Buck Boomer Jack	Doe Flyer Jill Roo	Troop
Leopard	Cub	Leopard	Leopardess	Leap
Mule	Foal	Jack	Hinney	Barren
Peafowl	Peachick	Peacock	Peahen	Muster
Pig	Piglet/Shoat/Farrow	Boar	Sow	Herd
Seal	Pup	Bull	Cow	Crash/Herd/Pod
Squirrel	Pup/Kit/Kitten	Buck	Doe	Dray
Swan	Cygnet/Flapper	Cob	Pen	Wedge

ANIMAL	YOUNG	MALE	FEMALE	GROUP
Toad	Tadpole	Male	Female	Knot
Turkey	Poult	Tom	Hen	Rafter
Wolf	Pup	Dog	Bitch	Rout

4. SUMMARY OF ANIMAL TISSUES

TISSUE	LOCATION	FUNCTIONS
Epithelial	Covering of body Lining internal organs	Protection Secretion
Muscle Skeletal Smooth Cardiac	 Attached to skeleton bones Walls of internal organs Walls of heart	 Voluntary movement Involuntary movement Pumping blood
Connective Binding Bone Adipose Cartilage	 Covering organs, in tendons and ligaments Skeleton Beneath skin and around internal organs Ends of bone, part of nose and ears	 Holding tissues and organs together Support, protection, movement Fat storage, insulation, cushion Reduction of friction, support
Nerve	Brain Spinal cord, nerves, ganglions	Interpretation of impulses, mental activity Carrying impulses to and from all organs
Blood	Blood vessels, heart	Carrying materials to and from cells, carrying oxygen, fighting germs, clotting

5. PERIODIC TABLE

THE PERIODIC TABLE

KEY

	Group Classification
Atomic Number →	4 / IVA / IVB
	22
	Ti ← Symbol
Atomic Weight →	47.88

( ) indicates most stable or best known isotope

METALS — NONMETALS

TRANSITIONAL METALS

1 IA/IA	2 IIA/IIA	3 IIIA/IIIB	4 IVA/IVB	5 VA/VB	6 VIA/VIB	7 VIIA/VIIB	8 VIIIA/VIII	9 VIIIA/VIII	10 VIIIA/VIII	11 IB/IB	12 IIB/IIB	13 IIIB/IIIA	14 IVB/IVA	15 VB/VA	16 VIB/VIA	17 VIIB/VIIA	18 VIII/0
1 H 1.008																	2 He 4.003
3 Li 6.941	4 Be 9.012											5 B 10.811	6 C 12.011	7 N 14.007	8 O 15.999	9 F 18.998	10 Ne 20.180
11 Na 22.990	12 Mg 24.305											13 Al 26.982	14 Si 28.086	15 P 30.974	16 S 32.066	17 Cl 35.453	18 Ar 39.948
19 K 39.098	20 Ca 40.078	21 Sc 44.956	22 Ti 47.88	23 V 50.942	24 Cr 51.996	25 Mn 54.938	26 Fe 55.847	27 Co 58.933	28 Ni 58.693	29 Cu 63.546	30 Zn 65.39	31 Ga 69.723	32 Ge 72.61	33 As 74.922	34 Se 78.96	35 Br 79.904	36 Kr 83.8
37 Rb 85.468	38 Sr 87.62	39 Y 88.906	40 Zr 91.224	41 Nb 92.906	42 Mo 95.94	43 Tc (97.907)	44 Ru 101.07	45 Rh 102.906	46 Pd 106.4	47 Ag 107.868	48 Cd 112.411	49 In 114.818	50 Sn 118.710	51 Sb 121.757	52 Te 127.60	53 I 126.905	54 Xe 131.29
55 Cs 132.905	56 Ba 137.327	57 La 138.906	72 Hf 178.49	73 Ta 180.948	74 W 183.84	75 Re 186.207	76 Os 190.23	77 Ir 192.22	78 Pt 195.08	79 Au 196.967	80 Hg 200.59	81 Tl 204.383	82 Pb 207.2	83 Bi 208.980	84 Po (208.982)	85 At (209.982)	86 Rn (222.018)
87 Fr (223.020)	88 Ra (226.025)	89 Ac (227.028)	104 Rf (261.11)	105 Db (262.114)	106 Sg (263.118)	107 Bh (262.12)	108 Hs (265)	109 Mt (266)	110 Uun (269)	111 Uuu (272)	112 Uub (285)		114 Uuq (289)		116 Uuh (292)		

Alkali Metals (Group 1) — **Alkaline Earth Metals** (Group 2) — **Halogens** (Group 17) — **Noble Gases** (Group 18)

LANTHANIDE SERIES

58 Ce 140.115	59 Pr 140.908	60 Nd 144.24	61 Pm (144.913)	62 Sm 150.36	63 Eu 151.965	64 Gd 157.25	65 Tb 158.925	66 Dy 162.50	67 Ho 164.930	68 Er 167.26	69 Tm 168.934	70 Yb 173.04	71 Lu 174.967

ACTINIDE SERIES

90 Th 232.038	91 Pa 231.036	92 U 238.029	93 Np (237.048)	94 Pu (244.064)	95 Am (243.061)	96 Cm (247.070)	97 Bk (247.070)	98 Cf (251.080)	99 Es (252.083)	100 Fm (257.095)	101 Md (258.1)	102 No (259.101)	103 Lr (262.11)

6. INDEX OF ELEMENTS

1. HYDROGEN	39. YTTRIUM	77. IRIDIUM
2. HELIUM	40. ZIRCONIUM	78. PLATINUM
3. LITHIUM	41. NIOBIUM	79. GOLD
4. BERYLLIUM	42. MOLYBDENUM	80. MERCURY
5. BORON	43. TECHNETIUM	81. THALLIUM
6. CARBON	44. RUTHENIUM	82. LEAD
7. NITROGEN	45. RHODIUM	83. BISMUTH
8. OXYGEN	46. PALLADIUM	84. POLONIUM
9. FLUORINE	47. SILVER	85. ASTATINE
10. NEON	48. CADMIUM	86. RADON
11. SODIUM	49. INDIUM	87. FRANCIUM
12. MAGNESIUM	50. TIN	88. RADIUM
13. ALUMINUM	51. ANTIMONY	89. ACTINIUM
14. SILICON	52. TELLURIUM	90. THORIUM
15. PHOSPHOROUS	53. IODINE	91. PROTACTINIUM
16. SULFUR	54. XENON	92. URANIUM
17. CHLORINE	55. CESIUM	93. NEPTUNIUM
18. ARGON	56. BARIUM	94. PLUTONIUM
19. POTASSIUM	57. LANTHANUM	95. AMERICUM
20. CALCIUM	58. CERIUM	96. CURIUM
21. SCANDIUM	59. PRASEODYMIUM	97. BERKELIUM
22. TITANIUM	60. NEODYMIUM	98. CALIFORNIUM
23. VANADIUM	61. PROMETHIUM	99. EINSTEINIUM
24. CHROMIUM	62. SAMARIUM	100. FERMIUM
25. MANGANESE	63. EUROPIUM	101. MENDELEVIUM
26. IRON	64. GADOLINIUM	102. NOBELIUM
27. COBALT	65. TERBIUM	103. LAWRENCIUM
28. NICKEL	66. DYSPROSIUM	104. RUTHERFORDIUM
29. COPPER	67. HOLMIUM	105. DUBNIUM
30. ZINC	68. ERBIUM	106. SEABORGIUM
31. GALLIUM	69. THULLUM	107. BOHRIUM
32. GERMANIUM	70. YTTERBIUM	108. HASSIUM
33. ARSENIC	71. LUTETIUM	109. MEITNERIUM
34. SELENIUM	72. HAFNIUM	110. UNUNNILIUM
35. BROMINE	73. TANTALUM	111. UNUNUNIUM
36. KRYPTON	74. TUNGSTEN	112. UNUNBIUM
37. RUBIDIUM	75. RHENIUM	114. UNUNQUADIUM
38. STRONTIUM	76. OSMIUM	116. UNUNHEXIUM

MATHEMATICS

1. MATHEMATICAL REFERENCE TABLE

Symbols and Their Meanings

=	is equal to	≤	is less than or equal to
≠	is unequal to	≥	is greater than or equal to
<	is less than	||	is parallel to
>	is greater than	⊥	is perpendicular to

2. FORMULAS

DESCRIPTION	FORMULA
Area (A) of a:	
square	$A = s^2$; where s = side
rectangle	$A = lw$; where l = length, w = width
parallelogram	$A = bh$; where b = base, h = height
triangle	$A = \frac{1}{2}\,bh$; where b = base, h = height
circle	$A = \pi r^2$; where $\pi = 3.14$, r = radius

Distance (d):

between two points in a plane

$$d = \sqrt{(x_2 - x_1)^2 + (y_2 - y_1)^2}$$

where (x_1, y_1) and (x_2, y_2) are two points in a plane

as a function of rate and time $d = rt$; where r = rate, t = time

Mean

$$\frac{x_1 + x2 + \ldots + x_n}{n}$$

where the x's are the values for which a mean is desired, and n = number of values in the series

Median   the point in an ordered set of numbers at which half of the numbers are above and half of the numbers are below this value

Perimeter (P) of a:

square	$P = 4s$; where s = side
rectangle	$P = 2l + 2w$; where l = length, w = width
triangle	$P = a + b + c$; where a, b, and c are the sides

circumference (C) of a circle $C = \pi d$; where $\pi = 3.14$, d = diameter = $2r$

Pythagorean Theorem	$c^2 = a^2 + b^2$; where c = hypotenuse, a and b are legs of a right triangle
Simple Interest (i)	$i = prt$; where p = principal, r = rate, t = time
Total Cost (c)	$c = nr$; where n = number of units, r = cost per unit

Volume (V) of a:
  cube $V = s^3$; where s = side
  rectangular container $V = lwh$; where l = length, w = width, h = height

3. THE METRIC SYSTEM

The prefixes commonly used in the metric system are:

Prefix	Meaning
kilo–	thousand (1,000)
deci–	tenth (0.1)
centi–	hundredth (0.01)
milli–	thousandth (0.001)

The basic unit of linear measure in the metric system is the meter, represented by m. The relationship among the commonly used linear units of measurement in the metric system is as follows:

1 kilometer (km)	1,000 m
1 meter (m)	1.0 m
1 decimeter (dm)	0.1 m
1 centimeter (cm)	0.01 m
1 millimeter (mm)	0.001 m

The basic unit of measurement for mass (or weight) in the metric system is the gram, represented by g. The relationship among the commonly used units of measurement for mass in the metric system is as follows:

1 kilogram (kg)	1,000 g
1 gram (g)	1.0 g
1 milligram (mg)	0.001 g

three

Practice Tests

Miller Analogies

Practice Test 1

Answer Sheet
Practice Test 1

1. (A) (B) (C) (D)
2. (A) (B) (C) (D)
3. (A) (B) (C) (D)
4. (A) (B) (C) (D)
5. (A) (B) (C) (D)
6. (A) (B) (C) (D)
7. (A) (B) (C) (D)
8. (A) (B) (C) (D)
9. (A) (B) (C) (D)
10. (A) (B) (C) (D)
11. (A) (B) (C) (D)
12. (A) (B) (C) (D)
13. (A) (B) (C) (D)
14. (A) (B) (C) (D)
15. (A) (B) (C) (D)
16. (A) (B) (C) (D)
17. (A) (B) (C) (D)
18. (A) (B) (C) (D)
19. (A) (B) (C) (D)
20. (A) (B) (C) (D)
21. (A) (B) (C) (D)
22. (A) (B) (C) (D)
23. (A) (B) (C) (D)
24. (A) (B) (C) (D)
25. (A) (B) (C) (D)
26. (A) (B) (C) (D)
27. (A) (B) (C) (D)
28. (A) (B) (C) (D)
29. (A) (B) (C) (D)
30. (A) (B) (C) (D)
31. (A) (B) (C) (D)
32. (A) (B) (C) (D)
33. (A) (B) (C) (D)
34. (A) (B) (C) (D)

35. (A) (B) (C) (D)
36. (A) (B) (C) (D)
37. (A) (B) (C) (D)
38. (A) (B) (C) (D)
39. (A) (B) (C) (D)
40. (A) (B) (C) (D)
41. (A) (B) (C) (D)
42. (A) (B) (C) (D)
43. (A) (B) (C) (D)
44. (A) (B) (C) (D)
45. (A) (B) (C) (D)
46. (A) (B) (C) (D)
47. (A) (B) (C) (D)
48. (A) (B) (C) (D)
49. (A) (B) (C) (D)
50. (A) (B) (C) (D)
51. (A) (B) (C) (D)
52. (A) (B) (C) (D)
53. (A) (B) (C) (D)
54. (A) (B) (C) (D)
55. (A) (B) (C) (D)
56. (A) (B) (C) (D)
57. (A) (B) (C) (D)
58. (A) (B) (C) (D)
59. (A) (B) (C) (D)
60. (A) (B) (C) (D)
61. (A) (B) (C) (D)
62. (A) (B) (C) (D)
63. (A) (B) (C) (D)
64. (A) (B) (C) (D)
65. (A) (B) (C) (D)
66. (A) (B) (C) (D)
67. (A) (B) (C) (D)
68. (A) (B) (C) (D)

69. (A) (B) (C) (D)
70. (A) (B) (C) (D)
71. (A) (B) (C) (D)
72. (A) (B) (C) (D)
73. (A) (B) (C) (D)
74. (A) (B) (C) (D)
75. (A) (B) (C) (D)
76. (A) (B) (C) (D)
77. (A) (B) (C) (D)
78. (A) (B) (C) (D)
79. (A) (B) (C) (D)
80. (A) (B) (C) (D)
81. (A) (B) (C) (D)
82. (A) (B) (C) (D)
83. (A) (B) (C) (D)
84. (A) (B) (C) (D)
85. (A) (B) (C) (D)
86. (A) (B) (C) (D)
87. (A) (B) (C) (D)
88. (A) (B) (C) (D)
89. (A) (B) (C) (D)
90. (A) (B) (C) (D)
91. (A) (B) (C) (D)
92. (A) (B) (C) (D)
93. (A) (B) (C) (D)
94. (A) (B) (C) (D)
95. (A) (B) (C) (D)
96. (A) (B) (C) (D)
97. (A) (B) (C) (D)
98. (A) (B) (C) (D)
99. (A) (B) (C) (D)
100. (A) (B) (C) (D)

Practice Test 1

TIME: 50 Minutes   **LENGTH:** 100 Analogies

DIRECTIONS: Read each of the following analogies carefully, and choose the BEST answer to each item. Fill in your responses in the answer sheets provided.

Note: The Miller Analogies Test consists of 120 questions to be completed in 60 minutes. Twenty of these questions are experimental items, which are not scored and thus not reflected in this practice test.

1.   MINERVA : THE ARTS :: (a. Pomona b. Flaura c. Gaia d. Demeter) : FRUITS

2.   COW : HEIFER :: FOX : (a. vixen b. gander c. bitch d. ewe)

3.   HALIFAX : CANADA :: O'HARE : (a. New York b. Ireland c. Chicago d. England)

4.   SCOPES : DARROW :: MCCARTHY : (a. Bailey b. Cohn c. Hutz d. Slotnick)

5.   EARL : JIMMY CARTER :: (a. Wilson b. Milhous c. Baines d. Herbert) : RONALD REAGAN

6.   BETTY : ELIZABETH :: (a. Jeremy b. Jeffrey c. Sean d. James) : JOHN

7.   UPI : AP :: Press Association : (a. Courier b. IPS c. AT&T d. Reuters)

8.   (a. Tar Heel b. Garden c. Buckeye d. Sunshine) : OHIO :: EMPIRE : NEW YORK

9.   MAGYAR : (a. Hungary b. China c. Madagascar d. Morocco) :: GAELIC : IRELAND

10. SAHARA : (a. Gobi b. Mojave c. Patagonia d. Arabian) :: AUSTRALIA : GREENLAND

11. SUPERIOR : CASPIAN :: (a. Mediterranean b. Coral c. Bering d. North) : ARABIAN SEA

12. MERCURY : JUPITER :: (a. Atlantic b. Indian c. Southern d. Arctic) : PACIFIC

13. CALF : WHALE :: (a. foal b. fawn c. chick d. cygnet) : SWAN

14. TALLAHASSEE : FLORIDA :: (a. Dover b. Newark c. Concord d. Annapolis) : DELAWARE

15. JUSTINIAN : (a. Macedonia b. Byzantium c. Athens d. Franks) :: AUGUSTUS : ROME

16. GINSBERG : KEROUAC :: HUGHES : (a. Hurston b. Walker c. Morrison d. Lee)

17. GALAPAGOS : (a. Greece b. Italy c. Ecuador d. India) :: AZORES : PORTUGAL

18. MARCO POLO : CHINA :: COLUMBUS : (a. North America b. Caribbean c. Central America d. Pacific Islands)

19. 1865 : EMANCIPATION OF AMERICAN SLAVES :: 1861 : (a. French Revolution b. Alaskan purchase c. emancipation of Russian serfs d. the passage of the Eighteenth Amendment)

20. 1799 : WASHINGTON :: 1865 : (a. Lincoln b. Buchanan c. McKinley d. Arthur)

21. LATITUDE : PARALLELS :: LONGITUDE : (a. line b. equator c. degree d. meridians)

22. LEIBNIZ : RATIONALISM :: LOCKE : (a. empiricism b. atomism c. idealism d. phenomenologism)

23. ORNITHOLOGY : BIRDS :: ICHTHYOLOGY : (a. cancer b. currency c. metals d. fish)

24. EIFFEL TOWER : GUSTAVE EIFFEL :: GUGGENHEIM MUSEUM :
(a. Solomon Guggenheim b. Frank Lloyd Wright c. Walter Gropius
d. Egon Schiele)

25. POUND : 16 OUNCES :: TROY POUND : (a. 8 oz. b. 24 oz. c. 12 oz. d. 17 oz.)

26. CHRONOMETER : TIME :: ANEMOMETER : (a. weight b. atmospheric
pressure c. wind speed d. distance)

27. EUROPE/RUSSIA : 13% OF THE WORLD POPULATION :: CHINA : (a. 35%
b. 20% c. 29% d. 17%)

28. ENGLISH : 460 MILLION SPEAKERS :: SPANISH : (a. 400 million
b. 80 million c. 125 million d. 357 million)

29. PRIMARY ECONOMIC ACTIVITY : FARMING :: SECONDARY
ECONOMIC ACTIVITY : (a. service b. information and research
c. manufacturing d. mining)

30. DONATELLO : BRONZE :: DÜRER : (a. copper b. titanium c. iron d. plaster)

31. BUONARROTI : MICHELANGELO :: REMBRANDT : (a. Donatello
b. Munch c. Lichtenstein d. Van Rijn)

32. PRIDE : LIONS :: (a. gaggle b. flock c. rafter d. herd) : TURKEYS

33. SWARM : BEES :: BUSINESS : (a. bears b. eagles c. ferrets d. elks)

34. ERATO : LOVE :: (a. Urania b. Terpsichore c. Euterpe d. Calliope) : DANCING

35. LAKOTA : SIOUX NATION :: (a. Mohawk b. Cherokee c. Navaho d. Lenape) :
IROQUOIS CONFEDERACY

36. *COMMON SENSE* : THOMAS PAINE :: (a. *Civil Disobedience* b. *Origin of
Species* c. *Wealth of Nations* d. *Poor Richard's Almanac*) : ADAM SMITH

37. HERTZ : FREQUENCY :: (a. joule b. tesla c. watt d. newton) : FORCE

38. FIRST ANNIVERSARY : SECOND ANNIVERSARY :: PAPER : (a. cotton
b. leather c. linen d. crystal)

39. VENTRICLE : AURICLE :: OCCIPITAL : (a. pylorus b. temporal c. thoracic d. nevus)

40. FEMUR : SKELETON :: (a. stomach b. brain c. skin d. heart) : ORGANS

41. BAROMETER : ATMOSPHERIC PRESSURE :: (a. anemometer b. bolometer c. galvanometer d. densitometer) : ELECTRICAL CURRENTS

42. BELL : TELEPHONE :: (a. Davy b. Deere c. Fitch d. Fulton) : STEAMBOAT

43. AMETHYST : OPAL :: LIMESTONE : (a. loam b. marble c. lava d. obsidian)

44. LEMONS : (a. vinegar b. aspirin c. batteries d. soap) :: ACID : BASE

45. POSITIVE : NEGATIVE :: CATION : (a. neutron b. anion c. proton d. electron)

46. 0° LATITUDE : EQUATOR :: 23.5° NORTH LATITUDE : (a. prime meridian b. tropic of Capricorn c. middle latitudes d. tropic of Cancer)

47. SPHYGMOMANOMETER : (a. doctor b. engineer c. photographer d. astronomer) :: COMPASS : NAVIGATOR

48. ENTOMOLOGIST : ARACHNOLOGIST :: GEOGRAPHER : (a. cartographer b. geologist c. archaeologist d. botanist)

49. *SANTA MARIA* : FRANCESO PINEDO :: *SPIRIT OF ST. LOUIS* : (a. Richard Byrd b. Charles Lindbergh c. Clarence Chamberlain d. Albert "Putty" Reed)

50. BARBARY COAST : NORTH AFRICA :: GOLD COAST : (a. Zimbabwe b. Chad c. South Africa d. Ghana)

51. ENDOCRINOLOGIST : (a. teeth b. eyes c. glands d. intestines) :: DERMATOLOGIST : SKIN

52. STRATFORD-ON-AVON : SHAKESPEARE :: BERDICHEV, UKRAINE : (a. Conrad b. Tolstoy c. Nabokov d. Solzhenitsyn)

53. JULIUS : REPUBLIC :: AUGUSTUS : (a. democracy b. aristocracy c. empire d. monarchy)

54. CORONATION : INAUGURATION :: (a. cardinal b. monarch c. bishop d. pope) : PRESIDENT

55. SAXOPHONE : (a. brass b. woodwind c. percussion d. horn) :: VIOLIN: STRING

56. SONNET : (a. 14 b. 16 c. 18 d. 10) :: HAIKU : THREE

57. KAFKA : SAMSA :: CAMUS : (a. Gregor b. Meursault c. *The Stranger* d. Franz)

58. APHRODITE : VENUS :: ZEUS : (a. Apollo b. Hecate c. Jupiter d. Mercury)

59. MICHELANGELO : LEONARDO :: (a. Dali b. Goya c. Cassatt d. Monet) : RENOIR

60. BOVARY : FLAUBERT :: CHATTERLY : (a. D.H. Lawrence b. V.S. Naipaul c. E.M. Forester d. Wyndham Lewis)

61. ELEANOR ROOSEVELT : FDR :: CLYTAEMNESTRA : (a. Lysistrata b. Antigone c. Agammemnon d. Caligula)

62. THATCHER : MAJOR :: AUGUSTUS : (a. Claudius   b. Julius c. Tiberius d. Nero)

63. K2 : EVEREST :: (a. Australia b. Africa c. Antarctica d. South America) : ASIA

64. TWAIN : CLEMENS :: (a. Eliot b. Dennisen c. Woolf d. Sand) : EVANS

65. VAN GOGH : *LUST FOR LIFE* :: (a. Frost b. Dali c. Bukowski d. Kerouac) : *BARFLY*

66. BYRON : ROMANTICISM :: (a. Melville b. Salinger c. Eliot d. Shelley) : TRANSCENDENTALISM

67. DEMOCRACY : CITIZENRY :: THEOCRACY : (a. church b. state c. populace d. monarch)

68. URSINE : BEAR :: CERVINE : (a. deer b. reptile c. fowl d. mule)

69. POSITIVE : NEGATIVE :: SHARP : (a. tone b. flat c. bass d. treble)

70. CONSTANTINE : CHRISTIANITY :: ASOKA : (a. Taoism b. Jainism c. Hinduism d. Buddhism)

71. FIBULA : TIBIA :: RADIUS : (a. sternum b. ulna c. femur d. mandibular)

72. CLAUSTRO : CLOSED SPACES :: (a. geno b. hydro c. mastigo d. xeno) : STRANGERS

73. MARAT : SADE :: JEFFERSON : (a. Robespierre b. Thoreau c. Franklin d. Hudson)

74. πr^2 : AREA :: $2\pi r$: (a. circumference b. width c. volume d. depth)

75. CALORIE : (a. pressure b. volume c. heat d. force) :: ACRE : AREA

76. SUNUNU : (a. Bush b. Reagan c. Meese d. Ford) :: PANETTA : CLINTON

77. Ag : SILVER :: Fe : (a. magnesium b. fermium c. iron d. zinc)

78. PLATO : THE ACADEMY :: GROPIUS : (a. Bauhaus b. Citadel c. Cambridge d. Montessori)

79. GODDARD : ROCKET :: BABBAGE: (a. Xerox b. fountain pen c. computer d. electric typewriter)

80. NILE : AFRICA :: (a. Yangtze b. Hwang Ho c. Yellow d. Ashikaga) : CHINA

81. LIVY : POLIO :: TURNER : (a. Limerick b. Influenza c. Prescott d. Moffit)

82. MAORI : NEW ZEALAND :: YANOMAMI : (a. Argentina b. Egypt c. Micronesia d. Brazil)

83. PLANCK : (a. rocketry b. physics c. quantum physics d. calculus) :: EUCLID : GEOMETRY

84. PLUTO : HADES :: (a.Vulcan b. Frigg c. Loki d. Isis) : HEPHAESTUS

85. MONTICELLO : (a. Adams b. Franklin c. Jackson d. Jefferson) :: FALLING WATER : WRIGHT

86. PRADO : (a. Rome b. Madrid c. Santa Fe d. Prague) :: GUGGENHEIM : NEW YORK

87. FRANKLIN : AMERICA :: (a. Goethe b. Baudelaire c. Le Corbusier d. Voltaire) : FRANCE

88. CONRAD : (a. Scotland b. England c. Ukraine d. Ireland) :: TWAIN : UNITED STATES

89. PHILATELIST : STAMPS :: LEPIDOPTERIST : (a. minerals   b. butterflies c. coins d. clocks)

90. GEORGE BUSH : RONALD REAGAN :: ANDREW JOHNSON : (a. John Q. Adams b. Abe Lincoln c. Rutherford Hayes d. Andrew Jackson)

91. HINDI : INDIA :: (a. Spanish b. English c. Portuguese d. French) : PERU

92. RUPEE : INDIA :: LIRA : (a. Egypt b. Greece c. Italy d. Spain)

93. BIBLIOPHILE : (a. bibles b. religion c. books d. music) :: ANGLOPHILE : ENGLAND

94. SLEUTH : (a. zebras b. horses c. worms d. bears) :: GAGGLE : GEESE

95. GYNOPHOBE : WOMAN :: ANDROPHOBE : (a. man b. homosexuals c. germs d. animals)

96. REFLECT : ABSORB :: CONVEX : (a. bend b. scatter c. converge d. concave)

97. SRI LANKA : CEYLON :: (a. Zimbabwe b. Zaire c. Ghana d. Uruguay) : BELGIAN CONGO

98. MELODIOUS : CACOPHONOUS :: (a. dry b. petulant c. sweet d. succulent) : ARID

99. 2 : 8 :: 4 : (a. 12 b. 17 c. 64 d. 24)

100. AVIARY : BIRDS :: FORMICARY : (a. fish b. reptiles c. insects d. ants)

Answer Key
Practice Test 1

1. (a)	26. (c)	51. (c)	76. (a)
2. (a)	27. (b)	52. (a)	77. (c)
3. (c)	28. (d)	53. (c)	78. (a)
4. (b)	29. (c)	54. (b)	79. (c)
5. (a)	30. (a)	55. (b)	80. (a)
6. (c)	31. (d)	56. (a)	81. (c)
7. (d)	32. (c)	57. (b)	82. (d)
8. (c)	33. (c)	58. (c)	83. (c)
9. (a)	34. (b)	59. (d)	84. (a)
10. (d)	35. (a)	60. (a)	85. (d)
11. (b)	36. (c)	61. (c)	86. (b)
12. (d)	37. (d)	62. (c)	87. (d)
13. (d)	38. (a)	63. (b)	88. (c)
14. (a)	39. (b)	64. (a)	89. (b)
15. (b)	40. (c)	65. (c)	90. (b)
16. (a)	41. (c)	66. (a)	91. (a)
17. (c)	42. (c)	67. (a)	92. (c)
18. (b)	43. (b)	68. (a)	93. (c)
19. (c)	44. (d)	69. (b)	94. (d)
20. (a)	45. (b)	70. (d)	95. (a)
21. (d)	46. (d)	71. (b)	96. (d)
22. (a)	47. (a)	72. (d)	97. (b)
23. (d)	48. (a)	73. (c)	98. (d)
24. (b)	49. (b)	74. (a)	99. (c)
25. (c)	50. (d)	75. (c)	100. (d)

Explanations
of Answers

Explanations of Answers
Practice Test 1

1. MINERVA : THE ARTS :: (**a. Pomona** b. Flaura c. Gaia d. Demeter) : FRUITS

   (**a**) is correct because Pomona is the Roman goddess of fruits as Minerva is the Roman goddess of the Arts and knowledge. (b) is incorrect because Flaura is the Roman goddess of flowers. (c) is incorrect because Gaia is the Greek goddess of the Earth. (d) is incorrect because Demeter, who is a goddess of fruits, is Greek, not Roman.

2. COW : HEIFER :: FOX : (**a. vixen** b. gander c. bitch d. ewe)

   (**a**) is correct because a vixen is a female fox as a heifer is a female bovine. (b) is incorrect because a gander is a male goose. (c) is incorrect because a bitch is a female dog. (d) is incorrect because a ewe is a female sheep.

3. HALIFAX : CANADA :: O'HARE : (a. New York b. Ireland **c. Chicago** d. England)

   (**c**) is correct because Chicago's international airport is named O'Hare, as Canada's international airport is named Halifax. (a) is incorrect because New York is home to JFK and LaGuardia international airports. (b) is incorrect because Ireland's international airport is Belfast. (d) is incorrect because England's international airport is Heathrow.

4. SCOPES : DARROW :: MCCARTHY : (a. Bailey **b. Cohn** c. Hutz d. Slotnick)

   (**b**) is correct because Roy Cohn defended Joseph McCarthy as Clarence Darrow defended John Scopes. (a) is incorrect because F. Lee Bailey is famous for defending the Boston Strangler. (c) is incorrect because Lionel Hutz is a fictional attorney. (d) is incorrect because Barry Slotnick is famous for defending Bernhard Goetz.

5. EARL : JIMMY CARTER :: (**a. Wilson** b. Milhous c. Baines d. Herbert) : RONALD REAGAN

   (**a**) is correct because Wilson is Ronald Reagan's middle name as Earl is Jimmy Carter's. (b) is incorrect because Milhous is the middle name of Richard Nixon. (c) is incorrect because Baines is the middle name of Lyndon Johnson. (d) is incorrect because Herbert is the middle name of George Bush.

6. BETTY : ELIZABETH :: (a. Jeremy b. Jeffrey **c. Sean** d. James) : JOHN

    (c) is correct because Sean is a form of John as Betty is a form of Elizabeth. (a) is incorrect because Jeremy is a form of Henry. (b) is incorrect because Geoff is the German form of Jeffrey. (d) is incorrect because James is a Latin form of Jacob.

7. UPI : AP :: Press Association : (a. Courier b. IPS c. AT&T **d. Reuters**)

    (d) is correct because Reuters and Press Association are based in London, just as United Press International and Associated Press are based in New York. (a) is incorrect because Courier is not an English news service. (b) is incorrect because IPS (International Press Service) is based in Rome. (c) is incorrect because AT&T is an American telecommunications firm.

8. (a. Tar Heel b. Garden **c. Buckeye** d. Sunshine) : OHIO :: EMPIRE : NEW YORK

    (c) is correct because Buckeye is the nickname for Ohio just as Empire is the nickname for New York. (a) is incorrect because Tar Heel is the nickname for North Carolina. (b) is incorrect because Garden is the nickname for New Jersey. (d) is incorrect because Sunshine is the nickname for Florida.

9. MAGYAR : (**a. Hungary** b. China c. Madagascar d. Morocco) :: GAELIC : IRELAND

    (a) is correct because Magyar is the main language of Hungary just as Gaelic is the main language of Ireland. (b) is incorrect because Mandarin and Cantonese are the main languages of China. (c) is incorrect because Malagasy is the main language of Madagascar. (d) is incorrect because Arabic is the official language of Morocco.

10. (SAHARA : (a. Gobi b. Mojave c. Patagonia **d. Arabian**) :: AUSTRALIA : GREENLAND

    (d) is correct because the Arabian Desert is the second largest desert to the Sahara as Greenland is the second largest island to Australia. (a) is incorrect because Gobi is the third largest desert. (b) is incorrect because Mojave is the sixth largest. (c) is incorrect because Patagonia is the fourth.

Explanations
of Answers

11. SUPERIOR : CASPIAN :: (a. Mediterranean **b. Coral** c. Bering d. North) : ARABIAN SEA

    (b) is correct because the Coral Sea is the largest sea with the Arabian Sea being the second largest, just as Superior is the second-largest lake to the Caspian Sea (actually a lake). (a) is incorrect because the Mediterranean is the fourth largest sea. (c) is incorrect because the Bering is the fifth-largest sea. (d) is incorrect because the North is the twenty-second largest sea.

12. MERCURY : JUPITER :: (a. Atlantic b. Indian c. Antarctic **d. Arctic**) : PACIFIC

    (d) is correct because the Arctic Ocean is the smallest and the Pacific Ocean is the largest as Mercury is the smallest planet and Jupiter is the largest. (a) is incorrect because the Atlantic is the second-largest ocean. (b) is incorrect because the Indian is the third-largest ocean. (c) is incorrect because the Southern Ocean is the fourth-largest ocean.

13. CALF : WHALE :: (a. foal b. fawn c. chick **d. cygnet**) : SWAN

    (d) is correct because a cygnet is a baby swan just as a calf is a baby whale. (a) is incorrect because a foal is a baby horse. (b) is incorrect because a fawn is a baby deer. (c) is incorrect because a chick is a baby chicken.

14. TALLAHASSEE : FLORIDA :: (**a. Dover** b. Newark c. Concord d. Annapolis) : DELAWARE

    (a) is correct because Dover is the capital of Delaware just as Tallahassee is the capital of Florida. (b) is incorrect because while Newark is a major city in both Delaware and New Jersey, it is the capital of neither state. (c) is incorrect because Concord is the capital of New Hampshire. (d) is incorrect because Annapolis is the capital of Maryland.

15. JUSTINIAN : (a. Macedonia **b. Byzantium** c. Athens d. Franks) :: AUGUSTUS : ROME

    (b) is correct because Justinian was the greatest ruler of Byzantium just as Augustus was the greatest ruler of Rome. (a) is incorrect because Philip was the greatest ruler of Macedonia. (c) is incorrect because the greatest ruler of Athens was Pericles. (d) is incorrect because the greatest ruler of the Frankish kingdom was Clovis I.

Explanations
of Answers

16. GINSBERG : KEROUAC :: HUGHES : (**a. Hurston** b. Walker c. Morrison d. Lee)

    (a) is correct because Zora Neale Hurston and Langston Hughes both emerged from the Harlem Renaissance just as Ginsberg and Kerouac both emerged from the Beat Movement. (b) and (c) are incorrect because both Alice Walker and Toni Morrison were born after the Harlem Renaissance. (d) is incorrect because Harper Lee was not part of the Harlem Renaissance.

17. GALAPAGOS : (a. Greece b. Italy **c. Ecuador** d. India) :: AZORES : PORTUGAL

    (c) is correct because the Galapagos Islands belong to Ecuador just as the Azores belong to Portugal. (a) is incorrect because the major island group of Greece is the Cyclades. (b) is incorrect because the major island group of Italy is the Aeloian. (d) is incorrect because the main island group of India is Andaman.

18. MARCO POLO : CHINA :: COLUMBUS : (a. North America **b. Caribbean** c. Central America d. Pacific Islands)

    (b) is correct because Columbus was the first non-indigenous person to land in the Caribbean Islands just as Marco Polo was the first European to journey to China. (a) is incorrect because the first non-indigenous person to land in North America was Leif Erikson. (c) is incorrect because Cortez was the first European to land in Central America. (d) is incorrect because Cook was the first European to land in the Pacific Islands.

19. 1865 : EMANCIPATION OF AMERICAN SLAVES :: 1861 : (a. French Revolution b. Alaskan purchase **c. emancipation of Russian serfs** d. the passage of the Eighteenth Amendment)

    (c) is correct because 1861 marked the emancipation of Russian serfs just as 1865 marked the emancipation of American slaves. (a) is incorrect because the French Revolution occurred in 1789. (b) is incorrect because the American purchase of Alaska occurred in 1867. (d) is incorrect because the Eighteenth Amendment was passed in 1920.

20. 1799 : WASHINGTON :: 1865 : (**a. Lincoln** b. Buchanan c. McKinley d. Arthur)

    (a) is correct because Lincoln died in 1865 just as Washington died in 1799. (b) is incorrect because Buchanan died in 1868. (c) is incorrect because McKinley died in 1901. (d) is incorrect because Arthur died in 1886.

Explanations
of Answers

21. LATITUDE : PARALLELS :: LONGITUDE : (a. line b. equator c. degree
    d. meridians)

    (d) is correct because *parallels* is another name for lines of latitude as *meridians*
    are another name for lines of longitude. (a) is incorrect because *line* is a gen-
    eral term and could apply to either longitude or latitude. (b) is incorrect because
    equator refers to a specific line of latitude. (c) is incorrect because degrees are a
    measurement of longitude and latitude.

22. LEIBNIZ : RATIONALISM :: LOCKE : (**a. empiricism** b. atomism c. idealism
    d. phenomenologism)

    (a) is correct because just as Leibniz was a rationalist, Locke was an empiricist.
    (b) is incorrect because atomism refers to the belief that all matter is composed
    of atoms. (c) is incorrect because an idealist believes the external world is a cre-
    ation of the mind. (d) is incorrect because phenomenology refers to a method of
    inquiry in which one closely inspects one's own thought processes.

23. ORNITHOLOGY : BIRDS :: ICHTHYOLOGY : (a. cancer b. currency
    c. metals **d. fish**)

    (d) is correct because just as a bird expert is an ornithologist, a fish expert is an
    ichthyologist. (a) is incorrect because a cancer expert is called an oncologist. (b)
    is incorrect because a numismatist is a currency expert. (c) is incorrect because a
    metalurgist is an expert in metals.

24. EIFFEL TOWER : GUSTAVE EIFFEL :: GUGGENHEIM MUSEUM :
    (a. Solomon Guggenheim **b. Frank Lloyd Wright** c. Walter Gropius d. Egon
    Schiele)

    (b) is correct because just as Gustave Eiffel designed the Eiffel Tower, Frank
    Lloyd Wright designed the Guggenheim Museum. (a) is incorrect because while
    the museum bears his name, he was not the designer of the building. (c) is incor-
    rect; Walter Gropius was the leader and designer of the Bauhaus School. (d) is
    incorrect because Egon Schiele is an artist, not an architect.

25. POUND : 16 OUNCES :: TROY POUND : (a. 8 oz. b. 24 oz. **c. 12 oz.** d. 17 oz.)

    (c) is correct because one standard pound is equal to 16 oz. just as one troy
    pound is equal to 12 oz. All other measurements, (a), (b), and (d), are irrelevant.

26. CHRONOMETER : TIME :: ANEMOMETER : (a. weight b. atmospheric pressure **c. wind speed** d. distance)

    (c) is correct because as a chronometer measures time, an anemometer measures wind speed. (a) is incorrect because a scale measures weight. (b) is incorrect because a barometer measures atmospheric pressure. (d) is incorrect because an odometer measures distance.

27. EUROPE/RUSSIA : 13% OF THE WORLD POPULATION :: CHINA : (a. 35% **b. 20%** c. 29% d. 17%)

    (b) is the correct answer. All of the others, (a), (c), and (d), are irrelevant.

28. ENGLISH : 460 MILLION SPEAKERS :: SPANISH : (a. 400 million b. 80 million c. 125 million **d. 357 million**)

    (d) is the correct answer because English has 460 million speakers worldwide and Spanish has approximately 357 million speakers globally. Choices (a), (b), and (c) are irrelevant.

29. PRIMARY ECONOMIC ACTIVITY : FARMING :: SECONDARY ECONOMIC ACTIVITY : (a. service b. information and research **c. manufacturing** d. mining)

    (c) is correct because as farming is a primary economic activity, manufacturing is a secondary economic activity. (a) is incorrect because service activity is a tertiary economic activity. (b) is incorrect because information and research involves a quarternary economic activity. (d) is incorrect because mining is a primary economic activity.

30. DONATELLO : BRONZE :: DÜRER : (**a. copper** b. titanium c. iron d. plaster)

    (a) is correct because Donatello was known for his bronze sculpture as Dürer was known for his copper engravings. (b), (c), and (d) are incorrect because Dürer did not work in these media.

31. BUONARROTI : MICHELANGELO :: REMBRANDT : (a. Donatello b. Munch c. Lichtenstein **d. Van Rijn**)

    (d) is correct because Buonarroti is the little used last name of Michelangelo as Van Rijn is the less known last name of Rembrandt. (a) is incorrect because Donatello was the name of an Italian sculptor. (b) is incorrect because Edvard Munch was a twentieth-century Norwegian expressionist painter. (c) is incorrect because Roy Lichtenstein was a twentieth-century American pop artist.

32. PRIDE : LIONS :: (a. gaggle b. flock **c. rafter** d. herd) : TURKEYS

(c) is correct because a group of turkeys is called a *rafter* just as a group of lions is called a *pride*. (a) is incorrect because *gaggle* refers to a group of geese. (b) is incorrect because *flock* is a generic term for a group of birds. (d) is incorrect because *herd* refers to a group of cattle.

33. SWARM : BEES :: BUSINESS : (a. bears b. eagles **c. ferrets** d. elks)

(c) is correct because *business* is a collective term for ferrets as swarm is a collective term for bees. (a) is incorrect because bears gather in sleuths. (b) is incorrect because a group of eagles is called a *convocation*. (d) is incorrect because a collective term for elks is *gang*.

34. ERATO : LOVE :: (a. Urania **b. Terpsichore** c. Euterpe d. Calliope) : DANCING

(b) is correct because Terpsichore was the Muse of dance as Erato was the Muse of love. (a) is incorrect because Urania was the Muse of astronomy. (c) is incorrect because Euterpe was the Muse of music. (d) is incorrect because Calliope was the Muse of poetry.

35. LAKOTA : SIOUX NATION :: (**a. Mohawk** b. Cherokee c. Navaho d. Lenape) : IROQUOIS CONFEDERACY

(a) is correct because Lakota is the name of a tribe in a confederation of tribes called the Sioux Nation as the Mohawk tribe is a member of the Iroquois Confederation. Choices (b), (c), and (d) are not part of the Iroquois Confederation.

36. *COMMON SENSE* : THOMAS PAINE :: (a. *Civil Disobedience* b. *Origin of Species* **c. Wealth of Nations** d. *Poor Richard's Almanac*) : ADAM SMITH

(c) is correct because *Wealth of Nations* is Smith's most famous work, as *Common Sense* is Thomas Paine's most famous work. (a) is incorrect because *Civil Disobedience* was penned by Henry David Thoreau. (b) is incorrect because *Origin of Species* was written by Charles Darwin. (d) is wrong because *Poor Richard's Almanac* was written by Benjamin Franklin.

37. HERTZ : FREQUENCY :: (a. joule b. tesla c. watt **d. newton**) : FORCE

(d) is the correct answer because a newton is a unit of force just as hertz is a unit of frequency. (a) is incorrect because a joule is a unit of energy. (b) is incorrect because a tesla is a unit of magnetic flux density. (c) is incorrect because a watt is a unit of power.

38. FIRST ANNIVERSARY : SECOND ANNIVERSARY :: PAPER : (**a. cotton** b. leather c. linen d. crystal)

(**a**) is correct because cotton is given for the second anniversary gift as paper is given for the first. (b) is incorrect because leather is given for the third anniversary. (c) is incorrect because linen is given for the fourth. (d) is incorrect because crystal is given for the fifteenth.

39. VENTRICLE : AURICLE :: OCCIPITAL : (a. pylorus **b. temporal** c. thoracic d. nevus)

(**b**) is correct because temporal and occipital are lobes (sections) of the brain as the ventricle and auricle are chambers of the heart. (a) is incorrect because the pylorus is the lower section of the stomach. (c) is incorrect because thoracic is the section of vertebrae between the neck and the abdomen. (d) is incorrect because a nevus is a birthmark.

40. FEMUR : SKELETON :: (a. stomach b. brain **c. skin** d. heart) : ORGANS

(**c**) is correct because the skin is the largest of the organs, just as the femur is the largest of the bones of the skeleton. (a), (b), and (d) are incorrect because these are not the largest of the body's organs.

41. BAROMETER : ATMOSPHERIC PRESSURE :: (a. anemometer b. bolometer **c. galvanometer** d. densitometer) : ELECTRICAL CURRENTS

(**c**) is the correct response because just as a barometer measures atmospheric pressure, a galvanometer measures electrical currents. (a) is incorrect because an anemometer measures wind speed. (b) is incorrect because a bolometer measures small amounts of radiant energy. (d) is incorrect because a densitometer measures the thickness or darkness of film.

42. BELL : TELEPHONE :: (a. Davy b. Deere **c. Fitch** d. Fulton) : STEAMBOAT

(**c**) is correct because John Fitch invented the first American steamboat as Alexander Bell invented the telephone. (a) is incorrect because Humphrey Davy invented the miner's lamp. (b) is incorrect because John Deere invented the steel plowshare. (d) is incorrect because Robert Fulton was erroneously credited with inventing the first steamboat. He actually improved upon Fitch's model.

Explanations
of Answers

43. AMETHYST : OPAL :: LIMESTONE : (a. loam **b. marble** c. lava d. obsidian)

(b) is correct because marble and limestone are both sedimentary rocks, just as amethyst and opal are both forms of quartz. (a) is incorrect because loam is a type of soil. (c) is incorrect because lava is molten rock. (d) is incorrect because obsidian is a glass that results from molten rock.

44. LEMONS : (a. vinegar b. aspirin c. batteries **d. soap**) :: ACID : BASE

(d) is the correct response because soap is basic while lemons are acidic; acids and bases are two forms of chemical composition classification. (a) is incorrect because vinegar is acetic acid. (b) is incorrect because aspirin is acetylsalicylic acid. (c) is incorrect because batteries are usually composed of sulfuric acid.

45. POSITIVE : NEGATIVE :: CATION : (a. neutron **b. anion** c. proton d. electron)

(b) is correct because a negatively charged ion is called an anion, just as a positively charged ion is called a cation. (a) is incorrect because a neutron is an uncharged particle. (c) is incorrect because a proton is a positively charged particle that exists in the atomic nucleus. (d) is incorrect because an electron is a negatively charged particle that orbits the atomic nucleus.

46. 0° LATITUDE : EQUATOR :: 23.5° NORTH LATITUDE : (a. prime meridian b. tropic of Capricorn c. middle latitudes **d. tropic of Cancer**)

(d) is correct because just as 0° latitude is also known as the equator, 23.5° north latitude is called the tropic of Cancer. (a) is incorrect because the prime meridian is 0° longitude. (b) is incorrect because the tropic of Capricorn lies at 23.5° south latitude. (c) is incorrect because the middle latitudes refers to the area between the tropics and their respective polar circles.

47. SPHYGMOMANOMETER : (**a. doctor** b. engineer c. photographer d. astronomer) :: COMPASS : NAVIGATOR

(a) is the correct response because a sphygmomanometer is an instrument used by a doctor (to measure blood pressure) just as a compass is an instrument used by a navigator. (b), (c), and (d) are incorrect because these occupations would have no use for this instrument.

48. ENTOMOLOGIST : ARACHNOLOGIST :: GEOGRAPHER :
(**a. cartographer** b. geologist c. archaeologist d. botanist)

(**a**) is correct because a cartographer (a map expert) is a more specific type of
geographer, just as an arachnologist (a spider expert) is a more specific type of
entomologist (insect expert). (b) is incorrect because a geologist studies rocks
and minerals. (c) is incorrect because an archaeologist studies past civilizations
and the history of humankind. (d) is incorrect because a botanist studies plants.

49. *SANTA MARIA* : FRANCESO PINEDO :: *SPIRIT OF ST. LOUIS* : (a. Richard
Byrd **b. Charles Lindbergh** c. Clarence Chamberlain d. Albert "Putty" Reed)

(**b**) is correct because the *Spirit of St. Louis* is the plane in which Charles
Lindbergh made his first trans-Atlantic flight, as the *Santa- Maria* is Pinedo's
trans-Atlantic plane. (a) Richard Byrd is incorrect because his plane was the
America. (c) Chamberlain's plane was the *Columbia*. (d) Reed's plane was the
Lame Duck.

50. BARBARY COAST : NORTH AFRICA :: GOLD COAST : (a. Zimbabwe
b. Chad c. South Africa **d. Ghana**)

(**d**) is correct because Ghana was formerly called the Gold Coast as most of
Northern Africa was called the Barbary Coast. (a) is incorrect because Zimbabwe was formerly known as Rhodesia. (b) is incorrect because Chad is part of
the Central African Republic. (c) is incorrect because South Africa was formerly
called the Union of South Africa by the Boers who colonized it.

51. ENDOCRINOLOGIST : (a. teeth b. eyes **c. glands** d. intestines) ::
DERMATOLOGIST : SKIN

(**c**) is correct because glands are the specialty of an endocrinologist as the skin
is the area of specialization for the dermatologist. (a) is incorrect because a specialist dealing with teeth is an orthodontist. (b) is incorrect because a specialist
dealing with eyes is an ophthalmologist. (d) is incorrect because a specialist
dealing with intestines is a gastroenterologist.

52. STRATFORD-ON-AVON : SHAKESPEARE :: BERDICHEV, UKRAINE :
(**a. Conrad** b. Tolstoy c. Nabokov d. Solzhenitsyn)

(**a**) is correct because Conrad was born in Berdichev just as Shakespeare was
born in Stratford-on-Avon. (b) is incorrect because Tolstoy was born in Yasnaya
Polyana, Russia. (c) is incorrect because Vladamir Nabokov was born in St. Petersburg, Russia. (d) is incorrect because Solzhenitsyn was born in Kislovodsk,
Russia.

Explanations of Answers

53. JULIUS : REPUBLIC :: AUGUSTUS : (a. democracy b. aristocracy **c. empire** d. monarchy)

     (c) is correct because Augustus was the first emperor following the decline of Julius' Republic. (a), (b), and (d) are incorrect because technically none of these forms of government existed during Rome's Golden Age.

54. CORONATION : INAUGURATION :: (a. cardinal **b. monarch** c. bishop d. pope) : PRESIDENT

     (b) is correct because a coronation is the ceremony during which a monarch receives a crown just as an inauguration is the induction ceremony for a president. (a), (c), and (d) are incorrect because all of the induction ceremonies are religiously based, not political.

55. SAXOPHONE : (a. brass **b. woodwind** c. percussion d. horn) :: VIOLIN: STRING

     (b) is correct because a saxophone belongs to the family of instruments known as woodwinds just as the violin belongs to the family of instruments known as the stringed instruments. (a) is incorrect because brass instruments do not use a reed, as does the saxophone. (c) is incorrect because percussion instruments, such as drums, are struck to produce sounds. (d) is incorrect because horn is a general term for any breath-propelled instruments.

56. SONNET : (**a. 14** b. 16 c. 18 d. 10) :: HAIKU : THREE

     (a) is correct because there are 14 lines in a sonnet and three in a haiku. (b), (c), and (d) are irrelevant.

57. KAFKA : SAMSA :: CAMUS : (a. Gregor **b. Meursault** c. *The Stranger* d. Franz)

     (b) is the correct answer because Meursault is the last name of the main character in Albert Camus' famous novel *The Stranger*. (a) is incorrect because Gregor is the first name of Kafka's main character Samsa, in the novel *The Metamorphosis*. (c) is incorrect because it is the title of Camus' famous novel, not the character. (d) is incorrect because Franz is Kafka's first name.

58. APHRODITE : VENUS :: ZEUS : (a. Apollo b. Hecate **c. Jupiter** d. Mercury)

    (c) is the correct answer because *Aphrodite* is the Roman name for the Greek goddess Venus and Zeus is the Roman name for the Greek god Jupiter. (a) is incorrect because Apollo is a Roman, not Greek, god. (b) is incorrect because Hecate is the goddess of witchcraft. (d) is incorrect because *Mercury* is the Greek name for Hermes.

59. MICHELANGELO : LEONARDO :: (a. Dali b. Goya c. Cassatt **d. Monet**) : RENOIR

    (d) is correct because just as Michelangelo and Leonardo were both Renaissance artists, Monet and Renoir were both impressionist painters. (a) is incorrect because Dali was a surrealist, not an impressionist. (b) is incorrect because Goya was a nineteenth-century artist known for his bleak outlook and imagery. (c) is incorrect because Cassatt was an impressionist.

60. BOVARY : FLAUBERT :: CHATTERLEY : (**a. D.H. Lawrence** b. V.S. Naipaul c. E.M. Forster d. Wyndham Lewis)

    (a) is correct because D.H. Lawrence was the author of *Lady Chatterley's Lover*, whose main character was Lady Chatterley, and Madame Bovary was the main character of Gustave Flaubert's novel of the same name. (b) is incorrect because V.S. Naipaul was a post-colonial author and not the author of *Lady Chatterley's Lover*. (c) is incorrect because, although E.M. Forster was a contemporary of Lawrence's, he did not write *Lady Chatterley's Lover*. (d) is incorrect because Wyndham Lewis, also a contemporary of Lawrence's, did not write the novel either.

61. ELEANOR ROOSEVELT : FDR :: CLYTAEMNESTRA : (a. Lysistrata b. Antigone **c. Agammemnon** d. Caligula)

    (c) is the correct answer because Clytaemnestra and Agammemnon were husband and wife as were Eleanor and Franklin Roosevelt. (a) is incorrect because *Lysistrata* is a work by Aristophanes. (b) is incorrect because *Antigone* was a drama written by Sophocles. (d) is incorrect because Caligula was a Roman emperor, not a fictional character.

62.   THATCHER : MAJOR :: AUGUSTUS : (a. Claudius b. Julius **c. Tiberius**
d. Nero

(c) is correct because Tiberius succeeded Augustus as emperor of Rome as John
Major succeeded Margaret Thatcher as prime minister of England. (a) is incorrect because Claudius was the third Roman emperor after Augustus. (b) is incorrect because Julius was emperor before Augustus. (d) is incorrect because Nero
was the fourth emperor following Augustus.

63.   K2 : EVEREST :: (a. Australia **b. Africa** c. Antarctica d. South America) : ASIA

(b) is correct because K2 is the second-tallest mountain to Everest as Africa is
the second largest continent to Asia. (a) is incorrect because Australia, part of
Oceania, is not the second-largest continent; it is the smallest. (c) is incorrect
because Antarctica is the fifth-largest continent. (d) is incorrect because South
America is the fourth-largest continent.

64.   TWAIN : CLEMENS :: (**a. Eliot** b. Dennisen c. Woolf d. Sand) : EVANS

(a) is correct because George Eliot was the pen name used by Mary Ann Evans,
as Mark Twain was the pseudonym used by Samuel Clemens. (b) is incorrect
because Isak Dennisen's real name is Karen Blixon. (c) is incorrect because
Virginia Woolf wrote under her own name. (d) is incorrect because George Sand
was the pseudonym for Amandine-Aurore-Lucie Dupin.

65.   VAN GOGH : *LUST FOR LIFE* :: (a. Frost b. Dali **c. Bukowski** d. Kerouac) :
BARFLY

(c) is the correct answer because *Lust for Life* was the biographical movie of
Vincent van Gogh as *Barfly* was the life story of the poet Charles Bukowski. (a)
is incorrect because Robert Frost was not the subject of the movie *Barfly*. (b) is
incorrect because Salvador Dali was not the subject of the movie *Barfly*. (d) is
incorrect because Jack Kerouac was not the subject of the movie *Barfly*.

66.   BYRON : ROMANTICISM :: (**a. Melville** b. Salinger c. Eliot d. Shelley) :
TRANSCENDENTALISM

(a) is correct because Byron was part of the Romantic movement in England,
and Melville was part of the parallel transcendental movement in the U.S. (b) is
incorrect because Salinger was a contemporary American novelist. (c) is incorrect because Eliot was an early twentieth-century Christian poet. (d) is incorrect
because Shelley was another Romantic poet.

Explanations
of Answers

67. DEMOCRACY : CITIZENRY :: THEOCRACY : (**a. church** b. state c. populace d. monarch)

    (**a**) is correct because democracy refers to a political system governed through the citizenry. In a theocracy, the church is the government. (b) is incorrect because state rule is characteristic of a totalitarian government. (c) is incorrect because populace is analogous to citizenry. (d) is incorrect because a monarchy is ruled by a royal family.

68. URSINE : BEAR :: CERVINE : (**a. deer** b. reptile c. fowl d. mule)

    (**a**) is correct because *cervine* is the adjective pertaining to the characteristics of a deer. (b) is incorrect because *reptilian* is the adjective for any classification of reptile. (c) is incorrect because *fowl* is the noun referring to any of the various birds of the order of Galliformes. (d) is incorrect because a mule cannot be classified as having cervine qualities because it is a hybrid of an ass and a horse.

69. POSITIVE : NEGATIVE :: SHARP : (a. tone **b. flat** c. bass d. treble)

    (**b**) is correct because *sharp* and *flat* are opposites as *positive* and *negative* are. (a) is incorrect because *tone* is a general term referring to the pitch, quality, or duration of a sound. (c) is incorrect because *bass* refers to the lowest musical register of a tone. (d) is incorrect because *treble* refers to a high pitch.

70. CONSTANTINE : CHRISTIANITY :: ASOKA : (a. Taoism b. Jainism c. Hinduism **d. Buddhism**)

    (**d**) is the correct answer because Asoka converted to Buddhism allowing it to spread throughout India. (a) is incorrect because Taoism is a philosophy based on the teachings of Lao Tsu. (b) is incorrect because Jainism was founded by Vardhamana Maravira in 600 B.C.E. (c) is incorrect because Hinduism already existed in India at the time of Asoka's conversion.

71. FIBULA : TIBIA :: RADIUS : (a. sternum **b. ulna** c. femur d. mandibular)

    (**b**) is the correct answer because the ulna is the corollary to the radius in the arm as the fibula is the correlative bone to the tibia in the leg. (a) is incorrect because sternum is the center bone of the rib cage. (c) is incorrect because the femur, the longest bone in the body, is found in the thigh, not the arm. (d) is incorrect because the mandibular is the jawbone.

72. CLAUSTRO : CLOSED SPACES :: (a. geno b. hydro c. mastigo **d. xeno**) : STRANGERS

    (d) is correct because *xeno-* is the prefix for people. (a) is incorrect because *geno-* is the prefix for sex. (b) is incorrect because *hydro-* is the prefix for water. (c) is incorrect because *mastigo-* is the prefix for flogging.

73. MARAT : SADE :: JEFFERSON : (a. Robespierre b. Thoreau **c. Franklin** d. Hudson)

    (c) is correct because Thomas Jefferson and Benjamin Franklin were political contemporaries in the New World, as were Jean Paul Marat and the Marquis de Sade during the French Revolution. (a) is incorrect because Robespierre was a French Revolutionary. (b) is incorrect because Thoreau was a transcendentalist poet. (d) is incorrect because Henry Hudson was a New World explorer.

74. πr^2 : AREA :: $2\pi r$: (**a. circumference** b. width c. volume d. depth)

    (a) is correct because πr^2 is the formula for the area of a circle and $2\pi r$ is the formula for circumference. (b) is incorrect because width is also known as the diameter of a circle. (c) is incorrect because it refers to a three-dimensional object. (d) is incorrect because it also refers to a three- dimensional object.

75. CALORIE : (a. pressure b. volume **c. heat** d. force) :: ACRE : AREA

    (c) is correct because a calorie is a unit of heat as an acre is a unit of measurement for area. (a) is incorrect because pressure is measured in p.s.i. (pounds per square inch). (b) is incorrect because the volume of an object refers to its internal capacity. (d) is incorrect because force is measured in foot-pounds.

76. SUNUNU : (**a. Bush** b. Reagan c. Meese d. Ford) :: PANETTA : CLINTON

    (a) is the correct answer because John Sununu was chief of staff during George H. W. Bush's presidency as Leon Panetta was chief of staff during Bill Clinton's first term. (b) is incorrect because John Sununu was not Ronald Reagan's chief of staff, Edwin Meese was. (c) is incorrect because Edwin Meese was not a president. (d) is incorrect because John Sununu was not Gerald Ford's chief of staff.

77. Ag : SILVER :: Fe : (a. magnesium b. fermium **c. iron** d. zinc)

    (c) is correct because the periodic abbreviation for iron is Fe. (a) is incorrect because the periodic abbreviation for magnesium is Mg. (b) is incorrect because the periodic abbreviation for fermium is Fm. (d) is incorrect because the periodic abbreviation for zinc is Zn.

Explanations of Answers

Explanations of Answers

78. PLATO : THE ACADEMY :: GROPIUS : (**a. Bauhaus** b. Citadel c. Cambridge d. Montessori)

    (**a**) is correct because Gropius established the school known as Bauhaus and Plato created the Academy. (b) is incorrect because the Citadel is a United States military institute, not established by Gropius. (c) is incorrect because Cambridge is an English university also not established by Gropius. (d) is incorrect because Montessori, a school of pedagogical method, was not established by Gropius, but by the woman whose name it bears.

79. GODDARD : ROCKET :: BABBAGE: (a. Xerox b. fountain pen **c. computer** d. electric typewriter)

    (**c**) is correct because Goddard invented the liquid fueled rocket as Babbage invented the computer. (a) is incorrect because Xerox is a trade name for a photostatic copier. (b) is incorrect because the fountain pen was invented by Lewis Waterman. (d) is incorrect because the electric typewriter was invented by Thomas A. Edison.

80. NILE : AFRICA :: (**a. Yangtze** b. Hwang Ho c. Yellow d. Ashikaga) : CHINA

    (**a**) is correct because the Nile is the largest river in Africa as the Yangtze is the largest in China. (b) and (c) are incorrect because the Hwang Ho is another name for the Yellow River, which is the second largest river in China. (d) is incorrect because Ashikaga was a Shogun, not a river.

81. LIVY : POLIO :: TURNER : (a. Limerick b. Influenza **c. Prescott** d. Moffit)

    (**c**) is correct because Turner and Prescott were Old Western historians and contemporaries like the ancient Roman historians Livy and Polio. (a) is incorrect because Patricia Limerick is a contemporary historian, considered among the New Western historians. (b) is incorrect because influenza is a disease, not a historian. (d) is incorrect because Moffit is a contemporary New Jersey historian and anthropologist.

82. MAORI : NEW ZEALAND :: YANOMAMI : (a. Argentina b. Egypt c. Micronesia **d. Brazil**)

    (**d**) is correct because an indigenous tribe, known as the Yanomami, reside in the Brazilian rain forests. (a) is incorrect because although Argentina is a South American country, it is not home to the Yanomami tribe. (b) is incorrect because the Yanomami do not live in Egypt. (c) is incorrect because the Yanomami do not live in Micronesia.

83. PLANCK : (a. rocketry b. physics **c. quantum physics** d. calculus) :: EUCLID : GEOMETRY

    (c) is correct because Planck is considered the father of quantum physics as Euclid is considered the father of geometry. (a) is incorrect because Goddard is known to be the founding theorist of rocketry. (b) is incorrect because Newton is considered the father of the study of physics. (d) is incorrect because Pascal invented the discipline known as calculus.

84. PLUTO : HADES :: (**a. Vulcan** b. Frigg c. Loki d. Isis) : HEPHAESTUS

    (a) Pluto is the Roman equivalent of Hades, the Greek god of the underworld, just as Vulcan is the Roman equivalent of the Hephaestus, the Greek god of fire and craftsmanship. (b) is incorrect because Frigg is the Norse goddess of marriage. (c) is incorrect because Loki is the Norse god of mischief. (d) is incorrect because Isis is the Egyptian queen of the gods.

85. MONTICELLO : (a. Adams b. Franklin c. Jackson **d. Jefferson**) :: FALLING WATER : WRIGHT

    (d) is correct because Monticello was established by Thomas Jefferson, as Falling Water was established by Frank Lloyd Wright. (a) is incorrect because John Adams had nothing to do with Monticello. (b) is incorrect because although Benjamin Franklin was a contemporary of Jefferson, he resided in Philadelphia, not Virginia, home to Monticello. (c) is incorrect because Andrew Jackson did not have any association with Monticello.

86. PRADO : (a. Rome **b. Madrid** c. Santa Fe d. Prague) :: GUGGENHEIM : NEW YORK

    (b) is correct because the Prado museum is located in Madrid, Spain. (a) is incorrect because Rome, although full of museums, does not house the Prado. (c) is incorrect because the Prado is not located in Santa Fe, New Mexico. (d) is incorrect because the Prado is not located in Prague, in the Czech Republic.

87. FRANKLIN : AMERICA :: (a. Goethe b. Baudelaire c. Le Corbusier **d. Voltaire**) : FRANCE

    (d) is correct because Voltaire is considered the leading French Enlightenment theorist, similar to his American Enlightenment counterpart, Benjamin Franklin. (a) is incorrect because Goethe was a German author. (b) is incorrect because Baudelaire was a French symbolist poet. (c) is incorrect because Le Corbusier was an architect.

Explanations
of Answers

88. CONRAD : (a. Scotland b. England **c. Ukraine** d. Ireland) :: TWAIN : UNITED STATES

    (c) is correct because Joseph Conrad was born in Ukraine as Mark Twain was born in the United States. (a) is incorrect because Conrad was not born in Scotland. (b) is incorrect because Conrad was not born in England. (d) is incorrect because Conrad was not born in Ireland.

89. PHILATELIST : STAMPS :: LEPIDOPTERIST : (a. minerals **b. butterflies** c. coins d. clocks)

    (b) is correct because a collector of butterflies is known as a lepidopterist, whereas a collector of stamps is known as a philatelist. (a) is incorrect because a connoisseur of minerals and gems is a lapidist. (c) is incorrect because a numismatist collects coins and (d) is incorrect because a collector of clocks is called a chronometist.

90. GEORGE H. W. BUSH : RONALD REAGAN :: ANDREW JOHNSON : (a. John Q. Adams **b. Abe Lincoln** c. Rutherford Hayes d. Andrew Jackson)

    (b) is correct because Andrew Johnson was Abe Lincoln's vice president as George H. W. Bush was Ronald Reagan's. (a) is incorrect because Adams was never vice president. (c) is incorrect because Hayes was never vice president. (d) is incorrect because Jackson was never vice president.

91. HINDI : INDIA :: (**a. Spanish** b. English c. Portuguese d. French) : PERU

    (a) is correct because Spanish is the main language of Peru as Hindi is of India. (b), (c), and (d) are incorrect because although these languages are spoken throughout the world none of them are the official language of Peru.

92. RUPEE : INDIA :: LIRA : (a. Egypt b. Greece **c. Italy** d. Spain)

    (c) is correct because Italy's basic monetary unit is the lira, as the rupee is the basic monetary unit of India. (a) is incorrect because Egypt's monetary unit is based on the Egyptian pound. (b) is incorrect because the drachma is Greece's basic monetary unit. (d) is incorrect because Spain uses the peseta as its basic monetary unit.

93. BIBLIOPHILE : (a. bibles b. religion **c. books** d. music) :: ANGLOPHILE : ENGLAND

    (c) is correct because bibliophiles have an interest in books as Anglophiles have an interest in England. (a) is incorrect because a bible is a type of book a bibliophile may collect. (b) is incorrect because a theologian would study or have a love of religion. (d) is incorrect because audiophiles have an interest in music.

94. SLEUTH : (a. zebras b. horses c. worms **d. bears**) :: GAGGLE : GEESE

    (d) is correct because bears gather in sleuths as geese fly in gaggles. (a) and (b) are incorrect because both zebras and horses gather in herds. (c) is incorrect because the collective term for worms is *clew*.

95. GYNOPHOBE : WOMAN :: ANDROPHOBE : (**a. man** b. homosexuals c. germs d. animals)

    (a) is correct because men are feared by androphobes as women are feared by gynophobes. (b) is incorrect because *homophobia* is the fear of homosexuals. (c) is incorrect because *spermaphobia* is the fear of germs. (d) is incorrect because *zoophobia* is a fear of animals.

96. REFLECT : ABSORB :: CONVEX : (a. bend b. scatter c. converge **d. concave**)

    (d) is correct because *concave* and *convex* are opposite lens shapes, as they curve in and out, respectively. *Reflect* and *absorb* are opposite reactions of light on a surface. (a) is incorrect because light that is bent is said to be *refracted*. (b) is incorrect because *scattered* refers to a haphazard arrangement of light. (c) is incorrect because *converge* refers to light rays coming together.

97. SRI LANKA : CEYLON :: (a. Zimbabwe **b. Zaire** c. Ghana d. Uruguay) : BELGIAN CONGO

    (b) is correct because Zaire is the new name of the region formerly known as the Belgian Congo as Ceylon is the former name of Sri Lanka. (a) is incorrect because Zimbabwe is a country in Africa. (c) is incorrect because Ghana is a North African country. (d) is incorrect because Uruguay is a South American country.

98. MELODIOUS : CACOPHONOUS :: (a. dry b. petulant c. sweet **d. succulent**) : ARID

    (d) is correct because *succulent*, "filled with water," is the opposite of *arid*, "void of water." *Melodious* is "full harmony," whereas *cacophonous* refers to discordant sound. (a) is incorrect because *dry* is a synonym for arid. (b) is incorrect because *petulant* refers to something or someone ill-tempered. (c) is incorrect because *sweet* refers to having a sugary taste.

99. 2 : 8 :: 4 : (a. 12 b. 17 **c. 64** d. 24)

    (c) is the correct response because 4 is the cube root of 64 just as 2 is the cube root of 8. All other responses are incorrect.

100. AVIARY : BIRDS :: FORMICARY : (a. fish b. reptiles c. insects **d. ants**)

    (d) is the correct response because just as birds are kept in an aviary, another name for an ant farm is a formicary. (a) is incorrect because fish are kept in an aquarium. (b) and (c) are incorrect because insects and reptiles are kept in a terrarium.

Miller Analogies

two
Practice Test 2

Answer Sheet
Practice Test 2

1. Ⓐ Ⓑ Ⓒ Ⓓ
2. Ⓐ Ⓑ Ⓒ Ⓓ
3. Ⓐ Ⓑ Ⓒ Ⓓ
4. Ⓐ Ⓑ Ⓒ Ⓓ
5. Ⓐ Ⓑ Ⓒ Ⓓ
6. Ⓐ Ⓑ Ⓒ Ⓓ
7. Ⓐ Ⓑ Ⓒ Ⓓ
8. Ⓐ Ⓑ Ⓒ Ⓓ
9. Ⓐ Ⓑ Ⓒ Ⓓ
10. Ⓐ Ⓑ Ⓒ Ⓓ
11. Ⓐ Ⓑ Ⓒ Ⓓ
12. Ⓐ Ⓑ Ⓒ Ⓓ
13. Ⓐ Ⓑ Ⓒ Ⓓ
14. Ⓐ Ⓑ Ⓒ Ⓓ
15. Ⓐ Ⓑ Ⓒ Ⓓ
16. Ⓐ Ⓑ Ⓒ Ⓓ
17. Ⓐ Ⓑ Ⓒ Ⓓ
18. Ⓐ Ⓑ Ⓒ Ⓓ
19. Ⓐ Ⓑ Ⓒ Ⓓ
20. Ⓐ Ⓑ Ⓒ Ⓓ
21. Ⓐ Ⓑ Ⓒ Ⓓ
22. Ⓐ Ⓑ Ⓒ Ⓓ
23. Ⓐ Ⓑ Ⓒ Ⓓ
24. Ⓐ Ⓑ Ⓒ Ⓓ
25. Ⓐ Ⓑ Ⓒ Ⓓ
26. Ⓐ Ⓑ Ⓒ Ⓓ
27. Ⓐ Ⓑ Ⓒ Ⓓ
28. Ⓐ Ⓑ Ⓒ Ⓓ
29. Ⓐ Ⓑ Ⓒ Ⓓ
30. Ⓐ Ⓑ Ⓒ Ⓓ
31. Ⓐ Ⓑ Ⓒ Ⓓ
32. Ⓐ Ⓑ Ⓒ Ⓓ
33. Ⓐ Ⓑ Ⓒ Ⓓ
34. Ⓐ Ⓑ Ⓒ Ⓓ

35. Ⓐ Ⓑ Ⓒ Ⓓ
36. Ⓐ Ⓑ Ⓒ Ⓓ
37. Ⓐ Ⓑ Ⓒ Ⓓ
38. Ⓐ Ⓑ Ⓒ Ⓓ
39. Ⓐ Ⓑ Ⓒ Ⓓ
40. Ⓐ Ⓑ Ⓒ Ⓓ
41. Ⓐ Ⓑ Ⓒ Ⓓ
42. Ⓐ Ⓑ Ⓒ Ⓓ
43. Ⓐ Ⓑ Ⓒ Ⓓ
44. Ⓐ Ⓑ Ⓒ Ⓓ
45. Ⓐ Ⓑ Ⓒ Ⓓ
46. Ⓐ Ⓑ Ⓒ Ⓓ
47. Ⓐ Ⓑ Ⓒ Ⓓ
48. Ⓐ Ⓑ Ⓒ Ⓓ
49. Ⓐ Ⓑ Ⓒ Ⓓ
50. Ⓐ Ⓑ Ⓒ Ⓓ
51. Ⓐ Ⓑ Ⓒ Ⓓ
52. Ⓐ Ⓑ Ⓒ Ⓓ
53. Ⓐ Ⓑ Ⓒ Ⓓ
54. Ⓐ Ⓑ Ⓒ Ⓓ
55. Ⓐ Ⓑ Ⓒ Ⓓ
56. Ⓐ Ⓑ Ⓒ Ⓓ
57. Ⓐ Ⓑ Ⓒ Ⓓ
58. Ⓐ Ⓑ Ⓒ Ⓓ
59. Ⓐ Ⓑ Ⓒ Ⓓ
60. Ⓐ Ⓑ Ⓒ Ⓓ
61. Ⓐ Ⓑ Ⓒ Ⓓ
62. Ⓐ Ⓑ Ⓒ Ⓓ
63. Ⓐ Ⓑ Ⓒ Ⓓ
64. Ⓐ Ⓑ Ⓒ Ⓓ
65. Ⓐ Ⓑ Ⓒ Ⓓ
66. Ⓐ Ⓑ Ⓒ Ⓓ
67. Ⓐ Ⓑ Ⓒ Ⓓ
68. Ⓐ Ⓑ Ⓒ Ⓓ

69. Ⓐ Ⓑ Ⓒ Ⓓ
70. Ⓐ Ⓑ Ⓒ Ⓓ
71. Ⓐ Ⓑ Ⓒ Ⓓ
72. Ⓐ Ⓑ Ⓒ Ⓓ
73. Ⓐ Ⓑ Ⓒ Ⓓ
74. Ⓐ Ⓑ Ⓒ Ⓓ
75. Ⓐ Ⓑ Ⓒ Ⓓ
76. Ⓐ Ⓑ Ⓒ Ⓓ
77. Ⓐ Ⓑ Ⓒ Ⓓ
78. Ⓐ Ⓑ Ⓒ Ⓓ
79. Ⓐ Ⓑ Ⓒ Ⓓ
80. Ⓐ Ⓑ Ⓒ Ⓓ
81. Ⓐ Ⓑ Ⓒ Ⓓ
82. Ⓐ Ⓑ Ⓒ Ⓓ
83. Ⓐ Ⓑ Ⓒ Ⓓ
84. Ⓐ Ⓑ Ⓒ Ⓓ
85. Ⓐ Ⓑ Ⓒ Ⓓ
86. Ⓐ Ⓑ Ⓒ Ⓓ
87. Ⓐ Ⓑ Ⓒ Ⓓ
88. Ⓐ Ⓑ Ⓒ Ⓓ
89. Ⓐ Ⓑ Ⓒ Ⓓ
90. Ⓐ Ⓑ Ⓒ Ⓓ
91. Ⓐ Ⓑ Ⓒ Ⓓ
92. Ⓐ Ⓑ Ⓒ Ⓓ
93. Ⓐ Ⓑ Ⓒ Ⓓ
94. Ⓐ Ⓑ Ⓒ Ⓓ
95. Ⓐ Ⓑ Ⓒ Ⓓ
96. Ⓐ Ⓑ Ⓒ Ⓓ
97. Ⓐ Ⓑ Ⓒ Ⓓ
98. Ⓐ Ⓑ Ⓒ Ⓓ
99. Ⓐ Ⓑ Ⓒ Ⓓ
100. Ⓐ Ⓑ Ⓒ Ⓓ

Practice Test 2

TIME: 50 Minutes   **LENGTH:** 100 Analogies

DIRECTIONS: Read each of the following analogies carefully, and choose the BEST answer to each item. Fill in your responses in the answer sheets provided.

Note: The Miller Analogies Test consists of 120 questions to be completed in 60 minutes. Twenty of these questions are experimental items, which are not scored and thus not reflected in this practice test.

1. PARTHENON : (a. Greece b. Athens c. Paris d. Dresden) :: SISTINE CHAPEL : ROME

2. H_2O : WATER :: CO_2 : (a. carbon dioxide b. carbon monoxide c. ammonia d. salt)

3. HENRY DAVID THOREAU : *CIVIL DISOBEDIENCE* :: RALPH WALDO EMERSON : (a. *Self-Reliance* b. *The Tell-Tale Heart* c. *Walden* d. *Leaves of Grass*)

4. AGGRAVATE : EXACERBATE :: MITIGATE : (a. legislate b. assuage c. abrachiate d. dissociate)

5. H : HYDROGEN :: Fe : (a. iron b. fluorine c. nickel d. sodium)

6. (a. Plantae b. Protista c. Chiroptera d. Fungi) : MUSHROOM :: ANIMALIA : MOUSE

7. FRANK LLOYD WRIGHT : (a. author b. sculptor c. architect d. choreographer) :: MICHELANGELO : PAINTER

8. HANDEL : *MESSIAH* :: ORFF : (a. *Carmina Burana* b. *Pomp and Circumstance* c. *The Nutcracker Suite* d. *The Rite of Spring*)

9. BARBARIC : (a. civilized b. savage c. content d. enraged) :: DIVINE : SACRED

10. PRESIDENT : DEMOCRACY :: (a. dictator b. emperor c. Parliament d. king) : MONARCHY

11. (a. cylinder b. circle c. triangle d. oval) : SQUARE :: πr^2 : L × H

12. MULTIPLICATION : DIVISION :: INTEGRATION : (a. substitution b. function c. equation d. derivation)

13. OCTAGON : (a. dodecahedron b. pentagon c. decagon d. polygon) :: 8 : 12

14. 3, 3 : 9, 9 :: –4, –4 : (a. 16, 16 b. –16, –16 c. 8, 8 d. –8, –8)

15. sin 90 degrees : 1 :: (a. cos 90 degrees b. tan 90 degrees c. cos 180 degrees d. tan 45 degrees) : 0

16. CRESCENDO : LOUDER :: (a. pianissimo b. fortissimo c. forte d. diminuendo) : SOFTER

17. LEONARDO DA VINCI : RENAISSANCE :: REMBRANDT : (a. baroque b. classical c. romantic d. impressionist)

18. ADAGIO : (a. largo b. allegretto c. presto d. mezzo-piano :: VIVACE : ALLEGRO

19. BEETHOVEN : *EROICA* :: MOZART : (a. *Hebrides Overture* b. *Rigoletto* c. *Don Giovanni* d. *Nocturne*)

20. TEMPO : SPEED :: BEAT : (a. metronome b. rhythm c. percussion d. meter)

21. *THE GRAPES OF WRATH* : (a. Steinbeck b. Dos Passos c. Hesse d. Heller) :: *FOR WHOM THE BELL TOLLS* : HEMINGWAY

22. HISTORY : RICHARD III :: (a. comedy b. romance c. tragedy d. fantasy) : ROMEO AND JULIET

23. MARX : COMMUNISM :: MUSSOLINI : (a. nazism b. nationalism c. fascism d. socialism)

24. RATIOCINATE : LOGICAL :: (a. deaminate b. fulminate c. sophistic
    d. monarchistic) : IRRATIONAL

25. MAHABHARATA : INDIAN :: GILGAMESH : (a. French b. English
    c. Sumerian d. Roman)

26. PLATO : *REPUBLIC* :: (a. More b. Socrates c. Coleridge d. Huxley) : *UTOPIA*

27. HENRY VIII : (a. 1400s b. 1500s c. 1600s d. 1700s) :: MOZART : 1700s

28. NIGHT : NOCTURNAL :: (a. evening b. morning c. day d. noon) : DIURNAL

29. AMERICA'S CUP : (a. soccer b. steeplechase c. yachting d. gymnastics) ::
    STANLEY CUP : HOCKEY

30. RIGHT TO KEEP AND BEAR ARMS : SECOND AMENDMENT :: RIGHT
    TO JURY TRIAL : (a. Fourth Amendment b. Fifth Amendment c. Sixth
    Amendment d. Seventh Amendment)

31. NOBEL PEACE PRIZE : MARTIN LUTHER KING, JR. :: (a. Nobel Prize in
    Physics b. Nobel Prize in Chemistry c. Nobel Prize in Medicine d. Nobel Prize
    in Literature) : IRENE JOILET-CURIE

32. NEIL ARMSTRONG : LUNAR LANDING :: CHUCK YEAGER : (a. first to
    break the speed of sound b. first to break the speed of light c. first American in
    space d. first in orbit)

33. IDAHO : ID :: MONTANA : (a. MN b. MO c. MS d. MT)

34. WASHINGTON : UNITED STATES :: (a. Berlin b. Munich c. Vienna
    d. Hamburg) : GERMANY

35. MOSCOW : RUSSIA :: (a. Perth b. Melbourne c. Sydney d. Canberra) :
    AUSTRALIA

36. ABOLITION OF SLAVERY : THIRTEENTH AMENDMENT :: WOMEN'S
    SUFFRAGE : (a. Eighteenth Amendment b. Nineteenth Amendment c. Twentieth
    Amendment d. Thirty-first Amendment)

37. (a. Roosevelt b. Coolidge c. Taft d. Ford) : TRUMAN :: WILSON : HARDING

38. QUANTUM THEORY : (a. Galileo b. Newton c. Planck d. Ramsay) ::
    RELATIVITY : EINSTEIN

39. WALT WHITMAN : *SONG OF MYSELF* :: NATHANIEL HAWTHORNE :
    (a. *Rappaccini's Daughter* b. *The Raven* c. *Gulliver's Travels* d. *Billy Budd*)

40. CASSIUS : (a. Polonius b. Laertes c. Brutus d. MacDuff) :: ANTONIO :
    OLIVIA

41. GERSHWIN : *RHAPSODY IN BLUE* :: BERNSTEIN : (a. *Adagio for Strings*
    b. *Porgy and Bess* c. *The Devil and Daniel Webster* d. *West Side Story*)

42. SOPHOCLES : *OEDIPUS REX* :: EURIPIDES : (a. *Prometheus Bound*
    b. *Lysistrata* c. *Medea* d. *Antigone*)

43. (a. Anton Chekhov b. Victor Hugo c. Oscar Wilde d. Henrik Ibsen) : *THE
    THREE SISTERS* :: GEORGE BERNARD SHAW : *SAINT JOAN*

44. KAFKA : *METAMORPHOSIS* :: (a. Coleridge b. Wordsworth c. Eliot
    d. Stoppard) : *THE WASTE LAND*

45. (a. Aesculapius b. Apollo c. Nike d. Selene) : MEDICINE :: CHAOS : VOID

46. (a. Tyche b. Thanatos c. Nyx d. Athena) : DEATH :: EROS : LOVE

47. MARS : WAR :: (a. Psyche b. Salacia c. Somnus d. Venus) : LOVE

48. CHROM : (a. motion b. color c. disease d. pain) :: DERM : SKIN

49. (a. anti b. aero c. acro d. arch) : TOP :: ANDRO : MAN

50. ETHNO : RACE :: (a. cardio b. crypto c. chrono d. choreo) : DANCE

51. (a. pronoun b. preposition, c. adjective d. article) : NOUN :: ADVERB : VERB

52. GERMAN SURRENDER : V-E DAY :: JAPANESE SURRENDER : (a. V-J Day
    b. Bastille Day c. Veterans Day d. Pearl Harbor Day)

53. LIE : LAY :: LAY : (a. laid b. laying c. lying d. lain)

54. WORK : *W=fd* :: VELOCITY : (a. *v=d/t* b. *V=fw* c. *Wt=mg* d. *R=V/I*)

55. (a. yellow b. red c. green d. indigo) : ORANGE :: BLUE : VIOLET

56. GINSBERG : *HOWL* :: (a. Burroughs b. Kesey c. Kerouac d. DiPrima) : *ON THE ROAD*

57. SYRIA : ASIA :: (a. Panama b. Colombia c. Venezuela d. Ecuador) : NORTH AMERICA

58. HEMI : (a. close b. under c. half d. outside) :: ANTE : BEFORE

59. $\frac{1}{2}$: 50% :: $\frac{2}{5}$: (a. 30% b. 35% c. 40% d. 45%)

60. PHENOTYPE : (a. molecular structure b. physical appearance c. heredity d. natural selection) :: GENOTYPE : GENETIC COMPOSITION

61. ELECTRON : NEGATIVE :: NEUTRON : (a. positive b. variable c. proton d. none)

62. C : CELSIUS :: (a. F b. f c. fh d. Fh) : FAHRENHEIT

63. OZ : OUNCE :: (a. tsp b. tbsp c. tasp d. pt) : TABLESPOON

64. 32 DEGREES FAHRENHEIT : 0 DEGREES CELSIUS :: (a. 100 degrees Fahrenheit b. 125 degrees Fahrenheit c. 212 degrees Fahrenheit d. 225 degrees Fahrenheit) : 100 DEGREES CELSIUS

65. BASEBALL : 9 :: FOOTBALL : (a. 9 b. 10 c. 11 d. 12)

66. VITAMIN A : CAROTENE :: (a. thiamine b. riboflavin c. niacin d. ascorbic acid) : VITAMIN C

67. FULMINATE : (a. cajole b. denounce c. exemplify d. placate) :: COMMEND : PRAISE

68. UNIX : (a. programming language b. computer system c. operating system d. peripheral) :: FORTRAN : LANGUAGE

69. ROSENCRANTZ : (a. Horatio b. Regan c. Gloucester d. Sebastian) :: DUNCAN : MALCOLM

70. DANTE : *INFERNO* :: (a. Byron b. Milton c. Wordsworth d. Shelley) : *PARADISE LOST*

71. HELLER : *CATCH-22* :: (a. Updike b. Pynchon c. Irving d. Kerouac) : *GRAVITY'S RAINBOW*

72. 8 : (a. 2 b. 4 c. 6 d. 8) :: DIAMETER : RADIUS

73. 2^3 : 3^3 :: 8 : (a. 18 b. 24 c. 27 d. 36)

74. CAT : KITTEN :: KANGAROO : (a. wallaby b. joey c. cub d. marsupial)

75. EAGLE : (a. feline b. equine c. bovine d. aquiline) :: DOG : CANINE

76. ANTELOPE : HERBIVORE :: OWL : (a. carnivore b. omnivore c. avian d. nocturnal)

77. KENNEDY : JOHNSON :: EISENHOWER : (a. Nixon b. Ford c. Kissinger d. Humphrey)

78. TOKYO : JAPAN :: (a. Tripoli b. Baghdad c. Aden d. Riyadh) : IRAQ

79. (a. Dallas b. Houston c. Fort Worth d. Austin) : TEXAS :: DENVER : COLORADO

80. SALT LAKE CITY : UTAH :: (a. Birmingham b. Huntsville c. Montgomery d. Tuscaloosa) : ALABAMA

81. BECOME : (a. became b. becoming c. becomed d. become) :: SHRINK : SHRANK

82. AURAL : ORAL :: EAR : (a. eyes b. nose c. mouth d. hand)

83. *FLYER* : WRIGHT BROTHERS :: (a. *Beagle* b. Galapagos c. Explorer d. *Calypso*) : DARWIN

84. SLOOP : 1 :: BARQUE : (a. 1 b. 2 c. 4 d. 7)

85. ACROPHOBIA : (a. blood b. heights c. food d. death) :: HYDROPHOBIA : WATER

86. REGICIDE : (a. king b. president c. friend d. child) :: PATRICIDE : FATHER

87. (a. feet b. yards c. inches d. meters) : MILE :: 1,760 : 1

88. (a. registration b. license c. patent d. statute) : INVENTION :: COPYRIGHT : NOVEL

89. HUMERUS : ARM :: (a. tarsus b. sternum c. clavicle d. femur) : LEG

90. FRONTAL LOBE : (a. touch b. speech c. memory d. hearing) :: OCCIPITAL LOBE : VISION

91. (a. teleologist b. theologist c. thanatologist d. zoologist) : NATURE :: ICTHYOLOGIST : FISH

92. *BEOWULF* : GRENDEL :: *HAMLET* : (a. Ophelia b. Polonius c. Gertrude d. Claudius)

93. CHROMOSOME : (a. gene b. RNA c. DNA d. enzyme) :: CELL : NUCLEUS

94. ORWELL : *1984* :: (a. Thoreau b. Emerson c. Burgess d. Huxley) : *BRAVE NEW WORLD*

95. (a. Coleridge b. Ibsen c. Tolstoy d. Wordsworth) : *KUBLA KHAN* :: YEATS : *SAILING TO BYZANTIUM*

96. SARTRE : (a. *A Streetcar Named Desire* b. *Our Town* c. *The Purloined Letter* d. *No Exit*) :: JOYCE : *ULYSSES*

97. BIBLE : CHRISTIANITY :: (a. Bhagavad-Gita b. New Testament c. Koran d. Talmud) : ISLAM

98. (a. *caveat emptor* b. *avant-garde* c. *primus inter pares* d. *tabula rasa*) : LET THE BUYER BEWARE :: *COGITO ERGO SUM* : I THINK, THEREFORE I AM

99. ANDROUS : MAN :: DENDRON : (a. movement b. blood c. skin d. tree)

100. I THINK, THEREFORE I AM : RENE DESCARTES :: THERE IS ONLY ONE GOOD, KNOWLEDGE, AND ONE EVIL, IGNORANCE : (a. Plato b. Socrates c. Machiavelli d. Nietzsche)

Answer Key
Practice Test 2

1. (b)	26. (a)	51. (c)	76. (a)
2. (a)	27. (b)	52. (a)	77. (a)
3. (a)	28. (c)	53. (a)	78. (b)
4. (b)	29. (c)	54. (a)	79. (d)
5. (a)	30. (d)	55. (b)	80. (c)
6. (d)	31. (b)	56. (c)	81. (a)
7. (c)	32. (a)	57. (a)	82. (c)
8. (a)	33. (d)	58. (c)	83. (a)
9. (b)	34. (a)	59. (c)	84. (c)
10. (d)	35. (d)	60. (b)	85. (b)
11. (b)	36. (b)	61. (d)	86. (a)
12. (d)	37. (a)	62. (a)	87. (b)
13. (a)	38. (c)	63. (b)	88. (c)
14. (a)	39. (a)	64. (c)	89. (d)
15. (a)	40. (c)	65. (c)	90. (b)
16. (d)	41. (d)	66. (d)	91. (a)
17. (a)	42. (c)	67. (b)	92. (d)
18. (a)	43. (a)	68. (c)	93. (a)
19. (c)	44. (c)	69. (a)	94. (d)
20. (b)	45. (a)	70. (b)	95. (a)
21. (a)	46. (b)	71. (b)	96. (d)
22. (c)	47. (d)	72. (b)	97. (c)
23. (c)	48. (b)	73. (c)	98. (a)
24. (c)	49. (c)	74. (b)	99. (d)
25. (c)	50. (d)	75. (d)	100. (b)

Explanations
of Answers

Explanations of Answers
Practice Test 2

1. PARTHENON : (a. Greece **b. Athens** c. Paris d. Dresden) :: SISTINE CHAPEL : ROME

   (b) is correct because the Parthenon is in Athens as the Sistine Chapel is in Rome. All other choices are irrelevant.

2. H_2O : WATER :: CO_2 : (**a. carbon dioxide** b. carbon monoxide c. ammonia d. salt)

   (a) is correct because H_2O is the chemical symbol for water just as CO_2 is the chemical symbol for carbon dioxide. Carbon monoxide (b) is CO, ammonia (c) is NH_3, and salt (d) is NaCl.

3. HENRY DAVID THOREAU : *CIVIL DISOBEDIENCE* :: RALPH WALDO EMERSON : (**a. *Self-Reliance*** b. *The Tell-Tale Heart* c. *Walden* d. *Leaves of Grass*)

   (a) is correct because Henry David Thoreau wrote *Civil Disobedience* just as Ralph Waldo Emerson wrote *Self-Reliance*. (b) is incorrect because Edgar Allan Poe wrote *The Tell-Tale Heart*. (c) is wrong because Henry David Thoreau wrote *Walden*, and (d) is incorrect because Walt Whitman wrote *Leaves of Grass*.

4. AGGRAVATE : EXACERBATE :: MITIGATE : (a. legislate **b. assuage** c. abrachiate d. dissociate)

   (b) is the correct response because *aggravate* and *exacerbate* are synonyms meaning "to worsen," just as *assuage* is a synonym for *mitigate* which means "to lessen or make milder." (a) is incorrect because *legislate* means "to create laws." An *abrachiate* (c) is an animal without gills, and *dissociate* (d) means "to separate."

5. H : HYDROGEN :: Fe : (**a. iron** b. fluorine c. nickel d. sodium)

   (a) is correct because H is the chemical symbol for hydrogen just as Fe is the chemical symbol for iron. (b) is incorrect because flourine is F; (c) is wrong because nickel is Ni; and (d) is incorrect because sodium is Na.

6. (a. Plantae b. Protista c. Chiroptera **d. Fungi**) : MUSHROOM :: ANIMALIA : MOUSE

   (d) is the correct response because a mushroom belongs to the kingdom Fungi as a mouse belongs to the kingdom Animalia. Plantae (a) refers to green plants, Protista (b) refers to acellular or unicellular organisms, and Chiroptera (c) refers to bats.

7. FRANK LLOYD WRIGHT : (a. author b. sculptor **c. architect** d. choreographer) :: MICHELANGELO : PAINTER

   (c) is correct because Frank Lloyd Wright was an architect just as Michelangelo was a painter.

8. HANDEL : *MESSIAH* :: ORFF : (**a. *Carmina Burana*** b. *Pomp and Circumstance* c. *The Nutcracker Suite* d. *The Rite of Spring*)

   (a) is the correct answer because Handel composed the *Messiah* as Orff composed *Carmina Burana*. (b) is incorrect because Elgar composed *Pomp and Circumstance*; (c) is incorrect because Tchaikovsky composed *The Nutcracker Suite*; and (d) is wrong because Stravinsky composed *The Rite of Spring*.

9. BARBARIC : (a. civilized **b. savage** c. content d. enraged) :: DIVINE : SACRED

   (b) is the correct response because *barbaric* is a synonym for *savage* just as divine is a synonym for *sacred*. (a) is not the correct choice because *civilized* means "refined." (c) is incorrect because *content* means "relaxed," and (d) is incorrect because *enraged* means "angry."

10. PRESIDENT : DEMOCRACY :: (a. dictator b. emperor c. Parliament **d. king**) : MONARCHY

    (d) is the correct choice because a president is the leader of a democracy in the same way that a king is the leader of a monarchy. (a) is incorrect because a dictator is a tyrannical ruler. An emperor (b) rules an empire, and Parliament (c) is the national legislature in England.

11. (a. cylinder **b. circle** c. triangle d. oval) : SQUARE :: πr^2 : L $\times$ H

    (b) is correct because the area of a circle is given by πr^2 just as the area of a square is given by L $\times$ H.

12. MULTIPLICATION : DIVISION :: INTEGRATION : (a. substitution
b. function c. equation **d. derivation**)

    (d) is the correct response because multiplication is the mathematical opposite
    of division just as integration is the mathematical opposite of derivation.

13. OCTAGON : (**a. dodecahedron** b. pentagon c. decagon d. polygon) :: 8 : 12

    (a) is the correct choice because an octagon has 8 sides and a dodecahedron has
    12 sides. A pentagon (b) has 5 sides, a decagon (c) has 10 sides, and a polygon
    (d) is a closed figure of 3 or more sides.

14. 3, 3 : 9, 9 :: –4, –4 : (**a. 16,** 16 b. –16, –16 c. 8, 8 d. –8, –8)

    (a) is the correct response because coordinate point 9, 9 is the square of coordi-
    nate point 3, 3 just as coordinate point 16, 16 is the square of coordinate point
    –4, –4. All other answer choices are irrelevant.

15. sin 90 degrees : 1 :: (**a. cos 90 degrees** b. tan 90 degrees c. cos 180 degrees
    d. tan 45 degrees) : 0

    (a) is correct because the sin of 90 degrees is 1 as the cos 90 degrees is 0. All
    other answer choices are irrelevant.

16. CRESCENDO : LOUDER :: (a. pianissimo b. fortissimo c. forte
    d. diminuendo) : SOFTER

    (d) is the correct response because *crescendo* means "to become louder" while
    diminuendo means "to become softer." *Pianissimo* (a) means "very soft or qui-
    et," and *fortissimo* (b) and *forte* (c) both mean "very loud."

17. LEONARDO DA VINCI : RENAISSANCE :: REMBRANDT : (**a. baroque**
    b. classical c. romantic d. impressionist)

    (a) is correct because Leonardo da Vinci was a Renaissance painter as Rem-
    brandt was a baroque painter. (b), (c), and (d) are incorrect because Rembrandt
    did not paint in these styles.

18. ADAGIO : (**a. largo** b. allegretto c. presto d. mezzo-piano :: VIVACE :
    ALLEGRO

    (a) is the correct answer because largo is of a slower tempo than adagio, as alle-
    gro is of a slower tempo than vivace. In order, from slowest to fastest tempo, the
    terms are: largo, grave, adagio, andante, moderato, allegretto, allegro, vivace,
    presto, and prestissimo.

19. BEETHOVEN : *EROICA* :: MOZART : (a. *Hebrides Overture* b. *Rigoletto*
    c. *Don Giovanni* d. *Nocturne*)

    (c) is the correct response because Beethoven wrote *Eroica* also called Symphony No. 3, just as Mozart wrote *Don Giovanni*. (a), (b), and (d) are incorrect because Mozart did not compose these works.

20. TEMPO : SPEED :: BEAT : (a. metronome **b. rhythm** c. percussion d. meter)

    (b) is correct because *tempo* is a musical term referring to speed as *beat* is a musical term referring to rhythm. A metronome (a) is a machine used for keeping rhythm; *percussion* (c) refers generally to the percussion section of an orchestra; and *meter* (d) refers to rhythm as it relates to poetry.

21. *THE GRAPES OF WRATH* : (**a. Steinbeck** b. Dos Passos c. Hesse d. Heller) ::
    FOR WHOM THE BELL TOLLS : HEMINGWAY

    (a) is the correct response because Steinbeck wrote *The Grapes of Wrath* and Hemingway wrote *For Whom the Bell Tolls*. (b) is incorrect because Dos Passos' most famous work is *Manhattan Transfer*. (c) is incorrect because Hesse's most famous work is *Siddhartha*, and (d) is incorrect because Joseph Heller's most famous work is *Catch 22*.

22. HISTORY : RICHARD III :: (a. comedy b. romance **c. tragedy** d. fantasy) :
    ROMEO AND JULIET

    (c) is the correct choice because William Shakespeare's play, *Richard III,* is a history just as Shakespeare's play *Romeo and Juliet* is a tragedy. Generally, Shakespeare's plays are divided into four catgories: the comedies, the histories, the romances, and the tragedies.

23. MARX : COMMUNISM :: MUSSOLINI : (a. nazism b. nationalism **c. fascism**
    d. socialism)

    (c) is the correct response because Marx founded modern communism just as Mussolini founded modern fascism. Nationalism (b) refers to extreme support of one's own country. Hitler founded Nazism (a), and Socialism (d) is an economic system used throughout the world.

Explanations
of Answers

24. RATIOCINATE : LOGICAL :: (a. deaminate b. fulminate **c. sophistic** d. monarchistic) : IRRATIONAL

(c) is the correct response because to ratiocinate is to think logically just as sophistic thinking is irrational. Deaminate (a) is to remove an amino group from an organic compound; fulminate (b) is to denounce; and monarchistic (d) refers to belief in a monarchy.

25. MAHABHARATA : INDIAN :: GILGAMESH : (a. French b. English **c. Sumerian** d. Roman)

(c) Mahabharata is an Indian epic just as Gilgamesh is a Sumerian epic. All other choices are irrelevant.

26. PLATO : *REPUBLIC* :: (**a. More** b. Socrates c. Coleridge d. Huxley) : *UTOPIA*

(a) is the correct response because Plato wrote the *Republic* just as Thomas More wrote *Utopia*. (b) is incorrect because Socrates produced no written works, but his philosophy is understood through the writings of Plato. Coleridge (c) is incorrect because he was a Romantic poet and literary critic, famous for long form poems such as *Christabel* and *Rime of the Ancient Mariner*. (d) is incorrect because Aldous Huxley's most famous work is *Brave New World*.

27. HENRY VIII : (a. 1400s **b. 1500s** c. 1600s d. 1700s) :: MOZART : 1700s

(b) is the right answer because King Henry VIII lived during the 1500s just as Mozart lived during the 1700s.

28. NIGHT : NOCTURNAL :: (a. evening b. morning **c. day** d. noon) : DIURNAL

(c) is the correct response because *nocturnal* refers to an animal active mainly at night as *diurnal* refers to an animal active mainly during the day.

29. AMERICA'S CUP : (a. soccer b. steeplechase **c. yachting** d. gymnastics) :: STANLEY CUP : HOCKEY

(c) is the correct response because the America's Cup is the championship prize for yachting just as the Stanley Cup is the championship prize for hockey. (a) is incorrect because the World Cup is the championship prize for soccer. (b) is incorrect because a steeplechase is an equestrian event. While gymnastics (d) is a competitive event it is not associated with the America's Cup.

30. RIGHT TO KEEP AND BEAR ARMS : SECOND AMENDMENT :: RIGHT TO JURY TRIAL : (a. Fourth Amendment b. Fifth Amendment c. Sixth Amendment **d. Seventh Amendment**)

    (d) is the correct response because the Second Amendment is the right to keep and bear arms just as the Seventh Amendment is the right to a jury trial. The Fourth Amendment (a) guarantees against unlawful search and seizure, and the Fifth Amendment (b) allows defendants to refuse to testify against themselves. The Sixth Amendment (c) guarantees a speedy trial.

31. NOBEL PEACE PRIZE : MARTIN LUTHER KING, JR. :: (a. Nobel Prize in Physics **b. Nobel Prize in Chemistry** c. Nobel Prize in Medicine d. Nobel Prize in Literature) : IRENE JOILET-CURIE

    (b) is correct because Martin Luther King, Jr., won the Nobel Peace Prize just as Irene Joliet-Curie won the Nobel Prize in Chemistry. (a), (c), and (d) are incorrect because Irene Joliet-Curie did not win these prizes.

32. NEIL ARMSTRONG : LUNAR LANDING :: CHUCK YEAGER : (**a. first to break the speed of sound** b. first to break the speed of light c. first American in space d. first in orbit)

    (a) is the correct response because Neil Armstrong was the first person to walk on the moon just as Chuck Yeager was the first person to break the speed of sound. (b) is incorrect because breaking the speed of light remains an impossibility. (c) is incorrect because the first American in space was Alan Shepard. (d) is incorrect because the first person in orbit was Yuri Gagarin.

33. IDAHO : ID :: MONTANA : (a. MN b. MO c. MS **d. MT**)

    (d) is correct because the postal abbreviation for Idaho is ID just as the postal abbreviation for Montana is MT. MN (a) is Minnesota, MO (b) is Missouri, and MS (c) is Mississippi.

34. WASHINGTON : UNITED STATES :: (**a. Berlin** b. Munich c. Vienna d. Hamburg) : GERMANY

    (a) is the correct response because Washington is the capital of the United States just as Berlin is the capital of Germany. (b) and (d) are incorrect because neither Munich nor Hamburg is a capital city. (c) is incorrect because Vienna is in another country.

Explanations
of Answers

35. MOSCOW : RUSSIA :: (a. Perth b. Melbourne c. Sydney **d. Canberra**) :
AUSTRALIA

    (d) Moscow is the capital of Russia as Canberra is the capital of Australia. Perth, Melbourne, and Sydney are all major cities in Australia, but none is the nation's capital.

36. ABOLITION OF SLAVERY : THIRTEENTH AMENDMENT :: WOMEN'S
SUFFRAGE : (a. Eighteenth Amendment **b. Nineteenth Amendment**
c. Twentieth Amendment d. Thirty-first Amendment)

    (b) The Thirteenth Amendment abolished slavery just as the Nineteenth Amendment gave women the right to vote. The Eighteenth Amendment (a) prohibited the use, manufacture, and sale of alcohol. The Twentieth Amendment (c) changed the date of inauguration. (d) is incorrect because there are 26 amendments to the Constitution.

37. (**a. Roosevelt** b. Coolidge c. Taft d. Ford) : TRUMAN :: WILSON : HARDING

    (a) is correct because Roosevelt was president before Truman just as Wilson was president before Harding. (b) is incorrect because Coolidge was the 30th president, preceding Hoover. (c) is incorrect because Taft was the 27th president, preceding Wilson. (d) is incorrect because Ford was the 38th president, preceding Carter.

38. QUANTUM THEORY : (a. Galileo b. Newton **c. Planck** d. Ramsay) ::
RELATIVITY : EINSTEIN

    (c) is correct because Planck discovered quantum theory as Einstein discovered the theory of relativity. (a) is incorrect because Galileo discovered the rules of planetary motion. (b) is incorrect because Newton described what has come to be called Newtonian physics, compared with Planck's quantum physics. (d) is incorrect because William Ramsay discovered helium.

39. WALT WHITMAN : *SONG OF MYSELF* :: NATHANIEL HAWTHORNE :
(**a. *Rappaccini's Daughter*** b. *The Raven* c. *Gulliver's Travels* d. *Billy Budd*)

    (a) is the correct response because Walt Whitman wrote *Song of Myself* just as Nathaniel Hawthorne wrote *Rappaccini's Daughter*. Herman Melville wrote *Billy Budd* (d), Jonathan Swift wrote *Gulliver's Travels* (c), and Edgar Allan Poe wrote *The Raven* (b).

40. CASSIUS : (a. Polonius b. Laertes **c. Brutus** d. MacDuff) :: ANTONIO : OLIVIA

    (c) is correct because Cassius and Brutus appear in Shakespeare's play *Julius Caesar* just as Antonio and Olivia appear in Shakespeare's play *Twelfth Night*. (a) and (b) are incorrect because Polonius and Laertes both appear in *Hamlet*, and (d) is incorrect because Macduff appears in *Macbeth*.

41. GERSHWIN : *RHAPSODY IN BLUE* :: BERNSTEIN : (a. *Adagio for Strings* b. *Porgy and Bess* c. *The Devil and Daniel Webster* **d. West Side Story**)

    (d) is correct because Gershwin wrote *Rhapsody in Blue* as Bernstein wrote *West Side Story*. Barber wrote *Adagio for Strings* (a), Gershwin wrote *Porgy and Bess* (b), and Moore wrote *The Devil and Daniel Webster* (c).

42. SOPHOCLES : *OEDIPUS REX* :: EURIPIDES : (a. *Prometheus Bound* b. *Lysistrata* **c. Medea** d. *Antigone*)

    (c) is correct because Sophocles wrote *Oedipus Rex* and Euripides wrote *Medea*. Aeschylus wrote *Prometheus Bound* (a), Aristophanes wrote *Lysistrata* (b), and Sophocles wrote *Antigone* (d).

43. (**a. Anton Chekhov** b. Victor Hugo c. Oscar Wilde d. Henrik Ibsen) : *THE THREE SISTERS* :: GEORGE BERNARD SHAW : *SAINT JOAN*

    (a) is the correct choice because Anton Chekhov wrote *The Three Sisters* and George Bernard Shaw wrote *Saint Joan*. Victor Hugo (b) wrote *Les Miserables*, Oscar Wilde (c) wrote *The Importance of Being Earnest*, and Henrik Ibsen (d) wrote *A Doll's House*.

44. KAFKA : *METAMORPHOSIS* :: (a. Coleridge b. Wordsworth **c. Eliot** d. Stoppard) : *THE WASTE LAND*

    (c) is the correct response because Kafka wrote the *Metamorphosis* and T. S. Eliot wrote *The Waste Land*. (a) is incorrect because Coleridge wrote *Lyrical Ballads*. (b) is incorrect because Wordsworth wrote *Poems Chiefly of Early and Late Years*, and (d) is incorrect because Stoppard wrote *Rosencrantz and Guildenstern Are Dead*.

45. (**a. Aesculapius** b. Apollo c. Nike d. Selene) : MEDICINE :: CHAOS : VOID

    (a) is correct because Aesculapius is the Greek god of medicine just as Chaos is the Greek god of the void. Apollo (b) is the god of the sun, Nike (c) is the goddess of victory, and Selene (d) is the goddess of the moon.

Explanations
of Answers

46. (a. Tyche **b. Thanatos** c. Nyx d. Athena) : DEATH :: EROS : LOVE

    (b) is the correct choice because Thanatos is the Greek god of death and Eros is the Greek god of love. Tyche (a) is the goddess of fortune, Nyx (c) is the goddess of night, and Athena (d) is the goddess of wisdom.

47. MARS : WAR :: (a. Psyche b. Salacia c. Somnus **d. Venus**) : LOVE

    (d) is the correct response because Mars is the Roman god of war just as Venus is the Roman goddess of love. Psyche (a) is the goddess of the soul, Salacia (b) is the goddess of the oceans, and Somnus (c) is the god of sleep.

48. CHROM : (a. motion **b. color** c. disease d. pain) :: DERM : SKIN

    (b) is the right answer because *-chrom* is a suffix meaning "color" and *-derm* is a suffix meaning "skin." *Kinesis* means "motion" (a), *pathos* is the term for "disease" (c), and *algia* means "pain" (d).

49. (a. anti b. aero **c. acro** d. arch) : TOP :: ANDRO : MAN

    (c) is the correct answer because *acro-* is a prefix meaning "top" just as *andro-* is a prefix meaning "man." *Anti-* (a) is the prefix meaning "against," *aero-* (b) means "air," and *arch-* (d) means "chief."

50. ETHNO : RACE :: (a. cardio b. crypto c. chrono **d. choreo**) : DANCE

    (d) is the correct response because *ethno-* is a prefix referring to race or ethnicity just as *choreo-* is a prefix referring to dance. *Cardio-* (a) means "relating to the heart," *crypto-* (b) means "hidden," and *chrono-* (c) means "time."

51. (a. pronoun b. preposition **c. adjective** d. article) : NOUN :: ADVERB : VERB

    (c) is the correct answer because an adjective modifies a noun in the same way that an adverb modifies a verb. A pronoun (a) substitutes for a noun, a preposition (b) defines the relationship of a noun to a verb, and an article (d) (a, an, or the) signals the presence of a noun.

52. GERMAN SURRENDER : V-E DAY :: JAPANESE SURRENDER :
(**a. V-J Day** b. Bastille Day c. Veterans Day d. Pearl Harbor Day)

(**a**) is correct because V-E Day, May 8, 1945, is the day the Germans surrendered to the Allied forces in World War II just as V-J Day, August 15, 1945, is the day the Japanese surrendered. (b) is incorrect because Bastille Day refers to the storming of a French prison by the proletariat of that nation, signaling the beginning of the French Revolution. Veteran's Day (c) is an American holiday remembering the war dead. Pearl Harbor Day (d) commemorates those who died in the Japanese attack on Pearl Harbor on December 7, 1941.

53. LIE : LAY :: LAY : (**a. laid** b. laying c. lying d. lain)

(**a**) is the correct response because *lay* is the past tense of the verb *lie* in the same way that *laid* is the past tense of the verb *lay*. *Laying* (b) is the present participle of *lay*, *lying* (c) is the present participle of *lie*, and *lain* (d) is the past participle of *lie*.

54. WORK : $W = fd$ :: VELOCITY : (**a.** $v = \dfrac{d}{t}$ b. $V = fw$ c. $Wt = mg$ d. $R = \dfrac{V}{I}$)

(**a**) is correct because $W = fd$ is the formula for determining work just as velocity is determined by the formula $v = \dfrac{d}{t}$. All other formulae are irrelevant.

55. (a. yellow **b. red** c. green d. indigo) : ORANGE :: BLUE : VIOLET

(**b**) is the right choice because red has a longer wavelength than orange just as blue has a longer wavelength than violet. In order from longest to shortest the colors in the visible spectrum are: red, orange, yellow, green, blue, indigo, violet.

56. GINSBERG : *HOWL* :: (a. Burroughs b. Kesey **c. Kerouac** d. DiPrima) : *ON THE ROAD*

(**c**) is correct because Allen Ginsberg wrote the poem *Howl* and Jack Kerouac wrote the novel *On the Road*. William Burroughs's (a) most famous work is *Naked Lunch*. Ken Kesey's (b) most famous work is *One Flew Over the Cuckoo's Nest*, and Diane DiPrima's most famous work is *Memoirs of a Beatnik*.

57. SYRIA : ASIA :: (**a. Panama** b. Colombia c. Venezuela d. Ecuador) : NORTH AMERICA

(**a**) is correct because the country Syria is a part of the Asian continent just as Panama is a part of the North American continent. Colombia (b), Venezuela (c), and Ecuador (d) are all part of the South American continent.

Explanations
of Answers

58. HEMI : (a. close b. under **c. half** d. outside) :: ANTE : BEFORE

    (c) is the correct response because the prefix *hemi-* means "half" just as the prefix *ante-* means "before." The prefix *para-* means "close" (a), *hypo-* means "under" (b), and *exo-* means "outside" (d).

59. $\frac{1}{2}$: 50% :: $\frac{2}{5}$: (a. 30% b. 35% **c. 40%** d. 45%)

    (c) is correct because the fraction $\frac{1}{2}$ expressed as a percentage is 50 percent, the same way that the fraction $\frac{2}{5}$ expressed as a percentage is 40 percent. All other fractions are irrelevant.

60. PHENOTYPE : (a. molecular structure **b. physical appearance** c. heredity d. natural selection) :: GENOTYPE : GENETIC COMPOSITION

    (b) is correct because an organism's phenotype describes its physical appearance just as its genotype describes its genetic composition. Molecular structure (a) is irrelevant because it is not confined to living things. Heredity (c) refers to the passage of genes from an organism to its offspring. Natural selection (d) refers to the extinction of certain species because they are less equipped to survive in a given environment than a competing species.

61. ELECTRON : NEGATIVE :: NEUTRON : (a. positive b. variable c. proton **d. none**)

    (d) is the correct choice because an electron is negatively charged in the same way that a neutron has no charge. A proton is positively charged so (a) and (c) are incorrect. Variable (b) is not relevant to this question.

62. C : CELSIUS :: (**a. F** b. f c. fh d. Fh) : FAHRENHEIT

    (a) is correct because C is the abbreviation for Celsius; F is the abbreviation for Fahrenheit. All other abbreviations are fictitious.

63. OZ : OUNCE :: (a. tsp **b. tbsp** c. tasp d. pt) : TABLESPOON

    (b) is correct because the abbreviation for ounce is oz; and the abbreviation for tablespoon is tbsp. The abbreviation for teaspoon is tsp, for pint is pt, for pound is lb, and for quart is qt.

Explanations
of Answers

64. 32 DEGREES FAHRENHEIT : 0 DEGREES CELSIUS :: (a. 100 degrees Fahrenheit b. 125 degrees Fahrenheit **c. 212 degrees Fahrenheit** d. 225 degrees Fahrenheit) : 100 DEGREES CELSIUS

    (c) is correct because the freezing point for water is 0 degrees Celsius or 32 degrees Fahrenheit; the boiling point for water is 100 degrees Celsius or 212 degrees Fahrenheit. All other temperatures are irrelevant.

65. BASEBALL : 9 :: FOOTBALL : (a. 9 b. 10 **c. 11** d. 12)

    (c) A baseball team fields 9 players simultaneously just as a football team fields 11 players simultaneously. All other numbers are incorrect.

66. VITAMIN A : CAROTENE :: (a. thiamine b. riboflavin c. niacin **d. ascorbic acid**) : VITAMIN C

    (d) is correct because another name for vitamin A is carotene and another name for vitamin C is ascorbic acid. Thiamine (a) is vitamin B1, riboflavin (b) is vitamin B2, and niacin (c) is also known as nicotinic acid.

67. FULMINATE : (a. cajole **b. denounce** c. exemplify d. placate) :: COMMEND : PRAISE

    (b) is the correct answer because *fulminate* means "to denounce" just as *commend* means "to praise." *Cajole* (a) means "to coax," *exemplify* (c) means "to make an example of," and *placate* (d) means "assuage."

68. UNIX : (a. programming language b. computer system **c. operating system** d. peripheral) :: FORTRAN : LANGUAGE

    (c) is correct because UNIX is a computer operating system just as FORTRAN is a computer programming language. (a) and (b) are general terms and do not refer to a specific language or system. Peripheral (d) refers to a device that works with a computer, but is not integral to the functioning of the computer, such as a printer.

69. ROSENCRANTZ : (**a. Horatio** b. Regan c. Gloucester d. Sebastian) :: DUNCAN : MALCOLM

    (a) is the right choice because Rosencrantz and Horatio are characters in Shakespeare's *Hamlet* just as Malcolm and Duncan are characters in Shakespeare's *Macbeth*. Regan (b) and Gloucester (c) appear in the play *King Lear*, and Sebastian (d) appears in *Twelfth Night*.

70. DANTE : *INFERNO* :: (a. Byron **b. Milton** c. Wordsworth d. Shelley) : *PARADISE LOST*

    (b) is correct because Dante wrote *Inferno* and Milton wrote *Paradise Lost*. (a), (c), and (d) were all Romantic poets.

71. HELLER : *CATCH-22* :: (a. Updike **b. Pynchon** c. Irving d. Kerouac) : *GRAVITY'S RAINBOW*

    (b) is the correct choice because Joseph Heller wrote *Catch-22* and Thomas Pynchon wrote *Gravity's Rainbow*. John Updike (a) wrote *The Witches of Eastwick*, Washington Irving (c) wrote *The History of New York*, and Jack Kerouac (d) wrote *Dharma Bums*.

72. 8 : (a. 2 **b. 4** c. 6 d. 8) :: DIAMETER : RADIUS

    (b) is correct because if the diameter of a circle is 8, then its radius will be 4. All other choices are irrelevant.

73. 2^3 : 3^3 :: 8 : (a. 18 b. 24 **c. 27** d. 36)

    (c) is the right answer because 2^3 is 8; 3^3 is 27. All other choices are irrelevant.

74. CAT : KITTEN :: KANGAROO : (a. wallaby **b. joey** c. cub d. marsupial)

    (b) is correct because a kitten is a baby cat and a joey is a baby kangaroo. A wallaby (a) is another animal. A cub (c) is a generic term for an animal that has not reached maturity. A marsupial (d) is the classification into which the kangaroo falls.

75. EAGLE : (a. feline b. equine c. bovine **d. aquiline**) :: DOG : CANINE

    (d) is correct because something with eagle-like features is aquiline just as something with dog-like features is canine. Feline (a) refers to cat-like, equine (b) refers to horse-like, and bovine (c) refers to cow-like.

76. ANTELOPE : HERBIVORE :: OWL : (**a. carnivore** b. omnivore c. avian d. nocturnal)

    (a) is the correct response because an antelope is an herbivore (plant eater) just as an owl is a carnivore (meat eater). *Omnivore* (b) refers to an animal (such as a human) that eats both meat and plants. *Avian* (c) is a general term for a bird. *Nocturnal* (d) refers to an animal that is active primarily at night.

77. KENNEDY : JOHNSON :: EISENHOWER : (**a. Nixon** b. Ford c. Kissinger
d. Humphrey)

(**a**) is the correct response because Johnson was Kennedy's vice president just as
Nixon was Eisenhower's vice president. Ford (b) was Nixon's vice president, and
became president when Nixon resigned. Kissinger (c) was never president or
vice president. Humphrey (d) was Lyndon Johnson's vice president.

78. TOKYO : JAPAN :: (a. Tripoli **b. Baghdad** c. Aden d. Riyadh) : IRAQ

(**b**) is the correct response because Tokyo is the capital of Japan just as Baghdad
is the capital of Iraq. Tripoli (a) is the capital of Libya, Aden (c) is the capital of
Yemen, and Riyadh (d) is the capital of Saudi Arabia.

79. (a. Dallas b. Houston c. Fort Worth **d. Austin**) : TEXAS :: DENVER :
COLORADO

(**d**) is the correct response because Austin is the capital of Texas just as Denver is
the capital of Colorado. All others are major cities in Texas, but not the capital.

80. SALT LAKE CITY : UTAH :: (a. Birmingham b. Huntsville **c. Montgomery**
d. Tuscaloosa) : ALABAMA

(**c**) is the correct response because Salt Lake City is the capital of Utah just as
Montgomery is the capital of Alabama. All others are major cities in Alabama,
but not the capital.

81. BECOME : (**a. became** b. becoming c. becomed d. become) :: SHRINK :
SHRANK

(**a**) is correct because the past tense of the verb *become* is *became* just as the
past tense of the verb *shrink* is *shrank*. All other choices are incorrect.

82. AURAL : ORAL :: EAR : (a. eyes b. nose **c. mouth** d. hand)

(**c**) is correct because just as *aural* relates to the ear; *oral* relates to the mouth.
Optical relates to the eyes (a), *nasal* refers to the nose (b), and *manual* refers to
the hand (d).

83. *FLYER* : WRIGHT BROTHERS :: (**a. *Beagle*** b. Galapagos c. Explorer
    d. *Calypso*) : DARWIN

    (**a**) is the correct choice because *Flyer* was the name of the Wright brothers' first
    airplane and *Beagle* was the name of Charles Darwin's ship. Galapagos (b) re-
    fers to the island group where Darwin did his research. Explorer (c) is a general
    term. The *Calypso* (d) is the name of the ship captained by the late Jacques Yves
    Cousteau.

84. SLOOP : 1 :: BARQUE : (a. 1 b. 2 **c. 4** d. 7)

    (**c**) is the correct response because a sloop is a sailing ship with a single mast
    and a barque is a sailing ship with 3–5 masts. All other choices are irrelevant.

85. ACROPHOBIA : (a. blood **b. heights** c. food d. death) :: HYDROPHOBIA :
    WATER

    (**b**) is correct because *acrophobia* is a fear of heights and *hydrophobia* is a fear
    of water. *Hemophobia* is a fear of blood (a), *sitophobia* is a fear of food (c), and
    necrophobia is a fear of death (d).

86. REGICIDE : (**a. king** b. president c. friend d. child) :: PATRICIDE : FATHER

    (**a**) is correct because killing a king is called regicide just as killing one's father
    is called patricide.

87. (a. feet **b. yards** c. inches d. meters) : MILE :: 1,760 : 1

    (**b**) is the correct response because there are 1,760 yards in a mile. There are
    5,280 feet (a) in a mile, there are 63,360 inches (c) in a mile, and roughly 1,500
    meters (d) in a mile.

88. (a. registration b. license **c. patent** d. statute) : INVENTION :: COPYRIGHT :
    NOVEL

    (**c**) is the correct response because just as a patent protects an invention, a copy-
    right protects a written work. Registration (a) and license (b) are general terms
    that are not specific to protection of ownership. A statute (d) refers to a law.

89. HUMERUS : ARM :: (a. tarsus b. sternum c. clavicle **d. femur**) : LEG

    (**d**) is correct because the humerus is a bone in the arm just as the femur is a
    bone in the leg. The tarsus (a) is the part of the foot between the metatarsus and
    the leg. The sternum (b) is commonly referred to as the breastbone. The clavicle
    (c) is commonly called the collarbone.

Explanations
of Answers

90. FRONTAL LOBE : (a. touch **b. speech** c. memory d. hearing) :: OCCIPITAL
    LOBE : VISION

    (b) is the correct response because the frontal lobe of the brain is responsible for
    speech just as the occipital lobe is responsible for vision. Touch (a) is a function
    of the parietal lobe, memory (c) and hearing (d) are functions of the temporal
    lobe.

91. (**a. teleologist** b. theologist c. thanatologist d. zoologist) : NATURE ::
    ICTHYOLOGIST : FISH

    (a) is correct because a teleologist studies nature as an icthyologist studies fish.
    (b) is incorrect because a theologist studies religion. (c) is incorrect because a
    thanatologist studies death, and (d) is incorrect because a zoologist studies animals.

92. *BEOWULF* : GRENDEL :: *HAMLET* : (a. Ophelia b. Polonius c. Gertrude
    d. Claudius)

    (d) is the correct response because Grendel is the primary antagonist in *Beowulf*
    just as Claudius is the primary antagonist in *Hamlet*. While Ophelia (a), Ger-
    trude (c), and Polonius (b) are characters in *Hamlet*, they are not the primary an-
    tagonists.

93. CHROMOSOME : (**a. gene** b. RNA c. DNA d. enzyme) :: CELL : NUCLEUS

    (a) is the correct response because a gene is a constituent part of a chromosome
    as a nucleus is a constituent part of a cell. RNA (b) and DNA (c) are compounds
    that carry information, and an enzyme (d) is a chemical that performs a specific
    function, so these are incorrect.

94. ORWELL : *1984* :: (a. Thoreau b. Emerson c. Burgess **d. Huxley**) : *BRAVE
    NEW WORLD*

    (d) is the correct response because George Orwell wrote *1984* based on Stalin's
    USSR as Aldous Huxley wrote *Brave New World* based on Roosevelt's USA. (a),
    (b), and (c) were all writers and social critics, however, they are not relevant to
    this question.

95. (**a. Coleridge** b. Ibsen c. Tolstoy d. Wordsworth) : *KUBLA KHAN* :: YEATS :
    SAILING TO BYZANTIUM

    (a) is correct because Coleridge wrote *Kubla Khan* just as Yeats wrote *Sailing to
    Byzantium*. Ibsen (b) is best known for *A Doll's House* and *Ghosts*, while Tolstoy
    (c) is best known for *War and Peace*. Wordsworth (d) is best known for his Ro-
    mantic poetry.

Explanations
of Answers

96. SARTRE : (a. *A Streetcar Named Desire* b. *Our Town* c. *The Purloined Letter*
    d. *No Exit*) :: JOYCE : *ULYSSES*

    (d) is correct because Sartre wrote *No Exit* and Joyce wrote *Ulysses*. *A Streetcar
    Named Desire* (a) was written by Tennessee Williams, *Our Town* (b) was written
    by Thornton Wilder, and *The Purloined Letter* (c) was written by Edgar Allan
    Poe.

97. BIBLE : CHRISTIANITY :: (a. Bhagavad-Gita b. New Testament **c. Koran**
    d. Talmud) : ISLAM

    (c) is correct because the Bible is the primary holy book of the Christian faith
    just as the Koran is the primary holy book of Islam. The Bhagavad-Gita (a) is a
    Hindu holy book, the New Testament (b) refers to a portion of the Bible, and the
    Talmud (d) is the book of Jewish law.

98. (**a. *caveat emptor*** b. *avant-garde* c. *primus inter pares* d. *tabula rasa*) : LET
    THE BUYER BEWARE :: *COGITO ERGO SUM* : I THINK, THEREFORE I AM

    (a) is the correct response because *caveat emptor* means let the buyer beware
    just as *cogito ergo sum* means I think, therefore I am.

99. ANDROUS : MAN :: DENDRON : (a. movement b. blood c. skin **d. tree**)

    (d) is the correct answer because *androus* is a suffix meaning "man" and *den-
    dron* is a suffix meaning "tree." *Kinesis* means "movement" (a), *emia* means
    "blood" (b), and *derm* means "skin" (c).

100. I THINK, THEREFORE I AM : RENE DESCARTES :: THERE IS ONLY
    ONE GOOD, KNOWLEDGE, AND ONE EVIL, IGNORANCE : (a. Plato
    b. Socrates c. Machiavelli d. Nietzsche)

    (b) Descartes said, "I think, therefore I am," just as Socrates said, "There is only
    one good, knowledge, and one evil, ignorance." All other choices are incorrect
    because these quotes are not attributable to these philosophers.

Miller Analogies

three

Practice Test 3

Answer Sheet
Practice Test 3

1. (A) (B) (C) (D)
2. (A) (B) (C) (D)
3. (A) (B) (C) (D)
4. (A) (B) (C) (D)
5. (A) (B) (C) (D)
6. (A) (B) (C) (D)
7. (A) (B) (C) (D)
8. (A) (B) (C) (D)
9. (A) (B) (C) (D)
10. (A) (B) (C) (D)
11. (A) (B) (C) (D)
12. (A) (B) (C) (D)
13. (A) (B) (C) (D)
14. (A) (B) (C) (D)
15. (A) (B) (C) (D)
16. (A) (B) (C) (D)
17. (A) (B) (C) (D)
18. (A) (B) (C) (D)
19. (A) (B) (C) (D)
20. (A) (B) (C) (D)
21. (A) (B) (C) (D)
22. (A) (B) (C) (D)
23. (A) (B) (C) (D)
24. (A) (B) (C) (D)
25. (A) (B) (C) (D)
26. (A) (B) (C) (D)
27. (A) (B) (C) (D)
28. (A) (B) (C) (D)
29. (A) (B) (C) (D)
30. (A) (B) (C) (D)
31. (A) (B) (C) (D)
32. (A) (B) (C) (D)
33. (A) (B) (C) (D)
34. (A) (B) (C) (D)

35. (A) (B) (C) (D)
36. (A) (B) (C) (D)
37. (A) (B) (C) (D)
38. (A) (B) (C) (D)
39. (A) (B) (C) (D)
40. (A) (B) (C) (D)
41. (A) (B) (C) (D)
42. (A) (B) (C) (D)
43. (A) (B) (C) (D)
44. (A) (B) (C) (D)
45. (A) (B) (C) (D)
46. (A) (B) (C) (D)
47. (A) (B) (C) (D)
48. (A) (B) (C) (D)
49. (A) (B) (C) (D)
50. (A) (B) (C) (D)
51. (A) (B) (C) (D)
52. (A) (B) (C) (D)
53. (A) (B) (C) (D)
54. (A) (B) (C) (D)
55. (A) (B) (C) (D)
56. (A) (B) (C) (D)
57. (A) (B) (C) (D)
58. (A) (B) (C) (D)
59. (A) (B) (C) (D)
60. (A) (B) (C) (D)
61. (A) (B) (C) (D)
62. (A) (B) (C) (D)
63. (A) (B) (C) (D)
64. (A) (B) (C) (D)
65. (A) (B) (C) (D)
66. (A) (B) (C) (D)
67. (A) (B) (C) (D)
68. (A) (B) (C) (D)

69. (A) (B) (C) (D)
70. (A) (B) (C) (D)
71. (A) (B) (C) (D)
72. (A) (B) (C) (D)
73. (A) (B) (C) (D)
74. (A) (B) (C) (D)
75. (A) (B) (C) (D)
76. (A) (B) (C) (D)
77. (A) (B) (C) (D)
78. (A) (B) (C) (D)
79. (A) (B) (C) (D)
80. (A) (B) (C) (D)
81. (A) (B) (C) (D)
82. (A) (B) (C) (D)
83. (A) (B) (C) (D)
84. (A) (B) (C) (D)
85. (A) (B) (C) (D)
86. (A) (B) (C) (D)
87. (A) (B) (C) (D)
88. (A) (B) (C) (D)
89. (A) (B) (C) (D)
90. (A) (B) (C) (D)
91. (A) (B) (C) (D)
92. (A) (B) (C) (D)
93. (A) (B) (C) (D)
94. (A) (B) (C) (D)
95. (A) (B) (C) (D)
96. (A) (B) (C) (D)
97. (A) (B) (C) (D)
98. (A) (B) (C) (D)
99. (A) (B) (C) (D)
100. (A) (B) (C) (D)

Practice Test 3

TIME: 50 Minutes   **LENGTH:** 100 Analogies

DIRECTIONS: Read each of the following analogies carefully, and choose the BEST answer to each item. Fill in your responses in the answer sheets provided.

Note: The Miller Analogies Test consists of 120 questions to be completed in 60 minutes. Twenty of these questions are experimental items, which are not scored and thus not reflected in this practice test.

1. CONSUMPTION : TUBERCULOSIS :: (a. the pox b. the clap c. the black death d. the flu) : BUBONIC PLAGUE

2. LEAGUE OF NATIONS : WILSON :: UNITED NATIONS : (a. Truman b. Roosevelt c. Eisenhower d. Kennedy)

3. PHILIP : VALOIS :: HENRY : (a. Windsor b. Saxe-Coburg c. Tudor d. Hanover)

4. JAMES VI OF SCOTLAND : JAMES I OF GREAT BRITAIN :: EDWARD VIII : (a. Edward I b. Elizabeth II c. Duke of Kent d. Duke of Windsor)

5. LINCOLN : JOHN WILKES BOOTH :: McKINLEY : (a. John Hinkley b. James Earl Ray c. Leon Czolgosz d. Charles Guiteau)

6. NICHOLAS II : RUSSIA :: (a. Louis XVI b. Louis XVIII c. Louis XIX d. Henri III) : FRANCE

7. CATHERINE THE GREAT : LATVIA :: NAPOLEON : (a. France b. Elba c. Corsica d. Waterloo)

8. PRAETORIAN GUARD : ROME :: SCOTS GUARD : (a. Great Britain b. Scotland c. Germany d. France)

9. WASHINGTON : ADAMS :: NIXON : (a. Carter b. Ford c. Reagan d. Johnson)

261

10. HUNDRED YEARS WAR : 116 YEARS :: THIRTY YEAR WAR : (a. 60 years b. 30 years c. 34 years d. 52 years)

11. PLUTO : TOMBAUGH :: LUCY : (a. Schultz b. Johanson c. Leakey d. Linus)

12. COUSTEAU : *CALYPSO* :: DARWIN : (a. Galapagos b. *Origin of Species* c. *Beagle* d. *Turtle*)

13. FRANKLIN ROOSEVELT : ELEANOR :: JAMES MADISON : (a. Martha b. Mary c. "Lady Bird" d. Dolley)

14. LUDWIG : NYMPHENBURG :: ARTHUR : (a. Camelot b. Versailles c. Guinevere d. Joyeus Gard)

15. U.S. SENATE : CONGRESS :: HOUSE OF COMMONS : (a. House of Lords b. Parliament c. Storting d. Cabinet)

16. TAUNG CHILD : DART :: LAOLTI FOOTPRINTS : (a. Richard Leakey b. Louis Leakey c. Mary Leakey d. Louise Leakey)

17. MAORI : TATTOOS :: CELTIC : (a. wode b. mead c. dirt d. saffron)

18. YURI GAGARIN : *VOSTOK I* :: NEIL ARMSTRONG : (a. *Apollo 8* b. *Apollo 11* c. *Apollo 17* d. *Gemini 3*)

19. APPELLATION : SOBRIQUET :: LOUIS XIV : (a. The Cruel b. The Sun King c. The Just d. The Confessor)

20. ALARIC : VISIGOTH :: (a. Caesar b. Clovis c. Attila d. Hadrian) : HUN

21. EARTH : MOON :: MARS : (a. Europa b. Oberon c. Phobos d. Nereid)

22. PYRAMIDS : EGYPT :: (a. Colossus b. Great Library c. Hanging Gardens d. Taj Mahal) : BABYLON

23. EUCLID : GEOMETRY :: HIPPOCRATES : (a. drama b. medicine c. sculpture d. astronomy)

24.   BLACK MONDAY : 1987 :: (a. Fat Tuesday b. Black Friday c. Black Tuesday d. Red Monday) : 1929

25.   S.B. ANTHONY : DOLLAR :: (a. A. Lincoln b. F. Roosevelt c. R. Nixon d. G. Washington) : DIME

26.   HOLY GRAIL : LANCELOT :: GOLDEN FLEECE : (a. Ulysses b. Orestes c. Jason d. Paris)

27.   BELL : TELEPHONE :: GALILEO : (a. wind tunnel b. zipper c. lightning rod d. water thermometer)

28.   GREEK : OLYMPUS :: NORSE : (a. Oden b. Thor c. Asgard d. Loki)

29.   AGENT ORANGE : VIETNAM :: MUSTARD GAS : (a. Civil War b. War of 1812 c. World War I d. World War II)

30.   FREQUENCY MODULATION : FM :: (a. attitude modulation b. amplitude modulation c. amplified modulation d. animated modulation) : AM

31.   DIAMOND : CUBIC ZIRCONIUM :: GOLD : (a. quartz b. silver c. alloy d. pyrite)

32.   EEG : (a. blood b. bone c. eye d. brain) :: EKG : HEART

33.   MARQUIS : MARCHIONESS :: (a. duke b. earl c. knight d. lord) : COUNTESS

34.   ASTHMA : LUNGS :: LEUKEMIA : (a. blood b. gall bladder c. liver d. immune system)

35.   EVERGLADES : FLORIDA :: GRAND CANYON : (a. Colorado b. Arizona c. Utah d. Nevada)

36.   MOUNT EVEREST : HIMALAYAS :: (a. Athos b. Montserrat c. Mount McKinley d. Matterhorn) : ALPS

Practice Test 3

37. HIGHLANDS : SCOTLAND :: BLACK FOREST : (a. France b. Belgium c. Germany d. Austria)

38. BOER WAR : SOUTH AFRICA :: CRIMEAN WAR : (a. Greece b. Russia c. Turkey d. Sweden)

39. HAVANA : CUBA :: (a. Kingston b. Montego Bay c. Ochos Rios d. Negril) : JAMAICA

40. PERSIA : IRAN :: PHRYGIA : (a. Egypt b. Turkey c. Spain d. India)

41. ALEUTIAN ISLANDS : ALASKA :: AUCKLAND ISLANDS : (a. Brazil b. China c. Argentina d. New Zealand)

42. LIVINGSTONE : AFRICA :: (a. Hudson b. Ponce de Léon c. La Salle d. Cabot) : LOUISIANA

43. LAKE OF LUCERNE : SWITZERLAND :: LAKE VICTORIA : (a. Great Britain b. Canada c. Australia d. Kenya)

44. BLACK FRIARS : DOMINICANS :: (a. Methodists b. Scientologists c. Jesuits d. Jehovah) : SOCIETY OF JESUS

45. SAPPHIRE : CORUNDUM :: AMETHYST: (a. graphite b. quartz c. feldspar d. garnet)

46. DESCARTES : SOLIPSISM :: (a. Xenophanes b. Zeno c. Pyrrho d. Epicurus) : STOICISM

47. BOXING DAY : DECEMBER 26 :: EARTH DAY : (a. April 19 b. May 19 c. April 22 d. May 22)

48. PORSCHE : VOLKSWAGEN :: FORD : (a. Lexus b. Model T c. Cadillac d. Jeep)

49. GRAM : MASS :: (a. cubit b. watt c. volume d. degree) : POWER

50. REVOLVER : COLT :: (a. cannon b. machine gun c. crossbow d. musket) : GATLING

51. JAPAN : YEN :: PORTUGAL : (a. peseta b. cruzeiro c. escudo d. rand)

52. AUSTRIA : GERMAN :: (a. France b. Sweden c. Norway d. Greenland) : DANISH

53. RIGEL : ORION :: (a. Sirus b. Capella c. Sol d. Polaris) : LITTLE DIPPER

54. AFRICA : KILIMANJARO :: NORTH AMERICA : (a. Mt. McKinley b. Mt. Helena c. Mt. Everest d. Boston Mountains)

55. ASIA : DEAD SEA :: NORTH AMERICA : (a. Grand Canyon b. Lake Michigan c. Death Valley d. Caribbean Sea)

56. AURORA BOREALIS : NORTHERN LIGHTS :: (a. Aurora Polaris b. Aurora Luminescence c. Aurora Australis d. Solar Winds) : SOUTHERN LIGHTS

57. PAPYRUS : EGPYT :: (a. stone tablets b. marble tablets c. clay tablets d. rice paper) : BABYLONIA

58. NOAH : JUDEO-CHRISTIAN :: (a. Gilgamesh b. Jason c. Deucalion d. Plato) : GREEK

59. TURPENTINE : PINE :: (a. soap b. ink c. rattan d. dye) : PALM

60. VICTORIA : BRITISH COLUMBIA :: (a. Toronto b. Montreal c. Hamilton d. Ottawa) : ONTARIO

61. UNIVERSITY OF ARIZONA : (a. Phoenix b. Flagstaff c. Prescott d. Tucson) :: FORDHAM : NEW YORK CITY

62. THE SNOW QUEEN : ANDERSEN :: UNCLE REMUS : (a. Grimm b. Faust c. Harris d. Disney)

63. LIGHT : SOUND :: (a. 186,000 feet per second b. 186,000 miles per second c. 1,860 miles per second d. 1,680 miles per second) : 1,088 FEET PER SECOND

64. BIO : LIFE :: HEMI : (a. half b. earth c. split d. world)

65. LIVY : HISTORY :: (a. Pindar b. Zeno c. Horace d. Sappho) : POETRY

66. WASHINGTON : MT. VERNON :: (a. Arthur b. Grant c. Roosevelt d. Cleveland) : HYDE PARK

67. *WALL STREET JOURNAL* : NEW YORK :: (a. *Sun Times* b. *Examiner* c. *Star* d. *Inquirer*) : PHILADELPHIA

68. PUERTO RICO : RICH PORT :: NEVADA : (a. flat land b. cold night c. snow clad d. new start)

69. HELIUM : SUN :: NEON : (a. new b. light c. bright d. extreme)

70. LUXEMBOURG : CONSTITUTIONAL MONARCHY :: ICELAND : (a. traditional monarchy b. constitutional monarchy c. independent commonwealth d. republic)

71. HYDROGEN : 1 :: CARBON : (a. 6 b. 8 c. 9 d. 12)

72. EMMY : TELEVISION :: (a. Nobel b. Tony c. Pulitzer d. Fermi) : JOURNALISM

73. (a. Throgs Neck b. Brooklyn c. George Washington d. Verrazano Narrows) : NEW YORK :: GOLDEN GATE : SAN FRANCISCO

74. PULLET : HEN :: ELVER : (a. wild fowl b. eel c. zebra d. hare)

75. EGYPT : PHILIPPINES :: POUND : (a. yen b. peso c. nuevo sol d. dinar)

76. JUPITER : PLANET :: (a. Io b. Moon c. Europa d. Ganymede) : SATELLITE

77. ESTROGEN : OVARIES :: GASTRIN : (a. stomach glands b. adrenal medulla c. thyroid d. pancreas)

78. MARGARET THATCHER : ELIZABETH II :: (a. Stanley Baldwin b. William Pitt, the younger c. Herbert Asquith d. Benjamin Disraeli) : VICTORIA

79. BRADLEY : HARTFORD :: (a. Gatwick b. Logan c. Dulles d. Midway) : WASHINGTON, D.C.

80. ROMAN CATHOLIC : POPE :: EPISCOPALIAN : (a. bishop b. archbishop c. cardinal d. apostle)

Practice Test 3

81. *HOMO HABILIS* : 2,000,000 :: NEANDERTHAL : (a. 10,000 b. 15,000 c. 75,000 d. 200,000)

82. NEST : VIPERS :: (a. gaggle b. band c. gross d. pack) : GORILLAS

83. CORAL SNAKE : BLACK WIDOW SPIDER :: GARDEN SNAKE : (a. harvest spider b. latrodectus geometricus c. brown recluse d. grey widow)

84. QUEENSLAND : AUSTRALIA :: (a. Texas b. Washington, D.C. c. Boston d. San Francisco) : UNITED STATES

85. KORAN : ISLAM :: BHAGAVAD-GITA : (a. Buddhism b. Confucianism c. Baha'i d. Hinduism)

86. ULNA : ARM :: (a. tarsals b. humerus c. mandible d. tibia) : LEG

87. DOG : CANIDAE :: (a. frog b. squirrel c. cat d. lizard) : RANIDAE

88. GAEA : TERRA :: HESTIA : (a. Juno b. Saturn c. Eros d. Vestia)

89. K : KAPPA :: (a. Z b. Q c. D d. L) : KOPPA

90. ARABIC : ROMAN :: 600 : (a. MD b. CC c. DC d. MX)

91. LEDA : HELEN :: (a. Metis b. Diona c. Themis d. Io) : APHRODITE

92. MACRO : LARGE :: HOMO : (a. small b. same c. male d. similar)

93. CZAR : RUSSIA :: KHAN : (a. Mongolia b. Egypt c. Turkey d. China)

94. BALL : MUSKET :: (a. wire b. nut c. bolt d. wood) : CROSSBOW

95. SITAR : STRING :: DOUMBEK : (a. keys b. pedals c. stick d. skin)

96. JOAN OF ARC : BURNING :: ROBESPIERRE : (a. hanging b. starvation c. guillotine d. firing squad)

97. FISSION : SPLITTING :: FUSION : (a. cooling b. heating c. combining d. melting)

98. SHIVA : KALI :: ODEN : (a. Frey b. Frigg c. Loki d. Thor)

99. SALVATION ARMY : WILLIAM BOOTH :: (a. Girl Scouts b. Boy Scouts c. Sierra Club d. Red Cross) : JEAN HENRI DURANT

100. AMNESIA : MEMORY :: (a. astigmatism b. tinnitus c. rhinitis d. othematoma) : VISION

Answer Key
Practice Test 3

1. (c)	26. (c)	51. (c)	76. (d)
2. (b)	27. (d)	52. (d)	77. (a)
3. (c)	28. (c)	53. (d)	78. (d)
4. (d)	29. (c)	54. (a)	79. (c)
5. (c)	30. (b)	55. (c)	80. (b)
6. (a)	31. (d)	56. (c)	81. (c)
7. (c)	32. (d)	57. (c)	82. (b)
8. (d)	33. (b)	58. (c)	83. (a)
9. (b)	34. (a)	59. (c)	84. (a)
10. (b)	35. (b)	60. (a)	85. (d)
11. (b)	36. (d)	61. (d)	86. (d)
12. (c)	37. (c)	62. (c)	87. (a)
13. (d)	38. (b)	63. (b)	88. (d)
14. (a)	39. (a)	64. (a)	89. (b)
15. (b)	40. (b)	65. (c)	90. (c)
16. (c)	41. (d)	66. (c)	91. (b)
17. (a)	42. (c)	67. (d)	92. (b)
18. (b)	43. (d)	68. (c)	93. (a)
19. (b)	44. (c)	69. (a)	94. (c)
20. (c)	45. (b)	70. (d)	95. (d)
21. (c)	46. (b)	71. (a)	96. (c)
22. (c)	47. (c)	72. (c)	97. (c)
23. (b)	48. (b)	73. (d)	98. (b)
24. (c)	49. (b)	74. (b)	99. (d)
25. (b)	50. (b)	75. (b)	100. (a)

Explanations of Answers
Practice Test 3

1. CONSUMPTION : TUBERCULOSIS :: (a. the pox b. the clap **c. the black death** d. the flu) : BUBONIC PLAGUE

   (c) is correct because *the black death* is the common name for the bubonic plague as consumption is for tuberculosis. (a) is incorrect because *the pox* is the common name for either small pox or syphilis. (b) is incorrect because it is the common name for venereal disease. (d) is incorrect because *the flu* is the common name for influenza.

2. LEAGUE OF NATIONS : WILSON :: UNITED NATIONS : (a. Truman **b. Roosevelt** c. Eisenhower d. Kennedy)

   (b) is correct because the United Nations was formed during Roosevelt's presidency as the League of Nations was under Wilson. (a), (c), and (d) are incorrect because the UN was not founded under these presidencies.

3. PHILIP : VALOIS :: HENRY : (a. Windsor b. Saxe-Coburg **c. Tudor** d. Hanover)

   (c) is correct because Henry was the founder of the House of Tudor as Philip was the founder of the House of Valois. (a) is incorrect because George V founded Windsor. (b) is incorrect because Edward VII founded Saxe-Coburg. (d) is incorrect because George I founded Hanover.

4. JAMES VI OF SCOTLAND : JAMES I OF GREAT BRITAIN :: EDWARD VIII : (a. Edward I b. Elizabeth II c. Duke of Kent **d. Duke of Windsor**)

   (d) is correct because Edward VIII became the Duke of Windsor, after he abdicated, as James VI of Scotland became James I of Great Britain after Elizabeth I died. (a), (b), and (c) are wrong, as Edward did not take those titles.

5. LINCOLN : JOHN WILKES BOOTH :: McKINLEY : (a. John Hinkley b. James Earl Ray **c. Leon Czolgosz** d. Charles Guiteau)

   (c) is correct because Leon Czolgosz shot William McKinley as Booth shot Lincoln. (a) is incorrect because Hinkley shot Reagan. (b) is incorrect because Ray shot King. (d) is incorrect because Guiteau shot Garfield.

6. NICHOLAS II : RUSSIA :: (**a. Louis XVI** b. Louis XVIII c. Louis XIX
   d. Henri III) : FRANCE

   (**a**) is correct because Louis XVI was the last king of France as Nicholas II was
   the last czar of Russia. (b), (c), and (d) are incorrect because these rulers were
   not the last king of France.

7. CATHERINE THE GREAT : LATVIA :: NAPOLEON : (a. France b. Elba
   c. Corsica d. Waterloo)

   (**c**) is correct because Napoleon was born in Corsica as Catherine was born in
   Latvia. (a) is incorrect because Napoleon ruled France. (b) is incorrect because
   he was exiled to Elba. (d) is incorrect because he was defeated at Waterloo.

8. PRAETORIAN GUARD : ROME :: SCOTS GUARD : (a. Great Britain
   b. Scotland c. Germany **d. France**)

   (**d**) is correct because the Scots guard was the personal guard of the kings of
   France as the Praetorian guard was the personal guard of the Roman emperors.
   (a), (b), and (c) are incorrect because the Scots Guard was not their personal
   guard.

9. WASHINGTON : ADAMS :: NIXON : (a. Carter **b. Ford** c. Reagan d. Johnson)

   (**b**) is correct because Nixon was followed by Ford in office, as Washington was
   followed by Adams. (a) is incorrect because Carter followed Ford. (c) is incorrect because Reagan followed Carter. (d) is incorrect because Johnson followed
   Kennedy.

10. HUNDRED YEARS WAR : 116 YEARS :: THIRTY YEARS WAR : (a. 60 years
    b. 30 years c. 34 years d. 52 years)

    (**b**) is correct because the Thirty Years War lasted 30 years, as the Hundred Years
    War lasted 116. (a), (c), and (d) are irrelevant.

11. PLUTO : TOMBAUGH :: LUCY : (a. Schultz **b. Johanson** c. Leakey d. Linus)

    (**b**) is correct because Lucy (*Australopithecus afarensis*) was discovered by
    Johanson and Taieb as Pluto was discovered by Tombaugh. (a) and (d) are in-
    correct because they refer to the comic strip "Peanuts." (c) is incorrect because
    Louis Leakey discovered *Homo habilis*.

12. COUSTEAU : *CALYPSO* :: DARWIN : (a. Galapagos b. *Origin of Species* **c. *Beagle*** d. *Turtl*

(c) is correct. Darwin's ship was the *Beagle* as Cousteau's was the *Calypso*. (a) is incorrect because the Galapagos were the islands to which he was traveling. (b) is incorrect because it is the title of his book. (d) is irrelevant.

13. FRANKLIN ROOSEVELT : ELEANOR :: JAMES MADISON : (a. Martha b. Mary c. "Lady Bird" **d. Dolley**)

(d) is correct because Dolley was Madison's wife as Eleanor was Roosevelt's. (a) is incorrect because Martha was Washington's wife. (b) is incorrect because Mary was Lincoln's wife. (c) is incorrect because Lady Bird was Johnson's wife.

14. LUDWIG : NYMPHENBURG :: ARTHUR : (**a. Camelot** b. Versailles c. Guinevere d. Joyeus Gard)

(a) is correct because Camelot was Arthur's castle, as Nymphenburg was Ludwig's. (b) is incorrect because it was the palace of the kings of France. (c) is incorrect because it is the name of Arthur's wife. (d) is incorrect because it is Lancelot's castle.

15. U.S. SENATE : CONGRESS :: HOUSE OF COMMONS : (a. House of Lords **b. Parliament** c. Storting d. Cabinet)

(b) is correct because the House of Commons is one of the two houses of Parliament as the Senate is one of the two houses of Congress. (a) is incorrect because it is a house of Parliament. (c) is incorrect because Storting is Norway's Parliament. (d) is incorrect because it refers to the appointed inner circle of the American president.

16. TAUNG CHILD : DART :: LAOLTI FOOTPRINTS : (a. Richard Leakey b. Louis Leakey **c. Mary Leakey** d. Louise Leakey)

(c) is correct because Mary Leakey found the Laolti footprints as Dart found the Taung child. (a) is incorrect because Richard Leakey made many important finds in East Africa. The Laolti footprints, however, were not among them. (b) is incorrect because Louis Leakey unearthed Zinjanthropus. (d) is incorrect because Louise Leakey is a fictitious name.

17. MAORI : TATTOOS :: CELTIC : (**a. wode** b. mead c. dirt d. saffron)

(a) is correct because the Celts would decorate their bodies with wode as the Maori would with tattoos. (b) is incorrect because it is a beverage. (c) is incorrect because the Celts did not decorate their bodies with dirt. (d) is incorrect because saffron is a spice.

18. YURI GAGARIN : *VOSTOK I* :: NEIL ARMSTRONG : (a. *Apollo 8* **b. *Apollo 11*** c. *Apollo 17* d. *Gemini 3*)

    (b) is correct because Armstrong was captain of the *Apollo 11* spacecraft as Gagarin was captain of *Vostok I*. (a), (c), and (d) are incorrect because Neil Armstrong did not command these missions. However, *Apollo 8* (a) was the first mission to accomplish a manned lunar orbit.

19. APPELLATION : SOBRIQUET :: LOUIS XIV : (a. The Cruel **b. The Sun King** c. The Just d. The Confessor)

    (b) is correct because the sobriquet of Louis XIV was the Sun King. (a), (c), and (d) are irrelevant because Louis XIV did not take these titles.

20. ALARIC : VISIGOTH :: (a. Caesar b. Clovis **c. Attila** d. Hadrian) : HUN

    (c) is correct because Attila was the ruler of the Huns as Alaric was the ruler of the Visigoths. (a) is incorrect because Caesar was the ruler of the Romans. (b) is incorrect because Clovis was the ruler of the Franks. (d) is incorrect because Hadrian was a ruler of Rome.

21. EARTH : MOON :: MARS : (a. Europa b. Oberon **c. Phobos** d. Nereid)

    (c) is correct because Phobos is a satellite of Mars as the Moon is a satellite of Earth. (a) is incorrect because Europa is a moon of Jupiter. (b) is incorrect because Oberon is a moon of Uranus. (d) is incorrect because Nereid is a moon of Neptune.

22. PYRAMIDS : EGYPT :: (a. Colossus b. Great Library **c. Hanging Gardens** d. Taj Mahal) : BABYLON

    (c) is correct because the wonder of the world that was located in Babylon was the Hanging Gardens as the pyramids were in Egypt. (a) and (b) are incorrect because even though they are wonders of the world they were not in Babylon. (d) is incorrect because it is not a wonder of the world nor in Babylon.

23. EUCLID : GEOMETRY :: HIPPOCRATES : (a. drama **b. medicine** c. sculpture d. astronomy)

    (b) is correct because Hippocrates was the founder of modern medicine as Euclid was the founder of geometry. (a), (c), and (d) are irrelevant because Hippocrates was not the founder of these disciplines.

24. BLACK MONDAY : 1987 :: (a. Fat Tuesday b. Black Friday **c. Black Tuesday** d. Red Monday) : 1929

    (c) is correct because Black Tuesday was the day that the stock market crashed in 1929 as Black Monday was the day the market fell in 1987. (a) is incorrect because Fat Tuesday is the day before Ash Wednesday. (b) and (d) are irrelevant.

25. S.B. ANTHONY : DOLLAR :: (a. A. Lincoln **b. F. Roosevelt** c. R. Nixon d. G. Washington) : DIME

    (b) is correct because Roosevelt is on the front of a dime as Anthony is on the front of the dollar coin. (a) is incorrect because Lincoln is on the penny. (c) is incorrect because Nixon is not on a coin. (d) is incorrect because Washington is on the quarter.

26. HOLY GRAIL : LANCELOT :: GOLDEN FLEECE : (a. Ulysses b. Orestes **c. Jason** d. Paris)

    (c) is correct because Jason's quest was the golden fleece as Lancelot's was the Holy Grail. (a) is incorrect because Ulysses's quest was to get home. (b) is incorrect because Orestes was the son of Agammemnon. (d) is incorrect because Paris was the ruler of Troy.

27. BELL : TELEPHONE :: GALILEO : (a. wind tunnel b. zipper c. lightning rod **d. water thermometer**)

    (d) is correct because Galileo invented the water thermometer as Bell invented the telephone. (a) is incorrect because Eiffel invented the wind tunnel. (b) is incorrect because Judson invented the zipper. (c) is incorrect because Franklin invented the lightning rod.

28. GREEK : OLYMPUS :: NORSE : (a. Oden b. Thor **c. Asgard** d. Loki)

    (c) is correct because Asgard was the home of the Norse gods as Olympus was the home of the Greek gods. (a), (b), and (d) are incorrect because they are the proper names of Norse gods.

29. AGENT ORANGE : VIETNAM :: MUSTARD GAS : (a. Civil War b. War of 1812 **c. World War I** d. World War II)

    (c) is correct because mustard gas was used during World War I as Agent Orange was used during the Vietnam War. (a), (b), and (d) are incorrect because these chemical weapons were not introduced during these conflicts.

Explanations of Answers

30. FREQUENCY MODULATION : FM :: (a. attitude modulation **b. amplitude modulation** c. amplified modulation d. animated modulation) : AM

   (b) is correct because *AM* stands for amplitude modulation as *FM* stands for frequency modulation. (a), (c), and (d) are incorrect.

31. DIAMOND : CUBIC ZIRCONIUM :: GOLD : (a. quartz b. silver c. alloy **d. pyrite**)

   (d) is correct because pyrite resembles gold as the cubic zirconium looks like a diamond. (a) is incorrect because quartz is a silicon mineral formation. (b) is incorrect because silver is an element. (c) is incorrect because an alloy is formed by mixing metals.

32. EEG : (a. blood b. bone c. eye **d. brain**) :: EKG : HEART

   (d) is correct because an EEG is a test for the brain as EKG is a test for the heart. (a), (b), and (c) are incorrect because an EEG does not measure their activity.

33. MARQUIS : MARCHIONESS :: (a. duke **b. earl** c. knight d. lord) : COUNTESS

   (b) is correct because the feminine form of *earl* is *countess* as the feminine form of *marquis* is *marchioness*. (a) is incorrect because *duchess* is the feminine form of *duke*. (c) is incorrect because *lady* is the feminine form of *knight*. (d) is incorrect because *lady* is the feminine form of *lord*.

34. ASTHMA : LUNGS :: LEUKEMIA : (**a. blood** b. gall bladder c. liver d. immune system)

   (a) is correct because leukemia directly affects the blood as asthma directly affects the lungs. (b), (c), and (d) are incorrect because leukemia does not directly affect these areas.

35. EVERGLADES : FLORIDA :: GRAND CANYON : (a. Colorado **b. Arizona** c. Utah d. Nevada)

   (b) is correct because the Grand Canyon National Park is in Arizona as the Everglades National Park is in Florida. (a), (c), and (d) are incorrect because the Grand Canyon is not in these states.

36. MOUNT EVEREST : HIMALAYAS :: (a. Athos b. Montserrat c. Mount McKinley **d. Matterhorn**) : ALPS

    (d) is correct because the Matterhorn is in the Alps as Mt. Everest is located in the Himalayas. (a) is incorrect because Athos is located in Greece. (b) is incorrect because Monserrat is located in Spain. (c) is incorrect because Mt. McKinley is located in the U.S.

37. HIGHLANDS : SCOTLAND :: BLACK FOREST : (a. France b. Belgium **c. Germany** d. Austria)

    (c) is correct because the Black Forest is an area of Germany as the Highlands is an area of Scotland. (a), (b), and (d) are incorrect because the Black Forest is not found in these nations.

38. BOER WAR : SOUTH AFRICA :: CRIMEAN WAR : (a. Greece **b. Russia** c. Turkey d. Sweden)

    (b) is correct because the Crimean War was fought in Russia as the Boer was fought in South Africa. (a), (c), and (d) are incorrect because the Crimean War was not fought in these places.

39. HAVANA : CUBA :: (**a. Kingston** b. Montego Bay c. Ochos Rios d. Negril) : JAMAICA

    (a) is correct because Kingston is the capital of Jamaica as Havana is the capital of Cuba. (b), (c), and (d) are incorrect because, although they are cities in Jamaica, they are not the capitals.

40. PERSIA : IRAN :: PHRYGIA : (a. Egypt **b. Turkey** c. Spain d. India)

    (b) is correct because ancient Phrygia is in modern Turkey as ancient Persia is in modern Iran. (a), (c), and (d) are incorrect because Phrygia was not included within their boundaries.

41. ALEUTIAN ISLANDS : ALASKA :: AUCKLAND ISLANDS : (a. Brazil b. China c. Argentina **d. New Zealand**)

    (d) is correct because the Auckland Islands are off the coast of New Zealand as the Aleutian Islands are off the coast of Alaska. (a) is incorrect because Fernando de Nororna Islands are located off the coast of Brazil. (b) is incorrect because Taiwan is located off the coast of China. (c) is incorrect because the Falkland Islands are located off the coast of Argentina.

Explanations of Answers

42. LIVINGSTONE : AFRICA :: (a. Hudson b. Ponce de Léon
    c. La Salle d. Cabot) : LOUISIANA

    (c) is correct because La Salle was known for his exploration of the Louisiana area as Livingstone was known for his exploration of Africa. (a) is incorrect because Hudson was known for exploring the Atlantic northeast. (b) is incorrect because Ponce de Léon was known for exploring the Florida area. (d) is incorrect because Cabot was known for exploring the coast of South America.

43. LAKE OF LUCERNE : SWITZERLAND :: LAKE VICTORIA : (a. Great Britain b. Canada c. Australia **d. Kenya**)

    (d) is correct because Lake Victoria is located in Kenya as the Lake of Lucerne is located in Switzerland. (a) is incorrect because, although Victoria rules Great Britain, there is no Lake Victoria. (b) is incorrect because Victoria Island is located in Canada. (c) is incorrect because the state of Victoria is located in Australia.

44. BLACK FRIARS : DOMINICANS :: (a. Methodists b. Scientologists **c. Jesuits** d. Jehovah) : SOCIETY OF JESUS

    (c) is correct because the *Jesuits* is another name for the Society of Jesus as the *Black Friars* was another name for the Dominicans. (a) is incorrect because Methodism is a sect of Protestantism. (b) is incorrect because Scientologists are those who follow the teachings of author L. Ron Hubbard. (d) is incorrect because this is one of the names humanity has given to its spiritual focus.

45. SAPPHIRE : CORUNDUM :: AMETHYST: (a. graphite **b. quartz** c. feldspar d. garnet)

    (b) is correct because amethyst is a variety of quartz as sapphire is a variety of corundum. (a) is incorrect because graphite is a form of carbon. (c) and (d) are incorrect because, although they are minerals, amethyst is not included among their varieties.

46. DESCARTES : SOLIPSISM :: (a. Xenophanes **b. Zeno** c. Pyrrho d. Epicurus) : STOICISM

    (b) is the correct answer because Zeno founded the school of stoicism as Descartes founded the school of solipsism. (a) is incorrect because Xenophanes founded the Eleatic school. (c) is incorrect because Pyrrho introduced skepticism. (d) is incorrect because Epicurus introduced hedonism.

47. BOXING DAY : DECEMBER 26 :: EARTH DAY : (a. April 19 b. May 19
    c. April 22 d. May 22)

    (c) is correct because Earth Day is on April 22 as Boxing Day is on December
    26. (a), (b), and (d) are incorrect because Earth Day is not observed on these
    days.

48. PORSCHE : VOLKSWAGEN :: FORD : (a. Lexus **b. Model T** c. Cadillac
    d. Jeep)

    (b) is correct because Henry Ford designed the Model T as Ferdinand Porsche
    designed the Volkswagen. (a), (c), and (d) are incorrect because Lexus is pro-
    duced by Toyota, Cadillac is made by General Motors, and Jeep is a Chrysler
    product.

49. GRAM : MASS :: (a. cubit **b. watt** c. volume d. degree) : POWER

    (b) is correct because watt is a unit of power as gram is a unit of mass. (a) is in-
    correct because cubit is a unit of length. (c) is incorrect because volume is a unit
    of capacity. (d) is incorrect because degree is a unit of temperature.

50. REVOLVER : COLT :: (a. cannon **b. machine gun** c. crossbow d. musket) :
    GATLING

    (b) is correct because Gatling invented the machine gun as Colt invented the re-
    volver. (a) is incorrect because the cannon was developed by Schwartz. (c) and
    (d) are incorrect because their inventors are unknown.

51. JAPAN : YEN :: PORTUGAL : (a. peseta b. cruzeiro **c. escudo** d. rand)

    (c) is correct because the escudo is the currency of Portugal as the yen is the
    currency of Japan. (a) is incorrect because the peseta is the currency of Spain.
    (b) is incorrect because the cruzeiro is the currency of Brazil. (d) is incorrect be-
    cause the rand is the currency of South Africa.

52. AUSTRIA : GERMAN :: (a. France b. Sweden c. Norway **d. Greenland**) :
    DANISH

    (d) is correct because the official language of Greenland is Danish as the official
    language of Austria is German. (a) is incorrect because the official language
    of France is French. (b) is incorrect because the official language of Sweden is
    Swedish. (c) is incorrect because the official language of Norway is Norwegian.

53. RIGEL : ORION :: (a. Sirus b. Capella c. Sol **d. Polaris**) : LITTLE DIPPER

    (d) is correct because Polaris is the brightest star in the Little Dipper as Rigel is the brightest star in Orion. (a) is incorrect because Sirus is located in Canis Major. (b) is incorrect because Capella is located in Auriga. (c) is incorrect because Sol is our sun.

54. AFRICA : KILIMANJARO :: NORTH AMERICA : (**a. Mt. McKinley** b. Mt. Helena c. Mt. Everest d. Boston Mountains)

    (a) is correct because Mt. McKinley is the highest point in North America as Kilimanjaro is the highest point in Africa. (b) and (d) are incorrect because, although in North America, they are not the highest points. (c) is incorrect because Mt. Everest is in Asia.

55. ASIA : DEAD SEA :: NORTH AMERICA : (a. Grand Canyon b. Lake Michigan **c. Death Valley** d. Caribbean Sea)

    (c) is correct because Death Valley is the lowest point in North America as the Dead Sea is the lowest point in Asia. (a), (b), and (d) are incorrect because, although in North America, they are not the lowest points.

56. AURORA BOREALIS : NORTHERN LIGHTS :: (a. Aurora Polaris b. Aurora Luminescence **c. Aurora Australis** d. Solar Winds) : SOUTHERN LIGHTS

    (c) is correct because *Aurora Australis* is another name for the southern lights as *Aurora Borealis* is another name for the northern lights. (a) is incorrect because it is the name for both southern and northern lights. (b) is incorrect because *Aurora Luminesence* is a general term, referring to either the northern or southern lights. (d) is incorrect because it refers to a stream of charged particles emanating from the upper atmosphere of the sun.

57. PAPYRUS : EGPYT :: (a. stone tablets b. marble tablets **c. clay tablets** d. rice paper) : BABYLONIA

    (c) is correct because clay tablets were used for writing in Babylonia as papyrus was in Egypt. (a), (b), and (d) are incorrect because these materials were not used in this capacity in Babylonia.

Explanations
of Answers

58. NOAH : JUDEO-CHRISTIAN :: (a. Gilgamesh b. Jason **c. Deucalion** d. Plato) : GREEK

    (c) is correct because Deucalion was the hero of the great flood myth in Greek mythology as Noah was in Judeo-Christian. (a) is incorrect because Gilgamesh is the protagonist of an ancient Sumerian epic of the same name. (b) is incorrect because Jason is a figure in Greek mythology. (d) is incorrect because Plato was an ancient Greek philosopher.

59. TURPENTINE : PINE :: (a. soap b. ink **c. rattan** d. dye) : PALM

    (c) is correct because rattan comes from the palm tree as turpentine comes from the pine tree. (a) is incorrect because soap, once made from animal products, is now synthetically produced. (b) is incorrect because ink, at its simplest, is a pigment suspended in a liquid. (d) is incorrect because *dye* generally refers to a pigment used to color fabrics.

60. VICTORIA : BRITISH COLUMBIA :: (**a. Toronto** b. Montreal c. Hamilton d. Ottawa) : ONTARIO

    (a) is correct because Toronto is the capital of Ontario as Victoria is the capital of British Columbia. (b), (c), and (d) are all incorrect because, although all are cities in Canada, they are not the capital of Ontario.

61. UNIVERSITY OF ARIZONA : (a. Phoenix b. Flagstaff c. Prescott **d. Tucson**) :: FORDHAM : NEW YORK CITY

    (d) is correct because the University of Arizona is located in Tucson as Fordham is located in New York City. (a), (b), and (c) are incorrect because, although all are cities in Arizona, the university is not located in any of them.

62. THE SNOW QUEEN : ANDERSEN :: UNCLE REMUS : (a. Grimm b. Faust **c. Harris** d. Disney)

    (c) is correct because Harris created Uncle Remus as Andersen created the Snow Queen. (a) and (d) are incorrect because, although they created many fictional characters, they did not create Uncle Remus. (b) is incorrect because Faust was a character in a novel by Goethe.

63. LIGHT : SOUND :: (a. 186,000 feet per second **b. 186,000 miles per second** c. 1,860 miles per second d. 1,680 miles per second) : 1,088 FEET PER SECOND

    (b) is correct because light travels at 186,000 miles per second in a vacuum as sound travels 1,088 feet per second in a vacuum. (a), (c), and (d) are irrelevant.

64. BIO : LIFE :: HEMI : (**a. half** b. earth c. split d. world)

    (**a**) is correct because *hemi* is Greek for "half" as *bio* is Greek for "like." (b), (c), and (d) are incorrect because none is the Greek word for "half."

65. LIVY : HISTORY :: (a. Pindar b. Zeno **c. Horace** d. Sappho) : POETRY

    (**c**) is correct because Horace was a Latin poet as Livy was a Latin historian. (a) is incorrect because Pindar was a Greek poet. (b) is incorrect because Zeno was a Greek philosopher. (d) is incorrect because Sappho was a Greek poet.

66. WASHINGTON : MT. VERNON :: (a. Arthur b. Grant **c. Roosevelt** d. Cleveland) : HYDE PARK

    (**c**) is correct because Franklin Roosevelt was buried at Hyde Park as Washington was buried at Mt. Vernon. (a) is incorrect because Arthur was buried in Albany. (b) is incorrect because Grant was buried in New York City. (d) is incorrect because Cleveland was buried in Princeton.

67. *WALL STREET JOURNAL* : NEW YORK :: (a. *Sun Times* b. *Examiner* c. *Star* **d. *Inquirer***) : PHILADELPHIA

    (**d**) is correct because the *Inquirer* is based in Philadelphia as the *Wall Street Journal* is based in New York. (a) is incorrect because the *Sun Times* is based in Chicago. (b) is incorrect because the *Examiner* is based in San Francisco. (c) is incorrect because the *Star* is a national tabloid.

68. PUERTO RICO : RICH PORT :: NEVADA : (a. flat land b. cold night **c. snow clad** d. new start)

    (**c**) is correct because the name *Nevada* comes from the Spanish for "snowclad" as *Puerto Rico* comes from the Spanish for "rich port." (a), (b), and (d) do not refer to this Western state.

69. HELIUM : SUN :: NEON : (**a. new** b. light c. bright d. extreme)

    (**a**) is correct because *neon* comes from the Greek word for "new" as *helium* comes from the Greek word for "sun." (b), (c), and (d) are irrelevant.

Explanations of Answers

Explanations
of Answers

70. LUXEMBOURG : CONSTITUTIONAL MONARCHY :: ICELAND :
(a. traditional monarchy b. constitutional monarchy c. independent
commonwealth **d. republic**)

(d) is correct because Iceland's form of government is a republic as Luxembourg's is a constitutional monarchy. (a), (b), and (c) are incorrect because, although all are forms of government, none applies to Iceland.

71. HYDROGEN : 1 :: CARBON : (**a. 6** b. 8 c. 9 d. 12)

(a) is correct because carbon's atomic number is 6 as hydrogen's atomic number is 1. (b) is incorrect because oxygen is atomic number 8. (c) is incorrect because fluorine is atomic number 9. (d) is incorrect because magnesium is atomic number 12.

72. EMMY : TELEVISION :: (a. Nobel b. Tony **c. Pulitzer** d. Fermi) :
JOURNALISM

(c) is correct because a Pulitzer is given as an award in the field of journalism as the Emmy is given in the field of television. (a) is incorrect because the Nobel Prize is awarded in the fields of physics, chemistry, medicine, literature, peace, and economic science. (b) is incorrect because the Tony is awarded in the field of Broadway theater. (d) is incorrect because the Fermi is awarded for achievement in atomic energy.

73. (a. Throgs Neck b. Brooklyn c. George Washington **d. Verrazano Narrows**) :
NEW YORK :: GOLDEN GATE : SAN FRANCISCO

(d) is correct because the Verrazano Narrows is the longest suspension bridge in New York, as the Golden Gate is the longest suspension bridge in San Francisco. (a), (b), and (c) are all incorrect because, although they are all suspension bridges in New York, they are not the longest.

74. PULLET : HEN :: ELVER : (a. wild fowl **b. eel** c. zebra d. hare)

(b) is correct because elver is the name for a young eel as pullet is the name for a young hen. (a) is incorrect because the name for a young wild fowl is a flapper. (c) is incorrect because the name for a young zebra is a foal. (d) is incorrect because the name for a young hare is a leveret.

75. EGYPT : PHILIPPINES :: POUND : (a. yen **b. peso** c. nuevo sol d. dinar)

   (b) is correct because the peso is the currency of the Philippines as the pound is the currency of Egypt. (a) is incorrect because the yen is the currency of Japan. (c) is incorrect because the nuevo sol is the currency of Peru. (d) is incorrect because the dinar is the currency of Algeria.

76. JUPITER : PLANET :: (a. Io b. Moon c. Europa **d. Ganymede**) : SATELLITE

   (d) is correct because Ganymede is the largest satellite in our solar system as Jupiter is the largest planet. (a), (b), and (c) are incorrect because, although all are satellites, they are not the largest.

77. ESTROGEN : OVARIES :: GASTRIN : (**a. stomach glands** b. adrenal medulla c. thyroid d. pancreas)

   (a) is correct because gastrin is a hormone produced by the stomach glands as estrogen is a hormone produced by the ovaries. (b) is incorrect because the adrenal medulla produces the hormone adrenaline. (c) is incorrect because the thyroid produces the hormones thyroxin and calcitonin. (d) is incorrect because the pancreas produces the hormone glucagon.

78. MARGARET THATCHER : ELIZABETH II :: (a. Stanley Baldwin b. William Pitt, the younger c. Herbert Asquith **d. Benjamin Disraeli**) : VICTORIA

   (d) is correct because Disraeli was prime minister under Victoria, as Thatcher was under Elizabeth II. (a) is incorrect because Baldwin was under George V. (b) is incorrect because Pitt, the younger was under George III. (c) is incorrect because Asquith was under George V.

79. BRADLEY : HARTFORD :: (a. Gatwick b. Logan **c. Dulles** d. Midway) : WASHINGTON, D.C.

   (c) is correct because Dulles Airport is located in Washington, D.C., as Bradley Airport is located in Hartford, Conn. (a) is incorrect because Gatwick is located in London. (b) is incorrect because Logan is located in Boston. (d) is incorrect because Midway is located in Chicago.

80. ROMAN CATHOLIC : POPE :: EPISCOPALIAN : (a. bishop **b. archbishop** c. cardinal d. apostle)

   (b) is correct because the Archbishop of Canterbury is the head of the Episcopalian faith as the Pope is the head of the Roman Catholic faith. (a), (c), and (d) are incorrect because they are all lower church offices.

Explanations of Answers

81. *HOMO HABILIS* : 2,000,000 :: NEANDERTHAL : (a. 10,000 b. 15,000 **c. 75,000** d. 200,000)

    (c) is correct because Neanderthal man existed circa 75,000 as *Homo hablis* existed circa 2,000,000. (a), (b), and (d) are insignificant.

82. NEST : VIPERS :: (a. gaggle **b. band** c. gross d. pack) : GORILLAS

    (b) is correct because *band* is the collective noun for "gorillas" as *nest* is the collective noun for "vipers." (a) is incorrect because it refers to geese. (c) is incorrect because it refers to oxen. (d) is incorrect because it refers to hounds.

83. CORAL SNAKE : BLACK WIDOW SPIDER :: GARDEN SNAKE : (**a. harvest** spider b. latrodectus geometricus c. brown recluse d. grey widow)

    (a) is correct because the harvest spider, like the garden snake, is harmless to humans, as the black widow spider and the coral snake are dangerous to humans. (b), (c), and (d) are all incorrect because they are spiders dangerous to humans.

84. QUEENSLAND : AUSTRALIA :: (**a. Texas** b. Washington, D.C. c. Boston d. San Francisco) : UNITED STATES

    (a) is correct because Texas is a state in the United States as Queensland is a state in Australia. (b), (c), and (d) are all incorrect because they are cities.

85. KORAN : ISLAM :: BHAGAVAD-GITA : (a. Buddhism b. Confucianism c. Baha'i **d. Hinduism**)

    (d) is correct because the Bhagavad-Gita is a work of Hinduism as the Koran is a work of Islam. (a) is incorrect because Tripitika is a work of Buddhism. (b) is incorrect because Analects is a work of Confucianism. (c) is incorrect because Bayán is a work of Baha'i.

86. ULNA : ARM :: (a. tarsals b. humerus c. mandible **d. tibia**) : LEG

    (d) is correct because the tibia is a bone in the leg as the ulna is an arm bone. (a) is incorrect because the tarsal bones are in the foot. (b) is incorrect because the humerus is a bone in the arm. (c) is incorrect because the mandible bone is in the head.

87. DOG : CANIDAE :: (**a. frog** b. squirrel c. cat d. lizard) : RANIDAE

    (a) is correct because the family name for frog is ranidae as the family name for dog is canidae. (b) is incorrect because the squirrel is in the sciurdae family. (c) is incorrect because the cat is in the felide family. (d) is incorrect because the lizard is in the squamata family.

Explanations of Answers

88. GAEA : TERRA :: HESTIA : (a. Juno b. Saturn c. Eros **d. Vestia**)

    (d) is correct because *Vestia* is the Roman name for "Hestia" as *Terra* is the Roman name for "Gaea." (a) is incorrect because *Juno* is the Roman name for "Hera." (b) is incorrect because *Saturn* is the Roman name for "Cronos." (c) is incorrect because *Eros* is the Roman name for "Cupid."

89. K : KAPPA :: (a. Z **b. Q** c. D d. L) : KOPPA

    (b) is correct because Q is the Roman letter for the Greek koppa as K is the Roman equivalent for the Greek kappa. (a) is incorrect because Z is Roman for zeta. (c) is incorrect because D is Roman for delta. (d) is incorrect because L is Roman for lambda.

90. ARABIC : ROMAN :: 600 : (a. MD b. CC **c. DC** d. MX)

    (c) is correct because Arabic numeral 600 is equivalent to Roman numeral DC. (a) is incorrect because the Arabic value of the Roman numeral MD is 1,500. (b) is incorrect because the Arabic equivalent of CC is 200. (d) is incorrect because MX equals 1,010.

91. LEDA : HELEN :: (a. Metis **b. Diona** c. Themis d. Io) : APHRODITE

    (b) is correct because Diona was the mother of Aphrodite as Leda was the mother of Helen. (a) is incorrect because Metis was the mother of Athena. (c) is incorrect because Themis was the mother of the Fates. (d) is incorrect because Io was the mother of Epaphus.

92. MACRO : LARGE :: HOMO : (a. small **b. same** c. male d. similar)

    (b) is correct because *homo* is Greek for "same" as *macro* is Greek for "large." (a) is incorrect because the Greek word for "small" is *micro*. (c) is incorrect because the Greek word for "male" is *andro*. (d) is incorrect because *homeo* is Greek for "similar."

93. CZAR : RUSSIA :: KHAN : (**a. Mongolia** b. Egypt c. Turkey d. China)

    (a) is correct because a khan was a ruler in Mongolia as a czar was a ruler in Russia. (b) is incorrect because a pharaoh ruled in Egypt. (c) is incorrect because a sultan ruled in Turkey. (d) is incorrect because an emperor ruled in China.

94. BALL : MUSKET :: (a. wire b. nut **c. bolt** d. wood) : CROSSBOW

    (c) is correct because a bolt is shot from a crossbow as a ball is shot from a musket. (a), (b), and (d) are incorrect because these objects were not fired from a crossbow.

95. SITAR : STRING :: DOUMBEK : (a. keys b. pedals c. stick **d. skin**)

   (d) is correct because sound is produced from the skin of the doumbek as it is produced from the string on a sitar. (a) and (b) are incorrect because they refer to a keyboard instrument, such as a piano, or an organ. (c) is incorrect because this is a general term, musically referring to a percussion implement.

96. JOAN OF ARC : BURNING :: ROBESPIERRE : (a. hanging b. starvation **c. guillotine** d. firing squad)

   (c) is correct because Robespierre was executed by guillotine as Joan of Arc was executed by burning. (a), (b), and (d) are incorrect because, although all are forms of execution, none apply here.

97. FISSION : SPLITTING :: FUSION : (a. cooling b. heating **c. combining** d. melting)

   (c) is correct because fusion creates energy by combining the nuclei as fission creates energy by splitting a nucleus. (a), (b), and (d) are incorrect because while these terms are used in the creation of nuclear energy, they do not specifically refer to fusion.

98. SHIVA : KALI :: ODEN : (a. Frey **b. Frigg** c. Loki d. Thor)

   (b) is correct because Frigg was the goddess consort of Oden in Norse mythology as Kali was to Shiva in Hindu mythology. (a) is incorrect because Frey was the god of prosperity. (b) is incorrect because Loki was the god of evil. (d) is incorrect because Thor was the god of thunder.

99. SALVATION ARMY : WILLIAM BOOTH :: (a. Girl Scouts b. Boy Scouts c. Sierra Club **d. Red Cross**) : JEAN HENRI DURANT

   (d) is correct because Durant was the founder of the Red Cross as Booth was the founder of the Salvation Army. (a) is incorrect because Juliette Low founded the Girl Scouts. (b) is incorrect because Sir Robert Powell founded the Boy Scouts. (c) is incorrect because John Muir founded the Sierra Club.

100. AMNESIA : MEMORY :: (**a. astigmatism** b. tinnitus c. rhinitis d. othematoma) : VISION

   (a) is correct because vision is affected by astigmatism as memory is affected by amnesia. (b) is incorrect because tinnitus affects the hearing. (c) is incorrect because rhinitis affects the sense of smell. (d) is incorrect because othematoma, cauliflower ear, affects the hearing.

Miller Analogies

Practice Test 4

Answer Sheet
Practice Test 4

1. Ⓐ Ⓑ Ⓒ Ⓓ
2. Ⓐ Ⓑ Ⓒ Ⓓ
3. Ⓐ Ⓑ Ⓒ Ⓓ
4. Ⓐ Ⓑ Ⓒ Ⓓ
5. Ⓐ Ⓑ Ⓒ Ⓓ
6. Ⓐ Ⓑ Ⓒ Ⓓ
7. Ⓐ Ⓑ Ⓒ Ⓓ
8. Ⓐ Ⓑ Ⓒ Ⓓ
9. Ⓐ Ⓑ Ⓒ Ⓓ
10. Ⓐ Ⓑ Ⓒ Ⓓ
11. Ⓐ Ⓑ Ⓒ Ⓓ
12. Ⓐ Ⓑ Ⓒ Ⓓ
13. Ⓐ Ⓑ Ⓒ Ⓓ
14. Ⓐ Ⓑ Ⓒ Ⓓ
15. Ⓐ Ⓑ Ⓒ Ⓓ
16. Ⓐ Ⓑ Ⓒ Ⓓ
17. Ⓐ Ⓑ Ⓒ Ⓓ
18. Ⓐ Ⓑ Ⓒ Ⓓ
19. Ⓐ Ⓑ Ⓒ Ⓓ
20. Ⓐ Ⓑ Ⓒ Ⓓ
21. Ⓐ Ⓑ Ⓒ Ⓓ
22. Ⓐ Ⓑ Ⓒ Ⓓ
23. Ⓐ Ⓑ Ⓒ Ⓓ
24. Ⓐ Ⓑ Ⓒ Ⓓ
25. Ⓐ Ⓑ Ⓒ Ⓓ
26. Ⓐ Ⓑ Ⓒ Ⓓ
27. Ⓐ Ⓑ Ⓒ Ⓓ
28. Ⓐ Ⓑ Ⓒ Ⓓ
29. Ⓐ Ⓑ Ⓒ Ⓓ
30. Ⓐ Ⓑ Ⓒ Ⓓ
31. Ⓐ Ⓑ Ⓒ Ⓓ
32. Ⓐ Ⓑ Ⓒ Ⓓ
33. Ⓐ Ⓑ Ⓒ Ⓓ
34. Ⓐ Ⓑ Ⓒ Ⓓ

35. Ⓐ Ⓑ Ⓒ Ⓓ
36. Ⓐ Ⓑ Ⓒ Ⓓ
37. Ⓐ Ⓑ Ⓒ Ⓓ
38. Ⓐ Ⓑ Ⓒ Ⓓ
39. Ⓐ Ⓑ Ⓒ Ⓓ
40. Ⓐ Ⓑ Ⓒ Ⓓ
41. Ⓐ Ⓑ Ⓒ Ⓓ
42. Ⓐ Ⓑ Ⓒ Ⓓ
43. Ⓐ Ⓑ Ⓒ Ⓓ
44. Ⓐ Ⓑ Ⓒ Ⓓ
45. Ⓐ Ⓑ Ⓒ Ⓓ
46. Ⓐ Ⓑ Ⓒ Ⓓ
47. Ⓐ Ⓑ Ⓒ Ⓓ
48. Ⓐ Ⓑ Ⓒ Ⓓ
49. Ⓐ Ⓑ Ⓒ Ⓓ
50. Ⓐ Ⓑ Ⓒ Ⓓ
51. Ⓐ Ⓑ Ⓒ Ⓓ
52. Ⓐ Ⓑ Ⓒ Ⓓ
53. Ⓐ Ⓑ Ⓒ Ⓓ
54. Ⓐ Ⓑ Ⓒ Ⓓ
55. Ⓐ Ⓑ Ⓒ Ⓓ
56. Ⓐ Ⓑ Ⓒ Ⓓ
57. Ⓐ Ⓑ Ⓒ Ⓓ
58. Ⓐ Ⓑ Ⓒ Ⓓ
59. Ⓐ Ⓑ Ⓒ Ⓓ
60. Ⓐ Ⓑ Ⓒ Ⓓ
61. Ⓐ Ⓑ Ⓒ Ⓓ
62. Ⓐ Ⓑ Ⓒ Ⓓ
63. Ⓐ Ⓑ Ⓒ Ⓓ
64. Ⓐ Ⓑ Ⓒ Ⓓ
65. Ⓐ Ⓑ Ⓒ Ⓓ
66. Ⓐ Ⓑ Ⓒ Ⓓ
67. Ⓐ Ⓑ Ⓒ Ⓓ
68. Ⓐ Ⓑ Ⓒ Ⓓ

69. Ⓐ Ⓑ Ⓒ Ⓓ
70. Ⓐ Ⓑ Ⓒ Ⓓ
71. Ⓐ Ⓑ Ⓒ Ⓓ
72. Ⓐ Ⓑ Ⓒ Ⓓ
73. Ⓐ Ⓑ Ⓒ Ⓓ
74. Ⓐ Ⓑ Ⓒ Ⓓ
75. Ⓐ Ⓑ Ⓒ Ⓓ
76. Ⓐ Ⓑ Ⓒ Ⓓ
77. Ⓐ Ⓑ Ⓒ Ⓓ
78. Ⓐ Ⓑ Ⓒ Ⓓ
79. Ⓐ Ⓑ Ⓒ Ⓓ
80. Ⓐ Ⓑ Ⓒ Ⓓ
81. Ⓐ Ⓑ Ⓒ Ⓓ
82. Ⓐ Ⓑ Ⓒ Ⓓ
83. Ⓐ Ⓑ Ⓒ Ⓓ
84. Ⓐ Ⓑ Ⓒ Ⓓ
85. Ⓐ Ⓑ Ⓒ Ⓓ
86. Ⓐ Ⓑ Ⓒ Ⓓ
87. Ⓐ Ⓑ Ⓒ Ⓓ
88. Ⓐ Ⓑ Ⓒ Ⓓ
89. Ⓐ Ⓑ Ⓒ Ⓓ
90. Ⓐ Ⓑ Ⓒ Ⓓ
91. Ⓐ Ⓑ Ⓒ Ⓓ
92. Ⓐ Ⓑ Ⓒ Ⓓ
93. Ⓐ Ⓑ Ⓒ Ⓓ
94. Ⓐ Ⓑ Ⓒ Ⓓ
95. Ⓐ Ⓑ Ⓒ Ⓓ
96. Ⓐ Ⓑ Ⓒ Ⓓ
97. Ⓐ Ⓑ Ⓒ Ⓓ
98. Ⓐ Ⓑ Ⓒ Ⓓ
99. Ⓐ Ⓑ Ⓒ Ⓓ
100. Ⓐ Ⓑ Ⓒ Ⓓ

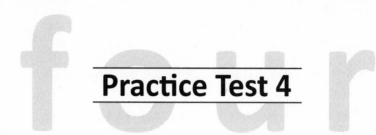

Practice Test 4

TIME: 50 Minutes   **LENGTH:** 100 Analogies

DIRECTIONS: Read each of the following analogies carefully, and choose the BEST answer to each item. Fill in your responses in the answer sheets provided.

Note: The Miller Analogies Test consists of 120 questions to be completed in 60 minutes. Twenty of these questions are experimental items, which are not scored and thus not reflected in this practice test.

1. CHARLES I : CROMWELL :: NICHOLAS II : (a. Rasputin b. Trotsky c. Stalin d. Lenin)

2. TRIANGLE : LEG :: CIRCLE : (a. radius b. side c. diameter d. arc)

3. CARBOXYLIC ACID PLUS ALCOHOL : (a. metal b. ester c. phenol d. amine) :: ACID PLUS BASE : SALT

4. POTATO : PEA :: (a. tomato b. cucumber c. beet d. corn) : BEAN

5. TANGENT : COTANGENT :: COSINE : (a. sine b. cosecant c. secant d. hypotenuse)

6. SODIUM : POTASSIUM :: ARGON : (a. calcium b. magnesium c. chlorine d. krypton)

7. TRANSPIRE : (a. occur b. pass c. weaken d. puncture) :: BREACH : BREAK

8. UNION : OR :: INTERSECTION : (a. both b. none c. all d. and)

9. (a. crest b. amplitude c. refraction d. edge) : TROUGH :: HIGH : LOW

10. PARE : APPLE :: (a. husk b. trim c. pollinate d. hybrid) : CORN

11. $x : x^2 + 3x :: xy :$ (a. $x^2 + 3y$ b. $x^2y + 3xy$ c. $x^2y^2 + 3y$ d. $x^2y^2 + 3xy$)

12. COLLUVIUM : SEDIMENTS :: GEOMETRIC MINERALS : (a. salts b. crystals c. tetrahedra d. mica)

13. INDUCTION : (a. suppression b. regulation c. promotion d. repression) :: LACTOSE OPERON : ARGININE OPERON

14. PRODUCT : FACTOR :: SUM : (a. integer b. quotient c. proctor d. addend)

15. (a. tranquilizer b. soporific c. stimulant d. analgesic) : SOMNOLENT :: ANXIOLYTIC : CALM

16. DONOR : (a. conjugation b. recipient c. HFR d. induction) :: F^+ : F^-

17. CORUSCATE : DIAMOND :: (a. shine b. soft c. flat d. refined) : GOLD

18. 8 : 2 :: 125 : (a. 15.65 b. 25 c. 5 d. 12.55)

19. GRADUATED CYLINDER : MILLILITER :: (a. pipette b. ounce c. scale d. analytical balance) : MILLIGRAM

20. SLED : RUNNER :: WAGON : (a. slat b. handle c. wheel d. wagoneer)

21. APERITIF : DRINK :: (a. chocolate b. dessert c. hors d'oeuvre d. soup) : FOOD

22. BREW : BEER :: (a. season b. leaf c. steep d. simmer) : TEA

23. ROCKSLIDE : HILL :: (a. fall b. flow c. creep d. slump) : CURVE

24. VIRGIL : *AENEID* :: (a. Chaucer b. Shakespeare c. Johnson d. Homer) : *ILIAD*

25. (a. acid rain b. distilled water c. baking soda d. litmus paper) : NEUTRAL :: VINEGAR : ACIDIC

26. 7 : 49 :: 11 : (a. 121 b. 144 c. 81 d. 13)

Practice Test 4

27. RANID : (a. fox b. frog c. rabbit d. grasshopper) :: CANID : WOLF

28. EDENTATE : TEETH :: ALBINO : (a. white b. fragile c. pigment d. small)

29. GENE : CHROMOSOME :: (a. bird b. feather c. flight d. bone) : WING

30. ABSORBED : SCATTERED :: SPECTROPHOTOMETER : (a. turbidity
     b. nephelometer c. voltmeter d. light)

31. BLINDERS : (a. partial b. central c. peripheral d. occasional) :: BLINDFOLD :
     TOTAL

32. IONIC : COLUMN :: GAMBREL : (a. ceiling b. mantel c. entry d. roof)

33. (a. lens b. microscope c. opera glasses d. telescope) : BINOCULARS ::
     SPINET : PIANO

34. $g : g^2 + 3g - 2 :: 3 : $ (a. 16 b. 2 c. −2 d. 10)

35. REYNARD : VIXEN :: (a. stallion b. doe c. steer d. jennet) : COW

36. PATTERN : GARMENT :: (a. DNA b. intellect c. hormones d. environment) :
     HEREDITY

37. pH : HYDROGEN ION :: (a. galvanometer b. current c. pH meter d. cuvette) :
     ELECTRONS

38. (a. Chaucer b. Ralph Waldo Emerson c. Joseph Heller d. James Joyce) :
     LOUISA MAY ALCOTT :: TRUMAN CAPOTE : PEARL S. BUCK

39. (a. Nathaniel Hawthorne b. Mark Twain c. Charles Dickens d. Ernest
     Hemingway) : MISSISSIPPI :: HENRY JAMES : NEW YORK

40. AMOEBA : (a. membranes b. gills c. cilia d. pseudopod) :: OCTOPUS :
     TENTACLE

41. NEOLOGISM : (a. book b. word c. property d. equation) :: INNOVATION :
     CONCEPT

42. DENSE : DISPERSE :: (a. release b. dilute c. erode d. inflict) : EXPAND

43. IMPROMPTU : MEMORIZED :: SPONTANEOUS : (a. impetuous b. static c. calculated d. glib)

44. IMPERVIOUS : AGITATED :: (a. enlightened b. depressive c. perturbed d. pretentious) : IGNORANT

45. JOHN KENNEDY : LYNDON BAINES JOHNSON :: GEORGE WASHINGTON : (a. John Adams b. Benjamin Harrison c. Andrew Jackson d. Benjamin Franklin)

46. BENEVOLENT : MALIGNANT :: COOPERATIVE : (a. deleterious b. resistant c. evasive d. eager)

47. $60°$: sin $60°$ :: $30°$: (a. b. $\frac{1}{2}$ c. 1 d.)

48. RIVER : ESTUARY :: (a. sand b. cove c. ocean d. land) : SHORE

49. PASSE PARTOUT : (a. code b. lock c. safe d. master key) :: NOUVEAU RICHE : NEWLY WEALTHY

50. (a. Patagonia b. Fierro c. Bolivar d. San Martin) : REVOLUTIONARY :: BORGES : AUTHOR

51. (a. absorbance b. adsorption c. reflection d. scattering) : TRANSMITTANCE :: INTAKE : OUTPUT

52. (a. grotesque b. imperfect c. pseudo d. exiguous) : COUNTERFEIT :: INCHOATE : SHAPELESS

53. WASP : HYMENOPTERA :: (a. dogs b. bears c. humans d. cats) : PRIMATES

54. SEDULOUS : (a. retreating b. habitual c. careless d. bored) :: PREEMPTORY : YIELDING

55. VALETUDINARIAN : (a. hypochondriac b. doctor c. hospital d. psychiatrist) :: VICTIM : PARANOIC

56.   MORTAR : (a. fire b. pestle c. brick d. cement) :: ANVIL : HAMMER

57.   GESTATION : (a. birth b. elimination c. conclusion d. resorption) ::
      LACTATION : WEANING

58.   Given

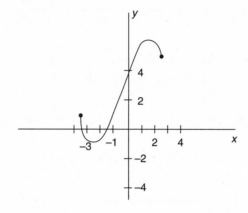

      (3, 8) : MAXIMUM :: (–2, –1) : (a. inflection point b. minimum c. slope
      d. intersection)

59.   (a. bacteria b. coliforms c. hepatitis virus d. rickettsia) : EOSIN METHYLENE
      BLUE AGAR :: YEASTS : SABOURAUD'S AGAR

60.   BLOOD : COAGULATE :: GRAVY : (a. rarefy b. congeal c. deepen d. separate)

61.   (a. Dali b. Cezanne c. Matisse d. Picasso) : CUBISM :: LICHTENSTEIN :
      POP ART

62.   RETROGRADE : ROTATION :: (a. object b. reverse c. circular d. method) :
      MOTION

63.   COCAINE : STIMULANT :: (a. amphetamines b. ritalin c. barbiturates
      d. LSD) : DEPRESSANT

64.   (a. shark b. whale c. flounder d. guppy) : FISH :: PLATYPUS : BIRD

65.   STREP THROAT : BACTERIA :: (a. Rocky Mountain spotted fever
      b. chickenpox c. amoebic dysentery d. tuberculosis) : VIRUS

66.   COMPLEX NUMBER : REAL NUMBER :: RATIONAL NUMBER :
      (a. irrational number b. imaginary number c. integer d. real number)

67. TRIVIAL : (a. minutia b. enigma c. levity d. palavar) :: CATHOLIC : UNIVERSALITY

68. VACILLATE : (a. switch b. divide c. endure d. waver) :: FLUCTUATE : MOVE

69. BLACKSMITH : FORGE :: PAINTER : (a. studio b. canvas c. brush d. mix)

70. (a. Skinner b. Freud c. Piaget d. Pavlov) : INTELLECTUAL DEVELOPMENT :: ERICKSON : EGO IDENTITY

71. VULGAR : CRUDE :: BIASED : (a. prejudiced b. charming c. rough d. just)

72. ANTI-PYROGENIC : ACETAMINOPHEN :: ANTI-INFLAMMATORY : (a. salicylates b. phenacetin c. caffeine d. codeine)

73. FERN : (a. seed b. leaf c. spore d. fruit) :: OAK : ACORN

74. ALBINISM : (a. albumin b. serotonin c. carotene d. melanin) :: MALNUTRITION : CALORIES

75. (a. $-COOH$ b. $-OH$ c. $R - C - OR$ d. $- C - N -$) : ALCOHOL :: $-NH_2$: AMINO

76. NaCl : ROCK SALT :: SiO_2 : (a. crystals b. ice c. calcareous rock d. quartz)

77. MERCURIAL : (a. erratic b. metaphorical c. meretricious d. penal) :: PENNYLESS : IMPOVERISHED

78. MERCER : (a. music b. animals c. textiles d. soldiers) :: RESTAURATEUR : FOOD

79. LIGATURE : (a. closing b. cutting c. binding d. arguing) :: HOOK : FISHING

80. BAROQUE : CLASSICAL :: (a. Renaissance b. Romanesque c. Medieval d. Classical) : ROMANTIC

81. PEREGRINATION : (a. flight b. walk c. flee d. wings) :: CRUISE : SAIL

82. MERGANSER : (a. penguin b. horse c. duck d. dog) :: GERNSEY : COW

83. BUDDHA : (a. China b. India c. Japan d. Cambodia) :: JESUS : ISRAEL

84. TACHYCARDIA : FAST :: (a. angina b. sphygmomanometer c. bradycardia d. cardiac arrhythmia) : SLOW

85. MORTARBOARD : COMMENCEMENT :: CROWN : (a. indoctrination b. ordination c. induction d. coronation)

86. TRANSMOGRIFY : LANGUAGE :: (a. form b. color c. size d. time) : TRANSLATE

87. AGNOSTIC : ATHEIST :: (a. question b. decision c. doubt d. definition) : STATEMENT

88. BARRIER : LINE :: ATOLL : (a. square b. triangle c. circle d. spiral)

89. FLEET : (a. quick b. ship c. ocean d. lugubrious) :: PENSIVE : THOUGHTFUL

90. BRACKISH : (a. murky b. unclean c. salty d. wet) :: FLAXEN : YELLOW

91. LEONINE : LION :: (a. cervine b. equine c. porcine d. bovine) : DEER

92. GRANT : (a. 15 b. 17 c. 22 d. 18) :: REAGAN: 40

93. HUBRIS : PRIDE :: (a. starvation b. satiation c. satisfaction d. nutrition) : HUNGER

94. COCCI : ROUND :: (a. bacilli b. spirochete c. mycoplasma d. spheroplast) : ROD

95. TRAVAIL : WORK :: (a. return b. pillage c. borrow d. kill) : STEAL

96. (a. blood b. milk c. table d. alcohol) : LACTOSE :: FRUIT : FRUCTOSE

97. UPBRAID : REPROACH :: (a. miniscule b. large c. enormous d. lower) : SMALL

98. ENDEMIC : (a. neighborhood b. planet c. region d. building) :: PANDEMIC : COUNTRY

99. FORGIVE : (a. pacify b. exculpate c. contemplate d. ruminate) :: FATAL : LETHAL

100. MORIBUND : (a. morbid b. dying c. laughing d. hungry) :: GERIATRIC : OLD

Answer Key
Practice Test 4

1. (d)	26. (a)	51. (a)	76. (d)
2. (d)	27. (b)	52. (c)	77. (a)
3. (b)	28. (c)	53. (c)	78. (c)
4. (c)	29. (b)	54. (c)	79. (c)
5. (c)	30. (b)	55. (a)	80. (d)
6. (d)	31. (c)	56. (b)	81. (b)
7. (b)	32. (d)	57. (a)	82. (c)
8. (d)	33. (c)	58. (b)	83. (b)
9. (a)	34. (a)	59. (b)	84. (c)
10. (a)	35. (c)	60. (b)	85. (d)
11. (d)	36. (a)	61. (d)	86. (a)
12. (b)	37. (b)	62. (b)	87. (a)
13. (d)	38. (b)	63. (c)	88. (c)
14. (d)	39. (b)	64. (b)	89. (a)
15. (b)	40. (d)	65. (b)	90. (c)
16. (b)	41. (b)	66. (c)	91. (a)
17. (a)	42. (c)	67. (a)	92. (d)
18. (c)	43. (c)	68. (d)	93. (a)
19. (d)	44. (a)	69. (a)	94. (a)
20. (c)	45. (a)	70. (c)	95. (b)
21. (c)	46. (b)	71. (a)	96. (b)
22. (c)	47. (b)	72. (a)	97. (a)
23. (d)	48. (d)	73. (c)	98. (c)
24. (d)	49. (d)	74. (d)	99. (b)
25. (b)	50. (d)	75. (b)	100. (b)

Explanations
of Answers

Explanations of Answers
Practice Test 4

1. CHARLES I : CROMWELL :: NICHOLAS II : (a. Rasputin b. Trotsky c. Stalin **d. Lenin**)

   (d) is correct because Charles I was an English ruler executed at the start of a revolution which resulted in non-royal leadership by Cromwell. Nicholas II was a Russian ruler executed at the start of a revolution which resulted in non-royal leadership by Lenin. Rasputin (a) preceded the revolution and was never an acknowledged leader. Trotsky (b) never had leadership of the Soviet Union and Stalin (c) was a leader after Lenin.

2. TRIANGLE : LEG :: CIRCLE : (a. radius b. side c. diameter **d. arc**)

   (d) The leg is part of the triangle, likewise, an arc (d) is part of a circle. The radius (a) and diameter (c) are parts of the circle, but they do not enclose the circle like the arcs do. A side (b) is a line which is part of a triangle, not a circle.

3. CARBOXYLIC ACID PLUS ALCOHOL : (a. metal **b. ester** c. phenol d. amine) :: ACID PLUS BASE : SALT

   (b) Ester is correct because when a carboxylic acid plus alcohol react, an ester results. When an acid and a base react, a salt results. A metal (a) is usually an element of two or more elements together, phenol (c) is an aromatic hydrocarbon, and an amine (d) will involve a nitrogen atom, so none of these fits the analogy of what results when any carboxylic acid is added to an alcohol.

4. POTATO : PEA :: (a. tomato b. cucumber **c. beet** d. corn) : BEAN

   (c) is correct because a potato and a beet are both root vegetables. A pea and a bean are both pod vegetables. Tomato (a) and cucumber (b) are both fruits. Corn (d) is neither a root nor a pod vegetable.

5. TANGENT : COTANGENT :: COSINE : (a. sine b. cosecant **c. secant** d. hypotenuse)

   (c) The cotangent is the complementary trigonometric function to tangent. Thus, the complementary function of cosine is secant (c). Sine (a) and cosecant (b) comprise the other pair of functions. The hypotenuse (d) is the longest leg of a right triangle. While the hypotenuse is used in calculating trigonometric functions, it is not one.

6. SODIUM : POTASSIUM :: ARGON : (a. calcium b. magnesium c. chlorine **d. krypton**)

    (d) Krypton is correct because sodium and potassium are found on the Periodic Table in Group IA, with sodium in Period 3 and potassium in Period 4. Argon and krypton are found in Group VIII, argon in Period 3 and krypton in Period 4. Calcium (a), magnesium (b), and chlorine (c) do not fit in a category with argon and therefore do not fit the analogy.

7. TRANSPIRE : (a. occur **b. pass** c. weaken d. puncture) :: BREACH : BREAK

    (b) is correct because *to transpire* is "to pass through a surface" just as *to breach* is "to break through a surface." *Occur* (a) does not specifically refer to breaking or passing through a surface. A substance that *transpires* does not necessarily weaken (c) or puncture (d) the surface.

8. UNION : OR :: INTERSECTION : (a. both b. none c. all **d. and**)

    (d) The union of sets includes all the elements of the sets. In contrast, the intersection of sets includes only the elements which are common to all the sets, i.e., the elements in one set and (d) in all other sets. Choices (a) both and (c) all are equivalent to the union, for cases of only two sets. Finally, none (b) would be the null set.

9. (**a. crest** b. amplitude c. refraction d. edge) : TROUGH :: HIGH : LOW

    (a) Crest is correct because the high part of a wave is the crest, while the low part is the trough. Amplitude (b) is one half of the distance between the crest and the trough. Refraction (c) is the change in direction of certain waves, while the edge (d) is the outer area. None of these three terms can be used to complete the analogy.

10. PARE : APPLE :: (**a. husk** b. trim c. pollinate d. hybrid) : CORN

    (a) is correct because to pare an apple is to remove its outer covering, just as to husk corn is to remove its outer covering. Trim (b) refers to cutting but not specifically to the removal of an outer covering. Pollinate (c) and hybrid (d) refer to breeding.

11. $x : x^2 + 3x :: xy : $ (a. $x^2 + 3y$ b. $x^2y + 3xy$ c. $x^2y^2 + 3y$ **d. $x^2y^2 + 3xy$**)

    (d) In this analogy, the term x is squared and added to 3 multiplied by x ($x^2 + 3x$). Thus, the term xy should also be squared and added to 3 multiplied by x^2y^2, or $x^2y^2 + 3xy$.

12. COLLUVIUM : SEDIMENTS :: GEOMETRIC MINERALS : (a. salts **b. crystals** c. tetrahedra d. mica)

    (b) *Crystals* is correct because *colluvium* is a collective term for "sediments deposited by mass movement." *Crystal* is a collective term for all geometric minerals. Not all salts (a) have a geometric pattern to their structure. Tetrahedra (c), although geometric, may not be minerals. Mica (d) does not have a regular geometric pattern.

13. INDUCTION : (a. suppression b. regulation c. promotion **d. repression**) :: LACTOSE OPERON : ARGININE OPERON

    (d) Repression is correct because the lactose operon works by induction, meaning that it functions only when the substrate lactose is present. The arginine operon works by repression, meaning that its function is repressed when too much arginine is present. The processes of suppression (a), regulation (b), and promotion (c) all impact on enzymatic gene regulation, but do not refer to the actual type of operon, and therefore do not complete the analogy.

14. PRODUCT : FACTOR :: SUM : (a. integer b. quotient c. proctor **d. addend**)

    (d) is correct because in math a product is the result of multiplying two or more factors, just as a sum is the result of adding two or more addends. Integers (a) are not exclusively numbers to be added and a quotient (b) is the result of division. Proctor (c) is incorrect because this refers to someone who oversees the administration of an exam.

15. (a. tranquilizer **b. soporific** c. stimulant d. analgesic) : SOMNOLENT :: ANXIOLYTIC : CALM

    (b) is correct because a soporific makes one somnolent or sleepy. An anxiolytic makes one calm. A tranquilizer (a) makes one calm but not necessarily sleepy. Stimulant (c) is incorrect because this has just the opposite effect. Analgesic (d) is incorrect because this refers to a pain reliever.

16. DONOR : (a. conjugation **b. recipient** c. HFR d. induction) :: F^+ : F^-

    (b) Recipient is correct because in the conjugation process, bacterial donor cells are referred to as F^+, while recipient cells are referred to as F^-. The process is conjugation (a), but this term does not complete the analogy. HFR (c) are high frequency recombination cells, but these cells donate. Induction (d) is a term which refers to the making of an enzyme only when its substrate is present.

17. CORUSCATE : DIAMOND :: (**a. shine** b. soft c. flat d. refined) : GOLD

(a) is correct because to coruscate is to sparkle as a diamond does. To shine is to be bright (but not sparkling) as gold is. Gold is soft (b) compared to a diamond but that isn't a visual attribute as both coruscate and sparkle are. (c) and (d) are incorrect because while they are physical attributes, they do not refer to their visual interaction with light.

18. 8 : 2 :: 125 : (a. 15.65 b. 25 **c. 5** d. 12.55)

(c) The cube root of 8 is 2; likewise, the cube root of 125 is 5.

19. GRADUATED CYLINDER : MILLILITER :: (a. pipette b. ounce c. scale **d. analytical balance**) : MILLIGRAM

(d) Analytical balance is correct because a graduated cylinder is a device used for measuring liquids in the unit known as the milliliter. The analogy is therefore completed by the device which measures things in the mass unit known as the milligram. The pipette (a) is a measuring device but measures in milliliters. The ounce (b) is a unit of measure, not a measuring device. The scale (c) technically measures weight, rather than mass. Thus, the analytical balance is the device which measures mass in the unit known as the milligram.

20. SLED : RUNNER :: WAGON : (a. slat b. handle **c. wheel** d. wagoneer)

(c) is correct because a sled moves on runners. A wagon moves on wheels. (a), (b), and (d) are incorrect because while they refer to the operation or parts of a wagon, they are not integral to its movement.

21. APERITIF : DRINK :: (a. chocolate b. dessert **c. hors d'oeuvre** d. soup) : FOOD

(c) is correct because an aperitif is by definition a drink served as an appetizer just as an hors d'oeuvre is by definition a food served as an appetizer. Chocolate (a) is a dessert (b), not an appetizer. Soup (d) may be served as an appetizer but is not exclusively an appetizer by definition.

22. BREW : BEER :: (a. season b. leaf **c. steep** d. simmer) : TEA

(c) is correct because you brew beer to prepare it as you steep tea to prepare it. You don't simmer (d) tea leaves (b)—you boil the water, then pour it over the leaves in a separate container. While it is optional to season (a) the tea or the beer, it is not a part of the creation of those beverages.

23. ROCKSLIDE : HILL :: (a. fall b. flow c. creep **d. slump**) : CURVE

(d) Slump is correct because a rockslide occurs because of a down slope move-ment of rocks on a hill. A slump is the sliding of rocks and other materials along a curve, usually due to erosion at the base of the curve. Flows (b) occur when materials have a semiliquid behavior, and do not have to be on curves. A fall (a) occurs from a high place such as a cliff and does not have to involve a curve. None of these words are related to the word curve and cannot be used to com-plete the analogy.

24. VIRGIL : *AENEID* :: (a. Chaucer b. Shakespeare c. Johnson **d. Homer**) : *ILIAD*

(d) is the correct response. Virgil wrote the *Aeneid*. (d) Homer wrote the *Iliad*. (a) Chaucer, (b) Shakespeare, and (c) Johnson are all incorrect because they are not authors of the *Iliad*.

25. (a. acid rain **b. distilled water** c. baking soda d. litmus paper) : NEUTRAL :: VINEGAR : ACIDIC

(b) is the correct answer. Vinegar is an acidic substance. Therefore, we are look-ing for a word that is a neutral substance. (b) distilled water is neutral. (a) is incorrect because acid rain is acidic. (c) is incorrect because baking soda is alka-line. (d) is wrong because litmus paper is used to test the pH of substances.

26. 7 : 49 :: 11 : (**a. 121** b. 144 c. 81 d. 13)

(a) Here, 49 is the square of 7. Therefore, the correct answer should be the square of 11, which is 121, (a). 144 (b) is the square of 12; 81 (c) is the square of 9. 13 (d) is the next prime number in the series, 7, 11, 13, . . .

27. RANID : (a. fox **b. frog** c. rabbit d. grasshopper) :: CANID : WOLF

(b) is correct because ranids are a family of animals consisting of types of frogs just as canids are a family of animals consisting of types of wolves and other doglike animals. The fox (a), rabbit (c), and grasshopper (d) are not even in the amphibian class as frogs are, so they couldn't be in the same family and are therefore incorrect.

28. EDENTATE : TEETH :: ALBINO : (a. white b. fragile **c. pigment** d. small)

(c) is correct because an edentate animal lacks teeth just as an albino animal lacks pigment. (a) is incorrect because an albino animal does not lack white. (b) and (d) are incorrect because there is nothing to suggest that an albino animal would be fragile or small.

29. GENE : CHROMOSOME :: (a. bird **b. feather** c. flight d. bone) : WING

   (b) is correct because many genes make up a chromosome. Many feathers make up a wing. (a) is incorrect because many birds do not comprise a wing. (c) is incorrect because flight is the function of the wing. Only a couple of bones (d) are needed for a wing and they are not the principal part of a wing.

30. ABSORBED : SCATTERED :: SPECTROPHOTOMETER : (a. turbidity **b. nephelometer** c. voltmeter d. light)

   (b) Nephelometer is correct because absorbed light is measured by a spectrophotometer, whereas scattered light is measured by a nephelometer. Turbidity (a) is the amount of light that is lost due to scattering, but it is not a measuring tool, and therefore does not complete the analogy. A voltmeter (c) is a measuring instrument, but it does not measure absorbed or scattered light. Although absorbed and scattered refer to light (d), the analogy cannot be completed with this term, since it is the device for measuring scattered light that is being sought.

31. BLINDERS : (a. partial b. central **c. peripheral** d. occasional) :: BLINDFOLD : TOTAL

   (c) is correct because blinders block peripheral vision. A blindfold blocks total vision. Blinders specifically block peripheral vision so partial (a), central (b), and occasional (d) are not precise enough.

32. IONIC : COLUMN :: GAMBREL : (a. ceiling b. mantel c. entry **d. roof**)

   (d) is correct because ionic is a style of column just as gambrel is a style of roof. Gambrel is a term used only for a roof. Ceiling (a), mantel (b), and entry (c) are general architectural terms to which gambrel does not refer, and are therefore incorrect.

33. (a. lens b. microscope **c. opera glasses** d. telescope) : BINOCULARS :: SPINET : PIANO

   (c) is correct because opera glasses are a compact low-powered type of binoculars. A spinet is a compact low-powered (in quantity and quality of sound) type of piano. A lens (a) is incorrect because it does not refer to the quality of the instrument that uses it. Microscope (b) and telescope (d) are general types of instruments that are not inherently low-powered.

34. $g : g^2 + 3g - 2 :: 3 :$ (**a. 16** b. 2 c. −2 d. 10)

   (a) This analogy defines g as a function of $g^2 + 3g - 2$. When 3 is substituted for g, then $3^2 + 3 \times 3 - 2 = 16$.

35. REYNARD : VIXEN :: (a. stallion b. doe **c. steer** d. jennet) : COW

(c) is the correct answer. A reynard is a male fox and a vixen is a female fox. Steer is the male and cow is the female version of an ox. (a) Stallion is the word for a male horse. (b) Doe is the female version and buck is the male version of deer. (d) Jennet is a female donkey.

36. PATTERN : GARMENT :: (**a. DNA** b. intellect c. hormones d. environment) : HEREDITY

(a) (a) is the correct response. A pattern is used as a blueprint for creating a garment. (a) DNA is the blueprint for heredity. (b) Intellect relates to your intelligence and is not a blueprint for heredity. (c) Hormones are a product of living cells that circulate and have an influence on other cells. (d) Environment is the outside influences on a person and does not have a direct effect on heredity.

37. pH : HYDROGEN ION :: (a. galvanometer **b. current** c. pH meter d. cuvette) : ELECTRONS

(b) is correct because pH is a measure of hydrogen ion concentration, while current is a measure of flow of electrons. The galvanometer (a) and the pH meter (c) are the instruments which are used to make the measurements and therefore do not complete the analogy to what is actually measured. The cuvette (d) is a tube which holds solutions to be measured and therefore does not complete the analogy to what is actually being measured.

38. (a. Chaucer **b. Ralph Waldo Emerson** c. Joseph Heller d. James Joyce) : LOUISA MAY ALCOTT :: TRUMAN CAPOTE : PEARL S. BUCK

(b) is the correct answer. Truman Capote and Pearl S. Buck were contemporaries. They both contributed to twentieth-century literature. (b) Ralph Waldo Emerson and Louisa May Alcott were writers in the nineteenth century. (a) Chaucer wrote in the thirteenth century. (c) Joseph Heller is a twentieth-century author. (d) James Joyce is also a twentieth-century author.

39. (a. Nathaniel Hawthorne **b. Mark Twain** c. Charles Dickens d. Ernest Hemingway) : MISSISSIPPI :: HENRY JAMES : NEW YORK

(b) is the correct answer. Henry James was an author who wrote about New York in his novels. Mark Twain was an author who wrote about the Mississippi in his books. (a) Nathaniel Hawthorne wrote about colonial New England. (c) Charles Dickens wrote about old England. (d) Ernest Hemingway wrote about the relationship between humans and their environment.

40.   AMOEBA : (a. membranes   b. gills   c. cilia   **d. pseudopod**) :: OCTOPUS : TENTACLE

(**d**) is the correct response. An octopus moves through the water using its tentacles. An amoeba moves by extending a (d) pseudopod. (a) Membranes are plant or animal tissues. (b) Gills are fish organs used to obtain oxygen from water. (c) Cilia are hairlike appendages found in some plants or animals.

41.   NEOLOGISM : (a. book   **b. word**   c. property   d. equation) :: INNOVATION : CONCEPT

(**b**) is correct because a neologism is a new word, just as an innovation is a new concept. Neologism refers specifically to words so all other answer choices are incorrect.

42.   DENSE : DISPERSE :: (a. release   b. dilute   **c. erode**   d. inflict) : EXPAND

(**c**) is correct because *dense* means "many things in one place," and *disperse* means "few things in one place," just as if something is eroding, it is becoming smaller, rather than expanding. (a) is incorrect because to release something is to let it go. (b) is incorrect because to dilute something is to make it less concentrated. (d) is incorrect because to inflict means to cause harm.

43.   IMPROMPTU : MEMORIZED :: SPONTANEOUS : (a. impetuous   b. static   **c. calculated**   d. glib)

(**c**) is correct because an impromptu performance is one that is not rehearsed or memorized, just as something that is spontaneous is not calculated. (a) is incorrect because something that is *impetuous* is "impulsive," and therefore a synonym. (b) is incorrect because *static* implies a lack of action, and action is implied in the analogy. (d) is incorrect because someone who is glib is thought to be superficial.

44.   IMPERVIOUS : AGITATED :: (**a. enlightened**   b. depressive   c. perturbed   d. pretentious) : IGNORANT

(**a**) is the correct answer. A person who is impervious (not capable of being affected or disturbed) cannot be agitated (excited, disturbed). A person who is (a) enlightened (instructed, informed) is not ignorant. (b) is incorrect because the relationship between the given words does not exist between a person who is depressive (sad) and ignorant. A depressive person may be ignorant. (c) perturbed (upset) and (d) pretentious are wrong because a perturbed or pretentious person may be ignorant.

45. JOHN KENNEDY : LYNDON BAINES JOHNSON :: GEORGE
    WASHINGTON : (**a. John Adams** b. Benjamin Harrison c. Andrew Jackson
    d. Benjamin Franklin)

    (**a**) is the correct response. John Kennedy was president and Lyndon Baines
    Johnson was his vice president. George Washington was president and (a) John
    Adams was his vice president. (b) Benjamin Harrison was the 23rd president.
    (c) Andrew Jackson was the 7th president. (d) Benjamin Franklin never held
    elected office.

46. BENEVOLENT : MALIGNANT :: COOPERATIVE : (a. deleterious
    b. resistant c. evasive d. eager)

    (**b**) is correct because *benevolent* and *malignant* are antonyms, as are *coopera-*
    tive and *resistant*. (a) is incorrect because *deliterious* means "harmful in a subtle
    way." (c) is incorrect because *evasive* means "vague." (d) is incorrect because
    eager is a synonym of cooperative.

47. 60° : sin 60° :: 30° : (a. **b.** $\frac{1}{2}$ c. 1 d.)

    (**b**) is correct because this analogy is a direct computation of the sign of the
    angle. Thus 30° = $\frac{1}{2}$. The cos 30° = (d), and thus is incorrect.

48. RIVER : ESTUARY :: (a. sand b. cove c. ocean **d. land**) : SHORE

    (**d**) is correct because the place where a river and an ocean meet is called an
    estuary. The place where land and ocean meet is called a shore. A shore is not
    always sand (a), and a cove (b) is just one type of place where land and ocean (c)
    meet.

49. PASSE PARTOUT : (a. code b. lock c. safe **d. master key**) :: NOUVEAU
    RICHE : NEWLY WEALTHY

    (**d**) is correct because a passe partout is something that allows passage through
    any obstacle, like a master key through any lock, just as someone who is said to
    be nouveau riche is disparaged because they have only recently become wealthy.
    (a), (b), and (c) are incorrect because they are the opposite of a passe partout.

50. (a. Patagonia b. Fierro c. Bolivar **d. San Martin**) : REVOLUTIONARY ::
    BORGES : AUTHOR

    (**d**) is correct because Jose de San Martin is a revolutionary from Argentina.
    Jorge Luis Borges is an author from Argentina. Patagonia (a) is a region. Fierro
    (b) was a gaucho—not a revolutionary—and Bolivar (c) was from Venezuela.

Explanations
of Answers

51. (**a. absorbance** b. adsorption c. reflection d. scattering) : TRANSMITTANCE ::
INTAKE : OUTPUT

(a) Absorbance is correct because intake is the taking of something internally, while output is the opposite. The analogy therefore is to be completed by the opposite of transmittance which is absorbance. Adsorption (b) implies the attachment of something to a surface, rather than the taking of something into the internal. Reflection (c) and scattering (d) are terms which refer to the action of light when it strikes a particle in liquid, but neither term is opposite to absorbance.

52. (a. grotesque b. imperfect **c. pseudo** d. exiguous) : COUNTERFEIT ::
INCHOATE : SHAPELESS

(c) is the correct answer. The relationship between the given words is that the words are synonyms of each other. If something is inchoate (incomplete), then it is shapeless (has no shape) because it is not finished. Something that is (c) pseudo (sham, showing a superficial resemblance) is counterfeit (not real, copied). (a) grotesque (bizarre) is wrong because if something is grotesque, it doesn't have to be counterfeit. (b) is incorrect because if something is imperfect it may or may not be counterfeit. The words are not necessarily synonyms. (d) is wrong because if something is exiguous (scanty in amount) it is not counterfeit.

53. WASP : HYMENOPTERA :: (a. dogs b. bears **c. humans** d. cats) : PRIMATES

(c) Humans is correct because the wasp belongs to the order Hymenoptera, while humans belong to the order Primates. Dogs (a), bears (b), and cats (d) belong to the order Carnivora, and therefore these choices cannot be used to complete the analogy.

54. SEDULOUS : (a. retreating b. habitual **c. careless** d. bored) :: PREEMPTORY :
YIELDING

(c) is correct because sedulous behavior is careful—the opposite of careless (c), just as preemptory behavior is urgent and doesn't permit contradiction—the opposite of yielding. (a) is incorrect because retreating is not necessarily related to the word careful. (b) is incorrect because *habitual* refers to something done out of habit. (d) is incorrect because it refers to a feeling of ennui.

55. VALETUDINARIAN : (**a. hypochondriac** b. doctor c. hospital d. psychiatrist) :: VICTIM : PARANOIC

(**a**) is correct because a valetudinarian is someone who is in poor health and is overly concerned about their ailments, as compared to a hypochondriac, who is overly concerned about imaginary ailments. This is analogous to someone who is the victim of an actual offense, as compared with someone who imagines that offenses are being plotted against them. (b), (c), and (d) are incorrect because while any of these people might need or want the services of those listed in the answer choices, they do not complete the analogy.

56. MORTAR : (a. fire **b. pestle** c. brick d. cement) :: ANVIL : HAMMER

(**b**) is correct because a mortar supports material that is being ground up by a pestle. An anvil supports material shaped with a hammer. Fire (a) is incorrect because it is used in conjunction with a hammer and anvil, not a mortar. A different type of mortar is used with a brick (c), but they don't reshape a third item. Cement (d) is incorrect because it is a building material, rather than a method of shaping that material.

57. GESTATION : (**a. birth** b. elimination c. conclusion d. resorption) :: LACTATION : WEANING

(**a**) is correct because completed gestation ends with birth just as completed lactation ends with weaning. Elimination and conclusion, (b) and (c) respectively, are general terms. Resorption (d) does not refer exclusively to gestation and occurs when gestation cannot be completed.

58. Given

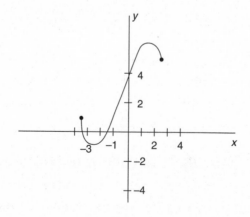

(3, 8) : MAXIMUM :: (−2, −1) : (a. inflection point **b. minimum** c. slope d. intersection)

Explanations of Answers

(b) The graph shows many points. The point (3, 8) is the maximum of this curve. The minimum point (b) is (–2, –1). The inflection point (a) is (0, 4). The intersection (d) of the *y*-axis is the point (0, 4) (in this case the same as the inflection point). The intersection with the *x*-axis are the points (–1, 0) and (–3, 0). The slope (c) is not defined as a point but a change in the rise of the curve.

59. (a. bacteria **b. coliforms** c. hepatitis virus d. rickettsia) : EOSIN METHYLENE BLUE AGAR :: YEASTS : SABOURAUD'S AGAR

(b) Coliforms is correct because eosin methylene blue agar is used to isolate coliforms from other bacterial species, especially in the testing of water for purity. Sabouraud's agar is used to isolate yeasts from bacterial species which might be growing with the yeasts. Bacteria (a) does not complete the analogy, since very few bacteria will grow on eosin methylene blue agar. Rickettsia (d) does not complete the analogy, since these are very fastidious organisms and require special conditions for growth. Hepatitis virus (c) is problematic in contaminated water supplies, and the presence of coliform agents in water is indicative that hepatitis virus could also be present, but this virus will not grow on eosin methylene blue agar and therefore this term does not complete the analogy.

60. BLOOD : COAGULATE :: GRAVY : (a. rarefy **b. congeal** c. deepen d. separate)

(b) is correct because the term used for the thickening of blood after it leaves the veins or arteries is coagulate. The term used for the thickening of gravy after it leaves the gravy boat is congeal. To rarefy (a) is to thin out and gravy does not deepen (c) or separate (d) after pouring.

61. (a. Dali b. Cézanne c. Matisse **d. Picasso**) : CUBISM :: LICHTENSTEIN : POP ART

(d) is the correct answer. Lichtenstein is a painter known for his works in pop art. (d) Picasso is the painter who is famous for Cubism. (a) Dali is known for surrealism. (b) Cézanne is know for impressionism. (c) Matisse is known for abstract painting.

62. RETROGRADE : ROTATION :: (a. object **b. reverse** c. circular d. method) : MOTION

(b) is correct because a retrograde type of rotation is a reverse type of motion. Object (a) is incorrect because it refers to that which is in motion, not to the motion itself. Circular (c) motion is not necessarily reverse. Method (d) is a general term not referring specifically to motion.

63. COCAINE : STIMULANT :: (a. amphetamines b. ritalin **c. barbiturates** d. LSD) : DEPRESSANT

(c) Barbiturates is correct because cocaine is a stimulant, while barbiturates are considered to be members of the depressant drugs. Amphetamines (a) and ritalin (b) are considered to be stimulants, not depressants. LSD (d) is also not a depressant, but rather a psychedelic drug. None of these fits the analogy.

64. (a. shark **b. whale** c. flounder d. guppy) : FISH :: PLATYPUS : BIRD

(b) is correct because a whale resembles a fish but is a mammal. A platypus resembles a bird (has a bill) but is a mammal. Other answer choices (a), (c), and (d) are fish.

65. STREP THROAT : BACTERIA :: (a. Rocky Mountain spotted fever **b. chicken pox** c. amoebic dysentery d. tuberculosis) : VIRUS

(b) Chicken pox is correct because strep throat is caused by a bacteria while chicken pox is caused by a virus. Rocky Mountain spotted fever (a) is caused by a rickettsial bacteria, amoebic dysentery (c) is caused by a protozoal parasite, and tuberculosis (d) is caused by a bacteria. These three answers cannot be used to complete the analogy.

66. COMPLEX NUMBER : REAL NUMBER :: RATIONAL NUMBER : (a. irrational number b. imaginary number **c. integer** d. real number)

(c) A real number is part of the set of complex numbers, which includes all numbers. The set of rational numbers includes natural numbers, counting numbers, and integers (c). Rational numbers and irrational numbers (a) comprise the set of real numbers. Real numbers (d) and imaginary numbers (b) comprise the set of complex numbers.

67. TRIVIAL : (**a. minutia** b. enigma c. levity d. palavar) :: CATHOLIC : UNIVERSALITY

(a) is the correct answer. The relationship between the given words could be stated as: If something is catholic (general) it has universality (it can be applied anywhere). If something is trivial (unimportant), then it deals with minutia (a minor detail). (b) enigma (riddles, puzzles) is wrong because if something is frivolous, it may or may not have universality. (d) is incorrect because palavar (word, speech) may or may not be trivial.

68. VACILLATE : (a. switch b. divide c. endure **d. waver**) :: FLUCTUATE : MOVE

    (d) is correct because to *vacillate* means "to waver between two courses of action in an indecisive manner," just as *fluctuate* means "to move from one area to another." (a) is incorrect because to *switch* means "to be decisive." (b) and (c) are incorrect because they are unrelated to the other terms.

69. BLACKSMITH : FORGE :: PAINTER : (**a. studio** b. canvas c. brush d. mix)

    (a) is correct because a blacksmith's place of work is a forge just as a painter's place of work is a studio. A forge is also the type of equipment a blacksmith works on but a painter's canvas (b) is not analogous to that type of forge, as a canvas is part of the finished product. Brush (c) is a tool used by a painter in the same way that a hammer would be by a blacksmith. Mix (d) is a general term that could apply to many crafts.

70. (a. Skinner b. Freud **c. Piaget** d. Pavlov) : INTELLECTUAL DEVELOPMENT :: ERICKSON : EGO IDENTITY

    (c) is the correct response. Erickson was a psychologist known for his study of ego identity. (c) Piaget was a psychologist known for his study of intellectual development. (a) Skinner was a behavioral psychologist. (b) Freud was a psychiatrist who studied the unconscious mind. (d) Pavlov was a psychologist who studied operant conditioning in dogs.

71. VULGAR : CRUDE :: BIASED : (**a. prejudiced** b. charming c. rough d. just)

    (a) is correct because *vulgar* and *crude* are synonyms, just as *biased* and *prejudiced* are synonyms. (b) is incorrect because *charming* is a positive quality, whereas *biased* is not. (c) is incorrect because although *rough* is a synonym for *vulgar* and *crude*, it is not a synonym for biased. (d) is incorrect because *just* implies impartiality, which is an antonym of *biased*.

72. ANTI-PYROGENIC : ACETAMINOPHEN :: ANTI-INFLAMMATORY : (**a. salicylates** b. phenacetin c. caffeine d. codeine)

    (a) Salicylates is correct because a specific anti-pyrogenic agent is acetaminophen, while a specific anti-inflammatory agent is the family referred to as salicylates. Phenacetin (b), caffeine (c), and codeine (d) do not have anti-inflammatory attributes, and do not complete the analogy.

73. FERN : (a. seed b. leaf **c. spore** d. fruit) :: OAK : ACORN

    (c) is correct because a fern reproduces by releasing spores. An oak reproduces by dropping acorns. A fern doesn't have seeds (a) or fruit (d).

Explanations
of Answers

74. ALBINISM : (a. albumin b. serotonin c. carotene **d. melanin**) ::
MALNUTRITION : CALORIES

   (d) is the correct answer. Malnutrition is caused by a lack of calories in the body. Albinism (lack of pigmentation) is caused by a lack of (d) melanin. (a) Albumin is the white substance found in an egg and has no relationship to albinism. (b) Serotonin is wrong. (c) Carotene is found in vegetables and provides vitamin A. It has no relation to albinism.

75. (a. –COOH **b. –OH** c. R – C – OR d. – C – N –) : ALCOHOL :: –NH$_2$: AMINO

   (b) –OH is correct because the –OH group is the functional alcohol group, while the –NH$_2$ is the functional amino group. –COOH (a) is a functional carboxylic acid. R—C—OR (c) is the functional ester. —C—N— (d) is a functional amide. None of the other answers can be used as an amino group.

76. NaCl : ROCK SALT :: SiO$_2$: (a. crystals b. ice c. calcareous rock **d. quartz**)

   (d) Quartz is correct because the common name for sodium chloride (NaCl) is rock salt, while the common name for silicon dioxide (SiO$_2$) is quartz. SiO$_2$ is a crystal (a), but this is a generic term and does not complete the analogy. Ice (b) is a form of crystal which does not depend on SiO$_2$ for its formation. Calcareous rock (c) is made of calcium and not SiO$_2$.

77. MERCURIAL : (**a. erratic** b. metaphorical c. meretricious d. penal) ::
PENNYLESS : IMPOVERISHED

   (a) is correct because *mercurial* refers to erratic behavior, just as someone who is penniless is said to be impoverished. (b) is incorrect because something that is metaphorical stands for something other than itself. (c) is incorrect because something that is meretricious is attractive in a vulgar way. (d) is incorrect because something that is penal involves punishment for a crime.

78. MERCER : (a. music b. animals **c. textiles** d. soldiers) :: RESTAURATEUR :
FOOD

   (c) is correct because a mercer is a dealer in textiles, just as a restaurateur sells food. All other answer choices are irrelevant.

79. LIGATURE : (a. closing b. cutting **c. binding** d. arguing) :: HOOK : FISHING

   (c) is correct because a ligature is a tool used for binding just as a hook is a tool used for fishing. All other answer choices are irrelevant because a ligature is not used to perform these tasks.

80. BAROQUE : CLASSICAL :: (a. Renaissance b. Romanesque c. Medieval
    d. Classical) : ROMANTIC

    (d) is correct because in music, the Baroque period immediately precedes the
    Classical period just as the Classical period immediately precedes the Romantic
    period. The Renaissance (a) and Medieval (c) periods precede the Baroque, and
    Romanesque (b) is an architecture term referring to a period around the 1000s.

81. PEREGRINATION : (a. flight **b. walk** c. flee d. wings) :: CRUISE : SAIL

    (b) is correct because a peregrination is a trip by foot as is a walk. A cruise is a
    travel by boat as is a sail. Peregrination is not specifically fleeing (c), and while
    wings (d) could be considered an aid in travel, they do not refer to the journey
    itself.

82. MERGANSER : (a. penguin b. horse **c. duck** d. dog) :: GERNSEY : COW

    (c) is correct because a merganser is a type of duck (having a long, narrow bill
    for fishing) just as a gernsey is a type of cow. There are many varieties of each of
    the other answer choices, however, merganser is not among them.

83. BUDDHA : (a. China **b. India** c. Japan d. Cambodia) :: JESUS : ISRAEL

    (b) is correct because Buddha was born in India just as Jesus was born in Israel.
    Buddhism is more common in some of the other countries such as China (a),
    Japan (c), and Cambodia (d), but Christianity, the religion based on Jesus's
    teachings, is also more common in countries other than his birth country.

84. TACHYCARDIA : FAST :: (a. angina b. sphygmomanometer **c. bradycardia**
    d. cardiac arrhythmia) : SLOW

    (c) Bradycardia is correct because tachycardia is an increase in heart rate above
    the normal rate, so it may be described as fast. Bradycardia is a decrease in heart
    rate and may be described as slow. Angina (a) is a pain in the chest due to in-
    adequate blood supply to the heart muscle, but is not necessarily related to the
    rhythm of the heart rate. The sphygmomanometer (b) is an instrument used to
    measure blood pressure and is not descriptive of heart rate. Cardiac arrhythmia
    (d) is a term which can refer to any change in heart rate—increase or decrease,
    and therefore does not fit the analogy.

Explanations of Answers

85. MORTARBOARD : COMMENCEMENT :: CROWN : (a. indoctrination
b. ordination c. induction **d. coronation**)

(d) is correct because a mortarboard is worn on one's head at commencement or graduation, just as a crown is placed on one's head during a coronation. (a) is incorrect because this refers to the installation of an idea into one's mind. (b) is incorrect because this applies to the clergy. (c) is incorrect because this applies to the armed forces.

86. TRANSMOGRIFY : LANGUAGE :: (**a. form** b. color c. size d. time) :
TRANSLATE

(a) is correct because *to transmogrify* means "to change form" just as to *translate* means "to change language." (b) and (c) can be said to be a change in form, but are too specific to complete the analogy. (d) is incorrect because time cannot be changed by external means.

87. AGNOSTIC : ATHEIST :: (**a. question** b. decision c. doubt d. definition) :
STATEMENT

(a) is correct because an agnostic questions the existence of god, just as the atheist decides that there is no god. (b) is incorrect because the agnostic has not made a clear cut decision, other than the decision to be an agnostic. (c) is incorrect because doubt does not have parity with the analogy. (d) is incorrect because definition implies a decision.

88. BARRIER : LINE :: ATOLL : (a. square b. triangle **c. circle** d. spiral)

(c) Circle is correct because a barrier reef is formed in a line. An atoll is a circle shaped reef surrounding a lagoon. A square (a) and a triangle (b) are not the correct shapes for an atoll. A spiral (d) is also not the shape of an atoll.

89. FLEET : (**a. quick** b. ship c. ocean d. lugubrious) :: PENSIVE : THOUGHTFUL

(a) is correct because something that is fleet (e.g., fleet-footed) is said to be quick and graceful, just as a pensive person is a thoughtful person. (b) is incorrect because a ship is a part of a different sort of fleet, or group of ships, that sails upon the ocean (c). Something that is lugubrious (d) is gloomy.

90. BRACKISH : (a. murky b. unclean **c. salty** d. wet) :: FLAXEN : YELLOW

(c) is correct because brackish water is salty and briny, just as something that is flaxen is yellow in color. (a) and (b) are incorrect because brackish water is not inherently dark or unclean. (d) is incorrect because all water is wet, and this term is therefore too general.

91.   LEONINE : LION :: (**a. cervine** b. equine c. porcine d. bovine) : DEER

(**a**) is correct because leonine means having the characteristics of a lion, just as cervine means having the characteristics of a deer. (b) is incorrect because equine refers to horses. (c) is incorrect because porcine refers to pigs. (d) is incorrect because bovine refers to cows.

92.   GRANT : (a. 15 b. 17 c. 22 **d. 18**) :: REAGAN: 40

(**d**) is correct because Grant was the 18th president just as Reagan was the 40th. All other answer choices are irrelevant.

93.   HUBRIS : PRIDE :: (**a. starvation** b. satiation c. satisfaction d. nutrition) : HUNGER

(**a**) is correct because hubris is an excessive form of pride, just as starvation is an excessive form of hunger. (b), (c), and (d) are incorrect because they are the opposite of hunger.

94.   COCCI : ROUND :: (**a. bacilli** b. spirochete c. mycoplasma d. spheroplast) : ROD

(**a**) Bacilli is correct because cocci are bacteria which have a round shape, while bacilli are bacteria which have a rod shape. Spirochetes (b) are spiral bacteria. Mycoplasma (c) and spheroplasts (d) do not have cell walls and therefore their shapes always appear round.

95.   TRAVAIL : WORK :: (a. return **b. pillage** c. borrow d. kill) : STEAL

(**b**) is correct because *travail* means "unpleasant, tiresome work," just as *pillage* is a severe form of *steal*. (a) is incorrect because it is an opposite of steal. (c) is incorrect because the word implies returning. (d) is incorrect because this is not a form of stealing.

96.   (a. blood **b. milk** c. table d. alcohol) : LACTOSE :: FRUIT : FRUCTOSE

(**b**) Milk is correct because the major sugar component found in fruit is fructose, while the major sugar component of milk is lactose. Alcohol (d), of itself, does not contain lactose. The sugar referred to as table (c) sugar is sucrose, and the sugar referred to as blood (a) sugar is glucose, and neither of these fit the analogy of where lactose is found.

97. UPBRAID : REPROACH :: (**a. miniscule** b. large c. enormous d. lower) :
SMALL

(a) is correct because *to upbraid* means "to reproach severely," just as something
that is miniscule is very small. (b) and (c) are incorrect because they are opposites of miniscule. (d) is incorrect because it is unrelated.

98. ENDEMIC : (a. neighborhood b. planet **c. region** d. building) :: PANDEMIC :
COUNTRY

(c) is correct because something that is endemic affects a single region, however,
is serious enough to be considered problematic, just as a pandemic is something
that effects an entire country. (a) and (d) are incorrect because they are too small
to foster something that could be considered endemic. (b) is incorrect because a
planet is too large to be considered an endemic.

99. FORGIVE : (a. pacify **b. exculpate** c. contemplate d. ruminate) :: FATAL :
LETHAL

(b) is correct because *to exculpate* means "to forgive," just as both *fatal* and *lethal* mean "to cause death." (a) is incorrect because *to pacify* means "to calm."
(c) is incorrect because *to contemplate* means "to consider deliberately." (d) is
incorrect because *to ruminate* means "to muse on a particular idea or thought."

100. MORIBUND : (a. morbid **b. dying** c. laughing d. hungry) :: GERIATRIC : OLD

(b) is correct because *to be moribund* means "to be dying" just as *to be geriatric*
means "to be old." (a) is incorrect because *morbid* means "in an unhealthy mental
state." (c) is incorrect because while one could be laughing while moribund, this
is unlikely. (d) is incorrect because someone in a dying state is rarely hungry, unless their hunger is the cause of their state, in which case this term is too specific.

Miller Analogies

five

Practice Test 5

Answer Sheet
Practice Test 5

1. (A) (B) (C) (D)
2. (A) (B) (C) (D)
3. (A) (B) (C) (D)
4. (A) (B) (C) (D)
5. (A) (B) (C) (D)
6. (A) (B) (C) (D)
7. (A) (B) (C) (D)
8. (A) (B) (C) (D)
9. (A) (B) (C) (D)
10. (A) (B) (C) (D)
11. (A) (B) (C) (D)
12. (A) (B) (C) (D)
13. (A) (B) (C) (D)
14. (A) (B) (C) (D)
15. (A) (B) (C) (D)
16. (A) (B) (C) (D)
17. (A) (B) (C) (D)
18. (A) (B) (C) (D)
19. (A) (B) (C) (D)
20. (A) (B) (C) (D)
21. (A) (B) (C) (D)
22. (A) (B) (C) (D)
23. (A) (B) (C) (D)
24. (A) (B) (C) (D)
25. (A) (B) (C) (D)
26. (A) (B) (C) (D)
27. (A) (B) (C) (D)
28. (A) (B) (C) (D)
29. (A) (B) (C) (D)
30. (A) (B) (C) (D)
31. (A) (B) (C) (D)
32. (A) (B) (C) (D)
33. (A) (B) (C) (D)
34. (A) (B) (C) (D)

35. (A) (B) (C) (D)
36. (A) (B) (C) (D)
37. (A) (B) (C) (D)
38. (A) (B) (C) (D)
39. (A) (B) (C) (D)
40. (A) (B) (C) (D)
41. (A) (B) (C) (D)
42. (A) (B) (C) (D)
43. (A) (B) (C) (D)
44. (A) (B) (C) (D)
45. (A) (B) (C) (D)
46. (A) (B) (C) (D)
47. (A) (B) (C) (D)
48. (A) (B) (C) (D)
49. (A) (B) (C) (D)
50. (A) (B) (C) (D)
51. (A) (B) (C) (D)
52. (A) (B) (C) (D)
53. (A) (B) (C) (D)
54. (A) (B) (C) (D)
55. (A) (B) (C) (D)
56. (A) (B) (C) (D)
57. (A) (B) (C) (D)
58. (A) (B) (C) (D)
59. (A) (B) (C) (D)
60. (A) (B) (C) (D)
61. (A) (B) (C) (D)
62. (A) (B) (C) (D)
63. (A) (B) (C) (D)
64. (A) (B) (C) (D)
65. (A) (B) (C) (D)
66. (A) (B) (C) (D)
67. (A) (B) (C) (D)
68. (A) (B) (C) (D)

69. (A) (B) (C) (D)
70. (A) (B) (C) (D)
71. (A) (B) (C) (D)
72. (A) (B) (C) (D)
73. (A) (B) (C) (D)
74. (A) (B) (C) (D)
75. (A) (B) (C) (D)
76. (A) (B) (C) (D)
77. (A) (B) (C) (D)
78. (A) (B) (C) (D)
79. (A) (B) (C) (D)
80. (A) (B) (C) (D)
81. (A) (B) (C) (D)
82. (A) (B) (C) (D)
83. (A) (B) (C) (D)
84. (A) (B) (C) (D)
85. (A) (B) (C) (D)
86. (A) (B) (C) (D)
87. (A) (B) (C) (D)
88. (A) (B) (C) (D)
89. (A) (B) (C) (D)
90. (A) (B) (C) (D)
91. (A) (B) (C) (D)
92. (A) (B) (C) (D)
93. (A) (B) (C) (D)
94. (A) (B) (C) (D)
95. (A) (B) (C) (D)
96. (A) (B) (C) (D)
97. (A) (B) (C) (D)
98. (A) (B) (C) (D)
99. (A) (B) (C) (D)
100. (A) (B) (C) (D)

Practice Test 5

TIME: 50 Minutes   **LENGTH:** 100 Analogies

DIRECTIONS: Read each of the following analogies carefully, and choose the BEST answer to each item. Fill in your responses in the answer sheets provided.

Note: The Miller Analogies Test consists of 120 questions to be completed in 60 minutes. Twenty of these questions are experimental items, which are not scored and thus not reflected in this practice test.

1.   BISHOP : MITER :: KING (a. throne b. scepter c. crown d. seal)

2.   DYNAMICS : TEMPO :: PIANO : (a. lento b. measure c. legato d. sforzando)

3.   MARY ANN EVANS : GEORGE ELIOT :: AUTHOR : (a. publisher b. editor c. character d. pseudonym)

4.   PROPOSE : SUGGESTION :: (a. propound b. query c. issue d. imply) : FIAT

5.   (a. 212 b. 451 c. 150 d. 32) : FAHRENHEIT :: 100 : CELSIUS

6.   ATTORNEY : DISBAR :: (a. nobleman b. professor c. prima donna d. priest) : UNFROCK

7.   HARPSICHORD : (a. viola b. harp c. cello d. violin) :: PIANO : HAMMERED DULCIMER

8.   LINE : FOOT :: (a. square b. distance c. cube d. weight) : CORD

9.   (a. granivorous b. frugivorous c. herbivorous d. omnivorous) : CARNIVOROUS :: CANARY : HAWK

10. L : (a. LL b. D c. XL d. C) :: X : XX

11. (a. works b. stem c. time d. crystal) : WATCH :: CRANKSHAFT : CAR

12. AENEAS : VIRGIL :: (a. Hercules b. Penelope c. Odysseus d. Dido) : HOMER

13. PUMICE : (a. lava b. porous c. volcano d. molten) :: AMBER : RESIN

14. CHAPTER : NOVEL :: (a. rhyme b. meter c. anthology d. stanza) : POEM

15. TROCHEE : IAMB :: TUESDAY : (a. Monday b. delay c. Wednesday d. day)

16. E.G. : N.B. :: FOR EXAMPLE : (a. and others b. by that fact c. note well d. and so forth)

17. (a. circumference b. diameter c. radius d. pi) : CIRCLE :: PERIMETER : SQUARE

18. GEORGIA O' KEEFFE : ANSEL ADAMS :: (a. choreography b. architecture c. sculpture d. painting) : PHOTOGRAPHY

19. (a. bread b. horseshoe c. boot d. furniture) : BLACKSMITH :: SHOE : COBBLER

20. (a. tadpole b. toad c. newt d. amphibian) : FROG :: NYMPH : DRAGONFLY

21. 12 : 144 :: (a. 2 b. 9 c. 6 d. 12) : 36

22. 6.4587 : 6 :: 10.28943 : (a. 28 b. 10 c. 9 d. 1)

23. GLUCOSE : STARCH :: (a. tricarboxylic acid b. carbonic acid c. amino acid d. triglyceride) : PROTEIN

24. ORATOR : LINGUIST :: (a. speech b. French c. language d. eloquence) : FLUENCY

25. CURRICULUM : CURRICULA :: ALUMNUS : (a. alumni b. alma mater c. senior d. alumna)

26. PHOTOSYNTHESIS : CHLOROPHYLL :: DIGESTION : (a. animal b. enzyme c. food d. energy)

27. MERCURY : Hg :: GOLD : (a. W   b. Pb   c. Au   d. O)

28. NYLON : POLYAMIDE :: (a. twill   b. cotton   c. wool   d. dacron) : POLYESTER

29. NUMERATOR : (a. quotient   b. denominator   c. product   d. hypotenuse) :: OVER : UNDER

30. POLIOMYELITIS : SALK :: SMALLPOX : (a. Blackwell   b. Fleming   c. Jenner   d. Langerhans)

31. NUCLEUS : (a. proton   b. electron   c. atom   d. neutron) :: PLANET : SATELLITE

32. (a. 4   b. 10   c. 5   d. 1) : 16 :: WASHINGTON : LINCOLN

33. (a. horse   b. griffin   c. minotaur   d. wolf) : FISH :: CENTAUR : MERMAID

34. Given

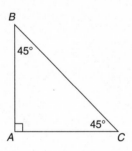

   $AB : AC :: BC :$ (a. AC^2 b. $\sqrt{(AB^2 + AC^2)}$ c. AB^2 d. $AB + AC$)

35. $(x, y) : \sqrt{xy^2} + 2x^2y - 4y :: (4, y) :$ (a. $2\sqrt{y}$ b. $6y$ c. $14\sqrt{y}$ d. $30y$)

36. 10 : (a. Downing St.   b. Broadway   c. Baker St.   d. 5th Avenue) :: 1600 : PENNSYLVANIA AVENUE

37. CONDUCTOR : (a. baton   b. orchestra   c. Bernstein   d. composer) :: TEACHER : CLASS

38. HUMERUS : PHALANGES :: ARM : (a. elbow   b. radius   c. toes   d. tibia)

39. SWITZERLAND : (a. Ceylon   b. Nepal   c. Madagascar   d. Portugal) :: ALPS : HIMALAYAS

Practice Test 5

40. (a. Elizabethan b. Edwardian c. eighteenth century d. Jacobian) : VICTORIAN :: SIXTEENTH CENTURY : NINETEENTH CENTURY

41. (a. epistemology b. existentialism c. ontology d. hermeneutics) : POSITIVISIM :: KIERKEGAARD : COMTE

42. PSYCHE : MIND :: EGO : (a. self b. the unconscious c. id d. mental)

43. (a. angel b. human c. animal d. misanthropist) : ANTHROPOMORPHIZE :: DEMON : DEMONIZE

44. TURNER : (a. England b. Germany c. Holland d. Brittany) :: VAN GOGH : HOLLAND

45. WOLVES : (a. pup b. canine c. pack d. prey) :: SEALS : POD

46. CITY : (a. architect b. advocate c. mayor d. journalist) :: WASHINGTON, D.C. : L'ENFANT

47. MESOZOIC : ERA :: (a. Jurassic b. Tertiary c. Pennsylvanian d. Paleozoic) : PERIOD

48. HABITAT : PLACE :: (a. carrying capacity b. competition c. niche d. predation) : ROLE

49. DENSITY : NUMBER :: (a. dispersion b. habitat c. cohort d. patches) : DISTRIBUTION PATTERN

50. ATHENS : OSLO :: GREECE : (a. Norway b. Crete c. Aegean d. Czech Republic)

51. $4 + 5 : (4 + 5)^5 - (4 - 5)^2 :: a + b :$ (a. $(a + b)^5 - (a + b)^2$ b. $(a + b)^4 - a^2 - 2ab - b^2$) c. $(a + b)^3$ d. $(a + b)^5 - a^2 + 2ab - b^2$)

52. VISUAL : AURAL :: MAGNIFYING GLASS : (a. telephone b. microscope c. hearing aid d. binoculars)

53. WAGNER : OPERA :: STRAUSS : (a. jazz b. Gregorian c. tarantella d. waltz)

54. ALGERIA : DINAR :: (a. Turkey b. Poland c. Israel d. Kuwait) : ZLOTY

55. (a. order b. addition c. quantity d. multiplication) : GROUPING :: COMMUTATIVE : ASSOCIATIVE

56. 2 : (a. circle b. circumference c. distance d. diameter) :: 1 : RADIUS

57. SHREW : RODENT :: (a. turtle b. antelope c. grasshopper d. swallow) : RUMINANT

58. (a. auxin b. cytokinin c. phytolexins d. glucose) : PHOTOTROPISM :: GIBBERELLIN : GROWTH

59. INCH : FOOT :: CENTIMETER : (a. millimeter b. meter c. liter d. gram)

60. Given graphs A and B:

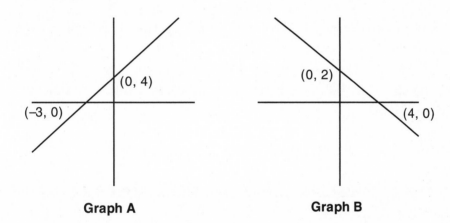

Graph A   **Graph B**

GRAPH A : (0, 4) :: GRAPH B : (a. (–3, 0) b. (2, 0) c. (4, 0) d. (0, 2))

61. (a. visible b. fluorescent c. ultraviolet d. quanta) : INFRARED :: SHORT : LONG

62. A : T :: C : (a. Y b. D c. M d. G)

63. BASIC : (a. saline b. acidic c. alkaline d. complex) :: BLUE : RED

64. (a. jetsam b. wharf c. land d. building) : DEFENESTRATE :: SHIP : JETTISON

65.   FUZZY : (a. texture b. touch c. furry d. tactile) :: PUNGENT : OLFACTORY

66.   (a. orange b. red c. purple d. brown) : BLUE :: RED : GREEN

67.   OCCUPY : VACANT :: (a. tenant b. fumigate c. undertake d. cultivate) : FALLOW

68.   DIAGONAL : RECTANGLE :: CHORD : (a. triangle b. circle c. hexagon d. rhombus)

69.   METER : YARD :: (a. liter b. inch c. pint d. milliliter) : QUART

70.   WHEREFORE : WHERE :: (a. location b. question c. person d. therefore) : PLACE

71.   RODIN : BRONZE :: STIEGLITZ : (a. oil b. stone c. tin d. film)

72.   SISYPHEAN : HERCULEAN :: ENDLESS : (a. labor b. difficult c. ongoing d. perpetual)

73.   (a. protein b. metabolism c. carbohydrate d. sugar) : LIPID :: AMINO ACID : FATTY ACID

74.   BLACK : WHITE :: (a. color b. mirror c. absorb d. red) : REFLECT

75.   (a. DeFoe b. Burney c. Cervantes d. Poe) : PICARESQUE :: RICHARDSON : EPISTOLARY

76.   (a. food b. quantity c. nutrition d. cuisine) : GOURMAND :: QUALITY : GOURMET

77.   Jane, Mary, and Todd all have money to go to the candy store. Jane buys chocolate drops and pays with only dimes. Mary buys a lollipop, and she only has pennies. Todd has a dollar bill but does not buy anything.

   MARY : PENNIES :: TODD : (a. dollar b. dimes c. chocolate drops d. lollipop)

78.   MONOCOT : (a. one b. two c. three d. four) :: DICOT : FIVE

79.   HUMAN BODY : 37° :: ROOM : (98.6° b. 32° c. 25° d. 0°)

80. HANDEL : MOZART :: (a. romantic b. operatic c. baroque d. modern) : CLASSICAL

81. FRUCTOSE : LACTOSE :: (a. cream b. fruit c. skim d. cereal) : MILK

82. BAY OF BENGAL : ARABIAN SEA :: EAST : (a. south b. north c. China d. west)

83. HOROWITZ : PIANO :: MA : (a. harp b. piccolo c. cello d. baritone)

84. REVOLUTIONARY : CIVIL :: (a. Bull Run b. Bunker Hill c. Alamo d. Wounded Knee) : GETTYSBURG

85. OLIGARCH : CHORISTER :: MONARCH : (a. conductor b. soloist c. section d. leader)

86. (a. thermostat b. kilowatt c. thermometer d. calorie) : HEAT :: NANOMETER : LENGTH

87. Given (k, m), then $g = 2$, if $k < 0$, $m < 0$
    $= 1$, if $k < 0$, $m = 0$
    $= 3$, if $k < 0$, $m > 0$
    $= 4$, if $k > 0$

    $(-1, 2) : 3 :: (4, -1) :$ (a. 1 b. 3 c. 4 d. 2)

88. BIZET : *CARMEN* :: MOZART : (a. *Eine Kleine Nachtmusik* b. *The Barber of Seville* c. *Don Giovanni* d. *Cherubino*)

89. NOCTURNAL : DIURNAL :: (a. lizard b. mammal c. bat d. hibernation) : SQUIRREL

90. SUCH IS LIFE : *C'EST LA VIE* :: (a. good day b. behold c. pen name d. such is war) : *NOM DE PLUME*

91. 2001 : 365 :: 2004 : (a. 52 b. 366 c. 1901 d. 3)

92. RIGHT : (a. correct b. ambidextrous c. dexter d. righteous) :: LEFT : SINISTER

93. MEXICO : CORTES :: (a. Argentina b. Bolivia c. El Salvador d. Peru) : PIZARRO

94. XYLEM : ROOTS :: (a. arteries b. veins c. phloem d. leaves) : HEART

95. TELESCOPE : BINOCULARS :: MONOCLE : (a. screen b. spectacles c. focus d. microscope)

96. KEY : TURNKEY :: (a. corkscrew b. drill c. spatula d. jackhammer) : SOMMELIER

97. PLANE : PERPENDICULAR :: FLOOR : (a. ceiling b. gable c. wall d. cellar)

98. 1215 : MAGNA CARTA :: 1789 : (a. Declaration of Independence b. *Common Sense* c. Twelfth Amendment d. U.S. Constitution)

99. 56 : EVEN :: (a. 12 b. 17 c. 150 d. 65) : PRIME

100. Given

x	y	z
4	10	22
2	15	33
2	20	44
4	25	55

($x = 2, y = 15$) : 33 :: ($x = 4, z = 55$) : (a. 44 b. 55 c. 25 d. 10)

Answer Key
Practice Test 5

1. (c)	26. (b)	51. (d)	76. (b)
2. (a)	27. (c)	52. (c)	77. (a)
3. (d)	28. (d)	53. (d)	78. (c)
4. (c)	29. (b)	54. (b)	79. (c)
5. (a)	30. (c)	55. (a)	80. (c)
6. (d)	31. (b)	56. (d)	81. (b)
7. (b)	32. (d)	57. (b)	82. (d)
8. (c)	33. (a)	58. (a)	83. (c)
9. (a)	34. (b)	59. (b)	84. (b)
10. (d)	35. (d)	60. (d)	85. (a)
11. (b)	36. (a)	61. (c)	86. (d)
12. (c)	37. (b)	62. (d)	87. (c)
13. (a)	38. (c)	63. (b)	88. (c)
14. (d)	39. (b)	64. (d)	89. (c)
15. (b)	40. (a)	65. (d)	90. (c)
16. (c)	41. (b)	66. (a)	91. (b)
17. (a)	42. (a)	67. (d)	92. (c)
18. (d)	43. (b)	68. (b)	93. (d)
19. (b)	44. (a)	69. (a)	94. (a)
20. (a)	45. (c)	70. (c)	95. (b)
21. (c)	46. (a)	71. (d)	96. (a)
22. (b)	47. (c)	72. (b)	97. (c)
23. (c)	48. (c)	73. (a)	98. (d)
24. (d)	49. (a)	74. (c)	99. (b)
25. (a)	50. (a)	75. (c)	100. (c)

Explanations
of Answers

Explanations of Answers
Practice Test 5

1. BISHOP : MITER :: KING (a. throne b. scepter **c. crown** d. seal)

   (c) is correct because a bishop's headdress is a miter, just as a king's headdress is a crown. All other choices (a), (b), and (d) are incorrect because while they are symbols of royalty, they are not headdresses.

2. DYNAMICS : TEMPO :: PIANO : (**a. lento** b. measure c. legato d. sforzando)

   (a) is correct because piano (meaning soft) describes the dynamics (volume) of a musical passage. Lento (slow) describes the tempo at which the piece is played. (b) is incorrect because a measure is a division in the written musical score. (c) is incorrect because legato refers to a manner of playing music that is smooth and connected. (d) is incorrect because sforzando refers to a forceful manner of playing, with strong stresses and accents.

3. MARY ANN EVANS : GEORGE ELIOT :: AUTHOR : (a. publisher b. editor c. character **d. pseudonym**)

   (d) is correct because Mary Ann Evans was an author, and George Eliot was her pseudonym. (a) and (b) are incorrect because they refer to the publishing process of a book, and (c) refers to the writing process.

4. PROPOSE : SUGGESTION :: (a. propound b. query **c. issue** d. imply) : FIAT

   (c) is correct because one proposes a suggestion just as one issues a fiat, or command. (a) is incorrect because to propound means to display. (b) is incorrect because to query means to ask a question. (d) is incorrect because to imply means to say something without conveying it directly.

5. (**a. 212** b. 451 c. 150 d. 32) : FAHRENHEIT :: 100 : CELSIUS

   (a) is correct because 212 is the temperature at which water boils on the Fahrenheit scale, just as 100 is the temperature at which water boils on the Celsius scale. All other answer choices are irrelevant.

6. ATTORNEY : DISBAR :: (a. nobleman b. professor c. prima donna **d. priest**) : UNFROCK

(d) is correct because attorneys who are banned from their profession are said to be disbarred, while priests who are banned from their profession are said to be unfrocked. (a) is incorrect because a nobleman derives power from an inherited line. (b) is incorrect because a professor would be fired from a teaching position. (c) is incorrect because a prima donna refers to the current most talented ballerina in a dance company, who would lose that title to a more talented dancer.

7. HARPSICHORD : (a. viola **b. harp** c. cello d. violin) :: PIANO : HAMMERED DULCIMER

(b) is correct because pianos and hammered dulcimers are instruments whose strings are struck. Harpsichords and harps are instruments with strings that are plucked. All other answers are generally played with a bow.

8. LINE : FOOT :: (a. square b. distance **c. cube** d. weight) : CORD

(c) is correct because a foot is a unit of linear measurement just as a cord is a unit of cubic measurement. (a) is incorrect because it is a geometric figure. (b) is incorrect because it refers to that which is measured rather than a unit of measure. (d) is incorrect because weight is another criteria for measuring a three-dimensional object.

9. (**a. granivorous** b. frugivorous c. herbivorous d. omnivorous) : CARNIVOROUS :: CANARY : HAWK

(a) is correct because a canary is a granivorous, or seed-eating, bird just as a hawk is a carnivorous bird. (b) is incorrect because a frugivorous bird is one that eats fruit. (c) is incorrect because an herbivorous animal would exclusively eat plants. (d) is incorrect because an omnivorous creature would eat both meat and plants.

10. L : (a. LL b. D c. XL **d. C**) :: X : XX

(d) is correct because C (the Roman numeral representing 100) is twice L (the Roman numeral representing 50). (a) is incorrect because the form of Roman numerals dictates that there should be as little repetition as possible. (b) is incorrect because D is the Roman numeral representing 500. (c) is incorrect because XL represents the Arabic numeral 40.

11. (a. works **b. stem** c. time d. crystal) : WATCH :: CRANKSHAFT : CAR

(b) is correct because in a car, the crankshaft transmits the motion generated by the engine, just as the stem transmits the motion of winding the watch. (a) is incorrect because the works measure time, but do not directly transmit motion produced by winding. (c) is incorrect because time is what the watch measures. (d) is incorrect because the crystal merely protects the face of the watch.

12. AENEAS : VIRGIL :: (a. Hercules b. Penelope **c. Odysseus** d. Dido) : HOMER

(c) is correct because Aeneas is the hero of Virgil's epic work, *The Aeneid*, just as Odysseus is the hero of Homer's epic *The Odyssey*. (a) is incorrect because Hercules is a hero of Greek mythology. (b) and (d) are incorrect because Penelope and Dido are minor characters in *The Odyssey*.

13. PUMICE : (**a. lava** b. porous c. volcano d. molten) :: AMBER : RESIN

(a) is correct because amber is a solid substance composed of hardened resin, just as pumice is a solid substance composed of hardened lava. (b) is incorrect because porous (meaning not water tight) may be a characteristic of rock, but not a rock itself. (c) is incorrect because a volcano is the source of igneous rocks, not the rocks themselves. (d) is incorrect because molten refers to the liquid state of rock.

14. CHAPTER : NOVEL :: (a. rhyme b. meter c. anthology **d. stanza**) : POEM

(d) is correct because just as a chapter is a section of a novel, a stanza is a section of a poem. (a) and (b) are incorrect because rhyme and meter may be characteristics of a poem, but neither is a section of one. (c) An anthology refers to a collection of works with a related theme. A poem may be part of an anthology, but an anthology cannot be a section of a poem.

15. TROCHEE : IAMB :: TUESDAY : (a. Monday **b. delay** c. Wednesday d. day)

(b) is correct because the word *Tuesday* is an example of a trochee—a pair of syllables with the accent on the first syllable, just as the word *delay* is an example of an iamb—a pair of syllables with the accent on the second syllable. All other choices are trochaic.

16. E.G. : N.B. :: FOR EXAMPLE : (a. and others b. by that fact **c. note well** d. and so forth)

(c) is correct because *e.g.* is an abbreviation for the Latin phrase *exempla gratia*, meaning for example just as *n.b.* is an abbreviation for the Latin phrase *nota bene*, meaning note well.

17. (**a. circumference** b. diameter c. radius d. pi) : CIRCLE :: PERIMETER : SQUARE

    (**a**) is correct because the perimeter of a square is the measure of a square's outer edge, just as the circumference of a circle is the measure of the circle's outer edge. The diameter of a circle (b) and the radius (c) are measurements within a circle, and are therefore incorrect. (d) is incorrect because pi, or π, is a number used to calculate the measurements of geometric shapes, roughly equal to 3.14159.

18. GEORGIA O' KEEFFE : ANSEL ADAMS :: (a. choreography b. architecture c. sculpture **d. painting**) : PHOTOGRAPHY

    (**d**) is correct because Ansel Adams was a photographer, just as Georgia O'Keeffe was a painter. These artists did not participate in these other disciplines, (a), (b), and (c), and they are therefore incorrect.

19. (a. bread **b. horseshoe** c. boot d. furniture) : BLACKSMITH :: SHOE : COBBLER

    (**b**) is correct because a cobbler (or shoemaker) produces shoes, while a blacksmith produces horseshoes. A blacksmith does not produce any of the other items, so (a), (c), and (d) are incorrect.

20. (**a. tadpole** b. toad c. newt d. amphibian) : FROG :: NYMPH : DRAGONFLY

    (**a**) is correct because an immature dragonfly is a nymph, just as an immature frog is a tadpole. (b) is incorrect because a toad is a mature type of amphibian. (c) is incorrect because a newt is another type of amphibian. (d) is incorrect because amphibian is a general term.

21. 12 : 144 :: (a. 2 b. 9 **c. 6** d. 12) : 36

    (**c**) is correct because 12 squared is 144 just as 6 squared is 36. All other answer choices are irrelevant.

22. 6.4587 : 6 :: 10.28943 : (a. 28 **b. 10** c. 9 d. 1)

    (**b**) is correct because the number 6.4587 is truncated to the integer 6. Therefore, 10.28943 when truncated becomes 10.

Explanations
of Answers

23. GLUCOSE : STARCH :: (a. tricarboxylic acid b. carbonic acid **c. amino acid** d. triglyceride) : PROTEIN

    (c) is correct because a monosaccharide is a unit of which the starch molecule is made. Amino acids are the units of which a protein is made. Triglycerides (d) are the units of which fatty acids are made, but they are not related to the protein. Tricarboxylic acid (a) and carbonic acid (b) are usually not considered to be structural units.

24. ORATOR : LINGUIST :: (a. speech b. French c. language **d. eloquence**) : FLUENCY

    (d) is correct because a successful linguist has the quality of fluency (in languages), just as a successful orator has the gift of eloquence (in public speaking). (a) is incorrect because speech is too general a term. (b) is incorrect because French is too specific a term. (c) is incorrect because language refers to the talent of both a linguist and an orator.

25. CURRICULUM : CURRICULA :: ALUMNUS : (**a. alumni** b. alma mater c. senior d. alumna)

    (a) is correct because *curricula* is the plural of *curriculum*, just as *alumni* is the plural of *alumnus*. (b) is incorrect because this refers to the school one attended. (c) is incorrect because this refers to a rank or position in that school. (d) is incorrect because *alumna* is the female form of *alumnus*.

26. PHOTOSYNTHESIS : CHLOROPHYLL :: DIGESTION : (a. animal **b. enzyme** c. food d. energy)

    (b) is correct because chlorophyll is the chemical necessary for plants to create food from sunlight and carbon dioxide (i.e., photosynthesis), just as an enzyme is necessary for digestion in animals. (a) is incorrect because an animal is the creature that carries out the process of digestion. (c) is incorrect because food is the raw material for digestion. (d) is incorrect because energy is the product of digestion.

27. MERCURY : Hg :: GOLD : (a. W b. Pb **c. Au** d. O)

    (c) is correct because Hg is the chemical symbol for mercury, just as Au is the symbol for gold. (a) is incorrect because W is the symbol for tungsten, (b) is incorrect because Pb is the symbol for lead, and (d) is incorrect because O is the symbol for oxygen.

28. NYLON : POLYAMIDE :: (a. twill b. cotton c. wool **d. dacron**) : POLYESTER

    (d) is correct because nylon is a type of polyamide and Dacron is a type of polyester. Both nylon and dacron are fabrics and therefore the choices of twill (a), cotton (b), and wool (c), appear appropriate at first, however, they are not types of polyester.

29. NUMERATOR : (a. quotient **b. denominator** c. product d. hypotenuse) :: OVER : UNDER

    (b) is correct because just as over is on top of under, so too is the numerator on top of the denominator. The quotient (a) is the answer to a division problem and therefore does not have a position under the numerator. The product (c) is the answer to a multiplication problem, and the hypotenuse (d) is the side of a right triangle which is across from the right angle. None of the other three terms show the over and under analogy.

30. POLIOMYELITIS : SALK :: SMALLPOX : (a. Blackwell b. Fleming **c. Jenner** d. Langerhans)

    (c) is correct because Jonas Salk discovered the vaccine for poliomyelitis just as Edward Jenner discovered a vaccine for smallpox. (a) is incorrect because Elizabeth Blackwell was the first woman in the United States to receive a medical degree. (b) is incorrect because Fleming shared the Nobel Prize for the development of penicillin. (d) is incorrect because Langerhans was a German anatomist.

31. NUCLEUS : (a. proton **b. electron** c. atom d. neutron) :: PLANET : SATELLITE

    (b) is correct because a satellite revolves around a planet just as electrons revolve around the nucleus of an atom. (a) and (d) are incorrect because these particles comprise the nucleus. (c) is incorrect because this term is too general to complete the analogy.

32. (a. 4 b. 10 c. 5 **d. 1**) : 16 :: WASHINGTON : LINCOLN

    (d) is correct because Abraham Lincoln was the sixteenth president, just as George Washington was the first. (a) is incorrect because the fourth president was Madison, the ninth (b) was Harrison, and the fifth (c) was Monroe.

33. (**a. horse** b. griffin c. minotaur d. wolf) : FISH :: CENTAUR : MERMAID

    (a) is correct because a mermaid is a mythical creature said to be part woman, part fish, just as a centaur was a creature said to be part man, part horse. (b) is incorrect because a griffin was said to be part eagle and part lion. (c) is incorrect because a minotaur was said to be part man and part bull. (d) is incorrect because the mythical creature associated with a wolf was a werewolf, said to be part wolf and part human.

34. Given

    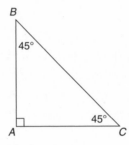

    $AB : AC :: BC :$ (a. AC^2 **b.** $\sqrt{(AB^2 + AC^2)}$ c. AB^2 d. $AB + AC$)

    (b) The triangle is a 45–45–90 right triangle. In this type of triangle the lengths of the sides opposite the 45° angles are equal in length, therefore $AB = AC$ and the analogy is one of equality. Also by the Pythagorean Theorem, in a right triangle the hypotenuse squared is equal to the sum of the individual legs squared: $BC^2 = AB^2 + AC^2$. In order to find the length of side BC, you must take the square root of the sum of the equation. Therefore, the answer is $\sqrt{(AB^2 + AC^2)}$.

35. $(x, y) : \sqrt{xy^2} + 2x^2y - 4y :: (4, y) :$ (a. $2\sqrt{y}$ b. $6y$ c. $14\sqrt{y}$ **d. 30y**)

    (d) This analogy is in the form of a function, the pair (x, y) is transformed into $\sqrt{xy^2} + 2x^2y - 4y$. When $(4, y)$ is substituted into the expression:

    $$4\sqrt{y^2} + 2(4)^2y - 4y =$$
    $$2y + 2 \times 16y - 4y =$$
    $$2y + 32y - 4y = 30y$$

36. 10 : (**a. Downing St.** b. Broadway c. Baker St. d. 5th Avenue) :: 1600 : PENNSYLVANIA AVENUE

    (a) is correct because 10 Downing St. is the address of the British Prime Minister just as 1600 Pennsylvania Ave. is the address of the President of the United States. (b) is incorrect because Broadway is associated with New York's musical theaters. (c) is incorrect because Baker St. is associated with fictional sleuth Sherlock Holmes. (d) is incorrect because Fifth Avenue in New York is associated with the American fashion industry.

37. CONDUCTOR : (a. baton **b. orchestra** c. Bernstein d. composer) :: TEACHER : CLASS

    (b) is correct because a conductor leads an orchestra in the same way that a teacher leads a class. (a) is incorrect because it is the object that a conductor uses. (c) is incorrect because Bernstein is the name of a famous American conductor. (d) is incorrect because a composer writes the music that orchestras and individual musicians perform.

38. HUMERUS : PHALANGES :: ARM : (a. elbow b. radius **c. toes** d. tibia)

    (c) is correct because the humerus is a bone of the upper arm just as phalanges are the bones of the toes and fingers. (a) is incorrect because elbow refers to a joint, not a bone. (b) is incorrect because the radius, along with the ulna, is a bone in the lower arm. (d) is incorrect because the tibia is a bone in the lower leg.

39. SWITZERLAND : (a. Ceylon **b. Nepal** c. Madagascar d. Portugal) :: ALPS : HIMALAYAS

    (b) is correct because the Alps are a mountain range in Switzerland just as the Himalayas are in Nepal. All other choices are irrelevant.

40. (**a. Elizabethan** b. Edwardian c. eighteenth century d. Jacobian) : VICTORIAN :: SIXTEENTH CENTURY : NINETEENTH CENTURY

    (a) is correct because the Victorian Age occurred in the ninteenth century as the Elizabethan Age occurred in the sixteenth century. The Jacobean Age (d) occurred in the seventeenth century, and Edwardian (b) occurred in the twentieth century.

41. (a. epistemology **b. existentialism** c. ontology d. hermeneutics) : POSITIVISIM :: KIERKEGAARD : COMTE

    (b) is correct because Auguste Comte originated positivism, a system of thought based on a hierarchy of the sciences, just as Sören Kierkegaard originated existentialism, a system of thought based on individual experience, freedom of choice, and responsibility for one's actions. (a) is incorrect because epistemology refers to the study of knowledge and its acquisition. (c) is incorrect because ontology refers to the debate surrounding the existence of god. (d) is incorrect because hermeneutics refers to the study of the principles of interpretation.

42. PSYCHE : MIND :: EGO : (**a. self** b. the unconscious c. id d. mental)

    (a) is correct because in the field of psychology, *psyche* is a synonym for "mind," just as *ego* is a synonym for "the self." (b) is incorrect because the unconscious is a part of the mind that one is rarely aware of but that has a strong influence on behavior. (c) is incorrect because *id* refers to the instinctual part of the mind. (d) is incorrect because *mental* is a general term that refers to the overall processes described by the other answer choices.

43. (a. angel **b. human** c. animal d. misanthropist) : ANTHROPOMORPHIZE :: DEMON : DEMONIZE

    (b) is correct because *demonizing* something means "to characterize as evil," just as to anthropomorphize something is to give human characteristics to an animal, plant, material object, etc. (a) is incorrect because an angel is a mythical creature said to be semi-divine. (c) is incorrect because an animal is a general term referring to something without total human characteristics. (d) is incorrect because a misanthrope is someone who hates humans.

44. TURNER : (**a. England** b. Germany c. Holland d. Brittany) :: VAN GOGH : HOLLAND

    (a) is correct because Van Gogh is a painter from Holland just as Turner is a painter from England. All other answer choices are irrelevant.

45. WOLVES : (a. pup b. canine **c. pack** d. prey) :: SEALS : POD

    (c) is correct because a group of seals is called a pod just as a group of wolves is called a pack. (a) is incorrect because a pup is an immature wolf or dog, or seal. (b) is incorrect because canine is a general term referring to the characteristics of a dog or wolf. (d) is incorrect because prey refers to a living creature eaten by another living creature.

46. CITY : (**a. architect** b. advocate c. mayor d. journalist) :: WASHINGTON, D.C. : L'ENFANT

    (a) is correct because the city of Washington, D.C., was designed by architect Pierre L'Enfant. (b) is incorrect because an advocate is someone who supports an idea or campaign. (c) is incorrect because a mayor is an elected official who functions as a city administrator. (d) is incorrect because a journalist reports the news of a city.

47.   MESOZOIC : ERA :: (a. Jurassic b. Tertiary **c. Pennsylvanian** d. Paleozoic) : PERIOD

(c) Pennsylvanian is correct because Mesozoic is an era defined on the Geological Time Scale, while Pennsylvanian is a period as defined on the Geological Time Scale. Jurassic (a) and Tertiary (b) are periods as defined on the Geological Time Scale. Paleozoic (d) is an era, not a period and therefore does not complete the analogy.

48.   HABITAT : PLACE :: (a. carrying capacity b. competition **c. niche** d. predation) : ROLE

(c) Niche is correct because the habitat of an organism is the place where it lives, while its niche is its role. Carrying capacity (a) refers to the number of individuals which an environment can support, and has nothing to do with the role of the individual. Competition (b) occurs between two individuals who need the same resources, but is not concerned with the role of the individual. Predation (d) is when one individual exploits another, usually as a food source, and this term does not relate to the role of the individual.

49.   DENSITY : NUMBER :: (**a. dispersion** b. habitat c. cohort d. patches) : DISTRIBUTION PATTERN

(a) Dispersion is correct because population density is the number of individuals per unit area, while dispersion is the distribution pattern of a population. Habitat defines where a population lives, not how it is distributed. Cohort (c) refers to a group of individuals who are together, not to the distribution of the group. Patches (d) refer to local areas of habitat, not to distribution patterns. Therefore, none of these words can complete the analogy.

50.   ATHENS : OSLO :: GREECE : (**a. Norway** b. Crete c. Aegean d. Czech Republic)

(a) is correct because Athens is the capital city of Greece just as Oslo is the capital city of Norway. (b) is incorrect because Crete is an island in the Greek archipelago. (c) is incorrect because Aegean is the sea surrounding many of the Greek islands. (d) is incorrect because Czech Republic is a nation whose capital is Prague.

Explanations
of Answers

Explanations
of Answers

51. $4 + 5 : (4 + 5)^5 - (4 - 5)^2 :: a + b :$ (a. $(a + b)^5 - (a + b)^2$ b. $(a + b)^4 - a^2 - 2ab - b^2$) c. $(a + b)^3$ **d. $(a + b)^5 - a^2 + 2ab - b^2$**)

   (d) The expression $(4 + 5)$ is transformed into the expression $(4 + 5)^5 - (4 + 5)^2$. Therefore, the expression $a + b$ then becomes $(a + b)^5 - (a - b)^2 = (a + b)^5 - a^2 + 2ab - b^2$.

52. VISUAL : AURAL :: MAGNIFYING GLASS : (a. telephone b. microscope **c. hearing aid** d. binoculars)

   (c) is correct because a magnifying glass magnifies visual images just as a hearing aid amplifies aural sounds. (a) is incorrect because a telephone transmits, rather than magnifies sound. (b) and (d) are incorrect because a microscope and binoculars magnify visual images.

53. WAGNER : OPERA :: STRAUSS : (a. jazz b. Gregorian c. tarantella **d. waltz**)

   (d) is correct because Wagner was a composer known for his operas just as Strauss was known for his waltzes. (a) is incorrect because jazz is an American musical form derived from ragtime and blues. (b) is incorrect because Gregorian refers to a mode of monastic chanting. (c) is incorrect because the tarantella is a dance.

54. ALGERIA : DINAR :: (a. Turkey **b. Poland** c. Israel d. Kuwait) : ZLOTY

   (b) is correct because the dinar is the basic unit of currency in Algeria, just as the zloty is the basic currency in Poland. (a) is incorrect because the basic unit of currency in Turkey is the Turkish lira. (c) is incorrect because the monetary unit of Israel is the shekel. (d) is incorrect because the monetary unit in Kuwait is the Kuwaiti dinar.

55. (**a. order** b. addition c. quantity d. multiplication) : GROUPING :: COMMUTATIVE : ASSOCIATIVE

   (a) is correct because in multiplication and addition, the associative principle states that grouping does not affect the computation of a group of numbers, just as the commutative property states that order does not affect the computation of a group of numbers. (b) and (d) are incorrect because addition and multiplication are implicit in the principles. (c) is incorrect because quantity is a general term.

Explanations
of Answers

56. 2 : (a. circle b. circumference c. distance **d. diameter**) :: 1 : RADIUS

(d) is correct because the diameter of a circle is twice the radius of a circle. That is, the proportion of diameter to radius is 2 to 1. (a) is incorrect because a circle is the general figure to which diameter and radius refer. (b) is incorrect because the circumference of a circle refers to the measure of its outer edge. (c) is incorrect because distance is a term referring to linear measure.

57. SHREW : RODENT :: (a. turtle **b. antelope** c. grasshopper d. swallow) : RUMINANT

(b) is correct because a shrew is a rodent just as an antelope is a member of the order of ruminants. (a) is incorrect because a turtle is of the order testudinata. (c) is incorrect because a grasshopper is of the order orthopterous. (d) is incorrect because a swallow is of the family hirundinidae.

58. (**a. auxin** b. cytokinin c. phytolexins d. glucose) : PHOTOTROPISM :: GIBBERELLIN : GROWTH

(a) Auxin is correct because gibberellin is a type of plant hormone which influences plant growth. Phototropism is influenced by the plant hormone auxin. Cytokinins (b) are responsible for binding transfer RNAs to ribosomes, phytolexins (c) are naturally occurring antibiotics produced by some plants to protect themselves, and glucose (d) is the food which plants make for energy. None of these plant chemicals influence phototropism, and none are hormones. They therefore cannot be used to complete the analogy.

59. INCH : FOOT :: CENTIMETER : (a. millimeter **b. meter** c. liter d. gram)

(b) An inch is smaller than a foot; 12 inches are in a foot. A centimeter is smaller than a meter; one hundred centimeters are in a meter. A millimeter (a) is smaller than the centimeter, not larger. The choices (c) liter and (d) gram are not units of length and therefore cannot be compared to the other units of length.

Explanations
of Answers

60. Given graphs A and B:

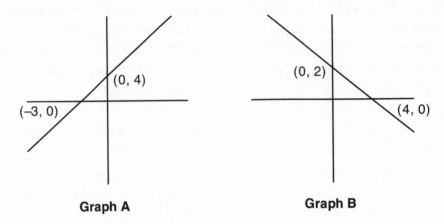

Graph A   **Graph B**

GRAPH A : (0, 4) :: GRAPH B : (a. (–3, 0) b. (2, 0) c. (4, 0) **d. (0, 2)**)

(d) The point (0, 4) in Graph A is the *y*-intercept. The *y*-intercept in Graph B is (0, 2) or choice (d). Choice (a), (–3, 0) is the *x*-intercept of Graph A. Choice (b) is not an intercept of either graph; while choice (c) is the *x*-intercept of Graph B.

61. (a. visible b. fluorescent **c. ultraviolet** d. quanta) : INFRARED :: SHORT : LONG

(c) Ultraviolet is correct because ultraviolet light has a short wavelength, whereas infrared has a long wavelength. The word wavelength does not complete the analogy which is a comparison of short to long. Visible (a) light falls in a medium wavelength range and therefore does not complete the analogy. Fluorescent light begins in UV wavelength ranges but then the electrons are excited to emit light in the visible ranges. Fluorescent (b) does not therefore complete the short: long analogy.

62. A : T :: C : (a. Y b. D c. M **d. G**)

(d) G is correct because A, the abbreviation for adenine, always pairs in DNA with T, which is the abbreviation for thymine. C, which is the letter for cytosine, always pairs with G for guanine. Y (a), D (b), and M (c) are not involved in DNA base pairing and therefore do not complete the analogy.

63. BASIC : (a. saline **b. acidic** c. alkaline d. complex) :: BLUE : RED

(b) is correct because litmus paper is blue when exposed to bases and red when it is exposed to acids. (a) is incorrect because saline is a solution of salt and water. (c) is incorrect alkaline is another name for a basic solution. (d) Complex is incorrect because it does not refer to the litmus paper, but rather to the substance the paper measures.

Explanations
of Answers

64. (a. jetsam b. wharf c. land **d. building**) : DEFENESTRATE :: SHIP : JETTISON

    (d) is correct because to defenestrate something is to toss it from a building, just as to jettison something is to toss it from a ship. (a) is incorrect because jetsam refers to the debris left by a shipwreck that sinks, compared with flotsam, which floats. (b) is incorrect because a wharf is a pier in a port. (c) is incorrect because land refers to that which is not sea.

65. FUZZY : (a. texture b. touch c. furry **d. tactile**) :: PUNGENT : OLFACTORY

    (d) is correct because a pungent scent is detected through the sense of smell, or the olfactory sense, just as something that feels fuzzy is detected through the tactile sense, or sense of touch. (a) is incorrect because texture is a general term which fuzzy might describe. (b) is incorrect because touch does not complete the analogy because it is not comparable to the form olfactory. (c) is incorrect because furry is a synonym for fuzzy.

66. (**a. orange** b. red c. purple d. brown) : BLUE :: RED : GREEN

    (a) is correct because red and green are opposite colors; that is, each contains the primary color or colors not included in the other, just as blue and orange are likewise opposite colors. All other answer choices are irrelevant.

67. OCCUPY : VACANT :: (a. tenant b. fumigate c. undertake **d. cultivate**) : FALLOW

    (d) is correct because a space that is not being occupied is vacant, just as a field which is not being cultivated is fallow. (a) is incorrect because tenant refers to someone occupying a building by renting rather than by owning. (b) is incorrect because fumigate refers to a process of treating a building with pesticides. (c) is incorrect because undertake means to begin a task.

68. DIAGONAL : RECTANGLE :: CHORD : (a. triangle **b. circle** c. hexagon d. rhombus)

    (b) A diagonal connects two vertices of a rectangle and divides the rectangle into two pieces. A chord connects two points on a circle (by definition) and divides the circle into two pieces. Chords are not found in triangles (a), hexagons (c), or rhombi (d).

69. METER : YARD :: (**a. liter** b. inch c. pint d. milliliter) : QUART

    (**a**) Liter is correct because a meter is the metric unit which is slightly larger than a yard. A liter is the metric unit which is slightly larger than a quart. An inch (b) is not a metric unit and it is a measure of length rather than a liquid. It also does not show the larger to smaller analogy. A pint (c) is a unit of liquid measure, but a pint is smaller than a quart and it is also not a metric unit. A milliliter is a metric unit (d) of liquid measure, but it does not show the larger to smaller part of the analogy.

70. WHEREFORE : WHERE :: (a. location b. question **c. person** d. therefore) :
    PLACE

    (**c**) is correct because "where" is used to inquire about a place, just as "wherefore" is used to inquire about a person. (a) is incorrect because a location would be a response to a "where" question. (b) is incorrect because question is too general a term to complete the analogy. (d) is incorrect because therefore is an adverb.

71. RODIN : BRONZE :: STIEGLITZ : (a. oil b. stone c. tin **d. film**)

    (**d**) is correct because Rodin was a sculptor whose primary artistic medium was bronze, just as Stieglitz's (a photographer) primary medium was film. All other answer choices are irrelevant.

72. SISYPHEAN : HERCULEAN :: ENDLESS : (a. labor **b. difficult** c. ongoing
    d. perpetual)

    (**b**) is correct because a Sisyphean task is one that is endless, just as a Herculean task is one which is very difficult. (a) is incorrect because both figures refer to labor. (c) and (d) are incorrect because both of these terms could be used to describe a Sisyphean task.

73. (**a. protein** b. metabolism c. carbohydrate d. sugar) : LIPID :: AMINO ACID :
    FATTY ACID

    (**a**) is correct because lipids are composed of fatty acids, just as proteins are composed of amino acids. (b) is incorrect because this refers to the rate at which the body processes food. (c) is incorrect because a carbohydrate is a compound of carbon, hydrogen, and oxygen. (d) is incorrect because sugar is another name for sucrose.

Explanations
of Answers

74. BLACK : WHITE :: (a. color b. mirror **c. absorb** d. red) : REFLECT

(c) is correct because objects that appear white reflect all the colors of the spectrum, just as objects which appear black absorb all the colors of the spectrum. (a) is incorrect because color is a general term that does not comment on absorption or reflection. (b) is incorrect because a mirror reflects an image, rather than a specific color. (d) is incorrect because red is a specific color.

75. (a. DeFoe b. Burney **c. Cervantes** d. Poe) : PICARESQUE :: RICHARDSON : EPISTOLARY

(c) is correct because just as Richardson wrote in an epistolary style (a story conveyed through letters), Cervantes wrote in a picaresque style (in which the characters' actions are conveyed in humorous episodes). All other answer choices used a variety of styles.

76. (a. food **b. quantity** c. nutrition d. cuisine) : GOURMAND :: QUALITY : GOURMET

(b) is correct because a gourmet desires quality in food, just as a gourmand desires quantity. (a) is incorrect because food is a general term that applies to either. (c) is incorrect because nutrition may or may not be a factor in the desires of either. (d) is incorrect because cuisine is another general term.

77. Jane, Mary, and Todd all have money to go to the candy store. Jane buys chocolate drops and pays with only dimes. Mary buys a lollipop, and she only has pennies. Todd has a dollar bill but does not buy anything**.**

MARY : PENNIES :: TODD : (**a. dollar** b. dimes c. chocolate drops d. lollipop)

(a) The analogy associates Mary with her type of money, in this case, pennies. Thus, Todd should also be associated with money, and the paragraph stated that he had a dollar bill (a). Jane had the dimes (b), not Todd. The remaining choices, (c) chocolate drops and (d) lollipop, were the candies that Jane and Mary purchased, and would not apply to Todd.

78. MONOCOT : (a. one b. two **c. three** d. four) :: DICOT: FIVE

(c) Three is correct because the angiosperm plants which are classified as dicot generally have flower parts in multiples of five, while monocot type of plants has flower parts in multiples of three. Other flower part arrangements do not exist, with the exception of a few dicots which have flower parts in multiples of four (d), but the analogy asks for the arrangement corresponding to monocots, so four will not complete the analogy. One (a) is the number of seed leaves which a monocot has, but this does not fit the analogy since dicot would then have to be paired with the word two (b).

79. HUMAN BODY : 37° :: ROOM : (98.6° b. 32° **c. 25°** d. 0°)

    (c) 25° is correct because human body temperature is 37° on the Celsius scale. Room temperature on the Celsius scale is 25°. The Fahrenheit scale records human body temperature as 98.6° (a), therefore this choice would not complete the analogy. The Fahrenheit Scale records freezing temperature as 32° (b), while the Celsius Scale records it as 0° (d). Therefore these two choices also do not complete the analogy.

80. HANDEL : MOZART :: (a. romantic b. operatic **c. baroque** d. modern) : CLASSICAL

    (c) is correct because Mozart was a composer in the classical style, just as Handel composed in the baroque style. All other answer choices are irrelevant.

81. FRUCTOSE : LACTOSE :: (a. cream **b. fruit** c. skim d. cereal) : MILK

    (b) is correct because lactose is sugar found in milk, just as fructose is sugar found in fruit. (a) and (c) are incorrect because they describe different types of milk. (d) is incorrect because this is a general term for a variety of grains.

82. BAY OF BENGAL : ARABIAN SEA :: EAST : (a. south b. north c. China **d. west**)

    (d) is correct because the Bay of Bengal is a body of water directly east of India, just as the Arabian Sea is just west of India. All other answer choices are irrelevant.

83. HOROWITZ : PIANO :: MA : (a. harp b. piccolo **c. cello** d. baritone)

    (c) is correct because Vladimir Horowitz was a classical pianist, just as Yo-Yo Ma is a classical cellist. All other answer choices are irrelevant.

84. REVOLUTIONARY : CIVIL :: (a. Bull Run **b. Bunker Hill** c. Alamo d. Wounded Knee) : GETTYSBURG

    (b) is correct because the Battle of Gettysburg was a major battle in the Civil War, just as the Battle of Bunker Hill was a major battle in the Revolutionary War. (a) is incorrect because Bull Run was a battle in the Civil War. (c) is incorrect because the Alamo was an American fort. (d) is incorrect because the Battle of Wounded Knee was a conflict between American and Native American forces.

85. OLIGARCH : CHORISTER :: MONARCH : (**a. conductor** b. soloist c. section
d. leader)

(**a**) is correct because an oligarch is one who rules a country as a member of a
relatively small ruling group, just as a chorister is a member of a relatively small
musical group. This is compared with a monarch, who alone guides a country,
just as a conductor alone guides an orchestra. (b) is incorrect because a soloist
would be analogous to a noble, someone who stands out, but is under the authority of the conductor. (c) and (d) are incorrect because section and leader are non-
specific terms.

86. (a. thermostat b. kilowatt c. thermometer **d. calorie**) : HEAT :: NANOMETER :
LENGTH

(**d**) is correct because a calorie is a unit of heat, just as a nanometer is a unit of
length. (a) is incorrect because a thermostat is used to regulate heat. (b) is incorrect because a kilowatt is a measure of energy. (c) is incorrect because a thermometer is used to measure heat.

87. Given (k, m), then $g = 2$, if $k < 0$, $m < 0$
$\qquad\qquad\qquad = 1$, if $k < 0$, $m = 0$
$\qquad\qquad\qquad = 3$, if $k < 0$, $m > 0$
$\qquad\qquad\qquad = 4$, if $k > 0$

$(-1, 2) : 3 :: (4, -1) :$ (a. 1 b. 3 **c. 4** d. 2)

(**c**) The given relationship defines the values of g, with respect to the values of k
and m. For $(-1, 2)$, $k < 0$, and $m > 0$, then by the definition, $g = 3$. For $(4, 1)$, $k >$
0, and the value of $g = 4$, regardless of the value of m.

88. BIZET : *CARMEN* :: MOZART : (a. *Eine Kleine Nachtmusik* b. *The Barber of
Seville* **c. Don Giovanni** d. *Cherubino*)

(**c**) is correct because just as Bizet composed the opera *Carmen*, so Mozart composed the opera *Don Giovanni*. Mozart also composed *Eine Kleine Nachtmusik*,
however this was not an opera.

89. NOCTURNAL : DIURNAL :: (a. lizard b. mammal **c. bat** d. hibernation) :
SQUIRREL

(**c**) is correct because a squirrel is a diurnal mammal, one that is active during the day, just as most bats are nocturnal mammals, and are active during the
night. (a) is incorrect because a lizard is a diurnal reptile. (b) is incorrect because it is too general. (d) is incorrect because it refers to seasonal sleep/activity
patterns, rather than to daily ones.

Explanations
of Answers

90. SUCH IS LIFE : *C'EST LA VIE* :: (a. good day b. behold **c. pen name** d. such is war) : *NOM DE PLUME*

    (c) is correct because "C'est la vie" is a French expression meaning "such is life," just as "Nom de plume" is a French expression meaning pen name. (a) is incorrect because French for good day is "bon jour." (b) is incorrect because French for behold is "viola." (d) is incorrect because French for such is war is "c'est la guerre."

91. 2001 : 365 :: 2004 : (a. 52 **b. 366** c. 1901 d. 3)

    (b) is correct because 2001, which is not divisible by four, will have 365 days, just as 2004 will be a leap year, and therefore will have 366 days. All other choices are irrelevant.

92. RIGHT : (a. correct b. ambidextrous **c. dexter** d. righteous) :: LEFT : SINISTER

    (c) is correct because sinister refers to something left-leaning, just as dexter refers to anything right-leaning. (a) is incorrect because there is nothing correct or incorrect about being on the left or right. (b) is incorrect because ambidextrous refers to someone with equal fluidity with the left or right hand. (d) is incorrect because it is unrelated to the analogy.

93. MEXICO : CORTES :: (a. Argentina b. Bolivia c. El Salvador **d. Peru**) : PIZARRO

    (d) is correct because Hernando Cortes was a Spanish explorer who conquered Mexico, just as Pizarro was the Spanish explorer who conquered Peru. All other choices are irrelevant.

94. XYLEM : ROOTS :: (**a. arteries** b. veins c. phloem d. leaves) : HEART

    (a) is correct because xylem is the tissue of a plant which conducts sap away from the roots, while arteries are the tissues of animals which conduct blood away from the heart. Veins (b) are the animal tissues which conduct blood toward the heart, while phloem (c) is the plant tissue which conducts sap toward the roots. Therefore, neither of these can be used to complete the analogy which is dependent on the concept of conduction "away from." Leaves (d) are not primarily involved with fluid conduction.

Explanations of Answers

95. TELESCOPE : BINOCULARS :: MONOCLE : (a. screen **b. spectacles** c. focus d. microscope)

    (b) is correct because a telescope is a magnifier for one eye and binoculars are a pair of magnifiers for both eyes, just as a monocle is a magnifier for one eye, and spectacles are magnifiers for both eyes. (a) is incorrect because a screen is something upon which an image is projected. (c) is incorrect because focus refers to the clarity of an image. (d) is incorrect because a microscope may be either for one or two eyes.

96. KEY : TURNKEY :: (**a. corkscrew** b. drill c. spatula d. jackhammer) : SOMMELIER

    (a) is correct because a key is the tool of a turnkey (warden), just as a corkscrew is the tool of a sommelier, or wine steward. All other choices are incorrect since a sommelier would have no use for these tools.

97. PLANE : PERPENDICULAR :: FLOOR : (a. ceiling b. gable **c. wall** d. cellar)

    (c) is correct because a floor is a plane, or flat surface, to which a wall is perpendicular. (a) is incorrect because a ceiling is also a plane to which a wall is perpendicular. (b) is incorrect because a gable refers to an arch over a doorway. (d) is incorrect because a cellar is a part of a building that is below ground level.

98. 1215 : MAGNA CARTA :: 1789 : (a. Declaration of Independence b. *Common Sense* c. Twelfth Amendment **d. U.S. Constitution**)

    (d) is correct because the Magna Carta was signed in 1215 just as the U.S. Constitution was signed in 1789. (a) is incorrect because the Declaration of Independence was signed in 1776. (b) is incorrect because *Common Sense* was a pamphlet written by Thomas Paine. (c) is incorrect because the Twelfth Amendment was not added in 1789.

99. 56 : EVEN :: (a. 12 **b. 17** c. 150 d. 65) : PRIME

    (b) is correct because 56 is an even number, meaning it is divisible by two, just as 17 is a prime number, meaning it is divisible by only itself and one. All other answer choices are irrelevant.

Explanations
of Answers

100. Given

x	y	z
4	10	22
2	15	33
2	20	44
4	25	55

$(x = 2, y = 15) : 33 :: (x = 4, z = 55) :$ (a. 44 b. 55 **c. 25** d. 10)

(c) The table provides the relationships between the variables x, y, and z. For $x = 2$ and $y = 15$, the z value is 33. Then for $x = 4$ and $z = 55$, the y value is 25 (c). Choice (d) is incorrect because while $x = 4$, $z = 22$, not 55. Choices (a) and (b) are z values and not y values.

Miller Analogies

six

Practice Test 6

Answer Sheet
Practice Test 6

1. Ⓐ Ⓑ Ⓒ Ⓓ
2. Ⓐ Ⓑ Ⓒ Ⓓ
3. Ⓐ Ⓑ Ⓒ Ⓓ
4. Ⓐ Ⓑ Ⓒ Ⓓ
5. Ⓐ Ⓑ Ⓒ Ⓓ
6. Ⓐ Ⓑ Ⓒ Ⓓ
7. Ⓐ Ⓑ Ⓒ Ⓓ
8. Ⓐ Ⓑ Ⓒ Ⓓ
9. Ⓐ Ⓑ Ⓒ Ⓓ
10. Ⓐ Ⓑ Ⓒ Ⓓ
11. Ⓐ Ⓑ Ⓒ Ⓓ
12. Ⓐ Ⓑ Ⓒ Ⓓ
13. Ⓐ Ⓑ Ⓒ Ⓓ
14. Ⓐ Ⓑ Ⓒ Ⓓ
15. Ⓐ Ⓑ Ⓒ Ⓓ
16. Ⓐ Ⓑ Ⓒ Ⓓ
17. Ⓐ Ⓑ Ⓒ Ⓓ
18. Ⓐ Ⓑ Ⓒ Ⓓ
19. Ⓐ Ⓑ Ⓒ Ⓓ
20. Ⓐ Ⓑ Ⓒ Ⓓ
21. Ⓐ Ⓑ Ⓒ Ⓓ
22. Ⓐ Ⓑ Ⓒ Ⓓ
23. Ⓐ Ⓑ Ⓒ Ⓓ
24. Ⓐ Ⓑ Ⓒ Ⓓ
25. Ⓐ Ⓑ Ⓒ Ⓓ
26. Ⓐ Ⓑ Ⓒ Ⓓ
27. Ⓐ Ⓑ Ⓒ Ⓓ
28. Ⓐ Ⓑ Ⓒ Ⓓ
29. Ⓐ Ⓑ Ⓒ Ⓓ
30. Ⓐ Ⓑ Ⓒ Ⓓ
31. Ⓐ Ⓑ Ⓒ Ⓓ
32. Ⓐ Ⓑ Ⓒ Ⓓ
33. Ⓐ Ⓑ Ⓒ Ⓓ
34. Ⓐ Ⓑ Ⓒ Ⓓ

35. Ⓐ Ⓑ Ⓒ Ⓓ
36. Ⓐ Ⓑ Ⓒ Ⓓ
37. Ⓐ Ⓑ Ⓒ Ⓓ
38. Ⓐ Ⓑ Ⓒ Ⓓ
39. Ⓐ Ⓑ Ⓒ Ⓓ
40. Ⓐ Ⓑ Ⓒ Ⓓ
41. Ⓐ Ⓑ Ⓒ Ⓓ
42. Ⓐ Ⓑ Ⓒ Ⓓ
43. Ⓐ Ⓑ Ⓒ Ⓓ
44. Ⓐ Ⓑ Ⓒ Ⓓ
45. Ⓐ Ⓑ Ⓒ Ⓓ
46. Ⓐ Ⓑ Ⓒ Ⓓ
47. Ⓐ Ⓑ Ⓒ Ⓓ
48. Ⓐ Ⓑ Ⓒ Ⓓ
49. Ⓐ Ⓑ Ⓒ Ⓓ
50. Ⓐ Ⓑ Ⓒ Ⓓ
51. Ⓐ Ⓑ Ⓒ Ⓓ
52. Ⓐ Ⓑ Ⓒ Ⓓ
53. Ⓐ Ⓑ Ⓒ Ⓓ
54. Ⓐ Ⓑ Ⓒ Ⓓ
55. Ⓐ Ⓑ Ⓒ Ⓓ
56. Ⓐ Ⓑ Ⓒ Ⓓ
57. Ⓐ Ⓑ Ⓒ Ⓓ
58. Ⓐ Ⓑ Ⓒ Ⓓ
59. Ⓐ Ⓑ Ⓒ Ⓓ
60. Ⓐ Ⓑ Ⓒ Ⓓ
61. Ⓐ Ⓑ Ⓒ Ⓓ
62. Ⓐ Ⓑ Ⓒ Ⓓ
63. Ⓐ Ⓑ Ⓒ Ⓓ
64. Ⓐ Ⓑ Ⓒ Ⓓ
65. Ⓐ Ⓑ Ⓒ Ⓓ
66. Ⓐ Ⓑ Ⓒ Ⓓ
67. Ⓐ Ⓑ Ⓒ Ⓓ
68. Ⓐ Ⓑ Ⓒ Ⓓ

69. Ⓐ Ⓑ Ⓒ Ⓓ
70. Ⓐ Ⓑ Ⓒ Ⓓ
71. Ⓐ Ⓑ Ⓒ Ⓓ
72. Ⓐ Ⓑ Ⓒ Ⓓ
73. Ⓐ Ⓑ Ⓒ Ⓓ
74. Ⓐ Ⓑ Ⓒ Ⓓ
75. Ⓐ Ⓑ Ⓒ Ⓓ
76. Ⓐ Ⓑ Ⓒ Ⓓ
77. Ⓐ Ⓑ Ⓒ Ⓓ
78. Ⓐ Ⓑ Ⓒ Ⓓ
79. Ⓐ Ⓑ Ⓒ Ⓓ
80. Ⓐ Ⓑ Ⓒ Ⓓ
81. Ⓐ Ⓑ Ⓒ Ⓓ
82. Ⓐ Ⓑ Ⓒ Ⓓ
83. Ⓐ Ⓑ Ⓒ Ⓓ
84. Ⓐ Ⓑ Ⓒ Ⓓ
85. Ⓐ Ⓑ Ⓒ Ⓓ
86. Ⓐ Ⓑ Ⓒ Ⓓ
87. Ⓐ Ⓑ Ⓒ Ⓓ
88. Ⓐ Ⓑ Ⓒ Ⓓ
89. Ⓐ Ⓑ Ⓒ Ⓓ
90. Ⓐ Ⓑ Ⓒ Ⓓ
91. Ⓐ Ⓑ Ⓒ Ⓓ
92. Ⓐ Ⓑ Ⓒ Ⓓ
93. Ⓐ Ⓑ Ⓒ Ⓓ
94. Ⓐ Ⓑ Ⓒ Ⓓ
95. Ⓐ Ⓑ Ⓒ Ⓓ
96. Ⓐ Ⓑ Ⓒ Ⓓ
97. Ⓐ Ⓑ Ⓒ Ⓓ
98. Ⓐ Ⓑ Ⓒ Ⓓ
99. Ⓐ Ⓑ Ⓒ Ⓓ
100. Ⓐ Ⓑ Ⓒ Ⓓ

Practice Test 6

TIME: 50 Minutes   **LENGTH:** 100 Analogies

DIRECTIONS: Read each of the following analogies carefully, and choose the BEST answer to each item. Fill in your responses in the answer sheets provided.

Note: The Miller Analogies Test consists of 120 questions to be completed in 60 minutes. Twenty of these questions are experimental items, which are not scored and thus not reflected in this practice test.

1. GRABEN : (a. faults b. lakes c. rivers d. cliffs) :: VALLEY : MOUNTAINS

2. HALCYON : (a. informal b. cautious c. tranquil d. peripheral) :: PALPABLE : MANIFEST

3. VII : XXI :: IX : (a. VI b. XXI c. XXVII d. XXIX)

4. FROND : FERN :: THREAD : (a. sewing b. cotton c. fiber d. needle)

5. 46 : CHROMOSOMES :: 206 : (a. muscles b. nerves c. bones d. teeth)

6. PEGASUS : HORSE :: ORION : (a. hunter b. bear c. bull d. dog)

7. (a. kindle b. garnish c. squander d. enumerate) : LIST :: RECLAIM : SALVAGE

8. COMPRESSED AIR : (a. shaft b. pneumatic c. diesel d. gas) :: LIQUID : TURBINE

9. ORNITHOLOGY : BIRDS :: (a. mycology b. cytology c. oncology d. biology) : FUNGI

10. (a. atom b. electron c. charge d. ferrous) : ELEMENT :: COMPOUND : MOLECULE

11. MARY ANN EVANS : (a. Willa Cather b. Silas Marner c. Emily Brontë d. George Eliot) :: SAMUEL CLEMENS : MARK TWAIN

12. 0.00036 : 3.6E–4 :: 1234.56 : (a. 1.23456E+3 b. 1.23456E+2 c. 123.456E+3 d. 1.23456E–3)

13. HIMALAYAS : (a. Australia b. North America c. South America d. Asia) :: ALPS : EUROPE

14. FACADE : PERSONALITY :: (a. lumber b. resin c. veneer d. leaf) : WOOD

15. HUMMINGBIRD : OSTRICH :: MERCURY : (a. Jupiter b. Earth c. Mars d. Venus)

16. LEWIS CARROLL : (a. Moby Dick b. Alice c. Hester Prynne d. Yossarian) :: CERVANTES : DON QUIXOTE

17. GLUCOSE : (a. vinegar b. honey c. vegetables d. poultry) :: ASCORBIC ACID : LEMON

18. SURGERY : (a. intelligence b. personality c. appearance d. emotions) :: CONDITIONING : BEHAVIOR

19. (a. adaptation b. restraint c. perception d. intelligence) : SURVIVAL :: CREATIVITY : GENIUS

20. (a. $\sqrt{250}$ b. $\sqrt{500}$ c. $\sqrt{625}$ d. $\sqrt{1000}$) : 25 :: $\sqrt{100}$: 10

21. DIMMER SWITCH : (a. shaft b. light c. elevator d. light bulb) :: THERMOSTAT : HEAT

22. (a. Civil War b. Desert Storm c. World War I d. Korean War) : TRUMAN :: WORLD WAR II : FRANKLIN ROOSEVELT

23. (a. names b. mixtures c. molecules d. elements) : FAMILIES :: FOOD : GROUPS

24. GOOSE : GOSLING :: (a. mallard b. swan c. owl d. osprey) : CYGNET

25. EQUATOR : NORTH POLE :: ZERO : (a. 90 b. 145 c. 180 d. 270)

26. ALGAE : (a. fungi b. molds c. agar d. protozoa) :: PENICILLIUM : ANTIBIOTIC

27. CONTRAVENE : HARMONIZE :: FUGUE : (a. opine b. demur c. vigilant d. intercede)

28. JAPAN : ISLANDS :: (a. Australia b. Italy c. France d. Switzerland) : PENINSULA

29. (a. bacteria b. radium c. nitrous oxide d. rabies) : PASTEUR :: TUBERCULOSIS : KOCH

30. VIRGIL : DANTE :: (a. Marley b. Dickens c. Cratchit d. ghosts) : SCROOGE

31. THYROID : (a. enzyme b. ligament c. joint d. gland) :: HEART : MUSCLE

32. MENDEL : GENETICS :: DARWIN : (a. evolution b. blood groups c. culture d. relative dating)

33. TEXTURE : SURFACE :: (a. size b. mass c. shape d. contents) : VOLUME

34. ECONOMICS : INCOME :: (a. geography b. genetics c. earth d. cultural anthropology) : POLITICS

35. Children in a classroom are assigned to different desks. The third grade girls are given blue seats while the third grade boys are given green seats. The second grade girls are seated in purple seats and the second grade boys in red seats. The first graders all have yellow seats.

     THIRD GRADE BOYS : GREEN :: FIRST GRADE GIRLS : (a. yellow b. purple c. red d. blue)

36. (a. trial by jury b. religious freedom c. income taxes d. 18-year-old vote) : I :: SLAVERY ABOLISHED : XIII

Practice Test 6

37. CUNEIFORM : HIEROGLYPHICS :: (a. phonics b. stylus c. drawing d. alphabet) : PICTOGRAM

38. (a. space travel b. color printing c. insurance d. human anatomy) : PROBABILITY THEORY :: BLOOD CIRCULATION : HUMAN PHYSIOLOGY

39. (a. population b. computer c. statistics d. validity) : SAMPLES :: DECK : CARDS

40. FUEL : POLLUTION :: WATER : (a. erosion b. energy c. congestion d. agriculture)

41. RNA : (a. one b. three c. five d. seven) :: DNA : SIX

42. (a. new moon b. crescent c. first quarter d. gibbous) : 30 :: FULL MOON : 15

43. FASCISM : DICTATORSHIP :: LAISSEZ-FAIRE : (a. free market economy b. historical development c. legal education d. scientific classification)

44. FRANCIS DRAKE : CALIFORNIA COAST :: (a. Hernando de Soto b. Hernando Cortes c. Ponce de Leon d. Jacques Cartier) : FLORIDA

45. HARTFORD : (a. Nebraska b. Connecticut c. Illinois d. New Jersey) :: AUSTIN : TEXAS

46. OPERCULUM : GILLS :: (a. pupil b. retina c. eyelid d. iris) : EYE

47. EMMA LAZARUS : (a. Liberty Bell b. America c. Red Cross d. Statue of Liberty) :: FRANCIS SCOTT KEY : NATIONAL ANTHEM

48. (a. verdant b. specious c. venerable d. nascent) : EXTINCT :: BLOOM : DEGENERATE

49. IGNEOUS : CRUST :: (a. granite b. cobalt c. ozone d. basalt) : OCEAN

50.   Given the graphs

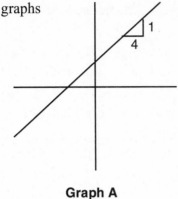

Graph A   **Graph B**

GRAPH B : $-\dfrac{2}{5}$ :: GRAPH A : (a. $-\dfrac{5}{2}$ b. 5 c. $\dfrac{2}{5}$ d. $\dfrac{1}{4}$)

51.   ARGOS : JASON :: (a. *Pequod* b. *Bounty* c. *Nautilus* d. *Enterprise*) : BLIGH

52.   *THE DIVINE COMEDY* : (a. essay b. abstract c. sonnet d. narrative) ::
      EVANGELINE : POEM

53.   CADMIUM : CORROSION :: (a. ions b. metal c. lead d. science) :
      RADIATION

54.   MONROE DOCTRINE : 1823 :: (a. Missouri Compromise b. Bill of Rights
      c. Louisiana Purchase d. Panama Canal) : 1803

55.   SARTRE : EXISTENTIALIST :: (a. Orwell b. Joyce c. Kipling d. Sandburg) :
      SATIRIST

56.   HENRY CLAY : (a. The Wizard of Menlo Park b. Iron Chancellor c. The Great
      Compromiser d. Old Hickory) :: LA GUARDIA : THE LITTLE FLOWER

57.   HYPOTHERMIA : BODY HEAT :: (a. humiliation b. controversy c. regret
      d. spirit) : STATURE

58.   (a. cabal b. exigency c. omen d. priority) : SECRET :: UNIVERSITY :
      ACADEMIC

59.   DIAGNOSIS : (a. remission b. controversy c. interpretation d. pronunciation) ::
      TRAVESTY : MISREPRESENTATION

60. DISEASE : TOXINS :: BANKRUPTCY : (a. money b. economics c. debts d. inflation)

61. CREEP : SLOW :: AVALANCHE : (a. snow b. water c. rapid d. debris)

62. DEER : HERD :: RABBIT : (a. colony b. flock c. pack d. litter)

63. (a. orator b. senator c. topic d. filibuster) : SPEECH :: NARRATIVE : EVENT

64. DIATOMS : CHLOROPHYLL :: BACTERIA : (a. cytoplasm b. cellulose c. nucleus d. carbon dioxide)

65. (a. the Doppler effect b. comets c. x-rays d. aurora) : RADIATION :: THE BLUE SHIFT : LIGHT

66. Given perpendicular lines with slopes m_1 and m_2 then

$$m_1 : -\frac{1}{m_2} :: m_1 = 5 : m_2 = (\text{a. } \frac{1}{5} \quad \text{b. } \frac{1}{2} \quad \text{c. } -\frac{1}{5} \quad \text{d. } -\frac{1}{2})$$

67. IMPECUNIOSITY : DEPRESSION :: (a. sorrow b. love c. passion d. anger) : JOY

68. COLLABORATION : (a. collusion b. notoriety c. cabal d. soloing) : FAME : INFAMY

69. OSMIUM : SILVER :: (a. steel b. oak c. balsa d. granite) : PINE

70. AESTHETICS : (a. literature b. philosophy c. psychology d. science) :: AGRONOMY : AGRICULTURE

71. NEBULA : (a. morning star b. protostar c. cloud d. crab) :: CONSTELLATION : URSA MINOR

72. CELESTIAL : (a. earthly b. visceral c. infernal d. divine) :: LOFTY : NETHER

73. BASEBALL PLAYER : DIAMOND :: (a. spelunker b. archaeologist c. researcher d. scientist) : CAVES

74. 10.2598 : 2598 :: 21.3926 : (a. 21 b. 0.3926 c. 3926 d. 39.26)

75. ROCKIES : NORTH :: (a. Appalachian b. Andes c. Alps d. Zagros) : SOUTH

76. BANAL : TRITE :: (a. ephemeral b. divine c. permanent d. unreal) : TEMPORARY

77. CONTRITE : (a. punctual b. dogmatic c. penitent d. pessimistic) : CONCISE : SUCCINCT

78. (a. endoplasmic reticulum b. mitochondrion c. ribosome d. chromosome) : CELL :: ACTIVE GALACTIC NUCLEUS : GALAXY

79. GAGGLE : GEESE :: (a. crew b. rafter c. class d. drift) : SWANS

80. (a. ligament b. muscle c. arm d. pauldron) : SHOULDER :: SKULL : BRAIN

81. PERIOD : ERA :: DISCONFORMITY : (a. conformity b. unconformity c. eon d. epoch)

82. CETACEA : WHALES :: FALCONIFORMES : (a. aves b. birds c. robin d. eagle)

83. PHILANTHROPIST : HUMANITARIAN :: (a. art b. money c. education d. medicine) : TIME

84. INTEGER : 5 :: PRIME NUMBER : (a. 1 b. 9 c. 3 d. 6)

85. THIEF : (a. implusive b. furtive c. irrational d. destitute) :: DELINQUENT : INTRACTABLE

86. SPECTROPHOTOMETRY: ABSORPTION OF LIGHT :: (a. coulometry b. potentiometry c. chromatography d. electrophoresis) :: CURRENT

87. MESOZOIC : REPTILES :: CENOZOIC : (a. mammals b. amphibians c. era d. succession)

88. SAUNTER : WALK :: (a. fortissimo b. fosse c. adagio d. arpeggio) : ANDANTE

89. Given arbitrary angles A and B

   COMPLEMENTARY : A + B = 90° :: SUPPLEMENTARY : (a. A − B = 90° b. A + B = 90° c. A − B = 180° d. A + B = 180°)

90. $\dfrac{f+g}{g-f} : \dfrac{g+f}{f-g} :: a + b - \dfrac{3}{2a} - 5b :$ (a. $b + a - \dfrac{3}{2b} - 5a$ b. $b + a - \dfrac{3}{2a} - 5b$ c. $a + b - \dfrac{3}{a+b}$ d. $\dfrac{b+a}{a-b}$)

91. (a. rod b. stylus c. mold d. kiln) : CLAY :: CHISEL : STONE

92. ISOAMYL ACETATE : BANANA :: (a. methyl salicylate b. ethyl butyrate c. benzyl acetate d. methyl anthranilate : WINTERGREEN

93. AREA : REAA :: TOYS : (a. YOTS b. TOZS c. TOYT d. TOY)

94. ARM : (a. tricep b. metacarpal c. tibia d. radius) :: LEG : FEMUR

95. WRITER : DRAFTS :: ARTIST : (a. notes b. studies c. sketches d. methods)

96. MINISTER : BIBLE :: CARPENTER : (a. plumb b. furnace c. book d. delimiter)

97. A coin is tossed 10 times.

   TAILS : 6 :: HEADS : (a. 5 b. 6 c. 10 d. 4)

98. GEOCHRONOLOGY : ISOTOPES :: BIOGENOUS DEPOSIT DATING : (a. rocks b. succession c. foraminiferal ooze d. magnetic minerals)

99. PORRINGER : BOWL :: (a. base b. meat c. platter d. dinner) : PLATE

100. FARROW : SOW :: (a. graze b. calf c. ruminate d. bull) : COW

Answer Key
Practice Test 6

1. (a)	26. (c)	51. (b)	76. (a)
2. (c)	27. (c)	52. (d)	77. (c)
3. (c)	28. (b)	53. (c)	78. (b)
4. (c)	29. (d)	54. (c)	79. (d)
5. (c)	30. (d)	55. (a)	80. (d)
6. (a)	31. (d)	56. (c)	81. (b)
7. (d)	32. (a)	57. (a)	82. (d)
8. (b)	33. (b)	58. (a)	83. (b)
9. (a)	34. (d)	59. (c)	84. (c)
10. (a)	35. (a)	60. (c)	85. (b)
11. (d)	36. (b)	61. (c)	86. (a)
12. (a)	37. (d)	62. (a)	87. (a)
13. (d)	38. (c)	63. (d)	88. (c)
14. (c)	39. (a)	64. (a)	89. (d)
15. (a)	40. (a)	65. (a)	90. (a)
16. (b)	41. (c)	66. (c)	91. (b)
17. (b)	42. (a)	67. (b)	92. (a)
18. (c)	43. (a)	68. (a)	93. (a)
19. (a)	44. (c)	69. (b)	94. (d)
20. (c)	45. (b)	70. (b)	95. (c)
21. (b)	46. (c)	71. (d)	96. (a)
22. (d)	47. (d)	72. (c)	97. (d)
23. (d)	48. (d)	73. (a)	98. (c)
24. (b)	49. (d)	74. (c)	99. (c)
25. (a)	50. (d)	75. (b)	100. (b)

Explanations
of Answers

Explanations of Answers
Practice Test 6

1. GRABEN : (**a. faults** b. lakes c. rivers d. cliffs) :: VALLEY : MOUNTAINS

   (**a**) is correct because a graben is a portion of the earth's crust that is surrounded on at least two sides by faults, just as a valley is surrounded by mountains. (b), (c), and (d) are incorrect because a graben is not formed by these structures.

2. HALCYON : (a. informal b. cautious **c. tranquil** d. peripheral) :: PALPABLE : MANIFEST

   (**c**) is the correct response. If something is palpable (capable of being touched, tangible), then it is manifest (obvious). If something is halcyon (calm, peaceful), then it is tranquil (calm). (a) Informal (casual) has no relationship to halcyon. (b) Cautious (careful) is not a synonym of halcyon. (d) Peripheral (covering a border area) has no relation to halcyon.

3. VII : XXI :: IX : (a. VI b. XXI **c. XXVII** d. XXIX)

   (**c**) is the correct answer. VII = 7, XXI = 21. What number is VII (7) multiplied by to get XXI (21)? The answer is 3. Therefore, IX (9) multiplied by 3 would give you (c) XXVII = 27. (a) VI = 6, (b) XXI = 21, and (d) XXIX = 29 are incorrect.

4. FROND : FERN :: THREAD : (a. sewing b. cotton **c. fiber** d. needle)

   (**c**) is the correct answer. A fern is made up of fronds (leaves). A (c) fiber is made up of strands of thread. (a) Thread is used in sewing, but sewing does not make up thread. (b) Cotton is a fabric. You can buy cotton thread, but the cotton is not a composite of the thread. (d) Needle is an instrument used with thread.

5. 46 : CHROMOSOMES :: 206 : (a. muscles b. nerves **c. bones** d. teeth)

   (**c**) is the correct response. There are 46 chromosomes in each cell. There are 206 (c) bones in the human body. (a) muscles and (b) nerves are incorrect. (d) There are 32 permanent teeth in the human body.

6. PEGASUS : HORSE :: ORION : (**a. hunter** b. bear c. bull d. dog)

   (**a**) is correct. Pegasus is the name of the constellation that represents a horse. Orion is the constellation that represents a (a) hunter. (b) Bear is Ursa Major. (c) Bull is Taurus. (d) Canus Major is a dog.

7. (a. kindle b. garnish c. squander **d. enumerate**) : LIST :: RECLAIM : SALVAGE

   (**d**) is the correct response. When you reclaim (claim back) something, you salvage it (rescue it from ruin). When you (d) enumerate something, you list it. (a) *Kindle* means "to start a fire or stir emotions." (b) *Garnish* means "to decorate something." (c) *Squander* means "to spend lavishly."

8. COMPRESSED AIR : (a. shaft **b. pneumatic** c. diesel d. gas) :: LIQUID : TURBINE

   (**b**) is correct. Power coming from the release of liquid under pressure is used in turbine engines. Power coming from compressed air is used to drive (b) pneumatic devices. (a) Shaft is a component of a machine. (c) Diesel is the type of fuel used for engines. (d) Gas is used to operate some machines, but is not associated with compressed air.

9. ORNITHOLOGY : BIRDS :: (**a. mycology** b. cytology c. oncology d. biology) : FUNGI

   (**a**) is correct. Ornithology is the study of birds. (a) Mycology is the study of fungi. (b) Cytology is a branch of biology for the study of cells. (c) Oncology is the branch of medicine dealing with cancer. (d) Biology is the study of life processes.

10. (**a. atom** b. electron c. charge d. ferrous) : ELEMENT :: COMPOUND : MOLECULE

    (**a**) is the right answer. The smallest part of a compound is a molecule. The smallest part of an atom (a) is the element. (b) An electron is a negatively charged particle and is not the smallest part of an element. A (c) charge tells you whether the particle is positive or negative. (d) Ferrous relates to an iron type of metal.

Explanations of Answers

11. MARY ANN EVANS : (a. Willa Cather b. Silas Marner c. Emily Brontë **d. George Eliot**) :: SAMUEL CLEMENS : MARK TWAIN

    (d) is correct. Samuel Clemens is the real name of the author who called himself Mark Twain. Mary Ann Evans is the real name of the author who called herself (d) George Eliot. (a) Willa Cather is the author of *My Antonia*. (b) *Silas Marner* is a book written by George Eliot. (c) Emily Brontë is the author of *Wuthering Heights*.

12. 0.00036 : 3.6E–4 :: 1234.56 : (**a. 1.23456E+3** b. 1.23456E+2 c. 123.456E+3 d. 1.23456E–3)

    (a) The analogy rewrites the decimal number in scientific notation. Therefore, 1234.56 written in scientific notation is 1.23456E+3.

13. HIMALAYAS : (a. Australia b. North America c. South America **d. Asia**) :: ALPS : EUROPE

    (d) is the correct response. The Alps are a mountain range in Europe. The Himalayas are a mountain range in (d) Asia. The Himalayas are not found in (a) Australia, (b) North America, or (c) South America.

14. FACADE : PERSONALITY :: (a. lumber b. resin **c. veneer** d. leaf) : WOOD

    (c) is correct. A facade (appearance that doesn't reflect the whole person) is only the outside appearance of a personality. A (c) veneer is the thin layer on the outside of wood. (a) lumber is logs cut into usable wood and does not have the same relationship as the given words. (b) Resin is a substance obtained from the sap of some trees. (d) A leaf is a stem of foliage and has no relationship to wood.

15. HUMMINGBIRD : OSTRICH :: MERCURY : (**a. Jupiter** b. Earth c. Mars d. Venus)

    (a) is the right answer. A hummingbird is the smallest type of bird. An ostrich is the largest bird. Mercury is the smallest planet, and Jupiter (a) is the largest planet. (b) Earth, (c) Mars, and (d) Venus are not as large as Jupiter.

16. LEWIS CARROLL : (a. Moby Dick **b. Alice** c. Hester Prynne d. Yossarian) :: CERVANTES : DON QUIXOTE

    (b) is the correct answer. Cervantes created a character named Don Quixote. Lewis Carroll created a character named (b) Alice. (a) Moby Dick was a whale in a book written by Melville. (c) Hester Prynne was a character in the *Scarlet Letter* written by Hawthorne. (d) Yossarian was a character in *Catch 22* written by Heller.

17. GLUCOSE : (a. vinegar **b. honey** c. vegetables d. poultry) :: ASCORBIC ACID : LEMON

    (b) is the correct response. Ascorbic acid is a natural substance found in lemon. (b) Glucose is a natural substance found in honey. (a) Glucose is not found in vinegar. (c) Vegetables may or may not contain glucose. (d) Poultry does not contain glucose.

18. SURGERY : (a. intelligence b. personality **c. appearance** d. emotions) :: CONDITIONING : BEHAVIOR

    (c) is correct. Conditioning (bringing about a response to a specific stimulus) alters behavior. Surgery alters (c) appearance. For the most part, surgery is not a means of altering (a) intelligence, (b) personality, or (d) emotions.

19. (**a. adaptation** b. restraint c. perception d. intelligence) : SURVIVAL :: CREATIVITY : GENIUS

    (a) is the correct response. Creativity is a necessary quality relating to genius. (a) Adaption is a necessary quality for survival. (b) Restraint (confinement or reserve) has nothing to do with survival. (c) Perception (insight) is a positive quality, but is not necessarily related to survival. (d) Intelligence is helpful but surely not necessary for survival.

20. (a. $\sqrt{250}$ b. $\sqrt{500}$ **c. $\sqrt{625}$** d. $\sqrt{1000}$) : 25 :: $\sqrt{100}$: 10

    (c) is the correct response. The square root of 100 is 10. The square root of 625 is 25. (a) The square root of 250 is not 25. (b) The square root of 500 is not 25. (d) The square root of 1,000 is not 25.

21. DIMMER SWITCH : (a. shaft **b. light** c. elevator d. light bulb) :: THERMOSTAT : HEAT

    (b) is the correct answer. A thermostat regulates heat as a dimmer switch regulates light. (a) A shaft is part of an automobile and it doesn't regulate speed. (c) An elevator is a machine which raises or lowers weight. (d) A lightbulb is not directly related to a dimmer switch.

22. (a. Civil War b. Desert Storm c. World War I **d. Korean War**) : TRUMAN :: WORLD WAR II : FRANKLIN ROOSEVELT

    (d) is the correct answer. World War II occurred under Franklin Roosevelt's administration. The Korean War occurred under Truman's administration. (a) The Civil War was associated with Lincoln. (b) Desert Storm occurred under Bush's administration. (c) World War I was under Wilson's administration.

23. (a. names b. mixtures c. molecules **d. elements**) : FAMILIES :: FOOD : GROUPS

    (d) is correct. Food can be classified into groups. (d) Elements can be classified into families. (a) Names doesn't have the same relationship as the given words. (b) Mixtures cannot be classified into families. (c) Molecules (smallest particles of matter) cannot be classified into families.

24. GOOSE : GOSLING :: (a. mallard **b. swan** c. owl d. osprey) : CYGNET

    (b) is the correct answer. A goose is a mature gosling, or gosling is the name of a young goose. A cygnet is the name for a young swan. (a) Mallard is a type of duck. Ducklings are baby ducks. (c) An owl is a bird and owlet is the word for an immature owl. (d) An osprey is a large hawk.

25. EQUATOR : NORTH POLE :: ZERO : (**a. 90** b. 145 c. 180 d. 270)

    (a) is the correct response. The equator is at a latitude of zero degrees. The north pole is at a latitude of 90 degrees. The north pole is not at a latitude of (b) 145 degrees, (c) 180 degrees, or (d) 270 degrees.

26. ALGAE : (a. fungi b. molds **c. agar** d. protozoa) :: PENICILLIUM : ANTIBIOTIC

    (c) Agar is made from algae, while some antibiotics are made from penicillium. Agar is not made from fungi (a), molds (b), or protozoa (c), and these terms do not therefore fit the analogy.

27. CONTRAVENE : HARMONIZE :: FUGUE : (a. opine b. demur **c. vigilant** d. intercede)

    (c) is the correct response. Contravene (go against someone's wishes) is the antonym of harmonize (agree). Fugue is a disturbed state of mind where a person unconsciously goes through an experience and has no recollection afterwards. (c) Vigilant means to be highly aware of your surroundings. (a) Opine means to have an opinion. (b) Demur means to object or protest. (d) Intercede means to intervene on someone's behalf.

28. JAPAN : ISLANDS :: (a. Australia **b. Italy** c. France d. Switzerland) : PENINSULA

    (b) is the correct response. Japan is a country composed of islands. (b) Italy is a country which is a peninsula. (a) Australia is a continent. (c) France is a country located in Europe. (d) Switzerland is on the European continent.

29. (a. bacteria b. radium c. nitrous oxide **d. rabies**) : PASTEUR ::
TUBERCULOSIS : KOCH

    (d) is the correct response. Koch, a German scientist, was famous for discovering a cure for tuberculosis. Pasteur was famous for discovering a vaccine for rabies. (a) Leeuwenhoek was famous for pioneering microscopy. Curie was famous for the discovery of (b) radium. (c) Priestley was famous for discovering nitrous oxide.

30. VIRGIL : DANTE :: (a. Marley b. Dickens c. Cratchit **d. ghosts**) : SCROOGE

    (d) is correct because Virgil was Dante's guide in the first two books of *The Divine Comedy* just as ghosts were Scrooge's guides in *A Christmas Carol*. Marley (a) is incorrect because while he was Scrooge's first visitor, he did not accompany him on his journey. Dickens (b) is the author of *A Christmas Carol*. Cratchit (c) is incorrect because he was Scrooge's assistant.

31. THYROID : (a. enzyme b. ligament c. joint **d. gland**) :: HEART : MUSCLE

    (d) is the correct answer. The heart is a muscle. The thyroid is a (d) gland. (a) An enzyme is a complex protein produced by living cells that induce or accelerate chemical reactions. (b) Ligaments are tissues that hold bones together. (c) Joint is the point of contact between bones.

32. MENDEL : GENETICS :: DARWIN : (**a. evolution** b. blood groups c. culture d. relative dating)

    (a) is the correct response. Mendel studied genetics. Darwin studied the process of (a) evolution. (b) Blood groups, (c) culture, and (d) relative dating were not studied by Darwin.

33. TEXTURE : SURFACE :: (a. size **b. mass** c. shape d. contents) : VOLUME

    (b) is the correct response. Texture relates to the nature of a material's surface. (b) Mass (quantity of matter that a material possesses) relates to the volume (space occupied as measured by cubic units) of a material. (a) Size is not related to volume as in the given words. (c) Shape has no relation to volume. (d) Contents tell you what is available.

Explanations
of Answers

34. ECONOMICS : INCOME :: (a. geography b. genetics c. earth **d. cultural anthropology**) : POLITICS

    (d) is correct. Economics is the science of production, distribution, and consumption of goods and services. (d) Cultural anthropology deals with patterns of social and cultural phenomena and includes the study of politics. (a) Geography is the study of the Earth's surface. (b) Genetics is the study of heredity and doesn't include politics. (c) Earth science is the study of the present features and past evolution of the Earth.

35. Children in a classroom are assigned to different desks. The third grade girls are given blue seats while the third grade boys are given green seats. The second grade girls are seated in purple seats and the second grade boys in red seats. The first graders all have yellow seats.

    THIRD GRADE BOYS : GREEN :: FIRST GRADE GIRLS : (**a. yellow** b. purple c. red d. blue)

    (a) The paragraph gives the relationships between the school children and their seat color. The analogy for third grade boys directly relates their seat color to them, third grade boys to green. Since all the first graders are in yellow seats, the sex of the first graders is not considered in the seat assignments. The first grade girls and boys all sit in yellow seats. The purple seats (b) are for the second grade girls, and the red (c) seats are for the second grade boys. The blue (d) seats are reserved for the third grade girls.

36. (a. trial by jury **b. religious freedom** c. income taxes d. 18-year-old vote) : I :: SLAVERY ABOLISHED : XIII

    (b) is the correct response. Slavery was abolished with the XIII (Thirteenth) Amendment to the U.S. Constitution. The First Amendment (b) I established, among other things, the right to religious freedom. (a) The right to trial by jury was established by the VII (Seventh) Amendment, which is part of the Bill of Rights. (c) Income taxes were authorized by the XVI (Sixteenth) Amendment. (d) The voting age was lowered to 18 by the XXVI (Twenty-sixth) Amendment.

37. CUNEIFORM : HIEROGLYPHICS :: (a. phonics b. stylus c. drawing **d. alphabet**) : PICTOGRAM

    (d) is the correct answer. Cuneiform is the Sumerian writing system and hieroglyphics is the Egyptian writing system. A pictogram is a writing system used in China and Japan and the (d) alphabet is a letter version of a writing system. (a) Phonics is the use of a letter-sound relationship in language. (b) Stylus is a writing instrument. (c) Drawing is a version of writing, but is not a formal writing system.

38. (a. space travel b. color printing **c. insurance** d. human anatomy) :
PROBABILITY THEORY :: BLOOD CIRCULATION : HUMAN
PHYSIOLOGY

(c) is the correct response. Blood circulation is explained by the study of human physiology. (c) Insurance is based on the study of probability theory. (a) Space travel has no relation to probability theory. (b) Color printing has no relation to probability theory. (d) Human anatomy cannot be explained by probability theory.

39. (**a. population** b. computer c. statistics d. validity) : SAMPLES :: DECK : CARDS

(a) is correct. When a dealer shuffles a deck of cards, he/she ensures that the cards from the whole deck are randomly distributed. When an experimenter wants to test a theory or find out information, he/she will use a sample (small number of cases) from the total population that are randomly distributed. (b) Computer is a machine and has no relation to the analogy. (c) Statistics is the science of gathering and interpreting data. (d) Validity is that the experiment is based on logical soundness.

40. FUEL : POLLUTION :: WATER : (**a. erosion** b. energy c. congestion d. agriculture)

(a) is correct. Fuel burning is a major source of air pollution. Water is the major source of soil erosion. Water is not the major source of (b) energy. Water is not the source of (c) congestion. Water is not the source of (d) agriculture. Water is a necessary ingredient in agriculture.

41. RNA : (a. one b. three **c. five** d. seven) :: DNA : SIX

(c) Five is correct because DNA contains the six-carbon sugar deoxyribose, whereas RNA contains the five-carbon sugar ribose. The numbers one, three, and seven have no related significance to RNA for this analogy.

42. (**a. new moon** b. crescent c. first quarter d. gibbous) : 30 :: FULL MOON : 15

(a) is the correct response. The full moon shows up 15 days in the cycle of the moon's orbit. The new moon occurs after 30 days in the moon's orbit. (b) The crescent moon occurs after $26\frac{1}{4}$ days. (c) The first quarter occurs after $7\frac{1}{2}$ days. (d) The gibbous moon occurs after $11\frac{1}{4}$ days and after $18\frac{3}{4}$ days.

43. FASCISM : DICTATORSHIP :: LAISSEZ-FAIRE : (**a. free market economy**
    b. historical development c. legal education d. scientific classification)

    (a) is the right answer. Fascism is a political movement that stands for a centralized autocratic government headed by a dictatorial leader. Fascism is associated with dictatorship. Laissez-faire is associated with a free market economy. (b) Historical development has no relation to laissez-faire. (d) Scientific classification has no relation to laissez-faire.

44. FRANCIS DRAKE : CALIFORNIA COAST :: (a. Hernando de Soto
    b. Hernando Cortes **c. Ponce de Leon** d. Jacques Cartier) : FLORIDA

    (c) is the correct answer. Francis Drake was an explorer of the California coast. (c) Ponce de Leon explored Florida. (a) Hernando de Soto explored the Mississippi River near Memphis. (b) Hernando Cortes explored Mexico. (d) Jacques Cartier explored the Gulf of St. Lawrence in Canada.

45. HARTFORD : (a. Nebraska **b. Connecticut** c. Illinois d. New Jersey) ::
    AUSTIN : TEXAS

    (b) is the right answer. Austin is the capital of Texas. Hartford is the capital of (b) Connecticut. Lincoln is the capital of (a) Nebraska. Springfield is the capital of (c) Illinois. Trenton is the capital of (d) New Jersey.

46. OPERCULUM : GILLS :: (a. pupil b. retina **c. eyelid** d. iris) : EYE

    (c) Eyelid is correct because the operculum is a covering which protects the gills, while the eyelid is a covering which protects the eye. The pupil (a), retina (b), and iris (d) are parts of the eye itself, and therefore could not complete the analogy, which is dependent on an independent structure.

47. EMMA LAZARUS : (a. Liberty Bell b. America c. Red Cross **d. Statue of
    Liberty**) :: FRANCIS SCOTT KEY : NATIONAL ANTHEM

    (d) is the correct answer. Francis Scott Key was famous for writing the poem that later became the *National Anthem*. Emma Lazarus was known for her poem "Colossus" on the (d) Statue of Liberty. (a) The Liberty Bell is in Independence Hall and was created to commemorate the 50th anniversary of the Commonwealth of Pennsylvania. (b) *America* was written by Rev. Samuel Francis Smith. (c) Red Cross is associated with Clara Barton.

48. (a. verdant b. specious c. venerable **d. nascent**) : EXTINCT :: BLOOM : DEGENERATE

    (d) is the correct answer. The opposite of bloom (to be in health) is to degenerate (to fall apart). The opposite of extinct (no longer exists) is to be (d) nascent (beginning to develop). (a) Verdant (green with growing plants) is not the opposite of extinct. (b) Specious (seeming to be genuine) has no relation to extinct. (c) Venerable (treated with respect) also has no relation to extinct.

49. IGNEOUS : CRUST :: (a. granite b. cobalt c. ozone **d. basalt**) : OCEAN

    (d) is the correct response. Igneous rock is found primarily in the Earth's crust. (d) Basalt rock is found on the ocean floors. (a) Granite is not usually found in the ocean. (b) Cobalt is not found primarily in the ocean. (c) Ozone is found primarily in the atmosphere.

50. Given the graphs

    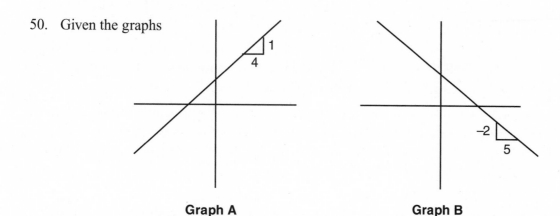

    GRAPH B : $-\dfrac{2}{5}$ :: GRAPH A : (a. $-\dfrac{5}{2}$ b. 5 c. $\dfrac{2}{5}$ **d. $\dfrac{1}{4}$**)

    (d) In graph B the slope of the line is change in *y* divided by the change in *x*, or $-\dfrac{2}{5}$. The slope on the line in graph A can be computed the same way. The change in *y* is 1, and the change in *x* is 4; therefore the slope is $\dfrac{1}{4}$.

51. ARGOS : JASON :: (a. *Pequod* **b. *Bounty*** c. *Nautilus* d. *Enterprise*) : BLIGH

    (b) is the correct answer. The *Argos* is the ship that Jason captained. The *Bounty* (b) is the ship that Bligh (*Mutiny on the Bounty*) captained. (a) The *Pequod* was Captain Ahab's ship from *Moby-Dick*. (c) The *Nautilus* was central to Verne's *20,000 Leagues Under the Sea*. (d) The *Enterprise* was Captain Kirk's ship from the *Star Trek* television serial.

Explanations
of Answers

52. *THE DIVINE COMEDY* : (a. essay b. abstract c. sonnet **d. narrative**) :: *EVANGELINE* : POEM

    (d) is the correct response. *Evangeline* is a poem written by Longfellow. *The Divine Comedy* is a descriptive narrative of an imaginary journey through the various levels of hell written by Dante. (a) An essay is a composition. (b) An abstract is a summary of a piece of work. (c) A sonnet is a type of poem.

53. CADMIUM : CORROSION :: (a. ions b. metal **c. lead** d. science) : RADIATION

    (c) is the correct response. Cadmium is used to plate metals and alloys to protect them from corrosion. (c) Lead is used to protect people and things from radiation. (a) Ions are electrically charged particles and don't protect from radiation. (b) Metal is an opaque, ductile, or lustrous substance, and is a chemical element. The term is too general to be a protection from radiation. (d) Science is not related to radiation as a protective device.

54. MONROE DOCTRINE : 1823 :: (a. Missouri Compromise b. Bill of Rights **c. Louisiana Purchase** d. Panama Canal) : 1803

    (c) is the correct answer. The date of the Monroe Doctrine was 1823. The date of the (c) Louisiana Purchase was 1803. The date of the (a) Missouri Compromise was 1820. The date of the (b) Bill of Rights was 1791. The Panama Canal (d) was built in 1914.

55. SARTRE : EXISTENTIALIST :: (**a. Orwell** b. Joyce c. Kipling d. Sandburg) : SATIRIST

    (a) is the correct answer. Sartre was an author who wrote books that dealt with existentialism. (a) Orwell was an author who wrote *Animal Farm*, this made him a satirist. (b) Joyce was known for his stream of consciousness writing style. (c) Kipling wrote about the British in India. (d) Sandburg was a poet who wrote about Chicago and the Midwest.

56. HENRY CLAY : (a. The Wizard of Menlo Park b. Iron Chancellor **c. The Great Compromiser** d. Old Hickory) :: LA GUARDIA : THE LITTLE FLOWER

    (c) is the right answer. Fiorello La Guardia was a former mayor of New York who was known as the Little Flower. Henry Clay was known as (c) the Great Compromiser. Thomas Alva Edison was known as (a) The Wizard of Menlo Park. Bismarck was known as the (b) Iron Chancellor. Andrew Jackson was known as (d) Old Hickory.

Explanations
of Answers

57. HYPOTHERMIA : BODY HEAT :: (**a. humiliation** b. controversy c. regret
d. spirit) : STATURE

    (**a**) is the correct response. Hypothermia is the loss of body heat from exposure
    to cold. (a) Humiliation (injury to self-respect) is the loss of stature. (b) Contro-
    versy has no relation to stature. (c) Regret is what you would feel after you lose
    stature. (d) Spirit is not related to stature as the given words.

58. (**a. cabal** b. exigency c. omen d. priority) : SECRET :: UNIVERSITY :
ACADEMIC

    (**a**) is correct. A university is an academic society. A (a) cabal is a secret society.
    An (b) exigency is an urgent need or requirement and has no relation to secret.
    An (c) omen is an event believed to be a sign or warning of a future occurrence
    and has no relation to secret. A (d) priority (something that takes precedence)
    has no relation to secret.

59. DIAGNOSIS : (a. remission b. controversy **c. interpretation** d. pronunciation) ::
TRAVESTY : MISREPRESENTATION

    (**c**) is the right answer. *Travesty* is a synonym for *misrepresentation. Diagno-
    sis* and (c) *interpretation* are synonyms. When a doctor makes a diagnosis, he/
    she interprets your symptoms. (a) *Remission* (release or abatement) is not a
    synonym of *diagnosis.* (b) *Controversy* (opposing views) and *diagnosis* are not
    synonyms. (d) *Pronunciation* (say or speak correctly) is not related to *diagnosis.*

60. DISEASE : TOXINS :: BANKRUPTCY : (a. money b. economics **c. debts**
d. inflation)

    (**c**) is the correct answer. Disease is caused by toxins in your body. Bankruptcy
    is caused by (c) debts (owing money to someone else). (a) Money doesn't cause
    bankruptcy by itself. The lack of money causes you to be bankrupt. (b) Econom-
    ics doesn't cause bankruptcy. (d) Inflation (the abnormal increase in the volume
    of money and credit resulting in a substantial and continuing rise in the general
    price level) doesn't directly cause bankruptcy.

61. CREEP : SLOW :: AVALANCHE : (a. snow b. water **c. rapid** d. debris)

    (**c**) Rapid is correct because a creep is a specific type of flow, an extremely slow,
    down-slope movement, while an avalanche is a rapid mass-movement process.
    Snow (a) and debris (d) are two types of avalanches, but do not form the speed
    dependent analogy. Water (b) may flow slowly or rapidly, but is not a specific
    type of flow.

62. DEER : HERD :: RABBIT : (**a. colony** b. flock c. pack d. litter)

   (**a**) is the correct answer. A group of deer is called a herd. A group of rabbit(s) is called a (a) colony. (b) A flock is a group of ducks. (c) A pack is a group of wolves or coyotes. (d) A litter is a group of cats.

63. (a. orator b. senator c. topic **d. filibuster**) : SPEECH :: NARRATIVE : EVENT

   (**d**) is the right answer. A narrative is an extended telling of an event. A (d) filibuster is an extensive speech. (a) An orator is a person who gives a speech. A (b) senator is a person who gives a speech. If she gives an extended speech that inhibits voting, she is known to be engaged in filibustering. (c) A topic is what a person gives a speech on.

64. DIATOMS : CHLOROPHYLL :: BACTERIA : (**a. cytoplasm** b. cellulose c. nucleus d. carbon dioxide)

   (**a**) is the right answer. One celled plants called diatoms contain chlorophyll. Bacteria contains (a) cytoplasm. (b) Cellulose is a plant material and bacteria are not plants. (c) A Nucleus is the center of the cell and doesn't have the same relationship with the given words. (d) Carbon dioxide is a byproduct of respiration.

65. (**a. the Doppler effect** b. comets c. x-rays d. aurora) : RADIATION :: THE BLUE SHIFT : LIGHT

   (**a**) The Doppler effect is correct because it is a change in the wavelength of radiation caused by a change in the position of the source and the observer. The blue shift is a change in the wavelength of light which is also caused by a change in the position of the source and the observer. Comets (b) are small icy bodies which orbit the sun, but there are no apparent wavelength changes as they orbit. X-rays (c) are a form of radiation, but the analogy is the change in wavelength which is observed due to the relationship of the source to the observer; therefore x-rays in and of themselves do not complete the analogy. An aurora (d) is a display of lights but the apparent changes which take place are not due to the relative positions of the source and observer, but rather are due to a guiding magnetic field.

66. Given perpendicular lines with slopes m_1 and m_2 then

   $$m_1 : -\frac{1}{m_2} :: m_1 = 5 : m_2 = (\text{a. } \frac{1}{5} \quad \text{b. } \frac{1}{2} \quad \textbf{c. } -\frac{1}{5} \quad \text{d. } -\frac{1}{2})$$

   (**c**) Perpendicular lines have slopes which are negative reciprocals of each other. This is also stated in the analogy as $m_1 : \frac{1}{m_2}$. Therefore if $m_1 = 5$, the slope of m_2 must be $-\frac{1}{5}$, choice (c).

67. IMPECUNIOSITY: DEPRESSION :: (a. sorrow **b. love** c. passion d. anger) : JOY

(b) is correct because impecuniosity, or poverty, can produce feelings of depression in much the same way that love can produce feelings of joy. (a) and (d) are incorrect because these are opposites of joy. (c) is incorrect because passion may be aroused by both positive and negative emotions.

68. COLLABORATION: (**a. collusion** b. notoriety c. cabal d. soloing) : FAME : INFAMY

(a) is correct because collusion refers to a form of collaboration in which the participants have dubious intentions, just as infamy refers to fame for negative things. (b) Notoriety is a general term for fame. (c) is incorrect because a cabal is a group of people doing something harmful; however, it is of a different form and does not complete the analogy. (d) Soloing is also an opposite of collaboration however, it is a general opposite, and not the specific opposite needed to complete the analogy.

69. OSMIUM : SILVER :: (a. steel **b. oak** c. balsa d. granite) : PINE

(b) is correct because osmium is a stronger metal than silver, just as oak is stronger than pine. (a) and (d) are incorrect because although they are stronger than pine, they are wholly different materials. (c) is incorrect because this type of wood is softer than pine.

70. AESTHETICS: (a. literature **b. philosophy** c. psychology d. science) :: AGRONOMY: AGRICULTURE

(b) is correct. Agronomy is a branch of agriculture dealing with raising crops and the care of soil. Aesthetics is a branch of philosophy (b) dealing with the nature and appreciation of beauty. (a) Literature is the study of written works. (c) Psychology is the study of human behavior. (d) Science is the study of the laws of the universe.

71. NEBULA: (a. morning star b. protostar c. cloud **d. crab**) :: CONSTELLATION : URSA MINOR

(d) Crab is correct because the crab is the name of a specific nebula while Ursa Minoris is the name of a specific constellation. The morning star (a) changes throughout the year and therefore does not complete the analogy of a specific name. A protostar (b) is the precursor to a star and therefore does not complete the analogy for a specific name. A nebula is a (c) cloud of gas and dust, but this does not complete the analogy of a specific name.

72. CELESTIAL : (a. earthly b. visceral **c. infernal** d. divine) :: LOFTY : NETHER

    (c) is correct because celestial is the direct opposite of infernal in the same way that lofty is the direct opposite of nether. (a) and (b) are incorrect because while they are temporal opposites, they are not direct opposites. (d) is incorrect because divine and celestial are synonyms.

73. BASEBALL PLAYER : DIAMOND :: (**a. spelunker** b. archaeologist c. researcher d. scientist) : CAVES

    (a) is correct because a spelunker explores caves *specifically* just as a baseball player needs specifically to play on a diamond. All other answer choices are related to the general idea framed by the question, but none of them provides the precise parallel that is required.

74. 10.2598 : 2598 :: 21.3926 : (a. 21 b. 0.3926 **c. 3926** d. 39.26)

    (c) The analogy relates the number 10.2598 to its decimal part, 2598. Then the decimal part of 21.3926 is 3926.

75. ROCKIES : NORTH :: (a. Appalachian **b. Andes** c. Alps d. Zagros) : SOUTH

    (b) Andes is correct because the Rockies are mountains which are found in North America, while the Andes are mountains which are found in South America. The Appalachian (a) mountains are found in North America, so this answer does not complete the analogy. The Alps (c) and the Zagros (d) are mountain ranges found in the Northern Hemisphere, so they also will not complete the analogy.

76. BANAL : TRITE :: (**a. ephemeral** b. divine c. permanent d. unreal) : TEMPORARY

    (a) is correct because both *banal* and *trite* mean "commonplace," just as *ephemeral* and *temporary* both mean "short-lived." (b) is incorrect because something that is divine is thought to be permanent (c), which is the opposite of temporary. (d) is incorrect because something that is temporary must have been real, if only for a short time.

77. CONTRITE : (a. punctual b. dogmatic **c. penitent** d. pessimistic) : CONCISE : SUCCINCT

    (c) is correct because both *contrite* and *penitent* mean "to be remorseful," just as *concise* and *succinct* both mean "brief." (a) is incorrect because *punctual* means "to be on time," (b) is incorrect because *dogmatic* means "stubborn," and (d) pessimistic is incorrect because this refers to someone who takes a negative perspective on a given situation.

78. (a. endoplasmic reticulum **b. mitochondrion** c. ribosome d. chromosome) :
CELL :: ACTIVE GALACTIC NUCLEUS : GALAXY

(b) Mitochondrion is correct because the active glactic nucleus is the central
energy source of a galaxy while the mitochondrion is the energy source of the
cell. The endoplasmic reticulum (a), ribosomes (c), and chromosomes (d) are not
responsible for energy production, nor are they central to the cell.

79. GAGGLE : GEESE :: (a. crew b. rafter c. class **d. drift**) : SWANS

(d) is correct because a group of geese is called a *gaggle*, just as a group of
swans is called a *drift*. *Crew* (a) and *class* (c) are general terms for a gathering,
and a *rafter* (b) refers to a group of turkeys.

80. (a. ligament b. muscle c. arm **d. pauldron**) : SHOULDER :: SKULL : BRAIN

(d) is correct because a pauldron is a piece of armor that protects the shoulder,
just as the skull protects the brain. (a) and (b) are parts of the shoulder, but are
not concerned with its protection. (c) is incorrect because this is the larger ap-
pendage of which the shoulder is a part.

81. PERIOD : ERA :: DISCONFORMITY : (a. conformity **b. unconformity** c. eon
d. epoch)

(b) Unconformity is correct because a period is a subdivision of an era while
disconformity is a subdivision of unconformity, which is a break in the geological time record. While eon (c) and epoch (d) are related to era and therefore
appear to be appropriate responses, they do not complete the analogy, which is
based on a part-to-whole relationship. (a) conformity would be the opposite of
unconformity and would therefore not complete the part-to-whole relationship.

82. CETACEA : WHALES :: FALCONIFORMES : (a. aves b. birds c. robin
d. eagle)

(d) Eagle is correct because Cetacea is the order to which whales belong and
eagles belong to the order falconiformes. Aves (a) is the class rather than the order to which all birds (b) belong, so neither aves nor birds complete the analogy.
Robins (c) belong to a different order.

83. PHILANTHROPIST : HUMANITARIAN :: (a. art **b. money** c. education
d. medicine) : TIME

(b) is correct because just as a philanthropist donates money to a given cause, a
humanitarian donates time. (a) is incorrect because while a philanthropist may
donate valuable art to help a cause, this is too specific to complete the analogy.
(c) is incorrect because while a philanthropist might donate money to a school,
he or she is not directly donating education, just as giving money to a hospital is
not directly giving medicine (d).

84. INTEGER : 5 :: PRIME NUMBER : (a. 1 b. 9 **c. 3** d. 6)

(c) The number 5 is an example of an integer. To complete the analogy, an example of a prime number is needed. A prime number is a number greater than 1
(therefore choice (a), 1, is incorrect) whose only factors are itself and 1. Choice
(b) has factors of 1, 3, and 9 and thus is not prime. Likewise, choice (d) has factors 1, 2, and 3. The only prime number choice is (c).

85. THIEF : (a. implusive **b. furtive** c. irrational d. destitute) :: DELINQUENT :
INTRACTABLE

(b) is correct because just as a delinquent must be intractable, or difficult to control, so a thief must be furtive and sly. (a) and (c) are incorrect because there is
nothing to suggest that a given thief is either impulsive or irrational. A thief may
be destitute (d); however, in the case of a successful thief this may not be the case.

86. SPECTROPHOTOMETRY: ABSORPTION OF LIGHT :: (**a. coulometry**
b. potentiometry c. chromatography d. electrophoresis) :: CURRENT

(a) Coulometry is correct because spectrophotometry is the measurement of the
absorption of light, while coulometry is a measurement of current. Potentiometry (b) measures the potential of an electrode compared to another electrode; it
does not measure current. Chromatography (c) separates dissolved solutes into
two phases, and it is therefore not a measurement technique. While it involves
the movement of charged particles in response to an electrical current, it is not a
measurement of current (d) and therefore does not complete the analogy of the
measurement technique to the thing measured.

87. MESOZOIC : REPTILES :: CENOZOIC : (**a. mammals** b. amphibians c. era
d. succession)

(a) Mammals is correct because the Mesozoic era was dominated by reptiles while
the Cenozoic era was dominated by mammals, but not by amphibians (b). While
the Mesozoic is an era, (c) this choice does not complete the analogy. Succession
(d) refers to a progression of life forms and not to the one which dominates an era.

88. SAUNTER : WALK :: (a. fortissimo b. fosse **c. adagio** d. arpeggio) :
ANDANTE

(**c**) is correct because adagio is slower in tempo than andante as a saunter is a
leisurely walk. *Fortissimo* (a) and *arpeggio* (d) are musical terms but do not fit
the analogy. *Fosse* may sound like a musical term but it refers to a ditch, especially a moat.

89. Given arbitrary angles A and B

COMPLEMENTARY : A + B = 90° :: SUPPLEMENTARY : (a. A − B = 90°
b. A + B = 90° c. A − B = 180° **d. A + B = 180°**)

(**d**) The analogy is a direct definition of complementary angles; complementary
angles are two angles whose sum is equal to 90°, such as two angles comprising
a right angle, or the two smaller angles in a right triangle. By definition, supplementary angles are those whose sum is 180°. Thus, for A and B to be supplementary, A + B = 180°.

90. $\dfrac{f+g}{g-f} : \dfrac{g+f}{f-g} :: a + b - \dfrac{3}{2a} - 5b : ($**a.** $b + a - \dfrac{3}{2b} - 5a$ b. $b + a - \dfrac{3}{2a} - 5b$
c. $a + b - \dfrac{3}{a+b}$ d. $\dfrac{b+a}{a-b}$)

(**a**) In the expression $\dfrac{f+g}{g-f}$, f and g are switched to yield $\dfrac{g+f}{f-g}$. Therefore in
the expression, $a + b - \dfrac{3}{2a} - 5b$, when a and b are switched, the expression becomes: $b + a - \dfrac{3}{2b} - 5a$.

91. (a. rod **b. stylus** c. mold d. kiln) : CLAY :: CHISEL : STONE

(**b**) is correct because a stylus is used to cut into clay just as a chisel is used to
cut into stone. (a) is incorrect because a rod is a general term for a long cylin-
drical object. (c) is incorrect because a mold is used to shape clay into a preset
form. (d) is incorrect because a kiln is an oven used to harden, or "fire" clay.

92. ISOAMYL ACETATE : BANANA :: (**a. methyl salicylate** b. ethyl butyrate
c. benzyl acetate d. methyl anthranilate : WINTERGREEN

(a) Methyl salicyate is correct because isoamylacetate provides the characteristic
flavor and taste of banana, while methyl salicylate provides the characteristic
flavor and taste of wintergreen. Ethyl butyrate (b) is the characteristic flavor of
pineapple, benzyl acetate (c) is the characteristic flavor of peach, and methyl
anthranilate (d) is the characteristic flavor of grape. None of these choices completes the analogy of the chemical to the characteristic flavor.

93. AREA : REAA :: TOYS : (**a. YOTS** b. TOZS c. TOYT d. TOY)

(a) The letters in *area* have been rearranged to form *reaa*. Likewise, the letters
in *toys* should be rearranged. Choice (a) rearranges them to form *yots*. The other
choices do not include all of the letters in *toys*.

94. ARM : (a. tricep b. metacarpal c. tibia **d. radius**) :: LEG : FEMUR

(d) is correct because the radius is a bone in the upper arm just as the femur is a
bone in the upper leg. (a) is incorrect because the tricep is the muscle at the rear
of the upper arm. (b) is incorrect because the metacarpals are the bones of the
hand. (c) is incorrect because this is a bone in the lower leg.

95. WRITER : DRAFTS :: ARTIST : (a. notes b. studies **c. sketches** d. methods)

(c) is correct because just as a writer may produce many drafts before a finished
product, an artist may produce many sketches before a final product is produced.
An artist may take notes (a), or study (b) before painting; however, this does not
take the same form as the finished product. An artist may also try different methods (d), but once again, this may not resemble the final product.

96. MINISTER : BIBLE :: CARPENTER : (**a. plumb** b. furnace c. book
d. delimiter)

(a) is correct because just as a minister uses a Bible in his or her work, so does
a carpenter use a plumb in his or her work. (b) is incorrect because the phase of
housebuilding in which a carpenter is involved would not include a furnace. (c)
is incorrect because while a carpenter may refer to a book, it is not something
that he/she always needs. (d) is incorrect because a delimiter is a character that
marks the beginning or end of a group of data on magnetic tape.

Explanations
of Answers

97. A coin is tossed 10 times.

    TAILS : 6 :: HEADS : (a. 5 b. 6 c. 10 **d. 4**)

    (d) When a coin is tossed, only two outcomes are possible, heads or tails. Since the number of tails is given as 6, then the number of heads must be equal to the total tosses minus the number of tails, or 10 − 6 = 4.

98. GEOCHRONOLOGY : ISOTOPES :: BIOGENOUS DEPOSIT DATING : (a. rocks b. succession **c. foraminiferal ooze** d. magnetic minerals)

    (c) Foraminiferal ooze is correct because geochronology is the science of dating which depends on the nuclear breakdown of isotopes. Biogenous deposit dating is the science of dating which depends on foraminiferal ooze. Rocks (a) are useful for dating but something within the rocks is used to identify the date of the rock formation. Succession (b) is used for dating, but biogenous deposit dating is dependent on the presence of foraminifera, not on the succession of species within sediments. Magnetic minerals (d) are used for magnetic reversal dating, but not for biogenous deposit dating and therefore this answer does not complete the analogy.

99. PORRINGER : BOWL :: (a. base b. meat **c. platter** d. dinner) : PLATE

    (c) is correct because a porringer is a type of bowl just as a platter is a type of plate. (a) is incorrect because base is a general term that can refer to anything upon which another thing rests. (b) is incorrect because while meat may be placed in either a porringer or a platter, it is not a type of plate. (d) is incorrect because while both of these objects would be useful at dinner, the term does not define a type of plate or a type of bowl.

100. FARROW : SOW :: (a. graze **b. calf** c. ruminate d. bull) : COW

    (b) is correct because just as a sow gives birth to a farrow (or young pig), so does a cow give birth to a calf. (a) is incorrect because this refers to the feeding of a cow. (c) is incorrect because this is a type of animal, e.g., an antelope. (d) is incorrect because this is the name for a male cow.

Miller Analogies

Practice Test 7

Answer Sheet
Practice Test 7

1. Ⓐ Ⓑ Ⓒ Ⓓ
2. Ⓐ Ⓑ Ⓒ Ⓓ
3. Ⓐ Ⓑ Ⓒ Ⓓ
4. Ⓐ Ⓑ Ⓒ Ⓓ
5. Ⓐ Ⓑ Ⓒ Ⓓ
6. Ⓐ Ⓑ Ⓒ Ⓓ
7. Ⓐ Ⓑ Ⓒ Ⓓ
8. Ⓐ Ⓑ Ⓒ Ⓓ
9. Ⓐ Ⓑ Ⓒ Ⓓ
10. Ⓐ Ⓑ Ⓒ Ⓓ
11. Ⓐ Ⓑ Ⓒ Ⓓ
12. Ⓐ Ⓑ Ⓒ Ⓓ
13. Ⓐ Ⓑ Ⓒ Ⓓ
14. Ⓐ Ⓑ Ⓒ Ⓓ
15. Ⓐ Ⓑ Ⓒ Ⓓ
16. Ⓐ Ⓑ Ⓒ Ⓓ
17. Ⓐ Ⓑ Ⓒ Ⓓ
18. Ⓐ Ⓑ Ⓒ Ⓓ
19. Ⓐ Ⓑ Ⓒ Ⓓ
20. Ⓐ Ⓑ Ⓒ Ⓓ
21. Ⓐ Ⓑ Ⓒ Ⓓ
22. Ⓐ Ⓑ Ⓒ Ⓓ
23. Ⓐ Ⓑ Ⓒ Ⓓ
24. Ⓐ Ⓑ Ⓒ Ⓓ
25. Ⓐ Ⓑ Ⓒ Ⓓ
26. Ⓐ Ⓑ Ⓒ Ⓓ
27. Ⓐ Ⓑ Ⓒ Ⓓ
28. Ⓐ Ⓑ Ⓒ Ⓓ
29. Ⓐ Ⓑ Ⓒ Ⓓ
30. Ⓐ Ⓑ Ⓒ Ⓓ
31. Ⓐ Ⓑ Ⓒ Ⓓ
32. Ⓐ Ⓑ Ⓒ Ⓓ
33. Ⓐ Ⓑ Ⓒ Ⓓ
34. Ⓐ Ⓑ Ⓒ Ⓓ

35. Ⓐ Ⓑ Ⓒ Ⓓ
36. Ⓐ Ⓑ Ⓒ Ⓓ
37. Ⓐ Ⓑ Ⓒ Ⓓ
38. Ⓐ Ⓑ Ⓒ Ⓓ
39. Ⓐ Ⓑ Ⓒ Ⓓ
40. Ⓐ Ⓑ Ⓒ Ⓓ
41. Ⓐ Ⓑ Ⓒ Ⓓ
42. Ⓐ Ⓑ Ⓒ Ⓓ
43. Ⓐ Ⓑ Ⓒ Ⓓ
44. Ⓐ Ⓑ Ⓒ Ⓓ
45. Ⓐ Ⓑ Ⓒ Ⓓ
46. Ⓐ Ⓑ Ⓒ Ⓓ
47. Ⓐ Ⓑ Ⓒ Ⓓ
48. Ⓐ Ⓑ Ⓒ Ⓓ
49. Ⓐ Ⓑ Ⓒ Ⓓ
50. Ⓐ Ⓑ Ⓒ Ⓓ
51. Ⓐ Ⓑ Ⓒ Ⓓ
52. Ⓐ Ⓑ Ⓒ Ⓓ
53. Ⓐ Ⓑ Ⓒ Ⓓ
54. Ⓐ Ⓑ Ⓒ Ⓓ
55. Ⓐ Ⓑ Ⓒ Ⓓ
56. Ⓐ Ⓑ Ⓒ Ⓓ
57. Ⓐ Ⓑ Ⓒ Ⓓ
58. Ⓐ Ⓑ Ⓒ Ⓓ
59. Ⓐ Ⓑ Ⓒ Ⓓ
60. Ⓐ Ⓑ Ⓒ Ⓓ
61. Ⓐ Ⓑ Ⓒ Ⓓ
62. Ⓐ Ⓑ Ⓒ Ⓓ
63. Ⓐ Ⓑ Ⓒ Ⓓ
64. Ⓐ Ⓑ Ⓒ Ⓓ
65. Ⓐ Ⓑ Ⓒ Ⓓ
66. Ⓐ Ⓑ Ⓒ Ⓓ
67. Ⓐ Ⓑ Ⓒ Ⓓ
68. Ⓐ Ⓑ Ⓒ Ⓓ

69. Ⓐ Ⓑ Ⓒ Ⓓ
70. Ⓐ Ⓑ Ⓒ Ⓓ
71. Ⓐ Ⓑ Ⓒ Ⓓ
72. Ⓐ Ⓑ Ⓒ Ⓓ
73. Ⓐ Ⓑ Ⓒ Ⓓ
74. Ⓐ Ⓑ Ⓒ Ⓓ
75. Ⓐ Ⓑ Ⓒ Ⓓ
76. Ⓐ Ⓑ Ⓒ Ⓓ
77. Ⓐ Ⓑ Ⓒ Ⓓ
78. Ⓐ Ⓑ Ⓒ Ⓓ
79. Ⓐ Ⓑ Ⓒ Ⓓ
80. Ⓐ Ⓑ Ⓒ Ⓓ
81. Ⓐ Ⓑ Ⓒ Ⓓ
82. Ⓐ Ⓑ Ⓒ Ⓓ
83. Ⓐ Ⓑ Ⓒ Ⓓ
84. Ⓐ Ⓑ Ⓒ Ⓓ
85. Ⓐ Ⓑ Ⓒ Ⓓ
86. Ⓐ Ⓑ Ⓒ Ⓓ
87. Ⓐ Ⓑ Ⓒ Ⓓ
88. Ⓐ Ⓑ Ⓒ Ⓓ
89. Ⓐ Ⓑ Ⓒ Ⓓ
90. Ⓐ Ⓑ Ⓒ Ⓓ
91. Ⓐ Ⓑ Ⓒ Ⓓ
92. Ⓐ Ⓑ Ⓒ Ⓓ
93. Ⓐ Ⓑ Ⓒ Ⓓ
94. Ⓐ Ⓑ Ⓒ Ⓓ
95. Ⓐ Ⓑ Ⓒ Ⓓ
96. Ⓐ Ⓑ Ⓒ Ⓓ
97. Ⓐ Ⓑ Ⓒ Ⓓ
98. Ⓐ Ⓑ Ⓒ Ⓓ
99. Ⓐ Ⓑ Ⓒ Ⓓ
100. Ⓐ Ⓑ Ⓒ Ⓓ

Practice Test 7

TIME: 50 Minutes   **LENGTH:** 100 Analogies

DIRECTIONS: Read each of the following analogies carefully, and choose the BEST answer to each item. Fill in your responses in the answer sheets provided.

Note: The Miller Analogies Test consists of 120 questions to be completed in 60 minutes. Twenty of these questions are experimental items, which are not scored and thus not reflected in this practice test.

1. BLUEPRINT : BUILDING :: SCORE : (a. contest b. exam c. symphony d. segment)

2. FINGER : KNUCKLE :: (a. joint b. ulna c. bone d. elbow) : ARM

3. RIDDLE : (a. question b. enigma c. problem d. query) :: MAZE : LABYRINTH

4. (a. red b. blue c. yellow d. green) : ENVY :: RED : RAGE

5. CRAVEN : (a. cowardly b. beautiful c. divided d. powerful) :: COLLOQUIAL : CASUAL

6. CHLOROPHYLL : GREEN :: HEMOGLOBIN : (a. bilirubin b. biliverdin c. red d. malachite green)

7. ESCHATOLOGY : (a. finality b. judgment c. death d. religion) :: EMPIRICISM : OBSERVATIONS

8. MARXISM : MARX :: GOLDEN MEAN : (a. Socrates b. Plato c. Aristotle d. Aristophanes)

9. SLOPE : LINE :: CURVATURE : (a. circle b. arc c. radius d. diameter)

10. BLASTULA : (a. heart b. novel c. embryo d. plant) :: ACORN : OAK

11. CALYX : (a. cup b. bowl c. rod d. sphere) :: BOX : SQUARE

12. HYPOCHONDRIAC : HEALTH :: (a. philanthropist b. miser c. millionaire d. philosopher) : MONEY

13. HALCYON : (a. martial b. hero c. tranquilizer d. passionate) :: PEACEFUL : WARLIKE

14. (a. celsius b. fahrenheit c. inch d. centimeter) : TEMPERATURE :: METER : LENGTH

15. PASSED : ELATION :: (a. present b. failed c. current d. rejection) : DEJECTION

16. HUGHES : ENKEPHALIN :: MENDEL : (a. genetics b. cloning c. x-rays d. hormones)

17. BRITTEN : *BILLY BUDD* :: VERDI : (a. *Aida* b. *Carmen* c. *La Straniera* d. *Norma*)

18. EMILY BRONTË : (a. Olivia Vernon b. Acton Bell c. Ellis Bell d. Alexandria Zenobia) :: STEPHEN KING : RICHARD BACHMAN

19. CAESURA : (a. stop b. poem c. stanza d. pause) :: CONCLUSION : END

20. LINE : LENGTH :: PLANE : (a. volume b. length c. width d. area)

21. ONOMATOPOEIA : BUZZ :: (a. road b. race car c. speedway d. meter) : PALINDROME

22. PHILOLOGIST : (a. thought b. conjecture c. language d. insects) :: ORNITHOLOGIST : BIRDS

23. REBUTTAL : SPEECH :: (a. applause b. commentary c. review d. renewal) : PERFORMANCE

24. *BEAU GESTE* : NOBLE GESTURE :: (a. *magnum opus* b. *mea culpa* c. *alma mater* d. *memento mori*) : FOSTERING MOTHER

25. ROMAN : STATUES :: BYZANTINE : (a. painting b. mosaic c. iconography d. sculpture)

26. (a. pulsar b. polaris c. zenith d. equinox) : NADIR :: NORTH : SOUTH

27. $f + g + h : f + g + \dfrac{h}{2}$ :: $a + b$: (a. $a + b + c$ b. $a + \dfrac{b}{2}$ c. $a + b + \dfrac{c}{2}$ d. $a - \dfrac{b}{2}$)

28. PAMPHLET : TEXTBOOK :: (a. view b. scope c. area d. aspect) : PANORAMA

29. BOAST : PRAISE :: ATONE : (a. commend b. compliment c. amend d. detract)

30. MISER : THRIFT :: (a. hedonist b. sadist c. socialist d. atheist) : PLEASURE

31. THICK : THIN :: AA LAVA : (a. tephra b. tubes c. pahoehoe d. pillows)

32. CEREBELLUM : BRAIN :: (a. veins b. arteries c. ventricles d. aorta) : HEART

33. COSMOGONY : (a. folktales b. creations c. mythology d. cosmology) :: BILDUNGSROMAN : COMING OF AGE

34. 2 : 8 :: 5 : (a. 25 b. 10 c. 125 d. 40)

35. OSSEUS : (a. teeth b. bones c. skull d. ribs) :: VISCERAL : BODY

36. ACID : 4 :: ALKALI : (a . 6 b. 0 c. 5 d. 8)

37. ANION : NEGATIVE :: (a. ion b. neutron c. cation d. proton) : POSITIVE

38. ANODE : POSITIVE :: (a. diode b. cathode c. LED d. transistor) : NEGATIVE

39. FORTRAN : (a. math b. graphics c. spreadsheets d. information processing) :: COBOL : BUSINESS

40. SOFTWARE : COMPUTER :: (a. textbooks b. chalk c. blackboard d. school) : TEACHER

41. SERENDIPITOUS : PLANNED :: INDEFATIGABLE : (a. slow b. industrious c. lazy d. sickly)

42. BOILING POINT : 100° :: FREEZING POINT : (a. celsius b. 212° c. 0° d. 32°)

43. $2x + y : 4x^2 + 4xy + y^2 :: a - b :$ (a. $a^2 - b^2$ b. $a^2 + b^2$ c. $a^2 - 2ab + b^2$ d. $2a^2 - 2b$)

44. POSTULATE : CLAIM :: (a. grieve b. cavil c. pike d. cabal) : CARP

45. MESTRAL : VELCRO :: (a. Bic b. Edison c. Biro d. Tupper) : BALLPOINT PEN

46. MILE : 5,280 :: ACRE : (a. $10,240^2$ b. $56,017^2$ c. $29,411^2$ d. $43,560^2$)

47. ODD NUMBER : 5 :: EVEN NUMBER : (a. 7 b. 2 c. 9 d. 1)

48. CORONA : SUN :: (a. stratosphere b. troposphere c. chromosphere d. thermosphere) : EARTH

49. CAPO : (a. coda b. denouement c. cadenza d. aria) :: BEGINNING : END

50. CENTENNIAL : 100 YEARS :: (a. sesquicentennial b. septennial c. sexennial d. decennial) : 7 YEARS

51. DIONYSUS : BACCHUS :: NOX : (a. Aurora b. Tyche c. Selene d. Nyx)

52. ALIAS : IDENTITY :: (a. name b. illusion c. idea d. appearance) : PERCEPTION

53. SANTAYANA : JAMES :: (a. Plato b. Aristotle c. Plotinus d. Arelius) : SOCRATES

54. AESTHETICS : BEAUTY :: PHENOMENALISM : (a. knowledge b. ethics c. appearances d. justice)

55. USURY : (a. money b. interest c. tax d. payment) :: VOLUBLE : FLUENT

56. LABOR : (a. field b. gestation c. yoke d. vex) :: URBANE : SUAVE

57. PARABLE : MORAL :: SATIRE : (a. ridicule b. irony c. myth d. disagreement)

58. ZERO-POINT ENERGY : MOTION :: ABSOLUTE ZERO : (a. force
     b. temperature c. speed d. joules)

59. Given triangles ABC ≈ DEF

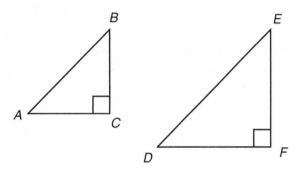

     $\overline{AB} : \overline{DE} :: \overline{BC} :$ (a. $\overline{DF}$ b. $\overline{AC}$ c. $\overline{DE}$ d. $\overline{EF}$)

60. HYPERBOLE : (a. curve b. exaggeration c. method d. fable) :: OXYMORON :
     CONTRADICTION

61. NICOTINE : TOBACCO :: (a. DDT b. NTE c. THC d. FAA) : MARIJUANA

62. RETARD : ADVANCE :: (a. postpone b. educate c. assist d. reschedule) :
     PROCEED

63. JOULE : ENERGY :: (a. newton b. pounds c. meter d. mass) : FORCE

64. GARRULOUS : (a. taciturn b. dour c. talkative d. bucolic) :: OFFEND :
     AGGRAVATE

65. PLAGIARIZE : STEAL :: (a. festoon b. baroque c. accessorize d. refurbish) :
     DECORATE

66. ORDER : DISORDER :: (a. mellifluous b. harmony c. euphony d. polyphony) :
     CACOPHONY

67. TYPO : SPELLING :: ANACHRONISM : (a. location b. method c. costume
     d. time)

68. VINEGAR : ACETIC ACID :: (a. carbonic acid b. baking soda c. sodium
     bicarbonate d. carbon tetrachloride) : SODA WATER

Practice Test 7

69. MOTIF : REFRAIN :: (a. novel b. song c. subplot d. prologue) : POEM

70. BIT : BYTE :: 1 : (a. 6 b. 16 c. 10 d. 8)

71. FORBEARANCE : (a. imposition b. impatience c. patience d. misery) ::
KNAVERY : TRICKERY

72. PEDESTRIAN : MUNDANE :: (a. petulant b. pedantic c. vivacious d. wry) :
INSOLENT

73. BRAIN : HUMAN :: (a. program b. CPU c. microprocessor d. memory) :
COMPUTER

74. JOLLY ROGER : (a. unions b. pirates c. missionaries d. seamen) :: MAPLE
LEAF : CANADA

75. LANGUR : (a. shark b. llama c. monkey d. tiger) :: BOTTLENOSE :
DOLPHIN

76. PARTISAN : TRAITOR :: (a. deluge b. pond c. famine d. storm) : DROUGHT

77. (a. potassium b. copper c. magnesium d. lithium) : RED :: SODIUM : YELLOW

78. $\frac{1}{3}$: 0.333 :: $\frac{9}{8}$: (a. 1.125 b. 125.0 $\times$ 10^{-2} c. $1\frac{1}{8}$ d. 0.777)

79. ESSENTIAL : SUPERFLUOUS :: SCURRILOUS : (a. vulgar b. refined
c. impetuous d. contumelious)

80. MEATUS : (a. body b. river c. canal d. ocean) :: STRAIT : WATER

81. ACEPHALOUS : (a. limb b. heart. c. head d. spouse) :: UNOPPOSED : RIVAL

82. FABACEOUS : (a. plant b. seed c. shrub d. bean) :: AQUILINE : EAGLE

83. MECCA : ISLAM :: (a. Medina b. Amristar c. Nepal d. Ganges) : HINDUISM

84. (a. conjunctiva b. tympanic membrane c. vestibulocochlear nerve d. cochlea) :
SOUND :: RETINA : LIGHT

85.   ALGEBRA : EQUATION :: GEOMETRY : (a. element b. proof c. set
      d. statistic)

86.   TIZANO VECELLIO : TITIAN :: DOMENIKOS THEOTOKOPOULOS :
      (a. Domenik b. El Greco c. Theo d. Poulous)

87.   WARHOL : POP ART :: (a. Picasso b. Pollack c. Mondrian d. Matisse) :
      CUBISM

88.   TIFFANY : GLASS :: CHRISTO JAVACHEF : (a. islands b. sculpture c. found
      objects d. painting)

89.   MYOPIC : NEARSIGHTED :: HABERDASHER : (a. soldier b. clothier
      c. educator d. editor)

90.   LAPIDARY : DIAMONDS :: COOPER : (a. jewelry b. beer c. casks d. cheese)

91.   TALMUD : JUDAISM :: (a. Tao Te Ching b. Koran c. Veda d. Sutra) :
      HINDUISM

92.   ASSOCIATIONS : (a. celestial sphere b. cosmic rays c. binary stars d. cardinal
      points) :: SCATTERED : BOUND

93.   WRIGHT : AIRPLANE :: (a. Garnerin b. Zeppelin c. Montgolfier d. Selfridge) :
      HOT AIR BALLOON

94.   NORSE : JUDEO-CHRISTIAN :: (a. Bragi b. Balder c. Buri d. Ask) : ADAM

95.   OEDIPUS : (a. Clytaemnestra b. Jocasta c. Antigone d. Cassandra) ::
      CLAUDIUS : GERTRUDE

96.   DARWIN : EVOLUTION :: BOHR : (a. atomic structure b. x-ray diffraction
      c. dynamite d. electrons)

97. Given that *B // C*,

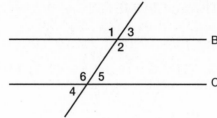

∠1 : ∠2 :: ∠4 : (a. 2 b. 3 c. 1 d. 6)

98. STEVENSON : EISENHOWER :: (a. Wilke b. Dewey c. Landon d. Davis) : COOLIDGE

99. FIFTEENTH AMENDMENT : VOTING RIGHTS :: NINETEENTH AMENDMENT : (a. prohibition b. cruel and unusual punishment c. voting rights d. succession)

100. EPICENE : (a. prehistoric b. artificial c. androgynous d. stubborn) :: ENTENTE : AGREEMENT

Answer Key
Practice Test 7

1. (c)	26. (c)	51. (d)	76. (a)
2. (d)	27. (b)	52. (b)	77. (d)
3. (b)	28. (d)	53. (a)	78. (a)
4. (d)	29. (c)	54. (c)	79. (b)
5. (a)	30. (a)	55. (b)	80. (a)
6. (c)	31. (c)	56. (c)	81. (c)
7. (a)	32. (d)	57. (d)	82. (d)
8. (c)	33. (b)	58. (b)	83. (d)
9. (b)	34. (c)	59. (d)	84. (d)
10. (c)	35. (b)	60. (b)	85. (b)
11. (a)	36. (d)	61. (c)	86. (b)
12. (b)	37. (c)	62. (a)	87. (a)
13. (a)	38. (b)	63. (a)	88. (a)
14. (a)	39. (a)	64. (c)	89. (b)
15. (b)	40. (a)	65. (a)	90. (c)
16. (a)	41. (c)	66. (c)	91. (c)
17. (a)	42. (c)	67. (d)	92. (c)
18. (c)	43. (c)	68. (a)	93. (c)
19. (d)	44. (b)	69. (a)	94. (d)
20. (d)	45. (c)	70. (d)	95. (b)
21. (b)	46. (d)	71. (c)	96. (a)
22. (c)	47. (b)	72. (a)	97. (b)
23. (a)	48. (d)	73. (b)	98. (d)
24. (c)	49. (a)	74. (b)	99. (c)
25. (c)	50. (b)	75. (c)	100. (c)

Explanations
of Answers

Explanations of Answers
Practice Test 7

1. BLUEPRINT : BUILDING :: SCORE : (a. contest b. exam **c. symphony** d. segment)

   (c) is correct because a blueprint is a written plan for a building just as a score is a written plan for a symphony. (a) and (b) are incorrect because while a score can be issued in a contest or an exam, this is an alternate definition. (d) is incorrect because a score represents an entire work, not just a segment.

2. FINGER : KNUCKLE :: (a. joint b. ulna c. bone **d. elbow**) : ARM

   (d) is correct because the joint of a finger is called the knuckle and the joint of the arm is called the elbow. (a) and (c) are incorrect because they are too general to complete the analogy. (b) is incorrect because this refers to one of the bones of the lower arm.

3. RIDDLE : (a. question **b. enigma** c. problem d. query) :: MAZE : LABYRINTH

   (b) is correct because *enigma* is a synonym for *riddle* just as *maze* is a synonym for *labyrinth*. (a), (c), and (d) are partial synonyms; however, they do not express the subtlety of a riddle, and are therefore incorrect.

4. (a. red b. blue c. yellow **d. green**) : ENVY :: RED : RAGE

   (d) is correct because green is the color associated with envy just as red is the color associated with rage. (a) is incorrect because, as we have seen, red is associated with rage. (b) is incorrect because blue is associated with sadness. (c) is incorrect because yellow is associated with cowardice.

5. CRAVEN : (**a. cowardly** b. beautiful c. divided d. powerful) :: COLLOQUIAL : CASUAL

   (a) is correct because *craven* and *cowardly* are synonyms just as *colloquial* and *casual* are synonyms. (b), (c), and (d) are unrelated.

6.   CHLOROPHYLL : GREEN :: HEMOGLOBIN : (a. bilirubin b. biliverdin
     c. red d. malachite green)

     (c) is correct because chlorophyll is the chemical found in plants which is green,
     while the heme pigment in hemoglobin is red. Bilirubin (a), biliverdin (b), and
     malachite green (d) are all pigments, but none of them contain the red color of
     hemoglobin, so none of them can complete the analogy.

7.   ESCHATOLOGY : (**a. finality** b. judgment c. death d. religion) ::
     EMPIRICISM : OBSERVATIONS

     (a) is correct because eschatology concerns itself with all final things just as em-
     piricism concerns itself with observable reality. (b), (c), and (d) may be concerns
     of the eschatologist, but only inasmuch as they represent and concern them-
     selves with finality.

8.   MARXISM : MARX :: GOLDEN MEAN : (a. Socrates b. Plato **c. Aristotle**
     d. Aristophanes)

     (c) is correct because Aristotle is the thinker who advocated the golden mean, a
     philosophy of moderation, just as Karl Marx advocated the idea that came to be
     known as Marxism.

9.   SLOPE : LINE :: CURVATURE : (a. circle **b. arc** c. radius d. diameter)

     (b) The slope is a property of a line. Likewise, the curvature is a property of an
     arc (b). Radius (c) and diameter (d) are parts of a circle (a). While a circle does
     have curvature, it is a closed object, while an arc, like a line, is open.

10. BLASTULA : (a. heart b. novel **c. embryo** d. plant) :: ACORN : OAK

     (c) is correct because a blastula is an early stage of an embryo just as an acorn
     is an early stage of an oak. (a) is incorrect because while the heart emerges from
     the blastula, this is too specific. (b) is incorrect because an early stage of a novel
     is a rough draft. (d) is incorrect because an early stage of a plant is a seedling.

11. CALYX : (**a. cup** b. bowl c. rod d. sphere) :: BOX : SQUARE

     (a) is correct because a calyx is a cup-shaped portion of a plant or animal organ,
     just as a box is generally rectangular in shape. (b), (c), and (d) are incorrect be-
     cause a calyx does not suggest this shape.

Explanations
of Answers

12. HYPOCHONDRIAC : HEALTH :: (a. philanthropist **b. miser** c. millionaire
    d. philosopher) : MONEY

    (b) is correct because just as a hypochondriac is overly concerned about his or
    her health, a miser is overly concerned about his or her money. (a) is incorrect
    because a philanthropist readily parts with his or her money. (c) is incorrect be-
    cause there is nothing inherent in the term millionaire to show that he or she is
    overly concerned about money. (d) is incorrect because a philosopher would be
    concerned with money in the context of its philosophical implications.

13. HALCYON : (**a. martial** b. hero c. tranquilizer d. passionate) :: PEACEFUL :
    WARLIKE

    (a) is correct because *halcyon* means "peaceful" and *martial* means "warlike."
    (b) is incorrect because there is no inherent connotation in the word *hero* to
    mean either "peaceful" or "warlike." (c) is incorrect because *tranquilizer* is a
    noun, rather than an adjective, and has a peaceful connotation. (d) *passionate* is
    incorrect because passion can be either peaceful or warlike.

14. (**a. celsius** b. fahrenheit c. inch d. centimeter) : TEMPERATURE :: METER :
    LENGTH

    (a) Celsius is correct because celsius is the metric unit for temperature while
    meter is the metric unit for length. Centimeter (d) is a division within the unit of
    meter and therefore does not complete the analogy. Fahrenheit (b) is a unit for
    measuring temperature, but it is not a metric unit. Inch (c) is an English unit for
    measuring length and therefore does not complete the analogy.

15. PASSED : ELATION :: (a. present **b. failed** c. current d. rejection) :
    DEJECTION

    (b) is correct because passing a test of some kind creates a feeling of elation,
    while failing creates a feeling of dejection. (a) and (c) are incorrect because they
    are unrelated. (d) is incorrect because while rejection would cause dejection, it is
    not parallel with passed, and therefore does not complete the analogy.

16. HUGHES : ENKEPHALIN :: MENDEL : (**a. genetics** b. cloning c. x-rays
    d. hormones)

    (a) is correct because just as John Hughes discovered the brain chemical en-
    kephalin, Mendel pioneered the science of genetics. (b) is incorrect because
    gene cloning was pioneered by the National Institutes of Health. (c) is incorrect
    because x-rays were discovered by Konrad and von Roentgen. (d) is incorrect
    because hormones were discovered by Bayliss and Starling.

17. BRITTEN : *BILLY BUDD* :: VERDI : (**a. *Aida*** b. *Carmen* c. *La Straniera* d. *Norma*)

    (**a**) is correct because *Billy Budd* is an opera written by Britten, just as *Aida* is an opera written by Verdi. (b) is incorrect because *Carmen* was written by Bizet. (c) and (d) are incorrect because these operas were written by Bellini.

18. EMILY BRONTË : (a. Olivia Vernon b. Acton Bell **c. Ellis Bell** d. Alexandria Zenobia) :: STEPHEN KING : RICHARD BACHMAN

    (**c**) is correct because this was Emily Brontë's pseudonym, just as Bachman was King's pseudonym. The remaining answer choices were pen names of Anne Brontë.

19. CAESURA : (a. stop b. poem c. stanza **d. pause**) :: CONCLUSION : END

    (**d**) is correct because in poetry, a caesura is a pause, just as a conclusion marks the end of a piece of writing. (a) is incorrect because a stop is more specific than a pause. (b) and (c) are incorrect because they are general terms for a work and its sections.

20. LINE : LENGTH :: PLANE : (a. volume b. length c. width **d. area**)

    (**d**) The measurement of a line (one dimension) is its length. The measurement of a plane (two dimensions) is the area. Volume (a) is a measurement in three dimensions. Width (c) is also a measurement of a line (in one dimension).

21. ONOMATOPOEIA : BUZZ :: (a. road **b. race** car c. speedway d. meter) : PALINDROME

    (**b**) is correct because *onomatopoeia* is a word whose sound suggests its meaning, as in *buzz*. This is analogous to a palindrome, which is a word, phrase, sentence fragment, or sentence spelled the same backward and forward; for example—race car. All other answer choices are incorrect because they are not palindromes.

22. PHILOLOGIST : (a. thought b. conjecture **c. language** d. insects) :: ORNITHOLOGIST : BIRDS

    (**c**) is correct because a philologist studies language just as an ornithologist studies birds. (a) is incorrect because someone who studies thought and thought systems would be a philosopher, a psychologist, or an epistemologist. (b) is incorrect because it is unrelated to the other segments of the analogy. (d) is incorrect because an entomologist studies insects.

Explanations
of Answers

23. REBUTTAL : SPEECH :: (**a. applause** b. commentary c. review d. renewal) :
PERFORMANCE

(a) is correct because applause usually follows a performance, just as a rebuttal
usually follows a speech. (b), (c), and (d) may all occur after a performance, but
not immediately.

24. *BEAU GESTE* : NOBLE GESTURE : (a. *magnum opus* b. *mea culpa* **c. alma
mater** d. *memento mori*) : FOSTERING MOTHER

(c) is correct because the literal translation of *alma mater* is fostering mother,
just as the literal translation of *beau geste* is a noble gesture. (a) is incorrect
because *magnum opus* means major work. (b) is incorrect because *mea culpa*
means my fault. (d) is incorrect because *memento mori* means reminder of death.

25. ROMAN : STATUES :: BYZANTINE : (a. painting b. mosaic **c. iconography**
d. sculpture)

(c) is correct because Byzantine art is characterized by its use of iconography
in its religious themes, just as Roman art used statues. All other answer choices
were known and used by the Byzantines, however not to the elevated status of
iconography.

26. (a. pulsar b. polaris **c. zenith** d. equinox) : NADIR :: NORTH : SOUTH

(c) Zenith is correct because the North is the direction toward the top of most
maps, while the South is the opposite or downward direction. The zenith is the
overhead direction in the sky while standing on Earth, while the nadir is the un-
derfoot direction or directly opposite the zenith. Pulsar (a) and equinox (d) are
not directional terms, nor are they opposite from the term nadir. Polaris (b) is the
name given to the North Star, but it does not fit into the analogy since it is the
name of a specific star and is not a term used specifically to imply direction.

27. $f + g + h : f + g + \dfrac{h}{2} :: a + b : ($a. $a + b + c$ **b. $a + \dfrac{b}{2}$** c. $a + b + \dfrac{c}{2}$
d. $a - \dfrac{b}{2})$

(b) In this analogy, the expression, $f + g + h$, is simply divided by 2. Then $a + b$
should also be divided by 2, giving $a + \dfrac{b}{2}$, choice (b).

Explanations
of Answers

28. PAMPHLET : TEXTBOOK :: (a. view b. scope c. area **d. aspect**) :
     PANORAMA

     (d) is correct because a pamphlet gives one a small amount of information,
     while a textbook gives one a great deal of information. This is analogous to an
     aspect giving one a small view of an area, and a panorama giving one a broad
     view of an area. (a), (b), and (c) are incorrect because they are too general to
     complete the analogy.

29. BOAST : PRAISE :: ATONE : (a. commend b. compliment **c. amend** d. detract)

     (c) is correct because to boast is to praise oneself, just as to atone is to make
     amends to oneself. (a) and (b) are incorrect because commend and compliment
     are synonyms meaning to praise. (d) is incorrect because to detract is an ant-
     onym of praise.

30. MISER : THRIFT :: (**a. hedonist** b. sadist c. socialist d. atheist) : PLEASURE

     (a) is correct because a hedonist is primarily concerned with his or her own
     pleasure, just as a miser is concerned with his or her own thrift. (b) is incorrect
     because a sadist is identified with cruelty. (c) is incorrect because a socialist is
     concerned with an economic system. (d) is incorrect because an atheist is one
     who believes that there is no god.

31. THICK : THIN :: AA LAVA : (a. tephra b. tubes **c. pahoehoe** d. pillows)

     (c) Pahoehoe is correct because *thick* can imply a very viscous fluid, while thin
     implies a fluid which is free flowing. AA lava is the name given to very viscous
     or thick lava, while the Hawaiian word *pahoehoe* is used worldwide to describe
     highly fluid or thin lava. *Tephra* (a), *tubes* (b), and *pillows* (d) are words which
     refer to lava, but they do not describe the fluidity of the lava and therefore can-
     not complete the analogy.

32. CEREBELLUM : BRAIN :: (a. veins b. arteries c. ventricles **d. aorta**) : HEART

     (d) is correct because the cerebellum is a part of the brain, just as the aorta is a
     part of the heart. (a) and (b) are part of the circulatory system, but not a direct
     part of the heart. (c) is not the best answer, because ventricles refer to two cham-
     bers of the heart, and therefore does not complete the analogy.

33. COSMOGONY : (a. folktales **b. creations** c. mythology d. cosmology) ::
· BILDUNGSROMAN : COMING OF AGE

(b) is correct because a cosmogony is a story of creation, such as Genesis, and a bildungsroman is a coming of age story, such as Joyce's *Portrait of the Artist as a Young Man.* (a) and (c) are too general, since folktales and mythologies may be concerned with creation, but they are not limited to that. (d) is incorrect because cosmology is the systematic study of the universe.

34. 2 : 8 :: 5 : (a. 25 b. 10 **c. 125** d. 40)

(c) The relationship in this analogy is that the second number is the first number cubed. Thus, 5 cubed is 125 (c). (a) is not the correct answer since 25 is 5 squared. (b) 10 and (d) 40 are only multiples of 5.

35. OSSEUS : (a. teeth **b. bones** c. skull d. ribs) :: VISCERAL : BODY

(b) is correct because osseus means relating to the bones just as visceral means relating to the body. (a), (c), and (d) are too specific to complete the analogy.

36. ACID : 4 :: ALKALI : (a . 6 b. 0 c. 5 **d. 8**)

(d) is correct because, on the pH scale, anything below 7 is an acid, and therefore anything above 7 is a base (alkali). The other choices are below 7 and are, therefore, acids.

37. ANION : NEGATIVE :: (a. ion b. neutron **c. cation** d. proton) : POSITIVE

(c) is correct because an anion is an ion with a negative charge, just as a cation is an ion with a positive charge. (a) is incorrect because it is too general. (b) is incorrect because a neutron is a particle without a charge. (d) is incorrect because a proton has a positive charge, but is not an ion.

38. ANODE : POSITIVE :: (a. diode **b. cathode** c. LED d. transistor) : NEGATIVE

(b) is correct because electrical currents flow from an anode (+) to a cathode (−). (a), (c), and (d) are incorrect because these are general terms that do not correspond to a specific negative or positive charge.

39. FORTRAN : (**a. math** b. graphics c. spreadsheets d. information processing) :: COBOL : BUSINESS

    (**a**) is correct because FORTRAN is a computer language geared toward math, just as COBOL is a computer language geared toward business. (b) is incorrect because FORTRAN is not designed to be a graphic-intensive language. (c) and (d) are incorrect because they refer to general applications of computer programs rather than languages.

40. SOFTWARE : COMPUTER :: (**a. textbooks** b. chalk c. blackboard d. school) : TEACHER

    (**a**) is correct because a computer uses software as a source for instructions just as a teacher uses a textbook as a source for instructions. (b) and (c) are incorrect because these would correspond to a computer's hardware. (d) is incorrect because this would refer to the building in which the computer is housed.

41. SERENDIPITOUS : PLANNED :: INDEFATIGABLE : (a. slow b. industrious **c. lazy** d. sickly)

    (**c**) is correct because something that is serendipitous is spontaneous rather than planned, just as someone who is indefatigable is industrious (b) rather than lazy. (a) and (d) are incorrect because neither of these terms implies laziness.

42. BOILING POINT : 100° :: FREEZING POINT : (a. celsius b. 212° **c. 0°** d. 32°)

    (**c**) 0° is correct because the boiling point of water is 100° on the Celsius scale, while the freezing point of water is 0° on the Celsius scale. The temperature of 212° (b) is the Fahrenheit temperature for boiling water and therefore does not relate to the freezing point. Celsius (a) is the name of the temperature scale which has the boiling point at 100° and does not complete the analogy for the corresponding freezing point. The temperature of 32° (d) is the freezing point of water, but it is on the Fahrenheit scale and therefore does not complete the analogy.

43. $2x + y : 4x^2 + 4xy + y^2 :: a - b :$ (a. $a^2 - b^2$ b. $a^2 + b^2$ **c. $a^2 - 2ab + b^2$** d. $2a^2 - 2b$)

    (**c**) The second expression, $4x^2 + 4xy + y^2$, is the square of the first expression, $2x + y$. Hence, the expression $a - b$, squared is $a^2 - 2ab + b^2$, (c).

Explanations
of Answers

44. POSTULATE : CLAIM :: (a. grieve **b. cavil** c. pike d. cabal) : CARP

    (b) is correct because *postulate* and *claim* have similar meanings (to state a position), just as cavil and carp have similar meanings. (a) is incorrect because *to grieve* means "to feel sadness over a loss." (c) is incorrect because a pike is a pointed stick. (d) is incorrect because a cabal is a group gathered to cause harm.

45. MESTRAL : VELCRO :: (a. Bic b. Edison **c. Biro** d. Tupper) : BALLPOINT PEN

    (c) is correct because just as Mestral invented velcro, so did the Biro brothers invent the ballpoint pen. (a) is incorrect because this is a brand name of a ballpoint pen, not its inventor. (b) is incorrect because although Edison invented a great many things, the ballpoint pen was not among them. (d) is incorrect because Earl Tupper invented Tupperware®.

46. MILE : 5,280 :: ACRE : (a. $10,240^2$ b. $56,017^2$ c. $29,411^2$ **d. $43,560^2$**)

    (d) is correct because a mile is 5,280 feet, just as an acre is 43,560 square feet. All other answer choices are irrelevant.

47. ODD NUMBER : 5 :: EVEN NUMBER : (a. 7 **b. 2** c. 9 d. 1)

    (b) The number 5 is an example of an odd number. Therefore, an example of an even number is needed to complete the analogy. The only even number amongst the choices is 2 (b). The other choices: 7 (a), 9 (c), and 1 (d) are all odd.

48. CORONA : SUN :: (a. stratosphere b. troposphere c. chromosphere **d. thermosphere**) : EARTH

    (d) Thermosphere is correct because the thermosphere is the outermost shell of the atmosphere of the Earth. The corona is the outermost layer of the atmosphere of the sun. The stratosphere (a) and the troposphere (b) are a part of the Earth's atmosphere, but they do not complete the analogy because they are not the outermost layer. The chromosphere (c) does not complete the analogy because it is a part of the atmosphere of the sun.

49. CAPO : (**a. coda** b. denouement c. cadenza d. aria) :: BEGINNING : END

    (a) is correct because the *capo* is the beginning of a musical piece and the *coda* is the end. (b) is incorrect because *denouement* refers to the action in a novel following the conclusion. (c) is incorrect because a cadenza is an ornamental passage near the end of a piece of music. (d) is incorrect because an aria is an extended vocal solo in an opera.

Explanations
of Answers

50. CENTENNIAL : 100 YEARS :: (a. sesquicentennial **b. septennial** c. sexennial d. decennial) : 7 YEARS

    (b) is correct because *centennial* refers to a period of 100 years just as *septennial* refers to a period of seven years. (a) is incorrect because sesquicentennial refers to a period of 150 years. (c) is incorrect because *sexennial* refers to a period of six years. (d) is incorrect because *decennial* refers to a period of ten years.

51. DIONYSUS : BACCHUS :: NOX : (a. Aurora b. Tyche c. Selene **d. Nyx**)

    (d) is correct because Dionysus is the Greek god of wine, and Bacchus is his Roman counterpart, just as Nox is the Greek goddess of night and Nyx is her Roman counterpart. (a) is incorrect because Aurora is the Greek goddess of the dawn. (b) is incorrect because Tyche is the goddess of fortune or fate. (c) is incorrect because Selene is the Greek goddess of the moon.

52. ALIAS : IDENTITY :: (a. name **b. illusion** c. idea d. appearance) : PERCEPTION

    (b) is correct because an alias is a false identity, just as an illusion is a false perception. (a) is incorrect because name corresponds to alias rather than perception. (c) and (d) are incorrect because an idea and appearance do not imply falsehood.

53. SANTAYANA : JAMES :: (**a. Plato** b. Aristotle c. Plotinus d. Arelius) : SOCRATES

    (a) is correct because Santayana was a student of William James as Plato was a student of Socrates. (b) is incorrect because Aristotle was a student of Plato. (c) is incorrect because Plotinus was an Egyptian and founder of Neoplatonism. (d) is incorrect because Marcus Arelius was a Roman emperor and Stoic.

54. AESTHETICS : BEAUTY :: PHENOMENALISM : (a. knowledge b. ethics **c. appearances** d. justice)

    (c) is correct because just as aesthetics are concerned with beauty, so phenomenalism is concerned with the notion that all that can be known are appearances, and that man cannot know the true nature of reality. (a) is incorrect because the study of knowledge is called epistemology. (b) and (d) are general terms, the nature of which has inspired many branches of philosophy.

55. USURY : (a. money **b. interest** c. tax d. payment) :: VOLUBLE : FLUENT

    (b) is correct because usury is another term for interest on a loan, just as voluble is
    another word for fluent. (a) and (d) are incorrect because they are general financial
    terms that do not exclusively apply to interest. (c) is incorrect because tax refers to
    money taken by the government to be used in the interest of the governed.

56. LABOR : (a. field b. gestation **c. yoke** d. vex) :: URBANE : SUAVE

    (c) is correct because yoke is synonymous with labor, just as urbane is synonymous
    with suave. (a) is incorrect because a field may be an area of labor, but not labor
    itself. (b) is incorrect because while labor can be said to be the culmination of ges-
    tation, it is not the process itself. (d) Vex means to annoy and is therefore incorrect.

57. PARABLE : MORAL :: SATIRE : (a. ridicule b. irony c. myth **d. disagreement**)

    (d) is correct because a parable illustrates a moral just as a satire illustrates a
    disagreement with a given condition. (a) is incorrect because while a satire may
    ridicule its subject, this is a method rather than an illustration. (b) is incorrect
    because a satire may contain irony; this is not inherent in the form. (c) is incor-
    rect because a myth is a story told to explain something that is not understood.

58. ZERO-POINT ENERGY : MOTION :: ABSOLUTE ZERO : (a. force
    b. temperature c. speed d. joules)

    (b) Temperature is correct because zero-point energy is the point at which all
    motion stops. Absolute zero is the zero energy point on the Kelvin temperature
    scale. Force (a), speed (c), and joules (d) are not related to the zero point of mo-
    tion and therefore do not complete the analogy.

59. Given triangles ABC ≈ DEF

    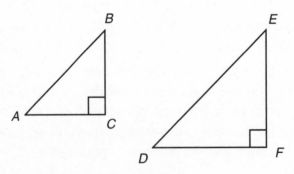

    $\overline{AB} : \overline{DE} :: \overline{BC} :$ (a. $\overline{DF}$ b. $\overline{AC}$ c. $\overline{DE}$ **d. $\overline{EF}$**)

    (d) These triangles are similar, thus corresponding sides are similar. Therefore,
    the ratio of $\overline{AB} : \overline{DE}$ is equivalent to the ratios $\overline{BC} : \overline{DE}$ (d) and $\overline{AC} : \overline{DF}$.

Explanations
of Answers

60. HYPERBOLE : (a. curve **b. exaggeration** c. method d. fable) :: OXYMORON : CONTRADICTION

   (b) is correct because *hyperbole* refers to exaggeration for effect just as an oxymoron (such as home office) uses contradiction for effect. (a) is incorrect because a curve refers to the mathematical construct of hyperbola. (c) is incorrect because it is too general. (d) is incorrect because a fable is a story that illustrates a moral.

61. NICOTINE : TOBACCO :: (a. DDT b. NTE **c. THC** d. FAA) : MARIJUANA

   (c) is correct because nicotine is the active drug in tobacco just as THC is the active drug in marijuana. (a) is incorrect because DDT was a pesticide removed from the market because of its carcinogenic properties. (b) is incorrect because NTE is an acronym for the National Teachers Examination. (d) is incorrect because the FAA is the Federal Aviation Administration.

62. RETARD : ADVANCE :: (**a. postpone** b. educate c. assist d. reschedule) : PROCEED

   (a) is correct because *retard* and *advance* are antonyms, just as *postpone* and *proceed* are antonyms. (b) and (c) are incorrect because in this context, both would mean "to aid or advance." (d) is incorrect because to *reschedule* does not inherently imply a delay.

63. JOULE : ENERGY :: (**a. Newton** b. pounds c. meter d. mass) : FORCE

   (a) Newton is correct because the joule is the SI unit for the measurement of energy. The Newton is the SI unit for the measurement of force. Pounds (b) are also used as a measure of force, but the pound is not the acceptable SI unit. Meter (c) is the SI unit for the measurement of length. Mass (d) is not a unit of measure and therefore could not complete the analogy.

64. GARRULOUS : (a. taciturn b. dour **c. talkative** d. bucolic) :: OFFEND : AGGRAVATE

   (c) is correct because *garrulous* is synonymous with *talkative*, just as *offend* and *aggravate* are synonymous. (a) and (b) are incorrect because they both mean "quiet" and "severe." (d) is incorrect because *bucolic* means rustic.

Explanations
of Answers

65. PLAGIARIZE : STEAL :: (**a. festoon** b. baroque c. accessorize d. refurbish) : DECORATE

    (a) is correct because to plagiarize something is, in effect, to steal it, just as to festoon is to decorate with flowers, ribbons, etc. (b) and (c) are incorrect because they refer a specific style of decoration. (d) is incorrect because to refurbish something is to completely redesign it.

66. ORDER : DISORDER :: (a. mellifluous b. harmony **c. euphony** d. polyphony) : CACOPHONY

    (c) is correct because *order* and *disorder* are antonyms, just as *euphony* (meaning harmonious sounds) and *cacophony* (meaning discordant sounds) are antonyms. (a) and (b) are incorrect because although their meanings are appropriate, they do not follow the form of the analogy. (d) is incorrect because polyphony means many voices.

67. TYPO : SPELLING :: ANACHRONISM : (a. location b. method c. costume **d. time**)

    (d) is correct because a typo is an error in spelling, just as an anachronism is a chronological impossibility. An example of an anachronism would be Shakespeare's inclusion of a clock in the play *Julius Caesar.* (a) and (c) are incorrect because although an anachronism could be exposed in the areas of location and costume, it is not restricted to these areas. (b) is incorrect because method is a general term that does not completely apply.

68. VINEGAR : ACETIC ACID :: (**a. carbonic acid** b. baking soda c. sodium bicarbonate d. carbon tetrachloride) : SODA WATER

    (a) is correct because acetic acid is the main ingredient in the food vinegar, but it is very dilute. Carbonic acid is likewise the main ingredient in the food soda water, and it is also very dilute. Baking soda (b) is made of a carbonate, but it is not a diluted chemical. Sodium bicarbonate (c) is the chemical found in baking soda, but it is not the diluted chemical for soda water. Carbon tetrachloride (d), is a very toxic chemical and is therefore not a food. None of the other three terms fit this analogy.

69. MOTIF : REFRAIN :: (**a. novel** b. song c. subplot d. prologue) : POEM

    (**a**) is correct because a motif is a recurring theme in a novel, just as a refrain is a recurring portion of a poem. (b) is incorrect because although songs have refrains, this section of the analogy is concerned with the motif. (c) is incorrect because a subplot is a secondary story within a larger story. (d) is incorrect because a prologue is an introductory speech or monologue.

70. BIT : BYTE :: 1 : (a. 6 b. 16 c. 10 **d. 8**)

    (**d**) is correct because when a computer processes information, it does so in bytes, each byte containing 8 bits, or binary digits.

71. FORBEARANCE : (a. imposition b. impatience **c. patience** d. misery) :: KNAVERY : TRICKERY

    (**c**) is correct because *forbearance* and *patience* are synonyms just as *knavery* and *trickery* are synonyms. (a) is incorrect because an imposition refers to an unwelcome request. (b) is incorrect because this is an antonym of the correct answer. (d) is incorrect because misery means extreme sadness.

72. PEDESTRIAN : MUNDANE :: (**a. petulant** b. pedantic c. vivacious d. wry) : INSOLENT

    (**a**) is correct because *pedestrian* and *mundane* have similar meanings ("mediocre or commonplace"), just as *petulant* and *insolent* have similar meanings ("peevish"). (b) is incorrect because its meaning is similar to *pedestrian*. (c) is incorrect because *vivacious* means "full of life." (d) is incorrect because *wry* means "cynical."

73. BRAIN : HUMAN :: (a. program **b. CPU** c. microprocessor d. memory) : COMPUTER

    (**b**) is correct because in a human, the brain is the center of information processing, just as the CPU, or central processing unit, is in a computer. (a) is incorrect because a program is a set of instructions along which the computer operates. (c) is incorrect because the microprocessor is too specific to complete the analogy. It would be analogous to a specific portion of the brain. (d) is incorrect because memory is too general.

74. JOLLY ROGER : (a. unions **b. pirates** c. missionaries d. seamen) :: MAPLE LEAF : CANADA

(b) is correct because the legendary pirate flag was adorned with a skull and crossbones, or Jolly Roger, just as the flag of Canada is adorned with a maple leaf. All other answer choices are incorrect because these groups did not have an independent flag.

75. LANGUR : (a. shark b. llama **c. monkey** d. tiger) :: BOTTLENOSE : DOLPHIN

(c) is correct because a langur is a specific type of monkey (found in Asia) just as a bottlenose is a specific type of dolphin. (a), (b), and (d) are incorrect because none of the animals have a subtype called a langur.

76. PARTISAN : TRAITOR :: (**a. deluge** b. pond c. famine d. storm) : DROUGHT

(a) is correct because a partisan is loyal to his or her party, and a traitor is disloyal to their party, just as a deluge is too much water in a given area, and a drought is not enough water in a given area. (b) is incorrect because a pond is not the direct opposite of a drought. (c) is incorrect because a famine refers to a lack of food or water in an area, and is therefore an indirect synonym of drought. (d) is incorrect because a drought is a severe shortage of water, and the word storm does not imply the severe conditions that deluge does.

77. (a. potassium b. copper c. magnesium **d. lithium**) : RED :: SODIUM : YELLOW

(d) is the correct answer. When placed in a flame, certain elements produce specific colors. Lithium produces a red flame, while sodium produces a yellow flame. Potassium (a) produces a violet flame, copper (b) produces a green flame, and magnesium (c) produces a white flame, so only lithium fits the analogy.

78. $\frac{1}{3}$: 0.333 :: $\frac{9}{8}$: (**a. 1.125** b. 125.0×10^{-2} c. $1\frac{1}{8}$ d. 0.777)

(a) The relationship is the decimal form of a fraction. The fraction ($\frac{9}{8}$) is written in decimal form as 1.125 (a). Choice (b) is given in scientific notation, not in decimal form. Choice (c) is in fraction format. While 0.777 (d) is in decimal form, it is not equivalent to $\frac{9}{8}$.

Explanations
of Answers

79. ESSENTIAL : SUPERFLUOUS :: SCURRILOUS : (a. vulgar **b. refined**
c. impetuous d. contumelious)

    (b) is correct because *essential* (meaning "necessary") and *superfluous* (meaning
    "unnecessary") are antonyms, just as *scurrilous* (meaning "vulgar") and *refined*
    are antonyms. (a) is incorrect because this is a synonym of *scurrilous*. (c) is in-
    correct because *impetuous* means "impulsive." (d) is incorrect because *contume-*
    lious means "incessantly annoying."

80. MEATUS : (**a. body** b. river c. canal d. ocean) :: STRAIT : WATER

    (a) is correct because a meatus is a natural passage in the body, just as a strait is
    a natural passage through bodies of water. (b) and (d) are incorrect because these
    are natural bodies of water. (c) is incorrect because a canal is a humanmade pas-
    sage between two bodies of water.

81. ACEPHALOUS : (a. limb b. heart. **c. head** d. spouse) :: UNOPPOSED : RIVAL

    (c) is correct because to be acephalous means to be without a head, just as to
    be unopposed means to be without a rival. (a) and (b) are incorrect because
    acephalous does not refer to these organs. (d) is incorrect because to be without
    a spouse is to be single.

82. FABACEOUS : (a. plant b. seed c. shrub **d. bean**) :: AQUILINE : EAGLE

    (d) is correct because *fabaceous* refers to the qualities of a bean, just as *aquiline*
    refers to the characteristics of an eagle. (a), (b), and (c) are incorrect because
    they are too general to sufficiently complete the analogy.

83. MECCA : ISLAM :: (a. Medina b. Amristar c. Nepal **d. Ganges**) : HINDUISM

    (d) is correct because Mecca is the holy city of the Islamic faith, just as the
    Ganges River is the holy place of Hinduism. (a) is incorrect because Medina is a
    holy city to Islam, not Hinduism. (b) is incorrect because Amristar is a holy city
    to the Sikhs. (c) is incorrect because Nepal is in Tibet.

84. (a. conjunctiva b. tympanic membrane c. vestibulocochlear nerve **d. cochlea**) :
    SOUND :: RETINA : LIGHT

    (d) Cochlea is correct because the cochlea is the organ of hearing, while the ret-
    ina is a membrane connected by the optic nerve to the brain, making sight pos-
    sible. The tympanic membrane (b) and the vestibulocochlear nerve (c) are found
    within the ear. But they are not the actual organ of hearing. The conjunctiva (a),
    which is not a sense organ, is found within the eye and therefore cannot be used
    to complete the analogy.

Explanations
of Answers

85. ALGEBRA : EQUATION :: GEOMETRY : (a. element **b. proof** c. set
d. statistic)

(b) The study of algebra involves solving equations, and the study of geometry
involves proofs of relations between lines, angles, and others. Elements (a) are
parts of sets and not found in geometry. Sets (c) are found in number theory, and
statistics (d) is a separate field of study.

86. TIZANO VECELLIO : TITIAN :: DOMENIKOS THEOTOKOPOULOS :
(a. Domenik **b. El Greco** c. Theo d. Poulous)

(b) is correct because the painter commonly known as Titian was, in fact, named
Tizano Vecellio, just as the painter commonly known as El Greco was in fact
named Domenikos Theotokopoulos. All other answer choices are ficticious.

87. WARHOL : POP ART :: (**a. Picasso** b. Pollack c. Mondrian d. Matisse) :
CUBISM

(a) is correct because as Warhol was considered the pioneer of Pop Art, so Picasso was considered the pioneer of Cubism. (b) is incorrect because Pollack
was an Abstract Expressionist. (c) is incorrect because Mondrian the master of
the De Stijl movement. (d) is incorrect because Matisse was an Expressionist.

88. TIFFANY : GLASS :: CHRISTO JAVACHEF : (**a. islands** b. sculpture c. found
objects d. painting)

(a) is correct because just as Tiffany is famous for his stained glass, Javachef is
famous for surrounding the islands of Biscayne Bay with pink fabric. (b), (c),
and (d) are incorrect because Javachef did not work in these media.

89. MYOPIC : NEARSIGHTED :: HABERDASHER : (a. soldier **b. clothier**
c. educator d. editor)

(b) is correct because *myopic* refers to a condition commonly called nearsighted-
ness, and a haberdasher is to a men's clothier. All other answer choices are irrelevant.

90. LAPIDARY : DIAMONDS :: COOPER : (a. jewelry b. beer **c. casks** d. cheese)

(c) is correct because a lapidary is someone who crafts precious stones, just as a
cooper is someone who makes barrels and casks. All other choices are irrelevant.

Explanations of Answers

91. TALMUD : JUDAISM :: (a. Tao Te Ching b. Koran **c. Veda** d. Sutra) :
    HINDUISM

    (c) is correct because the Veda are the holy writings of Hinduism, just as the Talmud is a holy book of the Jewish faith. (a) is incorrect because the Tao Te Ching contains the tenets of Taoism. (b) is incorrect because the Koran is the holy book of Islam. (d) is incorrect because a sutra is a Buddhist commentary.

92. ASSOCIATIONS : (a. celestial sphere b. cosmic rays **c. binary stars** d. cardinal points) :: SCATTERED : BOUND

    (c) Binary stars is correct because scattered objects are not held together by any force, whereas bound objects are held together by a common force. This analogy shows an opposite characteristic. Associations are scattered stars which are not bound by gravity, whereas binary stars are bound together through their orbiting of a common center of mass. This is a difficult analogy and requires the previous knowledge of the definition of association which at first glance seems to imply some type of a bond. Celestial sphere (a), cosmic rays (b), and cardinal points (d), while they are all terms applicable to astronomy, do not complete the opposite analogy and do not suggest an interrelationship with scattered versus bound.

93. WRIGHT : AIRPLANE :: (a. Garnerin b. Zeppelin **c. Montgolfier** d. Selfridge) :
    HOT AIR BALLOON

    (c) is correct because just as the Wright brothers engineered the first airplane flight, so did the Montgolfier brothers engineer the first hot air balloon flight. (a) is incorrect because Garnerin was credited with the first parachute jump. (b) is incorrect because Zeppelin was credited with the first rigid-frame airship flight. (d) is incorrect because Selfridge is noted as the first airplane fatality.

94. NORSE : JUDEO-CHRISTIAN :: (a. Bragi b. Balder c. Buri **d. Ask**) : ADAM

    (d) is correct because Adam is the first man in the Judeo-Christian faith, just as Ask was the first man in Norse mythology. (a) is incorrect because Bragi is the Norse god of poetry. (b) is incorrect because Balder is the Norse god of light. (c) is incorrect because Buri is the progenitor of the gods in Norse mythology.

Explanations
of Answers

95.   OEDIPUS : (a. Clytaemnestra **b. Jocasta** c. Antigone d. Cassandra) ::
CLAUDIUS : GERTRUDE

(b) is correct because Oedipus and Jocasta entered into a forbidden marriage
(mother to son) in Sophocles' Theban plays, just as Claudius and Gertrude entered into a forbidden marriage (brother-in-law to sister-in-law) in Shakespeare's
Hamlet. (a) is incorrect because Clytaemnestra was the wife of Agammemnon.
(c) is incorrect because Antigone was the daughter of Oedipus. (d) is incorrect
because Cassandra was a prophet in Greek mythology.

96.   DARWIN : EVOLUTION :: BOHR : (**a. atomic structure** b. x-ray diffraction
c. dynamite d. electrons)

(a) is correct because Charles Darwin was the first to establish a concrete theory
of evolution just as Niels Bohr was the first to establish an acceptable concrete
model of atomic structure. (b) is incorrect because x-ray diffraction was discovered by Max von Laue. (c) is incorrect because dynamite was first created by
Alfred Nobel. (d) is incorrect because electrons were first described by Joseph
Thompson.

97.   Given that *B // C*,

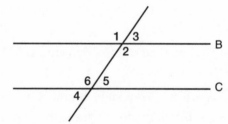

∠1 : ∠2 :: ∠4 : (a. 2 **b. 3** c. 1 d. 6)

(b) Angles 1 and 2 are vertical angles and thus are equal. Angles 4 and 5 are vertical angles, but 5 is not offered as a choice. Then what other angle is equal to 4?
The lines B and C are parallel, thus angles 3 and 5 are equal. Then angles 4 and
5 and 3 (b) are all equal.

98.   STEVENSON : EISENHOWER :: (a. Wilke b. Dewey c. Landon **d. Davis**) :
COOLIDGE

(d) is correct because John W. Davis unsuccessfully ran against Calvin Coolidge
for the presidency of the United States just as Adlai Stevenson unsuccessfully
ran against Dwight Eisenhower. (a), (b), and (c) are incorrect because all these
candidates unsuccessfully ran against Franklin Roosevelt.

99. FIFTEENTH AMENDMENT : VOTING RIGHTS :: NINETEENTH
    AMENDMENT : (a. prohibition b. cruel and unusual punishment **c. voting
    rights** d. succession)

    (c) is correct because the Fifteenth Amendment gave voting rights to men of all
    races, just as the Nineteenth Amendment gave voting rights to women. (a) is
    incorrect because prohibition was set in the Eighteenth Amendment. (b) is incor-
    rect because cruel and unusual punishment was prohibited in the Eighth Amend-
    ment. (d) is incorrect because the order of presidential succession was spelled
    out in the Twenty-fifth Amendment.

100. EPICENE : (a. prehistoric b. artificial **c. androgynous** d. stubborn) ::
     ENTENTE : AGREEMENT

     (c) is correct because *epicene* and *androgynous* mean "having both male and
     female characteristics," just as *entente* and *agreement* both mean "an understand-
     ing reached between parties." (a), (b), and (d) are unrelated to the meaning of
     these terms.

Miller Analogies

eight

Practice Test 8

Answer Sheet
Practice Test 8

1. Ⓐ Ⓑ Ⓒ Ⓓ
2. Ⓐ Ⓑ Ⓒ Ⓓ
3. Ⓐ Ⓑ Ⓒ Ⓓ
4. Ⓐ Ⓑ Ⓒ Ⓓ
5. Ⓐ Ⓑ Ⓒ Ⓓ
6. Ⓐ Ⓑ Ⓒ Ⓓ
7. Ⓐ Ⓑ Ⓒ Ⓓ
8. Ⓐ Ⓑ Ⓒ Ⓓ
9. Ⓐ Ⓑ Ⓒ Ⓓ
10. Ⓐ Ⓑ Ⓒ Ⓓ
11. Ⓐ Ⓑ Ⓒ Ⓓ
12. Ⓐ Ⓑ Ⓒ Ⓓ
13. Ⓐ Ⓑ Ⓒ Ⓓ
14. Ⓐ Ⓑ Ⓒ Ⓓ
15. Ⓐ Ⓑ Ⓒ Ⓓ
16. Ⓐ Ⓑ Ⓒ Ⓓ
17. Ⓐ Ⓑ Ⓒ Ⓓ
18. Ⓐ Ⓑ Ⓒ Ⓓ
19. Ⓐ Ⓑ Ⓒ Ⓓ
20. Ⓐ Ⓑ Ⓒ Ⓓ
21. Ⓐ Ⓑ Ⓒ Ⓓ
22. Ⓐ Ⓑ Ⓒ Ⓓ
23. Ⓐ Ⓑ Ⓒ Ⓓ
24. Ⓐ Ⓑ Ⓒ Ⓓ
25. Ⓐ Ⓑ Ⓒ Ⓓ
26. Ⓐ Ⓑ Ⓒ Ⓓ
27. Ⓐ Ⓑ Ⓒ Ⓓ
28. Ⓐ Ⓑ Ⓒ Ⓓ
29. Ⓐ Ⓑ Ⓒ Ⓓ
30. Ⓐ Ⓑ Ⓒ Ⓓ
31. Ⓐ Ⓑ Ⓒ Ⓓ
32. Ⓐ Ⓑ Ⓒ Ⓓ
33. Ⓐ Ⓑ Ⓒ Ⓓ
34. Ⓐ Ⓑ Ⓒ Ⓓ

35. Ⓐ Ⓑ Ⓒ Ⓓ
36. Ⓐ Ⓑ Ⓒ Ⓓ
37. Ⓐ Ⓑ Ⓒ Ⓓ
38. Ⓐ Ⓑ Ⓒ Ⓓ
39. Ⓐ Ⓑ Ⓒ Ⓓ
40. Ⓐ Ⓑ Ⓒ Ⓓ
41. Ⓐ Ⓑ Ⓒ Ⓓ
42. Ⓐ Ⓑ Ⓒ Ⓓ
43. Ⓐ Ⓑ Ⓒ Ⓓ
44. Ⓐ Ⓑ Ⓒ Ⓓ
45. Ⓐ Ⓑ Ⓒ Ⓓ
46. Ⓐ Ⓑ Ⓒ Ⓓ
47. Ⓐ Ⓑ Ⓒ Ⓓ
48. Ⓐ Ⓑ Ⓒ Ⓓ
49. Ⓐ Ⓑ Ⓒ Ⓓ
50. Ⓐ Ⓑ Ⓒ Ⓓ
51. Ⓐ Ⓑ Ⓒ Ⓓ
52. Ⓐ Ⓑ Ⓒ Ⓓ
53. Ⓐ Ⓑ Ⓒ Ⓓ
54. Ⓐ Ⓑ Ⓒ Ⓓ
55. Ⓐ Ⓑ Ⓒ Ⓓ
56. Ⓐ Ⓑ Ⓒ Ⓓ
57. Ⓐ Ⓑ Ⓒ Ⓓ
58. Ⓐ Ⓑ Ⓒ Ⓓ
59. Ⓐ Ⓑ Ⓒ Ⓓ
60. Ⓐ Ⓑ Ⓒ Ⓓ
61. Ⓐ Ⓑ Ⓒ Ⓓ
62. Ⓐ Ⓑ Ⓒ Ⓓ
63. Ⓐ Ⓑ Ⓒ Ⓓ
64. Ⓐ Ⓑ Ⓒ Ⓓ
65. Ⓐ Ⓑ Ⓒ Ⓓ
66. Ⓐ Ⓑ Ⓒ Ⓓ
67. Ⓐ Ⓑ Ⓒ Ⓓ
68. Ⓐ Ⓑ Ⓒ Ⓓ

69. Ⓐ Ⓑ Ⓒ Ⓓ
70. Ⓐ Ⓑ Ⓒ Ⓓ
71. Ⓐ Ⓑ Ⓒ Ⓓ
72. Ⓐ Ⓑ Ⓒ Ⓓ
73. Ⓐ Ⓑ Ⓒ Ⓓ
74. Ⓐ Ⓑ Ⓒ Ⓓ
75. Ⓐ Ⓑ Ⓒ Ⓓ
76. Ⓐ Ⓑ Ⓒ Ⓓ
77. Ⓐ Ⓑ Ⓒ Ⓓ
78. Ⓐ Ⓑ Ⓒ Ⓓ
79. Ⓐ Ⓑ Ⓒ Ⓓ
80. Ⓐ Ⓑ Ⓒ Ⓓ
81. Ⓐ Ⓑ Ⓒ Ⓓ
82. Ⓐ Ⓑ Ⓒ Ⓓ
83. Ⓐ Ⓑ Ⓒ Ⓓ
84. Ⓐ Ⓑ Ⓒ Ⓓ
85. Ⓐ Ⓑ Ⓒ Ⓓ
86. Ⓐ Ⓑ Ⓒ Ⓓ
87. Ⓐ Ⓑ Ⓒ Ⓓ
88. Ⓐ Ⓑ Ⓒ Ⓓ
89. Ⓐ Ⓑ Ⓒ Ⓓ
90. Ⓐ Ⓑ Ⓒ Ⓓ
91. Ⓐ Ⓑ Ⓒ Ⓓ
92. Ⓐ Ⓑ Ⓒ Ⓓ
93. Ⓐ Ⓑ Ⓒ Ⓓ
94. Ⓐ Ⓑ Ⓒ Ⓓ
95. Ⓐ Ⓑ Ⓒ Ⓓ
96. Ⓐ Ⓑ Ⓒ Ⓓ
97. Ⓐ Ⓑ Ⓒ Ⓓ
98. Ⓐ Ⓑ Ⓒ Ⓓ
99. Ⓐ Ⓑ Ⓒ Ⓓ
100. Ⓐ Ⓑ Ⓒ Ⓓ

Practice Test 8

TIME: 50 Minutes   **LENGTH:** 100 Analogies

DIRECTIONS: Read each of the following analogies carefully, and choose the BEST answer to each item. Fill in your responses in the answer sheets provided.

Note: The Miller Analogies Test consists of 120 questions to be completed in 60 minutes. Twenty of these questions are experimental items, which are not scored and thus not reflected in this practice test.

1. I. M. PEI : (a. architecture b. sculpture c. education d. illustration) :: ALVIN AILEY : CHOREOGRAPHY

2. NEMO : NAUTILUS :: AHAB : (a. Lusitania b. Nimitz c. Pequod d. Titanic)

3. PALEOCENE : CENOZOIC :: TRIASSIC : (a. Cambrian b. Silurian c. Devonian d. Mesozoic)

4. 10 : 1,000 :: 4 : (a. 16 b. 24 c. 48 d. 64)

5. COURAGEOUS : (a. pusillanimous b. victorious c. venerated d. vilified) :: VALOR : COWARDICE

6. HYDROGEN BOND : PAPER :: (a. disulfide linkages b. Van der Waals forces c. metallic bonds d. electrostatic attraction) : RUBBER

7. PRADO : MADRID :: HERMITAGE : (a. Paris b. New York c. St. Petersburg d. Vienna)

8. MALE : FEMALE :: TENOR : (a. alto b. soprano c. mezzo soprano d. bass)

9. STEER : COW :: GELDING : (a. horse b. mare c. foal d. colt)

10. COPERNICUS : SUN :: PTOLEMY : (a. Earth b. moon c. stars d. church)

11. *BROWN V. BOARD OF EDUCATION* : 1954 :: *ROE V. WADE* : (a. 1968 b. 1979 c. 1970 d. 1973)

12. (a. keratotomy b. demographics c. cartography d. topology) : MAPMAKING :: HAGIOGRAPHY : SAINTS

13. PERISSODACTYLA : HORSE :: ARTIODACTYLA : (a. pig b. cat c. monkey d. kangaroo)

14. SANCTION : PERMIT :: (a. argument b. tirade c. discussion d. debate) : HARANGUE

15. MCCARTHYISM : 1950 :: SALEM WITCH HUNTS : (a. 1730 b. 1580 c. 1692 d. 1800)

16. PIAGET : COGNITIVE DEVELOPMENT :: (a. Freud b. Jung c. Maslow d. Marcuse) : HIERARCHY OF HUMAN NEEDS

17. GARLIC : CLOVE :: GEAR : (a. tooth b. machine c. spin d. transfer)

18. HOMOGENEITY : INDIVIDUALISM :: (a. comprehension b. indoctrination c. education d. impartiality) : LEARNING

19. SYMMETRY : H :: ASYMMETRY : (a. E b. O c. J d. M)

20. BUS BOYCOTT : ALABAMA :: KENT STATE : (a. Massachusetts b. New Jersey c. California d. Ohio)

21. TEAPOT DOME : (a. gold b. oil c. uranium d. railroads) :: CREDIT MOBILIER : RAILROADS

22. BLANK VERSE : RHYME :: FREE VERSE : (a. form b. theme c. meter d. tone)

23. THORAX : (a. insect b. heart c. brain d. eyes) :: DIGIT : HAND

24. JUTE : SISAL :: TWINE : (a. fabric b. rope c. cotton d. sail)

25. ORIGINAL : REPLICA :: PUZZLE : (a. riddle b. question c. enigma
    d. solution)

26. AMPLE : ABUNDANT :: ENTHUSIASM : (a. happiness b. pleasure c. calm
    d. frenzy)

27. $\dfrac{3}{10}$: 0.30 :: $\dfrac{4}{3}$: (a. $1\dfrac{1}{3}$ b. 1.3 c. 1.33 d. 0.67)

28. COLLOQUIAL : (a. idiomatic b. pretentious c. aloof d. amiable) ::
    ALACRITY : ENTHUSIASM

29. ERSATZ : SUBSTITUTE :: PSEUDO : (a. approximate b. false c. partial
    d. genuine)

30. (a. errant b. arbitrary c. ignoble d. phlegmatic) : GERMANE :: NEFARIOUS :
    RIGHTEOUS

31. EBULLIENT : ENNUI :: (a. lecherous b. lustrous c. parochial d. quiescent) :
    LASCIVIOUS

32. MICHIGAN : GREAT LAKE STATE :: INDIANA : (a. Treasure State
    b. Bluegrass State c. Hoosier State d. Garden State)

33. EUTROPHY : NUTRITION :: ERGONOMICS : (a. finances b. comfort
    c. health d. movement)

34. BURNS : ALOE :: (a. sneezing b. headache c. backache d. nausea) :
    PEPPERMINT

35. VERISIMILITUDE : TRUTH :: (a. apparent b. obvious c. unknown
    d. unaware) : ACTUAL

36. LANGUAGE : PHILOGICAL :: (a. snake b. rodent c. fish d. bird) : OPHIDIAN

37. Give A = {1, 3, 4, 5, 7}
    B = {2, 4, 6, 8, 10}
    C = {4}
    D = {1, 2, 3, 4, 5, 6, 7, 8, 10}

    A ∩ B : C :: A ∪ B : (a. A b. B c. C d. D)

38. MYRMIDON : SYCOPHANT :: PROLETARIAT : (a. bourgeoise b. worker
    c. intellectual d. prolix)

39. GONG : CYMBAL :: (a. snare b. timpani c. bongo d. tom) : DRUM

40. SIMILACRUM : IMAGE :: ESTIMATE : (a. calculation b. guess c. opinion
    d. prospectus)

41. CRYPTOGRAPHER : CODES :: GLAZIER : (a. ice b. glass c. confections
    d. animals)

42. $3\frac{1}{4} : \frac{13}{4} :: 2\frac{1}{7} : $ (a. $\frac{14}{7}$ b. $\frac{10}{7}$ c. $\frac{15}{7}$ d. $\frac{22}{7}$)

43. CORNHUSKER STATE : NEBRASKA :: CONSTITUTION STATE :
    (a. Pennsylvania b. Massachusetts c. Connecticut d. Maryland)

44. CONFIDENCE : NARCISSISM :: FEAR : (a. apprehension b. worry
    c. welcome d. panic)

45. Given

f	h
1	3
2	5
3	7
9	9

$f : h - 1 :: 2 :$ (a. 5 b. 1 c. 4 d. 9)

46. (a. magnesium b. calcium c. strontium d. barium) : CHLOROPHYLL :: IRON : HEMOGLOBIN

47. PROTOSTOMES : SPIRAL :: DEUTEROSTOMES : (a. radial b. bilateral c. round d. helical)

48. UGA : CODON :: (a. TCG b. ACU c. UGT d. AAG) : ANTICODON

49. QUEBEC : (a. Edmonton b. Quebec City c. Winnipeg d. Toronto) :: BRITISH COLUMBIA : VICTORIA

50. SPIDER MONKEY : NEW WORLD :: (a. woolley monkey b. marmoset c. tamarin d. loris) : OLD WORLD

51. COMPLEX : FREUD :: ARCHETYPE : (a. Adler b. Jung c. James d. Campbell)

52. RENEGE : FULFILL :: RECANT : (a. declare b. absolve c. expose d. dissent)

53. $e^{2x} : 2x \log e :: \sqrt{8} : (\frac{1}{2} \log 8$ b. $8 \log 2$ c. $2 \log 8$ d. $4 \log 8)$

54. NIELS BOHR : QUANTUM THEORY :: ANNIE CANNON : (a. astronomer b. stellar spectral classification system c. Harvard College Observatory d. probability theory)

55. PLAINTIFF : LITIGANT :: (a. igneous b. stone c. weathered d. ancient) : ROCK

56. $x : \frac{1}{x}$ :: PERIOD : (a. amplitude b. $\frac{1}{\text{amplitude}}$ c. frequency, d. $\frac{1}{\text{frequency}}$)

57. SET : ELEMENT :: EQUATION : (a. division b. axiom c. variable d. Venn diagram)

58. WATER : DAM :: (a. livestock b. gas c. hair d. beer) : SNOOD

59. NANKING : (a. Beijing b. Canton c. Hong Kong d. Guangzhou) :: KYOTO : TOKYO

60. BALEFUL : (a. angelic b. masochistic c. malefic d. doleful) :: DULCET : MELLODIOUS

61. EXCULPATE : (a. absolve b. repay c. blame d. banish) :: EXALT : HONOR

62. PHILISTINE : (a. uncouth b. urbane c. laggard d. neophyte) :: ACRID : AROMATIC

63. BALTIMORE AND TEMIN : REVERSE TRANSCRIPTASE :: (a. Kornberg b. Newton and Leibniz c. Watson and Crick d. Thomson and Kelvin) : DNA

64. DEARTH : VACUOUS :: PENULTIMATE : (a. juxtaposition b. hiatus c. epitome d. terminus)

65. KR : KRYPTON :: CO : (a. chlorine b. copper c. cobalt d. carbon)

66. NASCENT : (a. incipient b. descant c. umbrage d. solace) :: INANIMATE : EXTINCT

67. GREGARIOUS : RECLUSIVE :: OBSEQUIOUS : (a. servile b. insolent c. petulent d. demure)

68. PROGENY : (a. genetics b. feminism c. genius d. offspring) :: PALLID : SALLOW

69. CREPUSCULAR : (a. twilight b. darkness c. sunrise d. noon) :: PEDAGOGICAL : EDUCATION

70. E : ECHO :: F : (a. fancy b. forest c. firefly d. fox-trot)

71. FRUCTOSE : (a. lactose b. sucrose c. glucose d. maltose) :: FRUIT : MILK

72. ANALOGOUS : (a. tautological b. similar c. tantamount d. opposite) :: LIQUESCENT : MELTING

73. PRIMA BALLERINA : BALLET :: DIVA : (a. opera b. art c. music d. dance)

74. ELUCIDATE : CLARIFY :: MAGISTRATE : (a. attorney b. police officer c. judge d. warden)

75. TRANSPOSONS : BARBARA MCCLINTOCK :: (a. HIV b. HTLV c. AIDS d. DNA polymerase) : LUC MONTAGNIER

76. PROSELYTE : (a. devotee b. concubine c. convert d. expert) :: NOVICE : NEOPHYTE

77. Given

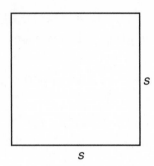 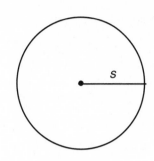

Then, $4s : s^2 :: 2\pi s :$ (a. $2\pi s^2$ b. πs^2 c. $(\frac{\pi}{2})s^2$ d. $\pi(\frac{s}{2})^2$)

78. MALE : FEMALE :: INCUBUS : (a. demon b. succubus c. distaff d. dowager)

79. $2x^2 + 4x + 3x^2 - 6x + 5 : 5x^2 - 2x + 5 :: 7x - 9x^2 + x^3 - 10x - 5 + 4x^4 + 7 :$ (a. $4x^4 + x^3 - 9x^2 - 3x + 2$ b. $5x^4 - 9x^2 - 3x$ c. $4x^4 + x^3 + 17x - 12$ d. $x^3 + 7x - 19x^2 - 2$)

80. *LAPSUS LINGUAE* : (a. tongue tied b. tongue twister c. lap dog d. slip of the tongue) :: *IN ABSENTIA* : IN ABSENCE

81. YATHRIB : MEDINA :: PERSIA : (a. Iraq b. Iran c. Saudi Arabia d. Mecca)

82. APOTHEGM : (a. touchstone b. maxim c. criticism d. praise) :: TRUCULENT : OVERBEARING

83. RED : BLUE :: (a. x-ray b. ultraviolet c. gamma radiation d. radio wave) : MICROWAVE

84. AMALIE NOETHER : PHYSICS :: ROSALIND FRANKLIN : (a. molecular biology b. x-ray crystallography c. organic chemistry d. transposons)

85. (a. voluble b. trite c. veracious d. accede) : FLUENT :: LACKADAISICAL : TARRY

86. DROMEDARY : CAMEL :: PACHYDERM : (a. ox b. tiger c. elephant d. whale)

87. TONI MORRISON : *BELOVED* :: (a. Jane Smiley b. John Updike c. Norman Mailer d. Alice Walker) : *RABBIT AT REST*

88. (a. glucose b. fructose c. sucrose d. deoxyribose) : GALACTOSE :: RIBOSE : ARABINOSE

89. SILENT SPRING : RACHEL CARSON :: THE DOUBLE HELIX : (a. Francis Crick b. Rosalind Franklin c. Maurice Wilkins d. James Watson)

90. SCURVY : VITAMIN :: (a. beriberi b. zwitterion c. kwashiorkor d. ketosis) : PROTEIN

91. NIXON : FORD :: GOLDA MEIR : (a. Itzhak Rabin b. Menachem Begin c. Shimon Peres d. Yitzhak Shamir)

92. SYCOPHANTIC : PANDERING :: DOGMATIC : (a. authoritarian b. unprincipled c. karmic d. innocuous)

93. SEPTADEKAPHILIA : 17 :: ARACHNAPHILIA : (a. people b. spiders c. strangers d. insects)

94. OBDURATE : (a. tenacious b. tacit c. succinct d. obstinate) :: UBIQUITOUS : OMNIPRESENT

95. RECANTATION : AFFIRMATION :: DEFY : (a. rebel b. challenge c. acquiesce d. dare)

96. PINEAL : MELATONIN :: KIDNEY : (a. glucagon b. insulin c. renin d. calcitonin)

97. Given A = {0, 1, 2, 3}
         B = {4, 5, 6, 7}
         C = {0, 1}
         D = {6, 7}
         E = {8, 9}

    C : A :: D : (a. A b. B c. C d. E)

98. CHOLERIC : CANTANKEROUS :: BOMBASTIC : (a. behoove b. affable
c. turgid d. pious)

99. APRIL : MAY :: (a. ruby b. sapphire c. garnet d. diamond) : EMERALD

100. UDOMETER : (a. rainfall b. age c. blood pressure d. RPMs) ::
CHRONOMETER : TIME

Answer Key
Practice Test 8

1. (a)	26. (d)	51. (b)	76. (c)
2. (c)	27. (c)	52. (a)	77. (b)
3. (d)	28. (a)	53. (a)	78. (b)
4. (d)	29. (b)	54. (b)	79. (a)
5. (a)	30. (b)	55. (a)	80. (d)
6. (a)	31. (c)	56. (d)	81. (b)
7. (c)	32. (c)	57. (c)	82. (b)
8. (b)	33. (b)	58. (c)	83. (d)
9. (a)	34. (d)	59. (a)	84. (a)
10. (a)	35. (a)	60. (c)	85. (a)
11. (d)	36. (a)	61. (a)	86. (c)
12. (c)	37. (d)	62. (b)	87. (b)
13. (a)	38. (b)	63. (c)	88. (a)
14. (b)	39. (b)	64. (d)	89. (d)
15. (c)	40. (a)	65. (c)	90. (c)
16. (c)	41. (b)	66. (a)	91. (a)
17. (a)	42. (c)	67. (b)	92. (a)
18. (b)	43. (c)	68. (d)	93. (b)
19. (c)	44. (d)	69. (a)	94. (d)
20. (d)	45. (c)	70. (d)	95. (c)
21. (b)	46. (a)	71. (a)	96. (c)
22. (c)	47. (a)	72. (b)	97. (b)
23. (a)	48. (b)	73. (a)	98. (c)
24. (b)	49. (b)	74. (c)	99. (d)
25. (d)	50. (a)	75. (a)	100. (a)

Explanations of Answers
Practice Test 8

1. I. M. PEI : (**a. architecture** b. sculpture c. education d. illustration) :: ALVIN AILEY : CHOREOGRAPHY

    (**a**) is correct because I. M. Pei is an architect just as Alvin Ailey is an choreographer. All other answer choices are incorrect because I. M. Pei was not active in these disciplines.

2. NEMO : NAUTILUS :: AHAB : (a. Lusitania b. Nimitz **c. Pequod** d. Titanic)

    (**c**) is correct because Nemo was the captain of the *Nautilus* in Jules Verne's *20,000 Leagues Under the Sea*, just as Ahab was the captain of the *Pequod* in Herman Melville's *Moby-Dick*. All other answer choices are incorrect because they are actual ships, not fictitious ones.

3. PALEOCENE : CENOZOIC :: TRIASSIC : (a. Cambrian b. Silurian c. Devonian **d. Mesozoic**)

    (**d**) is correct because the Cenozoic period marked the beginning of the Paleocene era, just as the Triassic period marked the beginning of the Mesozoic. All other choices were periods in the Paleozoic era.

4. 10 : 1,000 :: 4 : (a. 16 b. 24 c. 48 **d. 64**)

    (**d**) is correct because 1,000 is 10 cubed, just as 64 is 4 cubed. All other choices are insignificant to this analogy.

5. COURAGEOUS : (**a. pusillanimous** b. victorious c. venerated d. vilified) :: VALOR : COWARDICE

    (**a**) is correct because courageous is the opposite of pusillanimous (meaning cowardly), just as valor is the opposite of cowardice. (b) is incorrect because it is an indirect synonym of courageous. (c) is incorrect because something that is venerated is revered. (d) is incorrect because to be vilified means to be defamed.

6. HYDROGEN BOND : PAPER :: (**a. disulfide linkages** b. Van der Waals forces c. metallic bonds d. electrostatic attraction) : RUBBER

   (**a**) is correct because hydrogen bonds provide the cross linkages of cellulose in paper, while disulfide linkages provide the cross linkages in rubber. Van de Waals forces (b), metalic bonds (c), and electrostatic attraction (d) do not provide the cross linking forces in either of these situations and therefore do not provide a completion for the analogy.

7. PRADO : MADRID :: HERMITAGE : (a. Paris b. New York **c. St. Petersburg** d. Vienna)

   (**c**) is correct because the Prado is Madrid's most famous art museum just as the Hermitage is St. Petersburg's. (a) is incorrect because the most famous museum in Paris is the Louvre. (b) is incorrect because there are several famous museums in New York, including the Metropolitan and the Museum of Modern Art. (d) is incorrect because the most famous museum in Vienna is the Naturhistorices.

8. MALE : FEMALE :: TENOR : (a. alto **b. soprano** c. mezzo soprano d. bass)

   (**b**) is correct because tenor is the highest normal male voice just as soprano is the highest female voice. (a) is incorrect because alto is a lower female voice. (c) is incorrect because a mezzo soprano is lower than a soprano. (d) is incorrect because bass is the lowest male voice.

9. STEER : COW :: GELDING : (**a. horse** b. mare c. foal d. colt)

   (**a**) is correct because a castrated male cow is called a steer, just as a castrated male horse is called a gelding. (b) is incorrect because a mare is a female horse. (c) and (d) are incorrect because these are names for the offspring of horses.

10. COPERNICUS : SUN :: PTOLEMY : (**a. Earth** b. moon c. stars d. church)

    (**a**) is correct because in the Copernican model of the solar system, the Earth revolves around the sun, while in the Ptolemaic model, the sun revolved around the Earth. (b), (c), and (d) are incorrect because no credible scientist ever proposed that the Earth revolved around these bodies.

11. *BROWN V. BOARD OF EDUCATION* : 1954 :: *ROE V. WADE* : (a. 1968 b. 1979 c. 1970 **d. 1973**)

    (d) is correct because *Brown v. Board of Education* declaring segregation unconstitutional was decided in 1954 just as *Roe v. Wade* declaring prohibition of abortion unconstitutional was decided in 1973. All other answer choices are insignificant to this analogy.

12. (a. keratotomy b. demographics **c. cartography** d. topology) : MAPMAKING :: HAGIOGRAPHY : SAINTS

    (c) is correct because cartography refers to the science of mapmaking just as hagiography refers to the study of saints' lives. (a) is incorrect because keratotomy is a corrective operation on the lens of the eye. (b) is incorrect because demographics refers to the study of population distribution. (d) is incorrect because topology refers to a branch of calculus.

13. PERISSODACTYLA : HORSE :: ARTIODACTYLA : (**a. pig** b. cat c. monkey d. kangaroo)

    (a) Pig is correct because a horse is an ungulate and like all perissodactyla has an odd number of toes, while a pig is also an ungulate but has an even number of toes like all artiodactyla. Cats (b), Monkeys (c), and kangaroos (d) are not ungulates and therefore do not fit the analogy.

14. SANCTION : PERMIT :: (a. argument **b. tirade** c. discussion d. debate) : HARANGUE

    (b) is correct because permit and sanction are synonyms meaning to allow, just as harangue and tirade are synonyms meaning a bombastic rant. Argument (a), discussion (c), and debate (d) are incorrect because they convey a lesser degree of emotion.

15. MCCARTHYISM : 1950 :: SALEM WITCH HUNTS : (a. 1730 b. 1580 **c. 1692** d. 1800)

    (c) is correct because in 1950, the nation was gripped by the panic of McCarthyism, just as in 1692 the community of Salem, Massachusetts, was paralyzed by the Salem witch hunts. All other answer choices are insignificant to this analogy.

16. PIAGET : COGNITIVE DEVELOPMENT :: (a. Freud b. Jung **c. Maslow** d. Marcuse) : HIERARCHY OF HUMAN NEEDS

    (c) is correct because Jean Piaget developed a theory of cognitive development just as Abraham Maslow developed a hierarchy of human needs. (a) is incorrect because Freud developed a theory of psychoanalysis. (b) is incorrect because Jung is famous for his theory of collective unconscious. (d) is incorrect because Marcuse is well known for his theories on work and labor.

17. GARLIC : CLOVE :: GEAR : (**a. tooth** b. machine c. spin d. transfer)

    (a) is correct because a clove is a part of a garlic bulb as a tooth is a part of a gear. (b) is incorrect because a gear is part of a machine, and this reverses the whole/part relationship. (c) and (d) are incorrect because a gear spins (c) and by doing so transfers (d) power, however this is the function of a gear, not a part of its structure.

18. HOMOGENEITY : INDIVIDUALISM :: (a. comprehension **b. indoctrination** c. education d. impartiality) : LEARNING

    (b) is correct because homogeneity, or conformity on a social level, is the opposite of individualism, in much the same way that indoctrination, or the insertion of another's ideas and opinions into one's mind, is the opposite of learning. (a) and (c) are incorrect because they have similar meanings to learning. (d) is incorrect because to be impartial is to be unbiased.

19. SYMMETRY : H :: ASYMMETRY : (a. E b. O **c. J** d. M)

    (c) The letter *H* is symmetric both horizontally and vertically; as such, only *J* (c) is not symmetric, or it is asymmetric. However, the other choices are symmetric as shown.

20. BUS BOYCOTT : ALABAMA :: KENT STATE : (a. Massachusetts b. New Jersey c. California **d. Ohio**)

    (d) is correct because just as the bus boycott occurred in Montgomery, Alabama, a very influential student protest occurred at Kent State in Kent, Ohio. All other answer choices are insignificant to this analogy.

21. TEAPOT DOME : (a. gold **b. oil** c. uranium d. railroads) :: CREDIT
    MOBILIER : RAILROADS

    (b) is correct because the Teapot Dome Scandal involved the transfer of naval oil
    reserves, and the Credit Mobilier Scandal involved railroad tycoons establishing
    slush funds to defraud the government. All other choices are irrelevant to this
    analogy.

22. BLANK VERSE : RHYME :: FREE VERSE : (a. form b. theme **c. meter**
    d. tone)

    (c) is correct because just as blank verse poetry does not rhyme, free verse po-
    etry has no set meter. (a) is incorrect because free verse is a form in itself. (b)
    and (d) are incorrect because there is nothing inherent in the term free verse that
    would suggest that theme or tone are absent.

23. THORAX : (**a. insect** b. heart c. brain d. eyes) :: DIGIT : HAND

    (a) is correct because the thorax is part of an insect just as the digit is part of a
    hand. (b), (c), and (d) are incorrect because these are too specific to complete the
    analogy.

24. JUTE : SISAL :: TWINE : (a. fabric **b. rope** c. cotton d. sail)

    (b) is correct because jute is a plant material used to make twine just as sisal is a
    plant fiber used to make rope. (a), (c), and (d) are incorrect because neither jute
    nor sisal are used to make these materials.

25. ORIGINAL : REPLICA :: PUZZLE : (a. riddle b. question c. enigma
    d. solution)

    (d) is correct because an original is the opposite of a replica, just as a puzzle is
    the opposite of a solution. (a), (b), and (c) are incorrect because these are more
    or less synonymous with puzzle.

26. AMPLE : ABUNDANT :: ENTHUSIASM : (a. happiness b. pleasure c. calm
    d. frenzy)

    (d) is correct because *abundant* means "ample (sufficient) to a greater degree,"
    just as *frenzy* means "enthusiasm to a greater degree." (a) and (b) are incorrect
    because they do not convey a greater degree. (c) is incorrect because *calm* is the
    opposite of *frenzy*.

Explanations
of Answers

27. $\dfrac{3}{10}$: 0.30 :: $\dfrac{4}{3}$: (a. $1\dfrac{1}{3}$ b. 1.3 **c. 1.33** d. 0.67)

    (c) The fraction $\dfrac{3}{10}$ is rewritten as the decimal 0.30, with two decimal places. The fraction $\dfrac{4}{3}$ can also be written as a decimal, 1.33. Choice (a) is incorrect because the number is still in fraction form. In choice (b), the decimal is written with only one decimal place. Choice (d) is not equivalent to $\dfrac{4}{3}$.

28. COLLOQUIAL : (**a. idiomatic** b. pretentious c. aloof d. amiable) :: ALACRITY : ENTHUSIASM

    (a) is correct because *colloquial* and *idiomatic* are synonyms meaning "common" just as *alacrity* and *enthusiasm* are synonyms for "liveliness." (b) and (c) are incorrect because *pretentious* and *aloof* are opposites of *colloquial*. (d) is incorrect because *amiable* means "friendly."

29. ERSATZ : SUBSTITUTE :: PSEUDO : (a. approximate **b. false** c. partial d. genuine)

    (b) is correct because *ersatz* and *substitute* are synonymous, just as *pseudo* and *false* are synonymous. (a), (c), and (d) are incorrect because these are all relative antonyms of *pseudo*.

30. (a. errant **b. arbitrary** c. ignoble d. phlegmatic) : GERMANE :: NEFARIOUS : RIGHTEOUS

    (b) is correct because *arbitrary*, meaning "unimportant," is the antonym of *germane*, meaning "pertinent," just as *nefarious* and *righteous* are opposites. (a) is incorrect because *errant* means "wandering," (c) is incorrect because *ignoble* means "shameful," and (d) is incorrect because *phlegmatic* means "without interest or emotion."

31. EBULLIENT : ENNUI :: (a. lecherous b. lustrous **c. parochial** d. quiescent) : LASCIVIOUS

    (c) is correct because *parochial*, meaning "religiously moral," is the antonym of *lascivious*, meaning "immoral," just as *ebullient* and *ennui* are opposites meaning "excited" and "bored," respectively. (a) is incorrect because *lecherous* is a synonym for *lascivious*. (b) is incorrect because *lustrous* means "radiant." (d) is incorrect because *quiescent* means "inactive."

32. MICHIGAN : GREAT LAKE STATE :: INDIANA : (a. Treasure State
b. Bluegrass State **c. Hoosier State** d. Garden State)

(c) is correct because the nickname for Michigan is the Great Lake State just as
Indiana is the Hoosier State. (a) is incorrect because Montana is the Treasure
State. (c) is incorrect because the Bluegrass State is Kentucky. (b) is incorrect
because the Garden State is New Jersey.

33. EUTROPHY : NUTRITION :: ERGONOMICS : (a. finances **b. comfort**
c. health d. movement)

(b) is correct because just as geology is the scientific study of the earth's origin,
history, and structure, ergonomics is the science of human comfort. (a) is incorrect because the study of finances would be part of economics. (c) is incorrect
because the study of health would be medicine. (d) is incorrect because studies
of movement include kinesiology and eurythmics.

34. BURNS : ALOE :: (a. sneezing b. headache c. backache **d. nausea**) :
PEPPERMINT

(d) is correct because aloe is a natural treatment for burns just as peppermint is a
natural treatment for nausea. All other answer choices are incorrect because peppermint is not used for an antihistamine or an analgesic, appropriate treatments
for these ailments.

35. VERISIMILITUDE : TRUTH :: (**a. apparent** b. obvious c. unknown
d. unaware) : ACTUAL

(a) is correct because the relationship between *verisimilitude*, meaning "the appearance of truth," and *truth* is analogous to the relationship between *apparent*
and *actual*. (b) is incorrect because *obvious* refers to something clearly known.
(c) and (d) are incorrect because these terms imply a lack of knowledge rather
than a perceived, though flawed, knowledge.

36. LANGUAGE : PHILOGICAL :: (**a. snake** b. rodent c. fish d. bird) : OPHIDIAN

(a) is correct because *philogical* is an adjective meaning "pertaining to language," just as *ophidian* is an adjective meaning "pertaining to snakes." (b) is
incorrect because a rodent is a suborder of mammals. (c) is incorrect because an
adjective meaning pertaining to fish would be ichtyian. (d) is incorrect because
an adjective meaning pertaining to birds would be either ornithian or avian.

Explanations
of Answers

37. Given A = {1, 3, 4, 5, 7}
    B = {2, 4, 6, 8, 10}
    C = {4}
    D = {1, 2, 3, 4, 5, 6, 7, 8, 10}

    A ∩ B : C :: A ∪ B : (a. A b. B c. C **d. D**)

    (d) This analogy uses set theory. A « B is interpreted as the intersection of sets A and B, which is set C. The element {4} occurs in both sets. A » B is the union of both sets, which should include the elements of both sets. Only set D includes all the elements.

38. MYRMIDON : SYCOPHANT :: PROLETARIAT : (a. bourgeoisie **b. worker** c. intellectual d. prolix)

    (b) is correct because both *myrmidon* and *sycophant* refer to someone who obeys an authority without question, just as *proletariat* refers to a member of the working class. (a) is incorrect because *bourgeoisie* refers to the middle class (c) is incorrect because there is nothing inherent in the term *intellectual* that would denote specifically a class standing. (d) is incorrect because *prolix* means "wordy and tedious."

39. GONG : CYMBAL :: (a. snare **b. timpani** c. bongo d. tom) : DRUM

    (b) is correct because a gong is a large version of a cymbal, just as a timpani is a large version of a drum. (a), (c), and (d) are incorrect because a snare, a bongo, and a tom are smaller drums.

40. SIMILACRUM : IMAGE :: ESTIMATE : (**a. calculation** b. guess c. opinion d. prospectus)

    (a) is correct because a similacrum is a vague image, just as an estimate is a vague calculation. (b), (c), and (d) are incorrect because they are all relatively synonymous with estimate.

41. CRYPTOGRAPHER : CODES :: GLAZIER : (a. ice **b. glass** c. confections d. animals)

    (b) is correct because a glazier is someone who works with glass in the same way that a cryptographer is someone who works with codes. (a) is incorrect because it is irrelevant to this analogy. (c) is incorrect because someone who works with confections is a baker or pastry chef. (d) is incorrect because a zoologist, veterinarian, or farmer might work with animals.

42. $3\frac{1}{4} : \frac{13}{4} :: 2\frac{1}{7} :$ (a. $\frac{14}{7}$ b. $\frac{10}{7}$ **c.** $\frac{15}{7}$ d. $\frac{22}{7}$)

(c) is correct because just as $\frac{13}{4}$ is the improper fractional representation of the mixed number $3\frac{1}{4}$, $\frac{15}{7}$ is the improper fractional representation of $2\frac{1}{7}$. (a) is incorrect because this improper fraction is equivalent to the whole number 2. (c) is incorrect because its mixed number representation is $1\frac{3}{7}$. (d) is incorrect because this is the fractional equivalent of π.

43. CORNHUSKER STATE : NEBRASKA :: CONSTITUTION STATE :
(a. Pennsylvania b. Massachusetts **c. Connecticut** d. Maryland)

(c) is correct because Connecticut's nickname is the "Constitution State," just as Nebraska's is the "Cornhusker State." (a) is incorrect because Pennsylvania's nickname is the "Keystone State." (b) is incorrect because Massachusetts's nickname is the "Bay State." (d) is incorrect because Maryland's nickname is the "Old Line State;" it's also known as the "Free State."

44. CONFIDENCE : NARCISSISM :: FEAR : (a. apprehension b. worry
c. welcome **d. panic**)

(d) is correct because narcissism is an extreme form of confidence just as panic is an extreme form of fear. (a) and (b) are incorrect because they convey a lesser degree of fear than panic. (c) is incorrect because welcome would be an opposite of fear.

45. Given

f	h
1	3
2	5
3	7
9	9

$f : h - 1 :: 2 :$ (a. 5 b. 1 **c. 4** d. 9)

(c) The given table provides the relationship between f and h. For the analogy, 2 is substituted for f, and h is then 5; thus, $h - 1 = 5 - 1 = 4$. The choice (a) is the direct value of h (5) in the table.

Explanations of Answers

Explanations
of Answers

46. (**a. magnesium** b. calcium c. strontium d. barium) : CHLOROPHYLL :: IRON : HEMOGLOBIN

    (**a**) Magnesium is correct because magnesium is the central ion in the chlorophyll molecule, while iron is the central ion in the hemoglobin molecule. Calcium (b), strontium (c), and barium (d) all belong to the same group on the Periodic Table, but they cannot be effectively used in the chlorophyll molecule.

47. PROTOSTOMES : SPIRAL :: DEUTEROSTOMES : (**a. radial** b. bilateral c. round d. helical)

    (**a**) Radial is correct because protostomes have a spiral cleavage pattern at the third cleavage, while deuterostomes have a radial cleavage pattern at the third cleavage. Bilateral (b) is not a type of cleavage, but indicates a type of symmetry, but spiral is not a type of symmetry and therefore an analogy would not be formed. Round (c) is a shape but spiral is a twisting pattern. Helical (d) is a term similar to spiral and therefore would not complete an analogy.

48. UGA : CODON :: (a. TCG **b. ACU** c. UGT d. AAG) : ANTICODON

    (**b**) ACU is correct because UGA is one codon of the possible 64 codons which can be found on messenger RNA. Because of the strict base pairing which occurs, ACU is the only transfer RNA anticodon which should fit with this codon. Therefore, the other three choices cannot be used to complete the analogy.

49. QUEBEC : (a. Edmonton **b. Quebec City** c. Winnipeg d. Toronto) :: BRITISH COLUMBIA : VICTORIA

    (**b**) is the correct answer because Quebec City is the provincial capital of the Canadian province of Quebec, just as Victoria is the capital of British Columbia. (a) is incorrect because Edmonton is the capital of Alberta. (c) is incorrect because Winnipeg is the capital of Manitoba. (d) is incorrect because Toronto is the capital of Ontario.

50. SPIDER MONKEY : NEW WORLD :: (**a. woolley** monkey b. marmoset c. tamarin d. loris) : OLD WORLD

    (**a**) is correct because only the woolley monkey is an Old World monkey. All others are New World monkeys.

Explanations of Answers

51. COMPLEX : FREUD :: ARCHETYPE : (a. Adler **b. Jung** c. James d. Campbell)

    (b) is correct because Freud is noted for originating the psychological concept of a complex, just as Jung is credited with the concept of the archetype. All other answer choices are irrelevant.

52. RENEGE : FULFILL :: RECANT : (**a. declare** b. absolve c. expose d. dissent)

    (a) is correct because to renege is to go back on a promise, the opposite of fulfilling it. To recant is to reverse a decision about a belief, as to declare is to affirm it. (b) is incorrect because to absolve means to forgive. (c) is incorrect because to expose something means to reveal it. (d) is incorrect because to dissent from something is to go against a popular idea.

53. $e^{2x} : 2x \log e :: \sqrt{8} :$ (**a. $\frac{1}{2} \log 8$** b. $8 \log 2$ c. $2 \log 8$ d. $4 \log 8$)

    (a) Another way of writing e^{2x} is $2x \log e$, therefore, can be written as $8^{\frac{1}{2}} = \left(\frac{1}{2}\right) \log 8$.

54. NIELS BOHR : QUANTUM THEORY :: ANNIE CANNON : (a. astronomer **b. stellar spectral classification system** c. Harvard College Observatory d. probability theory)

    (b) Stellar spectral classification system is correct because Bohr discovered quantum theorem, while Annie Cannon discovered the stellar spectral classification system. While Cannon was indeed an astronomer (a) and she did work at the Harvard College Observatory (c), these two choices do not show the discovery analogy. Probability theory (d) was discovered by Pascal and Fermat.

55. PLAINTIFF : LITIGANT :: (**a. igneous** b. stone c. weathered d. ancient) : ROCK

    (a) is correct because a plaintiff is a more specific type of litigant, or party in a lawsuit, just as igneous refers to a specific type of rock. (b), (c), and (d) are all adjectives that might describe a rock, but are too general to complete the analogy.

56. $x : \frac{1}{x} ::$ PERIOD : (a. amplitude b. $\frac{1}{\text{amplitude}}$ c. frequency, **d. $\frac{1}{\text{frequency}}$**)

    (d) In this analogy, $\frac{1}{x}$ is the inverse of x. Likewise, the inverse of the period is $\frac{1}{\text{frequency}}$.

57. SET : ELEMENT :: EQUATION : (a. division b. axiom **c. variable** d. Venn diagram)

    (c) A set is composed of elements, and thus an equation contains variables and coefficients. Division (a) is an operation done on variables. An axiom (b) is a statement, or a part of a theorem. A Venn diagram (d) is used to shown relationships between sets.

58. WATER : DAM :: (a. livestock b. gas **c. hair** d. beer) : SNOOD

    (c) is correct because a dam is built to confine water to a particular place just as a snood is designed to hold hair in a specific style. (a) is incorrect because a barn or stable would contain livestock. (b) is incorrect because gas is contained in tanks. (d) is incorrect because beer is contained in kegs.

59. NANKING : **(a. Beijing** b. Canton c. Hong Kong d. Guangzhou) :: KYOTO : TOKYO

    (a) is correct because Nanking is the past capital of China and Beijing is the current capital just as Kyoto was once the capital of Japan; an office now filled by Tokyo. (b), (c), and (d) are all incorrect because although they are cities in China, they are not and have never been the capital.

60. BALEFUL : (a. angelic b. masochistic **c. malefic** d. doleful) :: DULCET : MELODIOUS

    (c) is correct because malefic and baleful both describe something evil and are synonyms just as dulcet and melodious are synonyms for that which is pleasant sounding. (a) is incorrect because angelic is the opposite of baleful. (b) is incorrect because masochistic describes someone who enjoys abuse. (d) is incorrect because doleful means sorrowful.

61. EXCULPATE : **(a. absolve** b. repay c. blame d. banish) :: EXALT : HONOR

    (a) is correct because to *exculpate* means "to remove blame," and so is synonymous with absolve. This is analogous to the synonymous relationship between *exalt* and *honor*. (b) is incorrect because to repay an offense would be to punish rather than absolve. (c) and (d) are incorrect because they are relative antonyms of exculpate.

Explanations
of Answers

62. PHILISTINE : (a. uncouth **b. urbane** c. laggard d. neophyte) :: ACRID : AROMATIC

    (b) is correct because *urbane*, meaning "cultured," is the opposite of *philistine*, meaning "uncultured." *Acrid*, "foul-smelling," is the antonym of *aromatic* which means "pleasant in aroma." (a) is incorrect because *uncouth* is a synonym for *philistine*. (c) is incorrect because a laggard is a lazy person. (d) is incorrect because a neophyte is a novice or beginner.

63. BALTIMORE AND TEMIN : REVERSE TRANSCRIPTASE :: (a. Kornberg b. Newton and Leibniz **c. Watson and Crick** d. Thomson and Kelvin) : DNA

    (c) Watson and Crick is correct because Baltimore and Temin worked cooperatively to discover the enzyme known as reverse transcriptase. Watson and Crick worked cooperatively to discover DNA. Kornberg (a) discovered the DNA polymerase enzyme, but he alone is credited with the initial discovery. Newton and Leibniz (b) discovered calculus, but independently of each other. William Thomson and Lord Kelvin (d) are the two names of the same individual.

64. DEARTH : VACUOUS :: PENULTIMATE : (a. juxtaposition b. hiatus c. epitome **d. terminus**)

    (d) is correct because *penultimate* means "next to last or near completion," and *terminus* is defined as "completion or conclusion." *Dearth* means "scarcity or shortage," followed by *vacuous*, meaning "completely empty or void." (a) is incorrect because *juxtaposition* is "the placement of something side-by-side." (b) is incorrect because a hiatus is only a break in activity, not an end. (c) is incorrect because *epitome* means "typification."

65. KR : KRYPTON :: CO : (a. chlorine b. copper **c. cobalt** d. carbon)

    (c) is the correct answer because the periodic abbreviation for cobalt is Co, just as Kr is for krypton. (a) is incorrect because chlorine's chemical abbreviation is Cl. (b) is incorrect because the periodic abbreviation of copper is Cu. (d) is incorrect because the periodic abbreviation for carbon is C.

66. NASCENT : (**a. incipient** b. descant c. umbrage d. solace) :: INANIMATE : EXTINCT

    (a) is correct because *incipient* and *nascent* both mean "to come into being or existence" just as *inanimate* and *extinct* are synonyms for "lifelessness." (b) is incorrect because *descant* means "to talk at length." (c) is incorrect because *umbrage* means "resentful displeasure." (d) is incorrect because *solace* means "comfort."

Explanations
of Answers

67. GREGARIOUS : RECLUSIVE :: OBSEQUIOUS : (a. servile **b. insolent** c. petulant d. demure)

    (b) is correct because *obsequious*, meaning "overly attentive," and *insolent*, meaning "overly rude and abrasive," are antonyms just as *gregarious*, meaning "sociable," and *reclusive*, meaning "solitary," are antonyms. (a) is incorrect because *servile* is synonymous with *obsequious*. (c) is incorrect because *petulant* means "impatient." (d) is incorrect because *demure* means "shy."

68. PROGENY : (a. genetics b. feminism c. genius **d. offspring**) :: PALLID : SALLOW

    (d) is correct because *progeny* and *offspring* are synonyms for "descendents" just as *pallid* and *sallow* are synonyms for "paleness." (a) is incorrect because *genetics* is the study of genes and chromosomes. (b) is incorrect because *feminism* is a political belief in gender equality. (c) is incorrect because a genius is defined as an exceptionally smart person with a high IQ.

69. CREPUSCULAR : (**a. twilight** b. darkness c. sunrise d. noon) :: PEDAGOGICAL : EDUCATION

    (a) is correct because *crepuscular* means "pertaining to twilight," just as *pedagogical* means "pertaining to education." All other answer choices are incorrect because they refer to states other than twilight.

70. E : ECHO :: F : (a. fancy b. forest c. firefly **d. fox-trot**)

    (d) is correct because in the International Radio Alphabet, E is clarified as echo, just as F is clarified as fox-trot. All other choices are incorrect.

71. FRUCTOSE : (**a. lactose** b. sucrose c. glucose d. maltose) :: FRUIT : MILK

    (a) is correct because fructose is sugar found in fruit as lactose is sugar found in milk. (b) and (c) are incorrect because sucrose and glucose are derived from sugar cane. (d) is incorrect because maltose is derived from malt.

72. ANALOGOUS : (a. tautological **b. similar** c. tantamount d. opposite) :: LIQUESCENT : MELTING

    (b) is correct because *similar* is synonymous with *analogous*, just as *liquescent*, meaning "becoming liquid," is synonymous with *melting*. (a) is incorrect because *tautological* refers to an overstatement of the truth. (c) is incorrect because *tantamount* means "equal to a given thing or idea." (d) is incorrect because, of course, it is the opposite of *analogous*.

Explanations of Answers

73. PRIMA BALLERINA : BALLET :: DIVA : (**a. opera** b. art c. music d. dance)

    (**a**) is correct because a prima ballerina is the lead female dancer in a ballet, just as a diva is the lead female voice in an opera. All other answer choices are incorrect because, traditionally, the term diva refers to operatic performers.

74. ELUCIDATE : CLARIFY :: MAGISTRATE : (a. attorney b. police officer **c. judge** d. warden)

    (**c**) is correct because *elucidate* and *clarify* are synonyms, just as *magistrate* and *judge* are synonyms. (a), (b), and (d) are incorrect because while these are court-related professions, they are not synonymous with *magistrate*.

75. TRANSPOSONS : BARBARA MCCLINTOCK :: (**a. HIV** b. HTLV c. AIDS d. DNA polymerase) : LUC MONTAGNIER

    (**a**) Montagnier is correct because Barbara McClintock discovered the "jumping genes" or transposons, while Luc Montagnier discovered HIV, the causative agent of AIDS. AIDS (c) is an incorrect answer because Montagnier did not discover the disease itself but rather its causative agent. HTLV (b) is a virus that causes an AIDS-like illness, and DNA polymerase (d) is an enzyme that was discovered by Kornberg.

76. PROSELYTE : (a. devotee b. concubine **c. convert** d. expert) :: NOVICE : NEOPHYTE

    (**c**) is correct because a proselyte is a convert from one creed to another just as a novice and a neophyte both refer to a recent convert. (a) and (d) are incorrect because these terms do not imply conversion. (b) is incorrect because a concubine is a consort.

77. Given

    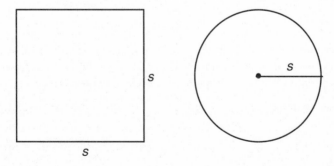

    Then, $4s : s^2 :: 2\pi s :$ (a. $2\pi s^2$ **b.** πs^2 c. $(\frac{\pi}{2})s^2$ d. $\pi(\frac{s}{2})^2$)

    (**b**) This relationship is the perimeter of the square to the area of the square. Therefore, the perimeter (or circumference) of the circle is $2\pi s$, and the area will be πs^2.

Explanations of Answers

78.   MALE : FEMALE :: INCUBUS : (a. demon **b. succubus** c. distaff d. dowager)

(b) is correct because an incubus is a male demon, just as a succubus is a female demon. (a) is incorrect because it is not gender specific. (c) is incorrect because while it means pertaining to a female, it has no demonic connotations. (d) is incorrect because a dowager is an older unmarried woman.

79. $2x^2 + 4x + 3x^2 - 6x + 5 : 5x^2 - 2x + 5 :: 7x - 9x^2 + x^3 - 10x - 5 + 4x^4 + 7 :$ **(a. $4x^4 + x^3 - 9x^2 - 3x + 2$** b. $5x^4 - 9x^2 - 3x$ c. $4x^4 + x^3 + 17x - 12$ d. $x^3 + 7x - 19x^2 - 2$)

(a) Part of the analogy, $5x^2 - 2x + 5$, is the simplified form of

$2x^2 + 4x + 3x^2 - 6x + 5.$

Thus simplifying

$$7x - 9x^2 + x^3 - 10x - 5 + 4x^4 + 7$$
$$= 4x^4 + x^3 - 9x^2 + 7x - 10x - 5 + 7$$
$$= 4x^4 + x^3 - 9x^2 - 3x + 2$$

80.   *LAPSUS LINGUAE* : (a. tongue tied b. tongue twister c. lap dog **d. slip of the tongue**) :: *IN ABSENTIA* : IN ABSENCE

(d) is correct because *lapsus linguae* is Latin for slip of the tongue, just as *in absentia* is Latin for in absence. (a), (b), and (c) are insignificant to this analogy.

81.   YATHRIB : MEDINA :: PERSIA : (a. Iraq **b. Iran** c. Saudi Arabia d. Mecca)

(b) is correct because Yathrib is the old name of the city of Medina, just as Persia is the old name of Iran. All other choices are not significant to this analogy.

82.   APOTHEGM : (a. touchstone **b. maxim** c. criticism d. praise) :: TRUCULENT : OVERBEARING

(b) is correct because both *apothegm* and *maxim* both refer to short, pithy dictum, just as *truculent* and *overbearing* are synonymous. (a) is incorrect because a touchstone is some criterion against which something is judged. (c) and (d) are incorrect because neither an apothegm nor a maxim is inherently critical or praising.

83.   RED : BLUE :: (a. x-ray b. ultraviolet c. gamma radiation **d. radio wave**) : MICROWAVE

(d) is correct because light in the red wavelength is long, whereas light in the blue wavelength is short. Radio waves are long, whereas the microwave is short. X-ray (a), ultraviolet (b), and gamma radiation (c) are long wavelengths and therefore do not complete the analogy.

84. AMALIE NOETHER : PHYSICS :: ROSALIND FRANKLIN : (**a. molecular biology** b. x-ray crystallography c. organic chemistry d. transposons)

    (**a**) Molecular biology is correct because the work of Amalie Noether became a guiding principle in the field of physics. The work of Rosalind Franklin lead to the discovery of DNA structure which became the guiding principle in the field of molecular biology (a). X-ray crystallography (b) is a technique which Franklin used in her work. Organic chemistry (c) is a branch of science which deals with the chemical molecules which make up living matter. Transposons (d) are a type of genetic material which moves around within the DNA of a cell.

85. (**a. voluble** b. trite c. veracious d. accede) : FLUENT :: LACKADAISICAL : TARRY

    (**a**) is correct because *voluble* is a synonym for *fluent*, which means "well versed or able to communicate." *Lackadaisical* and *tarry* both describe something lacking vigor or enthusiasm. (b) is incorrect because *trite* means "commonplace." (c) is incorrect because *veracious* means "accurate." (d) is incorrect because *accede* means "to comply with."

86. DROMEDARY : CAMEL :: PACHYDERM : (a. ox b. tiger **c. elephant** d. whale)

    (**c**) is correct because dromedary is another name for a camel just as pachyderm is another name for an elephant. (a) is incorrect because an ox is bovine. (b) is incorrect because a tiger is feline. (d) is incorrect because a whale is cetaceous.

87. TONI MORRISON : *BELOVED* :: (a. Jane Smiley **b. John Updike** c. Norman Mailer d. Alice Walker) : *RABBIT AT REST*

    (**b**) is correct because John Updike won the 1991 Pulitzer Prize for his novel *Rabbit at Rest*, just as Toni Morrison won the coveted award in 1988 for her book, *Beloved*. (a), (c), and (d) are all incorrect because, although Smiley, Mailer, and Walker are all Pulitzer winners, they won for the books *A Thousand Acres, The Executioner's Song,* and *The Color Purple*, respectively.

88. (**a. glucose** b. fructose c. sucrose d. deoxyribose) : GALACTOSE :: RIBOSE : ARABINOSE

    (**a**) Glucose is correct because glucose and galactose are diasteriomers, ribose and arabinose are also diasteriomers. Fructose (b), sucrose (c), and deoxyribose (d) are not diasteriomers of galactose and therefore they do not fit the analogy.

Explanations
of Answers

89. SILENT SPRING : RACHEL CARSON :: THE DOUBLE HELIX : (a. Francis Crick b. Rosalind Franklin c. Maurice Wilkins **d. James Watson**)

    (d) James Watson is correct because *Silent Spring* is a book written by Rachel Carson about the care of the environment, while *The Double Helix* is a book written about the discovery of DNA by James Watson. Francis Crick (a), Rosalind Franklin (b), and Maurice Wilkins (c) all played a role in the discovery of DNA, but they did not write this book.

90. SCURVY : VITAMIN :: (a. beriberi b. zwitterion **c. kwashiorkor** d. ketosis) : PROTEIN

    (c) Kwashiorkor is correct because scurvy is caused by a vitamin C deficiency. Kwashiorkor is caused by a protein deficiency. Beriberi (a) is caused by a vitamin deficiency and is not associated with protein. Zwitterion (b) is not associated with vitamins, proteins, or deficiencies and does not fit into the analogy. Ketosis (d) is associated with faulty fat metabolism and is therefore not protein related.

91. NIXON : FORD :: GOLDA MEIR : (**a. Itzhak Rabin** b. Menachem Begin c. Shimon Peres d. Yitzhak Shamir)

    (a) is the correct answer because Rabin succeeded Meir as prime minister of Israel in 1974 until 1977. Nixon and Meir both served as leaders of their respective countries from 1969–1974 just as Ford and Rabin served from 1974–1977 for their countries, the U.S. and Israel, respectively. (b) is incorrect because Begin was prime minister from 1977–1983. (c) is incorrect because Peres was prime minister from 1984–1988. (d) is incorrect because Shamir was leader from 1988–1992. Rabin was re-elected in 1992.

92. SYCOPHANTIC : PANDERING :: DOGMATIC : (**a. authoritarian** b. unprincipled c. karmic d. innocuous)

    (a) is correct because *dogmatic* and *authoritarian* are synonyms just as *sycophantic* and *pandering* are. (b) is incorrect because *unprincipled* is the opposite of *dogmatic*. (c) is incorrect because *karmic* describes actions seen as bringing upon oneself inevitable results. (d) is incorrect because *innocuous* describes something that is unlikely to cause damage.

93. SEPTADEKAPHILIA : 17 :: ARACHNAPHILIA : (a. people **b. spiders** c. strangers d. insects)

    (b) is correct because *septadekaphilia* means an "affinity for the number 17," just as *arachnaphilia* refers to an affinity for spiders. (a) and (c) are incorrect because an affinity for people, especially strangers, would be *xenophilia*. An affinity for insects would be *entophilia* (d).

Explanations
of Answers

94. OBDURATE : (a. tenacious b. tacit c. succinct **d. obstinate**) :: UBIQUITOUS :
     OMNIPRESENT

     (d) is correct because both *obdurate* and *obstinate* mean "stubborn or unwaver-
     ing," just as *ubiquitous* and *omnipresent* mean "everywhere at once." (a) is incor-
     rect because *tenacious* means "holding to something." (b) is incorrect because
     tacit describes something that goes unexpressed. (c) is incorrect because *suc-
     cinct* means concise.

95. RECANTATION : AFFIRMATION :: DEFY : (a. rebel b. challenge **c. acquiesce**
     d. dare)

     (c) is correct because a recantation is a reversal of a past assertion, while an
     affirmation is a restatement of a previously held position. This relationship is
     analogous to that of defy, meaning to challenge (b), and acquiesce, meaning to
     concede. (a) and (d) are incorrect because these are synonymous with defy.

96. PINEAL : MELATONIN :: KIDNEY : (a. glucagon b. insulin **c. renin**
     d. calcitonin)

     (c) Renin is correct because the pineal gland secretes the chemical melatonin
     which regulates the biological clock, while the kidney secretes renin which helps
     to regulate blood pressure. Glucagon (a) and insulin (b) are secreted by the pan-
     creas and calcitonin (d) is secreted by the thyroid, so none of these can complete
     the analogy.

97. Given A = {0, 1, 2, 3}
            B = {4, 5, 6, 7}
            C = {0, 1}
            D = {6, 7}
            E = {8, 9}

     C : A :: D : (a. A **b. B** c. C d. E)

     (b) C is a subset of set A, and thus D is a subset of set B. D is not a subset of any
     of the other choices, set A (a), set C (c), or set E (d). Set D is a subset of itself,
     but this choice is not given.

98. CHOLERIC : CANTANKEROUS :: BOMBASTIC : (a. behoove b. affable
     c. turgid d. pious)

     (c) is correct because *bombastic* and *turgid* are both adjectives describing pomp-
     ousness just as *choleric* and *cantankerous* are synonyms for *cranky*. (a) is incorrect
     because *behoove* means "advantageous." (b) is incorrect because *affable* describes
     friendliness. (d) is incorrect because *pious* is an antonym for *bombastic*.

Explanations
of Answers

99. APRIL : MAY :: (a. ruby b. sapphire c. garnet **d. diamond**) : EMERALD

     (d) is correct because the birthstone for April is the diamond just as the birthstone for May is the emerald. (a) is incorrect because the ruby is the gem for July. (b) is incorrect because the sapphire is the birthstone for September. (c) is incorrect because the garnet is the birthstone for January.

100. UDOMETER : (**a. rainfall** b. age c. blood pressure d. RPMs) ::
     CHRONOMETER : TIME

     (a) is correct because an udometer measures rainfall, just as a chronometer measures time. (b) is incorrect because there is no gauge that measures age. (c) is incorrect because blood pressure is measured with a sphymanomometer. (d) is incorrect because in a combustion engine, revolutions per minute are measured with a tachometer.

REA's Study Guides

Review Books, Refreshers, and Comprehensive References

Problem Solvers®

Presenting an answer to the pressing need for easy-to-understand and up-to-date study guides detailing the wide world of mathematics and science.

High School Tutors®

In-depth guides that cover the length and breadth of the science and math subjects taught in high schools nationwide.

Essentials®

An insightful series of more useful, more practical, and more informative references comprehensively covering more than 150 subjects.

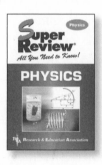

Super Reviews®

Don't miss a thing! Review it all thoroughly with this series of complete subject references at an affordable price.

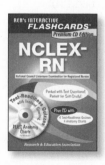

Interactive Flashcard Books®

Flip through these essential, interactive study aids that go far beyond ordinary flashcards.

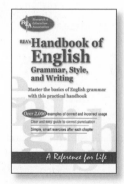

Reference

Explore dozens of clearly written, practical guides covering a wide scope of subjects from business to engineering to languages and many more.

For information about any of REA's books, visit
www.rea.com

Research & Education Association
61 Ethel Road W., Piscataway, NJ 08854
Phone: (732) 819-8880

INSTALLING REA's TestWare®

SYSTEM REQUIREMENTS

Pentium 75 MHz (300 MHz recommended), or a higher or compatible processor; Microsoft Windows 95, 98, NT 4 (SP6), ME, 2000, or XP; 64 MB Available RAM; Internet Explorer 5.5 or higher (Internet Explorer 5.5 is included on the CD); minimum 60 MB available hard-disk space; VGA or higher-resolution monitor, 800x600 resolution setting; Microsoft Mouse, Microsoft Intellimouse, or compatible pointing device.

INSTALLATION

1. Insert the TestWare® for the Miller Analogies Test CD-ROM into the CD-ROM drive.
2. If the installation doesn't begin automatically, from the Start Menu, choose the RUN command. When the RUN dialog box appears, type d:\setup (where D is the letter of your CD-ROM drive) at the prompt and click OK.
3. The installation process will begin. A dialog box proposing the directory "Program Files\REA\MAT" will appear. If the name and location are suitable, click OK. If you wish to specify a different name or location, type it in and click OK.
4. Start the MAT TestWare® application by double-clicking on the icon.

REA's MAT TestWare® is **EASY** to **LEARN AND USE**. To achieve maximum benefits, we recommend that you take a few minutes to go through the on-screen tutorial on your computer.

TECHNICAL SUPPORT

REA's TestWare® is backed by customer and technical support. For questions about **installation or operation of your software**, contact us at:

Research & Education Association
Phone: (732) 819-8880 (9 a.m. to 5 p.m. ET, Monday–Friday)
Fax: (732) 819-8808
Website: http://www.rea.com
E-mail: info@rea.com

Note to Windows XP Users: In order for the TestWare® to function properly, please install and run the application under the same computer-administrator level user account. Installing the TestWare® as one user and running it as another could cause file access path conflicts.